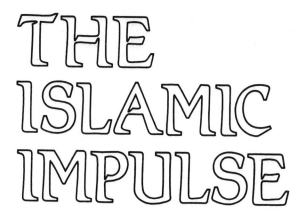

THE ISLAMIC IMPULSE

Edited by Barbara Freyer Stowasser

CENTER FOR CONTEMPORARY ARAB STUDIES
Georgetown University
Washington, DC

©1987 Center for Contemporary Arab Studies,
Georgetown University, Washington, DC 20057
Croom Helm Ltd, Provident House, Burrell Row, Beckenham,
Kent BR3 1AT
Croom Helm Australia Pty Ltd, Suite 4, 6th Floor,
64-76 Kippax Street, Surry Hills, NSW 2010, Australia
Second paperback printing, 1989, by Center for Contemporary Arab
Studies.

British Library Cataloguing in Publication Data

The Islamic impulse.
  1. Islam and politics—Near East
  I . Stowasser, Barbara Freyer
  II. Georgetown University. *Center for*
  Contemporary Arab Studies
297'.1977'0956   BP173.7

  ISBN 0-7099-3394-0

Library of Congress Cataloging-in-Publication Data

The Islamic impulse.

  Bibliography: p.
  Includes index.
  1. Islam—20th century. I. Stowasser, Barbara
Freyer.
BP163.I775   1986   297'.09'04   86-18802
ISBN 0-932568-12-2

CONTENTS

ACKNOWLEDGEMENTS

The editor wishes to acknowledge all those who assisted in the coordination of the Center for Contemporary Arab Studies 1983 Symposium, "New Perspectives on Islam and Politics in the Middle East," on which this book is based, and in the editing and production of this volume. They include the faculty and staff of the Center, the symposium steering committee, panel chairpersons, and external readers of the papers. Special thanks are extended to Center Director Michael C. Hudson, Symposium Manager Michael Baker, Publications Manager Zeina Azzam Seikaly, Publications Assistants John D. Lawrence and B. Lynne Barbee, and Text Editor J. Coleman Kitchen, Jr.

This paperback edition of the book, published in 1989, is a reprint of the first paperback edition, which was published in 1987. The Editor and the Center for Contemporary Arab Studies would like to express their profound gratitude to Mr. Abdullah Borek, whose generosity has made the second printing possible.

1 INTRODUCTION

Barbara Freyer Stowasser

The large number of scholarly and popular publications on Islam that have appeared in the West in recent years not only indicate our cognizance of the importance of the Muslim world to our own political and economic interests, but reflect a strong reaction to the visible regeneration of the Islamic ethos and the intensified role of Islam in the political process in the Muslim world today. We in the West have come to use different labels to describe this phenomenon of greater visibility and politicization of Islam: Islamic Fundamentalism, Islamic Resurgence, Islamic Revival, or Militant Islam. Overall, our responses to it have been characterized by confusion, by a lack of careful investigation, hence by overreaction and fear. We have given little thought to the problem of what, if anything, in all this Islamic ferment we so recently "discovered" is really new. Specifically, therefore, we have been inclined to perceive the Islamic revolution that toppled the Shah as the harbinger of a new chapter in the history of Islam and have come to view the activism of Muslim groups as a disconcerting and even ominous challenge.

This volume brings together a number of approaches, both new and traditional, to the problematic of contemporary Islam. While many of the contributors are secularists, some speak from the vantage point of Islamic modernism, and others from that of Islamic fundamentalism. Taken together, their analyses of the genesis, ideological structure, political and social orientation and organization, and the goals of contemporary Islam in the Middle East present a multifaceted interpretation of the complex issues that underlie and constitute contemporary Islamic thought and action. Only a broad approach like the one attempted in this book, which enlists the energy and vision of many different types of interpreters, can lead beyond one-dimensionality, bias, or mere reactiveness to a full understanding of contemporary Islam. At first sight, the many and varied definitions of the nature of modern Islam, Islamic revival, and Islamic fundamentalism presented here may appear as bewildering as the fact that the secularist and the religiously-committed contributors to this volume seem to speak in different languages. Careful reading, however, will show some important

1

insights they share, such as the awareness that the Islamic revival is largely not reactionary, but rather is caused by the desire in many Islamic societies to modernize within a religious context which is in harmony with the indigenous culture and whose historical roots, therefore, lie in the nineteenth century. The contributors to this volume were participants in a symposium on Islam and politics in the Middle East, convened in 1983 by the Center for Contemporary Arab Studies at Georgetown University, in order to provide a forum for in-depth discussion relating to the role of religion in the Middle Eastern political and social process. The participants in this conference were both Muslim and non-Muslim. They came from the Middle East, Europe, and the United States, and represented the disciplines of theology, political science, history, sociology, anthropology, and law.

The Role of Colonialism in the Genesis of Contemporary Islam

The contributors to this volume approach the issue of Islam and politics in many different ways. One theme, however, is advanced by all: that Islam is an important — for some the most important or even the only legitimate — force of solidarity and cohesion in the Middle East today that has evolved into its contemporary form as a response to the traumatic experience of Western colonialism. Whether its foremost current trait is perceived as renewed religious vision, reformist zeal, or dynamic political force, its innermost nature is described as defensive against the wrenching impact of alien forces whose influence in economic, political, and cultural permutations has not abated to this day. Some (e.g., Chatty) see Islam as an ideal, divinely inspired system that was disturbed and dislocated only temporarily by the colonial experience which overpowered it when Muslims had fallen into the weaknesses of ritualism and lethargy. But after a hundred years of internal rejuvenation, reformism, and indigenous modernism, aided by the economic recovery and the increased political importance of the Muslim world, Islam is now coming into its own again and is shedding the inferiority complex foisted upon it by an expansionist, oppressive West. Others (e.g., Faruqi) also see Islam as an all-inclusive, God-given (and implicitly static) order, but perceive the colonial experience as far from over. In the face of this unholy legacy that remains an overpowering reality in the Muslim world,

Islam, with its divinely legislated spiritual, political, social, and economic values, provides the believers with a blueprint for action. When they heed the call for equality, equity, and justice, as contained and exemplified in the Qur'an and the Sunna, contemporary Muslims can alleviate the harmful effects of Westernization and ensure that the Islamic world will be made whole once again.

The secularist contributors to this book (e.g., Davis, Tibi, Lawrence, Mitchell) view the colonialist experience as even more important. In their view, contemporary Islam is not reconstituting its strength toward the attainment of another "Golden Age," nor is the question one of whether the Qur'anic and Sunnaic ideal paradigm can or does provide a realistic blueprint for Muslim action now to overcome the trauma of colonialist oppression and exploitation. Rather, the colonialist experience is seen as responsible for the rise of a whole new brand of politicized Islamic response that uses some of the old symbols and problem-solving approaches of the past, but is in essence and even in form unlike anything that preceded it. Islam is operative in a new "cultural milieu"[1] now, the global society of industrialized nations, in which its role is as different from the classical past as the challenges it encounters. And even within the post-colonialist Islam, careful distinctions must be made, since even modern Islam is not a unified ideology in abstract terms, but must be seen within a well-differentiated, finely tuned sociohistorical framework which alone provides the referent for correct analysis of Islam's various stages and permutations (Davis).

The Historical Context of Islamic Resurgence

Both groups, those who see the Islamic political movements of the present as carriers of the vision of Ideal Muslim Society, and those who demand that such movements be analyzed in terms of the specific nature of specific societies at specific times, view the history of Islam as one of ebb and flow, strengthening and decline. The Islamic past is studded with periods of resurgence, sparked by religious thinkers and religio-political avant-garde groups who called the believers "to return from the abyss" (Mitchell) by demanding that they seriously reexamine their heritage as an alternative mode of action, or who translated such visions into political reform. For those who regard Islamic history as the record of attempts on the part of the *umma* to translate the Qur'anic and

Sunnaic ideal paradigm of Muslim society into reality, the Kharijites (or Khawarij, seventh century), the Wahhabis (eighteenth century), and the Muslim Brothers (twentieth century) have much in common. They share the fact that a religious vision propelled them into political action, just as they share the fact that they were doomed to failure through their own "fanaticism, isolation, and narrow puritanism" (Ayoub). As this historical cyclical experience of weakness and reform, of challenge and response continues unaltered into the twentieth century, it provides direct lessons to be learned, and failed experiments to be studied by contemporary Muslims (Ayoub). This is not so for critics who concern themselves with the specific sociohistoric settings of Islamic movements and not with Islam as a theology of universalism, a monolithic religion, a perfect blueprint for a just society. While they too perceive a cyclical pattern of decline and reexamination, weakening and resurgence in the past—e.g., during the eras of Ibn Taymiyya (thirteenth century) and of the Wahhabi movement (eighteenth century)—these critics see these experiences as belonging to a different order than today's events. For it is only since the beginnings of the colonial encounter with the technologically and militarily superior West that the Islamic world, now part of world society, has come to face the utterly foreign concept of secularism that was foisted upon it from abroad. This experience, then, was both unprecedented and more traumatic in a multiplicity of dimensions. For Muslims everywhere, it entailed the bitterness of knowing that foreigners and their client local elites were—and are—in charge of their destiny and even the definition of that destiny; that efforts to modernize and reform from within brought not strength, but increased weakness and domination by the West; and, worst and most important of all, that the concept of secularism, a completely alien and hence most threatening notion, challenged—and challenges—the very core of Islam as expressed in the Islamic doctrine of *tawhid,* the unity of life (Mitchell). These features set the contemporary Islamic experience apart from all that occurred in pre-modern history. They constitute a crisis of unprecedented magnitude which has to be dealt with by Islamic societies on a global scale, and one to which the lessons learned from past experiences have little or no relevance. Islam now has "to search for its *qibla*" (Hasan Turabi as quoted by Mitchell) as never before since its birth some fourteen centuries ago.

What is Contemporary Islamic Fundamentalism?

For those who view Islam as an ideal system of faith and action revealed once and for all in historical time, the contemporary Islamic movements are contemporary armies struggling to reestablish the divinely legislated, original order of Islam, albeit in a modern way. For secularist analysts, on the other hand, Islamic fundamentalism cannot be seen in terms of a theology translated once again into activism, of an archetypal constant functioning once again as the motor propelling political action in a contemporary setting. Rather, Islamic fundamentalism must be seen as a modern acculturationist ideology (Tibi).[2] It is shaped by the forces of the modern world to which it responds, while attempting to develop an idiom in which to do so. In the process, it bypasses and disregards its own theological past and often takes a clear stance against the official theological establishment, the *'ulama,* who are viewed as having sold out to the political establishment, i.e., the secularized nationalized governments in power in the Islamic world. Thus, unencumbered by intervening tradition, by the theological interpretation developed over centuries, fundamentalism as a modern ideology sets out to "rediscover the original meaning of the Islamic message" (Fazlur Rahman as cited by Lawrence) and to translate it into action as a direct response to the challenges of the post-industrial, post-colonial age. It is noteworthy that no indigenous word for "fundamentalism" exists in Arabic, and that Muslims do not define themselves as fundamentalists or define others as such (Lawrence). Maybe the reason for this is that fundamentalism is not a well-defined program as much as it is a mood. It is a multifaceted, often opaque search for an Islamic meaning in the modern world. It is characterized by mass involvement and, lately, by messianic ambitions among some of its leaders. It is anti-modern, anti-intellectual, and anti-mystic. In their quest for legitimate government, a moral economy, equity and justice for all, its activists are activists with scriptural shibboleths (Lawrence). Their visions are meant to be a challenge to the world in general—and the West in particular—and as such have become powerful beacons for large numbers of disenfranchised, impoverished, frustrated Muslims living in an overcrowded, cruel, and uncertain world. Crucial as the socioeconomic ills underlying the rise of Islamic activism may be, its primary cause must be found in the deficiencies of coercive political systems which exclude the masses from political participation (Ibrahim).

Staticity vs. Dynamism

The Islamic fundamentalists who demand a radical transformation of the contemporary sociopolitical, legal, and economic realities of the Muslim world do so under the banner of "pure Islam," i.e., the Islam of the Qur'an and Sunna. They defend the legitimacy of their platforms by arguing that they are derived from "the basics" of Islam. While they hoist the flag of "pure Islam" to carry it into battle against twentieth-century external and internal enemies, these fundamentalists do not pause to consider Islam in its historical dimension as interpreted through the centuries by generations upon generations of lawyer-theologians, and thus seemingly present an Islam that is *static* and lacking the dimension of internal evolution. In reality, however, fundamentalists of this type are highly selective in their approach to and their use of this "pure Islam." Even those who claim to speak with the voice of pure and original Islam reinterpret (as well as circumvent) Qur'anic and Sunnaic texts in their endeavor to establish a basis for irrefutable contemporary argument. This has resulted in "distortions" of what other Muslims consider to be "Islamic," such as Khomeini's application of what he considers to be Islamic criminal justice, which is to other Muslims contrary to the basic tenets of Islamic criminal justice (Bassiouni). Similarly, these fundamentalists' anti-capitalist stance is based on reinterpretation of the early Islamic sources, *ijtihad* (Beinin). Thus, in their methods — albeit not in their goals — they have more in common with the progressivists or reformists or modernists than either group would care to admit. In contradistinction to the fundamentalists, the modernists openly proclaim Islam to be a flexible, *dynamic* system that was and should always be interpreted and molded from within to accommodate the social and political changes of the ages. From this vantage point, constitutional democracy (Badr), a unified, complex, and modern system of criminal justice (Bassiouni), and the equality of the sexes (Stowasser) are among the features of the Islamic order, either on the basis of its classical development, i.e., the *ijtihad* of the past, or on the basis of contemporary and future interpretation. What separates the modernists from the fundamentalists here is the desire of the former to work toward a development of the Islamic order (perceived by them as dynamic) through the processes of rational reinterpretation of general Islamic directives, outside the pressures of political considerations such as the desire for radical sociopolitical and economic transformation of Islamic society.

Islamic Fundamentalism and Secular Ideologies

As viewed by many fundamentalist ideologues, Islam is a system of universalism, not regionalism. The *umma* envelops all Muslims both as believers and citizens, and thus should be the single focus of their undivided religio-political loyalty. The splintering of this *umma* into national entities with their rival claims upon this loyalty was as much the result of foreign meddling as were the ensuing regional tensions and conflicts. Until the greater Islamic unity is once again achieved in actuality, it should at least inspire Muslim political life and action "in potentiality and tendency" by inspiring organic relations and cooperation among Muslim states everywhere. In addition to universalism, the fully realized Islamic *umma* is characterized by the sovereignty of the *shari'a* in its complete form, without any admixture of foreign systems as regarding the legal order itself or its application. The Islamic world will remain impotent against outside imperialist pressures as long as it exists in a situation of nation-splintering, and will have to suffer autocracy, oppression, illiteracy, social delinquency, and the disintegration of the family unless and until the *shari'a* is applied once again in its entirety within its borders (Faruqi). While Islam is thus the only legitimate force of political and social cohesion, it is also the only guarantee against economic exploitation, materialism, and greed. Islam condemns economic competition, exploitation of the poor, class privileges, monopolies, and other aspects of capitalism (which is, by nature, nothing but a dimension of imperialism). True Islam provides for economic justice and equity. It envisages communal ownership of all resources, which means, in practical terms, such modern things as the nationalization of public utilities (Beinin). Islam, however, is not compatible with socialism because the latter is a materialist system of Western origin and as such is *jahili*, i.e., the product of disbelief and polytheism (Sayyid Qutb as quoted by Beinin and others).

This fundamentalist interpretation of Islam as a universalist system of political, social, and economic strength, equity, and justice which provides the only legitimate alternative to the ideologies of nationalism, socialism, and communism "as championed by the West" is to secularist interpreters the reason why they perceive contemporary Islamic fundamentalism as an acculturationist ideology. Fundamental Islam, in their view, is a contemporary ideology that responds to internal realities as well as to other ideologies challenging it at home and from abroad. Recognition of the dialectic relationship of sociopolitical reality to the "ideal superstructure" of Islam is the key to correct interpretation of contemporary Islamic thought and development (Tibi and others). Therefore, the borders between nationalism and Islam, socialism and Islam, Marxism and Islam are not drawn along the lines of either-or. Rather, the universality of the problems and of the search for their solution creates common features in the Islamic and secularist alternatives and, thereby, acculturationist interference. The whole concept of "political system" which feeds into the notion of the *umma* as defined by the Islamic fundamentalists is an acculturationist phenomenon, as are those schools of thought which see Islam and nationalism, or Islam and Arabism, as inseparable. All are the result of the same crisis situation. While the spokesmen of Arabism are being strengthened by Islamic fundamentalism as an ideology of revolution, even the incumbent regimes use Islamic language as a legitimizing device in support of the status quo (Michael C. Hudson as cited by Tibi). The same pattern applies to the anti-capitalist attitudes of the Islamic fundamentalists. While Islam was tolerant of protocapitalist activities during its classical past, it adopted an increasingly anti-capitalist stance during its exposure to colonialism, and passed through a stage of support for socialism by Islamic modernists. The contemporary fundamentalists assert that they reject socialism as a Western, *jahili* ideology. All the while, however, their platform, which includes such items as social security, the right to work, and so forth, usually subsumed under the fundamentalists' concept of "mutual social responsibility," clearly marks fundamentalism as both a response to internal economic and political pressures, and an alternative to Western-inspired socialism. This interpretation of fundamentalist Islam as an acculturationist ideology even permits one to draw close parallels between Islam and Marxism. While Marxism by its materialist nature is of course unacceptable to the Islamic mind-set, and while its spokesmen in the Muslim world failed to elicit large-scale support because of prevalent social and economic factors (Gran), Marxism and fundamentalist Islam share a vision of "holy war" of the exploited against the exploiters, or, Islamically speaking, of the weak on earth against the corrupt and unjust. Eventually, the proletariat will win out over the capitalists, or, the faithful will triumph over those who have gone astray. Not only the programmatic language but even the organizational structures of both sets of believers bear important similarities.[3] In this fashion, secularist interpreters see Islamic fundamentalism as closely linked both to the socioeconomic realities in the Islamic world and to Western secular ideologies. The fundamentalists' assertion that all association of Islam with secular thought is "pagan" is not an obstacle to this interpretation, but rather proves its validity. Reactiveness and defensiveness, in the secularists' view, are important characteristics of this acculturationist ideology.

The Polycentric Nature of Contemporary Islam

Whether committed to piety in their own individual lives, or engaged in Islamic activism, contemporary Muslims are influenced by the visions of recent interpreters of Islam. Among the voices that are important today and are translated into the platforms of a variety of Islamic movements are those of Abu al-'Ala' al-Mawdudi, Hasan al-Banna, Sayyid Qutb, and Ayatollah Ruhollah Khomeini. The theoreticians among them — Mawdudi and Qutb — are often interpreted loosely today, but remain inspirational and thus powerful. Of the activists, al-Banna is regarded as weaker than Khomeini because the Muslim Brothers under his guidance were never able to translate their vision into reality, i.e., their vision was not tried in an actual modern nation-state (Ayoub), while Khomeini was able to lead a successful Islamic revolution, or at least fall heir to one after it was already under way (Farhang). This last fact, indeed, has had enormous influence on Muslims everywhere. For one, the Iranian Revolution has "moved the Islamic movement from the realm of theoretical outline of goals to the practical level of application. As in all revolutionary situations, this fact has raised the level and quality of debate about means as well as ends" (Mitchell). It has made it possible for Muslims in general to focus more sharply on the question of representative government: who should be the leader, how he should accede to power, and how the resulting polity should function within the parameters of (at least) limited democracy (Mitchell). The Iranian Revolution has thus become a powerful experience that inspires even Muslims given not to activism but to contemplation and an individual quest for the Islamic vision. Even they have come to feel that "perhaps Shi'i hopes and patient struggle, with that revolution, may bear fruits for all Muslims to enjoy" (Ayoub). There is, then, a strong transnational Islamic awareness at work in the Muslim world today. It is, however, spiritual and not organizational in nature. To date, "there exists no single revolutionary or organizational epicenter or single charismatic leader who would provide some focus in terms of spiritual unity and revolutionary activity."[4] Specific, local socioeconomic, and political conditions endow the Islamic movement with special dimensions of concern, and thus localize it to a large degree. Very important in this localization process are the independence and leadership function — or the lack thereof — of the local religious establishment, and even the overall situation of religious ideology or of the Muslim community within a given political system (Antoun, Dessouki, Batatu, Özbudun, Harik).

Conclusion

Nevertheless, it must be understood that contemporary Islam, though not a unified and centrally organized plan for action, is a widely shared, transnational mood that is eliciting renewed personal commitment and, occasionally, political activism on the part of Muslims in all Islamic countries. This mood's central theme is that Islam was established on earth not to redeem and liberate the individual, but to establish a community living under God's guidance and His law. A renewed commitment to faith and action, individual or collective, private or public, is therefore understood by Muslims not only as an act of defense against the decadence and immorality of the modern age, but as the precondition for the building of a strong, united Islam as the only road of salvation for the world.

Notes

1. Hans Freyer, *Schwelle der Zeiten* (Stüttgart: Deutsche Verlags-Anstalt, 1965).
2. This term is used here to describe the nature of contemporary Islamic fundamentalist thought and is not intended to convey the meaning ascribed to it by Yvonne Haddad in her *Contemporary Islam and the Challenge of History* (Albany, NY: State University of New York Press, 1982, pp. 7ff.). While she defines modernists, secularists, and Westernizers as "acculturationists," her equivalent to our "fundamentalism" is "neo-normativism." Similarities of interpretation, however, surpass these differences in terminology, as Haddad also sees the "neo-normativist" interpretation of Islam as the result of discussions between "normativists" and "acculturationists," i.e., as a fresh new interpretation of Islam for modern man by

the former under the influence of the latter. That this is truly the case is *not* conceptualized on their part, however. "The literature they have produced evidences assimilation and integration of some new tools of hermeneutics and explication, but the content of what is affirmed is the eternal message of Islam, the same message given to man at creation, valid for today and forever. What is being advocated is a new articulation of the faith, relevant for modern challenges, but not a new Islam" (p. 11).

3. Maxime Rodinson, *Marxism and the Muslim World* (New York and London: Monthly Review Press, 1981), pp. 92ff., 103ff.

4. Richard Dekmejian, "Anatomy of Islamic Revival," *Middle East Journal*, XXXIV, 1 (1980), p. 2.

PART I: SECULARIST ANALYSES

2 MUSLIM FUNDAMENTALIST MOVEMENTS: REFLECTIONS TOWARD A NEW APPROACH

Bruce B. Lawrence

There has been much to-do in the United States about Islamic fundamentalism of late. Countless newspaper articles have bemoaned the appearance of radical, militant, fundamentalist groups in the Muslim/Arab world. Their members, in photographic glimpses of them, look strangely like Palestinian terrorists of the 1960s: shadow figures, haranguing, declaiming, killing. Verbal by-lines — oral and written — complement as well as confirm the visual impressions: these people are not like us; they are against us; they are against those whom we are for. They are unthinking, unflinching, dangerous. We should be afraid of them. We are.

This portrait of Islamic fundamentalism will strike many readers as a caricature. In fact, it comes very close to the perception of my students and other Americans like them, well educated, internationally oriented, eager to understand the actors and activities that characterize contemporary Muslim society.

It is not enough to deride all these observers as misguided products of solipsistic capitalism, with its innate anti-religious and parochial bias. Something else is happening here. In part, it relates to the pace of modern life, the rapid circulation of a variety of opinions and images not only in the press and classrooms but at many levels of U.S. society. To look at the popular conception of Islamic fundamentalism is to recognize it as a recycled form of the dragon labeled "Islam" which has been with us for a very long time. Concern about "Islamic fundamentalism" is a very recent phenomenon in U.S. public life. This notion's antecedents are "Islamic revivalism" or "Islamic resurgence," terms that still compete with it for media attention. The implicit overlap of these terms is confirmed by the frequent conjoining of papers or articles which deal with fundamentalism, resurgence, revivalism, Islamization.

Yet there is a danger that none of these names may directly correspond to a cognitive reality that reflects the moods and moments of actual Muslims. As Clifford Geertz has noted about "the revival of Islam," it "tends to divert attention from its referent to itself. The question becomes whether there really is such a thing out there in 'Islamdom' demanding special explanation or whether there is not, and our sense that there *is* grows out of tuning in late to a historical process, faith-driven politics, that has been going on for a very long time and has come to our attention only because it has begun directly to touch our interests."[1]

The difficulty is that many of us — and not merely journalists, Defense Department analysts, or U.S. embassy officials stationed in Middle Eastern countries — have become riveted to faith-driven politics. We introduce copulatives (the revival of Islam, the militancy of Islam, the fundamentalism of Islam) wildly and randomly to come to terms with something that will not be simply understood or quickly subdued.

Yet our copulatives are informative, if we but listen to the pulse rate of popular anxiety that they project. Their life spans, like those of many aspects of contemporary American life, are very brief. Islamic revivalism, or the resurgence of Islam, only became a serious public preoccupation in the United States after 1973, though some trace its origin back to 1967 and the aftermath of the June war. Islamic fundamentalism, revivalism's companion and successor, only occupied center stage after 1979. Both were linked to crucial events that occurred within the Muslim world and came to have portentous international significance: the OPEC oil price rise after late 1972, and then, barely six years later, the Iranian Revolution deposing the Shah and heralding an Islamic theocracy in early 1979. No one would dispute the economic significance of the former, or the political impact of the latter. What does seem to be still very much in question is the connection of either event to Islam, specifically to clichéd apparitions such as Islamic revivalism or Islamic fundamentalism.

To date, there have been three main scholarly approaches to Islamic fundamentalism: (1) to dismiss it outright as inappropriate to discourse on contemporary Muslim society; (2) to assume its viability and to invoke it as a descriptive category in discussing particular Muslim groups; or (3) to wrestle with its applicability as a thought-form eliciting loyalty/allegiance among Muslims, mostly by comparing Muslim fundamentalism to other ideologies with which it is said to be competitive.

All three approaches have their advocates; all stake out a claim to interpret, rather than merely describe, that entity known as the Arab/Muslim world. Before outlining our own view of Islamic fundamentalist movements, let us consider what has been said elsewhere by others.

The Dismissive Approach

The dismissive approach is fashionable among certain enlightened journalists, who go beyond fads and try to isolate the elusive core identity of their quarry. Hence Edward Mortimer, who has produced a highly readable account of some features of present-day Muslim states, writes about the familiar cast of Islamic reformers — Afghani, 'Abduh, Rida — and carefully avoids using the term "fundamentalist" until he comes to Rida. He then poses the rhetorical question: "Was he [Rida] a fundamentalist?" And goes on to answer his own question:[2]

> If . . . "fundamentalism" means an effort to define the fundamentals of one's religion and refusal to budge from them once defined, then Rida was a fundamentalist indeed. (But surely anybody with serious religious beliefs of any sort must be a fundamentalist in this sense?)

The parentheses are Mortimer's; they attempt to frame and justify his exclusion of further attention to fundamentalism. His too brief caveat is elaborated by Yvonne Haddad, but not in her recent work, *Contemporary Islam and the Challenge of History*. There she does not even broach the term fundamentalism, offering in its stead a tripartite model of Islamic thought: normative, neo-normative, and acculturationist. Neo-normativist represents the major group in the dialectical dance of Islamic ideology which Haddad choreographs. They seem to resemble traditionalists, conservatives, or fundamentalists, just as their opponents, the acculturationists, resemble those known to most as Westernizers or modernizers.

Haddad's implicit exclusion of fundamentalism in her book is later defended in an article on the theme of "The Islamic Alternative."[3] She rejects fundamentalism as a descriptive category because:

> . . . it has become fashionable in Western circles to refer to the Islamization process evident in various parts of the world as

"fundamentalism" or Muslim "fanaticism." The term neo-
normative is utilized . . . to avoid the tendency of Western
readers to dismiss "fanaticism" and "fundamentalism" as passing
fads that need to be ignored because of their transient nature.

In short, Haddad rejects Islamic fundamentalism as a descriptive
category not because it would be inappropriate to label certain
conditions in the Muslim world as "fundamentalist" but because the
label "fundamentalist" implies fanaticism and transiency in the
Western mind. The fact that Haddad's neo-normative Muslims act
like fundamentalists is made evident later in the same article when
she states that "they seek similar goals to those of the Moral
Majority and attempt to replicate the perfect society [of seventh
century A.D. Arabia]."

Mortimer's demurral at the term "fundamentalism" is partly due
to his having reordered his thinking about the Muslim world
through the prism of Edward Said's *Orientalism*. According to the
Gramsci/Foucault/post-*Orientalism* canon, one cannot use terms
that are inappropriate to a culture without practicing a kind of guile-
less, intellectual imperialism; one must ever be alert to cultural
presuppositions that inform and distort every attempt to approach,
to know, to deal with the "Other," or those "others" coming from
civilizational, social, and religious backgrounds divergent from
one's own.

Such a supersensitized cross-cultural hermeneutics may also be at
play in Haddad's effort to redefine categories for analyzing contemporary Muslim society. But with reference to Islamic fundamentalism, the argument for dismissing it seems to warrant at least two
further subsidiary lines of support:

1. *Empirical.* No group exists in the contemporary Arab Muslim
world that calls itself fundamentalist. Various phrases are used but
none translates as fundamentalist. A Pakistani scholar/journalist,
who heard me give a preliminary talk on Islamic fundamentalism in
June 1982, counseled me to drop the term altogether because even
nonfundamentalist Muslims found the term offensive. An
anthropologist in Toronto offered similar advice. They, and others,
have a simple, blunt point to make: Don't apply words to describe
people that they would not accept and apply to themselves.
Fundamentalism is not, never has been, nor ever will be a term used
by most Muslims to describe either their own religious outlook or
the religious outlook of other Muslims with whom they disagree.

2. *Etymological*: There exists no Arabic word for fundamentalism. A comparison with the terms "Islamic reform" and "Islamic revivalism" is illustrative. Both *islah* and *nahda* are Arabic words used respectively to describe what are assumed to be two major moods in the modern phase of Islamic history. The historical usage of both is often at variance with the current interpretation provided by their advocates, but the existence of approximate terms, and their immediate acceptance among all Arabic-speaking Muslims and non-Muslims, is evident. The case with fundamentalism is different. One can find neither a neologism nor a revalidated term by which to talk of it. An effort has been mounted in certain journalistic quarters to perpetrate terms such as *usuliyya* (lit., "that which pertains to rudiments or fundamentals," in Gulf Arabic) or *bunyan parasti* (lit., "worship of the foundation" of faith, in Pakistani Urdu) as if they connoted fundamentalism in English. Others use the terms *mutadayyinun* ("those committed to religion") or *mutatarrifun* ("those inclined to extremism") to differentiate ardent believers, the so-called militant Muslims, from their co-religionists. Yet these terms apply equally well to conservatives or traditionalists, as Fadwa al-Guindi earlier illustrated.[4]

The two nouns most often invoked to describe fundamentalism are *salafiyya* and *Islamiyya*. The first, meaning "that which pertains to ancestors," has time-honored sanctity, bordering on nostalgia, because it harks back to the ancestors of faith, the first generation of Muslims, who supported and fought alongside the Prophet Muhammad in seventh-century A.D. Arabia. Ironically, its contemporary usage derives from the inspiration of Muhammad 'Abduh, a turn-of-the-century Egyptian reformer, now categorized as a modernist and hence the opposite of a fundamentalist. The term *Islamiyya*, like *usuliyya*, is a neologism of uncertain origin, but intended to distinguish those who aspire to create an Islamic or Medinan state from those who are content to live within a modern-day Muslim nation-state. The *Islamiyyun* (as proponents of *Islamiyya* are called) commit themselves to the full implementation of Islamic ideals (e.g., as in post-1979 Iran), while *Muslimun* are "mere" Muslims, those who have only the formal qualities of Muslim identity. The majority of the inhabitants of *Muslimun* states profess Islam, as do the ruling elite; Islam is enshrined as the state ideology and is said to be integral to all public and private features of life. But in reality a corrosive competing ideological formation — whether disguised secularism, diluted socialism, or corrupt capitalism — shapes the life of the state, according to the *Islamiyyun*.

In Arabic nomenclature there are no safe or easy solutions to the question: how does one define Islamic fundamentalism? It remains an idea transported from another cultural context and lacking any secure resting place in the Islamic fabric.

It would be easy to agree with the many who have argued that the term "Islamic fundamentalism" ought to be dropped. Yet, in the same manner that Muslim countries have become integral to a larger global culture, many "isms" exist in the Islamic world that do not originate from the Qur'an, the Sunna, or any pre-modern category of Islamic history. Their existence is too stubborn to be denied. What they represent must be admitted and discussed. Just as Arab nationalism is a reality crisscrossed with Islamic loyalty in over twenty nations of the Middle East and North Africa, so fundamentalism is a religious force no less real but decidedly more mysterious in its origin and its continuous manifestation.

The Smother Approach and the Arm's-Length Survey

Those analysts who are willing to use the term "Islamic fundamentalism" when writing or speaking in English[5] separate out into two camps: (a) those who ignore its definition but use it extensively (on the assumption that its meaning is either too obvious or too subtle to be spelled out), and (b) those who wrestle with its suitability as an alternative thought-form/motivation/category at least among some persons or groups — peripheral but related to the nexus of political power — in certain Muslim/Arab countries.

Those who use the term "fundamentalism" unreflectively scamper quickly into the fact forest of contemporary political life in Muslim/Arab society. Often they use "conservative," "fundamentalist," and "revivalist" as interchangeable adjectives.

Expositors of fundamentalism as a full-blown ideology, by contrast, perhaps because they struggle to locate its integrity as a conceptual system, tend to stay on the high plateau of analytical discourse; they eschew formulaic resolutions of complex issues. They resort to historical examples to document their views. Seldom do they illustrate the contemporaneity of Islamic fundamentalism with reference to specific groups, named leaders, and country contexts.

Because of the similar language but opposite approach of the two groups, let us try to clarify the differences between them by labeling the first of them "the smother approach" and the second "the arm's-length survey."

The Smother Approach

Perhaps the best example of an author who uses the word "fundamentalism" with rapt inattention to its meaning is Fouad Ajami. His work, *The Arab Predicament*, contains frequent insights into aspects of the contemporary Arab world. But on certain subjects he wallows in conceptual opaqueness. One is the supposed distinction between what he infelicitously calls "radical fundamentalism" and its symbiotic cousin, "conservative fundamentalism." The differentiation is strictly in terms of the economic viewpoint advocated by select authors, though it is not clear on what basis they were selected. "Radical" derives from egalitarian or socialist approaches to the economic order, while "conservative" implies a paradoxical embrace of capital formation and private property. Both somehow rate as "fundamentalist," it appears, because of the respective authors' repeated emphasis on the need for Islamic rule and derision of those who are corrupt (for radicals, the conformist wealthy in power are corrupt; for conservatives, it is the revolutionary socialists discrediting Islam in the name of Islam who are corrupt). The problem of language is compounded by Ajami's facile literary style; he lumps fundamentalism with "reactionary theocrats" among radicals and with "diehard traditionalists" among conservatives.

That fundamentalism has a fluid rather than constant valence for Ajami becomes clear toward the end of *The Arab Predicament*. This valence is negative for both the radical and conservative forms of fundamentalism. Ibrahim Abu-Lughod was right when he noted that Ajami fails to map out the full range of the Arab predicament because he both ignores the role of Western/U.S. imperialism along with the multitiered threat of Israel and also assumes fundamentalism to be flawed utopianism, a kind of lower-grade nostalgia doomed to failure.[6] The end of Ajami's book provides its own glaring criticism of what precedes it. After having discoursed on fundamentalism at length without ever defining it, he cites on the last page an anonymous Japanese informant who had suggested to him that he replace fundamentalism with "nativism." Not commenting on this gloss directly, Ajami concludes:[7]

At the root of the nativist [read: fundamentalist] view of the world is a utopia . . . In the modern world utopias can serve as a corrective. But utopias can be pushed too far. Our imagined utopias turn out to be the source of much of our misery: We never quite approximate them, and we feel all the more diminished for failing to replicate the glories of our ancestors or the perfection of our plans.

This is a none too subtle rebuke of all forms of Islamic fundamentalism. And it may have been the casuistry of Ajami, in the company of a host of other writers, which prompted Abu-Lughod to note elsewhere that most books on contemporary Islam "represent the stubborn weight of a barren tradition"; i.e., they ignore economic change and development, while reducing the cultural struggle of Muslims to an endless tug-of-war between "two primary poles of attraction, that of Islam in whatever form — dynamic, stultified, reformed or folk — and that of the West which is both the object of hostility and the primary cause of the challenge which Muslims have to face, cope, and come to terms with, or transcend" (i.e., these writers assume the primacy of ideas, imagining that alternatives are determined by what people think or are led to think rather than by objective social, structural, and material conditions).[8]

Abu-Lughod criticizes overattention to ideology and yet he readily admits that it cannot be ignored. Moreover, the source of its infusion into contemporary life cannot easily be separated out into Islamic-non-Islamic, East-West. The name Ajami, for instance, is a Lebanese Shi'i *nisba* yet the views of Fouad Ajami resemble those of a Western student of political, social, and cultural philosophy.

Ajami's assertion about nativism is perhaps the strongest evidence of "Western" influence. Michael M.J. Fischer, whose article on "Islam and the Revolt of the Petite Bourgeoisie" also treats Islamic fundamentalism superficially, begins that same article with a quotation from Barrington Moore that differs little from Ajami's conclusion:[9]

. . . 20th century religious conflict and fanaticism are qualitatively different [writes Moore]. They resemble more closely the well known phenomenon of nativism. In many parts of the world, when an established culture was beginning to erode, threatening some of the population, people have responded by reaffirming the traditional way of life with increasing and frantic vigor. Often the reaffirmation has but tenuous connection with historical reality.

Moore does not go on to say that the nativist revolt (read: fundamentalist protest) is doomed to failure but he clearly implies its futility, as does Fischer in his highly literate essay. Among those who practice the art of dialectical dance, Fischer rivals Ajami in the skill of gathering a maze of references to delineate a target, the omnipresent fundamentalist, who is pursued but never defined. Fischer's article begins with a litany of social upheavals in numerous parts of the Muslim world — Africa as well as the Middle East, extending to Turkey and, of course, his own area of special interest and expertise, Iran. That litany is followed by a unique chronology that highlights the role of Islamic fundamentalism. Labeled "Contributions and Failings of the Five Generations," it divides recent Muslim history into the following five periods:[10]

1. Puritanical religious reformism: pre-modern fundamentalism — eighteenth-nineteenth centuries
2. Modernist reformism: the expected cast of actors — Afghani, 'Abduh, Ahmad Khan, Atatürk, Iqbal — early twentieth century
3. Neo-fundamentalists: Muslim Brotherhood, Mawdudi's Jama'at-i Islami — 1930s, 1940s
4. Islamic socialism: Nasser, Destour, Ba'th, Bhutto — post World War II
5. Islamic resurgence of the 1970s and 1980s

It is a neat, in my view too neat, scheme into which many parts can be fit, for it serves as a backdrop to analyzing the current drama of resurgence, highlighted by the emergence of petit bourgeois fundamentalists in Iran. Fundamentalism, in Fischer's view, never loses its reformist edge. It is fundamentalist reformism which appeals to former rural ignoramuses, shopkeepers, clerks, teachers, craftsmen, all of whom have been drawn into the urban cockpit (whether by hope of economic profit or by military/political compulsion) and henceforth struggle to maintain rural values in defiance of the European life-style aped by the technological and bureaucratic elites among their countrymen.

But beware the generation gap! The tide of potential dissidence swells among the children of the same urban petite bourgeoisie, for the children have benefited from expanded educational and cultural horizons. They know of a world different from that of their fathers and forefathers. Yet there are fewer jobs, in some cases none, for this generation. Out of their frustration emerges an urge for social and religious change. Hence both Marxist revolutionaries and religious fundamentalists recruit members from this same class: the second-generation members (male and female) of the urban petite bourgeoisie.

The historical review and ideological profile of Muslim society presented by Fischer seems to be a curious admixture of modified class analysis and anthropological dilettantism. Its early sections are interesting chiefly because of the manner in which he culls and compares a broader sampling of secondary sources than is available to most readers. The final section, however, shifts gears, and the reader is presented first with Muammar Qaddafi and then Ayatollah Khomeini as examples of how contemporary Islamic fundamentalisms work: they are not simply regressive atavisms but modern ideologies using "time-honored disguises." The elliptical citation from Karl Marx is elucidated in a footnote (41), to the effect that spokesmen of the Islamic movement often consciously speak two languages, one for the general public and one for use among Muslims.[11] This, of course, echoes the charge that Elie Kedourie never tires of leveling at Jamal al-Din al-Afghani, and that his younger disciple, Daniel Pipes, aims at a host of other contemporary Muslim leaders. It is impossible to refute, but also impossible to confirm, since few of the cited leaders have denied the West as an implicit source of inspiration — only as an object of unthinking imitation and servile compliance. More interesting is Fischer's attempt to show how the persona of Khomeini appeals to both the subproletariat of unemployed new urban immigrants and the traditional (that is, second-generation) urban petite bourgeoisie, groups which previously have been in conflict with one another.

Yet none of his sleight-of-hand arguments amount to a holistic analysis of Muslim society or a baring of Islamic fundamentalism. Rather, we are left with Barrington Moore's caveat, to wit, that "aspects of nativism . . . can be seen in the charismatic leadership and sectarian forms used by contemporary Islamic fundamentalism."[12] Old-style tribal revolts take place only at peripheries; though they may affect the center, they do not originate there. What does derive from the center are "ademocratic mass politics," that is to say, dictatorships, either theocratic or secular, which define

Islam in a state obedience context, and against which Islamic fundamentalists vigorously protest.

Hamid Enayat, whose book *Modern Islamic Political Thought* poses unique perspectives on a variety of issues precisely because its author moves easily in both Sunni and Shi'i primary source material, nonetheless stands in the tradition of Ajami and Fischer on the question of Islamic fundamentalism: He repeatedly refers to what he understands to be fundamentalism yet never ventures to define it. More self-conscious in his methodology than either Ajami or Fischer, he tries to adduce a model of historical development in Islamic thought that is fuller than Fischer's skeleton precisely because it is interactive: a prodigious textualist, Enayat looks at the range of views within the writings of each major figure, some well known, some scarcely known, and he then elaborates their attempts to be consistent with what they presume to be core Islamic principles. His is a sympathetic rather than a carping approach. Perhaps for that reason he never uses the word "reform," which, despite its repeated invocation by other writers, is riddled with ambiguity in the context of contemporary Islam. Instead, Enayat sees two phases of contemporary fundamentalism: the period through the emergence of Rashid Rida, and the era of his successors. In the first phase, fundamentalism appeared as "the most political manifestation of Islamic religious thought from the mid-twenties onwards, serving as the meeting ground between the puritanism of the Wahhabis, and the teachings of the Salafiyya."[13] But, beginning with Rashid Rida, these twin wings of Islamic fundamentalism, as Enayat calls them, drifted apart, the Salafiyya being increasingly represented by activist and revolutionary trends, while Wahhabism retreated to a staunch conservatism. All later fundamentalists are then depicted as descendants ("continuators") of the trend initiated by the Muslim Brothers, namely, to deny the parallel existence of religious and political spheres and to insist on the subordination of the former to the latter. Enayat locates the most graphic examples of present-day Islamic fundamentalist movements in Egypt, Iran, and Pakistan, and contrasts them first with each other on fine points, and then collectively on a broad plane with the traditional type of fundamentalism exemplified by the Saudi model.[14]

While applauding Enayat's fine attention to textual data, one must wonder by what leap of faith in historical methodology he posited the Wahhabis and the Salafiyya as belonging to a common movement. However much they might be identified as anticolonialists, they were fighting on different ground against different enemies, even using different tools and espousing different goals. He broadens their role as dissenters beyond clear and cogent definitional boundaries.

The Arm's-Length Survey

Among current scholars who are aware of the ambiguities of Islamic ideology in general and fundamentalism in particular, three are outstanding for their effort to come to terms with what fundamentalism connotes as a thought-form and how it relates to both contemporary and earlier thought-forms. Since each of them has written extensively on the issue, it seems preferable to deal with them serially before attempting to present a summary thumbnail definition of Islamic fundamentalism that may be reasonably applied to present-day Muslim movements.

Detlev Khalid, in an early article titled, "The Phenomenon of Re-Islamization,"[15] depicted Islam as a multifaceted cultural process, with two major tendencies: the formalism of the urban *'ulama* and the Sufism of the rural masses. Fundamentalism as a minority strand evolved only in the modern context, in response to challenges of Westernization and often through the subtle co-optation of Western sources. Hence, in his view, puritan Wahhabis in Arabia and mystical Sanusis in Libya represent two kindred wings of nascent Islamic fundamentalism, "due to a kindred geo-political situation (desert Islam, with little acculturation) plus a special historical affinity (loyalty to the Hanbali *madhhab*)." Each exemplifies Islamic fundamentalism, which he then deductively describes:[16]

> As both interpretations [that is, the dominant interpretations, formalism and Sufism] found it difficult to cope with the increasing challenges of modernity, there merged a third force which is commonly called fundamentalism or integralist Islam. It is re-invigorated formalism . . . It militates against fatalistic quietism and endeavors to substitute this with the belief in Islam as a political ideology. Hence this Muslim fundamentalism is also called Islamism, because it visualized itself as a rival to all "foreign" ideologies such as socialism, communism, fascism, nationalism and liberalism . . . Fundamentalism is suspicious of both mysticism and theology, not to mention philosophy. The Islamists regard all of these as intrusions upon the fundamental message of Islam as enshrined in primary sources, i.e., Qur'an

and hadith. Their attitude is characterized by a longing for simplicity which is presumed to be found in the original nature of Islam. As a reaction to these complexities of modern life, they proffer nativistic solutions. In this they are to be viewed in the wider context of third world attitudes, all of which have as a common denominator the crisis of identity. As for Muslims, this pride in the "pristine" simplicity as well as in the finality and all-comprehensiveness of the Islamic message has been fostered by many of the writings of European orientalists . . . A number of their [the orientalists'] contentions are all too eagerly pounced upon by Muslim fundamentalists. While they sincerely believe that they are propagating nothing but the pure Islam of the days of the Prophet and his first "rightly guided" Caliphs, their teachings are in reality conditioned to a fair extent by the challenges of their assumed adversary, Western civilization.

This definition of Islamic fundamentalism is intriguing. Advanced prior to the Iranian Revolution, it contains no allusion to any group in Iran. The seminal, guiding notion is identity crisis, not only Muslim but Third World, and this point is developed further in a later article by Khalid, "Islam and the Future of Civilization."[17] Its major weakness is the same as that which Ibrahim Abu-Lughod attributed to Ajami: unflinching, unqualified faith in the primacy of ideas, and the development of rival positions in a too-sequestered, uncluttered ideological vacuum.

The chief historical question that Khalid avoids is the relationship between fundamentalism as an anti-Western, anti-modernist faith stance and the early Wahhabi, Sanusi movements which were anti-centrist but not anti-Western. The problem is averted altogether by a second member of the arm's-length survey school, Fazlur Rahman, in his article "Roots of Islamic Neo-Fundamentalism."[18] His is an essay of incomparable clarity and logic. It delineates schools of thought, liaisons, and contrasts, with a skill that few possess, and even fewer exercise. The early reformers or revivalists were Arabian, Indian, Libyan, Nigerian, and Sudanese. Rahman does not distinguish between them on the basis of historical context, choosing instead to emphasize their commonality as Islamic positivists, present-day successors to the tradition inaugurated by Ibn Khaldun. Yet they all neglected the tradition of *ijtihad* ("individual inquiry and juridical judgment"), which the next generation of Muslim thinkers — Muslim modernists — developed to a remarkable degree, writing "a brilliant new chapter in the history of Islamic thought." Their influence did not hold the day, however, and they were succeeded in the 1930s by a new breed that Rahman calls the neo-fundamentalists. Not that there weren't lingering modernists (e.g., in Egypt) or vigorous secularists (chiefly in Turkey) or traditionalists (in several quarters), but neo-fundamentalists were the newest emergent group, all the more important because they competed with the traditionalist-conservative *'alim* ("religious functionary"). (The contrast between Rahman's approach and lumping together of fundamentalism, traditionalism, and conservatism under the label "neo-normative" could not be more direct.) If the pattern sounds familiar, it is because the three phases or generations of Rahman were recycled in Fischer's "five-generations" model of Islamic history. To "puritan reformers," "modernists," and "neo-fundamentalists," Fischer simply appended socialism in the 1950s and Islamic resurgence in the 1970s and 1980s.

Like Khalid, Rahman stresses that neo-fundamentalism is above all a reaction to the threat of modernism, neither equivocal nor two-faced, as Khalid implies, but rigorously atavistic and consistently anti-intellectual. It is the anti-intellectual tone that irritates Rahman, for the neo-fundamentalist assumes that "Muslims can straighten out the practical world without serious intellectual effort, with the aid only of catchy slogans. Hence they oppose the traditional learning of Islam as well as imported ideologies." In rejecting neo-fundamentalism, Rahman also offers the clearest definition of its tenets. It is, in his words,[19]

> . . . an Islamic bid to rediscover the original meaning of the Islamic message without historic deviations and distortions and without being encumbered by the intervening tradition, this being meant not only for the benefit of the Muslim community but as a challenge to the world and to the West in particular.

Rahman also underscores the intensity of this new bid on the part of Islamic neo-fundamentalists. "It is vibrant, it pulsates with anger and enthusiasm, and it is exuberant and full of righteous hatred. Its ethical dynamism is genuine, its integrity remarkable."

Steve Humphreys is a third scholar who surveys fundamentalism at arm's length. Like Khalid and Rahman, he treats fundamentalism as being part of a spectrum of intellectual traditions that it both complements and rivals. Unlike Khalid and Rahman, Humphreys unabashedly offers secularism as the total context for all Middle Eastern Muslim nations. And it is with reference to secularism that he analyzes fundamentalism and modernism as interrelated but divergent tangents.[20]

Humphreys' work is a brilliant tour de force. Of all the approaches reviewed in this article, his is the only one that highlights the difference between modern and earlier contexts. Hence Humphreys does not have to cite apologetically the Mahdi revolt, Libyan Sanusis, or Arabian Wahhabis as precursors to modern-day Islamic fundamentalism. They belong to a previous era with its own concerns and limitations. All of them have been reshaped by the experience of colonialism, the Great Western Transmutation (to quote M.G.S. Hodgson), of which two offshoots are tradition (some might say archaism) reaffirmed in a different light, which is fundamentalism, or society redefined in a future dimension, which is modernism.

In effect, Humphreys has shifted the context of the debate about Islamic fundamentalism. It does not have to be traced to a lineal development from the desert monarchies of Arabia and Libya, and then somehow wrenched and shifted into line to serve as an opposition to the complexities of modern life.

Fundamentalism arose in the modern era. Like every other aspect of Muslim life, it was shaped by the overwhelming and new character of secularization, much of which permeated only the elite classes of Muslim countries but permanently shaped all residents of the Muslim/Arab world through the emergence of such new institutions as communications, health care, education, and, above all, nationalism. Nationalism was not and never will be a Muslim institution in origin, but it was adopted by many Muslim elites as a strategy for coping with the otherwise intractable authority of colonial governments, economies, and armies. What emerged with nationalism in nearly every country was the state as an obedience context, with the kind of Islam advocated by the government enforced on the majority as a symbol of political loyalty as well as religious orthodoxy.[21]

Fundamentalism then began as a dissident movement against both foreign power and foreign ideas perpetrated by indigenous elites. Yet it took cognizance of the power of both. The seductiveness of nationalism as an ideology was due to the illusion it gave that indigenous elites playing out the European theme of national liberation had somehow achieved an indigenous, an "Islamic" victory. The further courtship with socialism (Nasser, Ba'th, Fischer's "fourth generation," etc.) took that illusion one step further.

Fundamentalists, in the form of the Ikhwan and Jama'at, opposed Western-style nationalism in the name of Islam. But precisely because they recognized the strength of the enemy — *not* because they were trying to cloak the locus of their instrumentalities (as Khalid and Fischer, in the manner of Kedourie, have implied) — they did not hesitate to use Western writings, Western means of communications, and aspects of Western ideologies to achieve their own ends.

In other words, once Humphreys' postulation is accepted (and I accept it unqualifiedly), a whole new series of evaluations comes into play. Secularism equals nationalism, or nationalism equals secularism; it does not matter which comes first, or that only certain elites in all the concerned countries are actors in that drama. To extend the homologies, as fundamentalists were prone to do, nationalism equals secularism equals reinterpretation of religion equals devaluation of Islam as religious polity. By their very background, the new governing elites in each country have had to be Muslim; but by the nature of the institutions they were supporting, their version of Islam would be different from that of any past era, especially to the extent that they had access to means of enforcing conformity, of making the state the obedience context.

As Humphreys alone makes compellingly clear, fundamentalism took cognizance of the changed context. The fundamentalists opposed colonialism while at the same time recognizing the power of colonial institutions. Much of the motivational élan which characterized fundamentalists was unconscious rather than conscious. They have defied explanation because they do not fit into a convenient generational or typological model of Islamic history. They have implicitly recognized the novelty of the conditions facing all post-colonial, newly-independent Muslim nations in the twentieth century, yet they explicitly oppose both the expression of that novelty by modernists and also the neglect of that novelty by traditionalists. (Rahman, in particular, focuses on the bitterness between fundamentalists and the traditional *'ulama.*) It is this alienation of fundamentalists from other Muslims which belies Haddad's valiant effort to embrace conservatism/traditionalism as well as fundamentalism within the single category of "neo-normative." Both reformers and *'ulama* are castigated, their leadership eschewed. Of the two, the *'ulama* pose the greater threat to Islamic ideals. To ignore change, as they have done, is, in the fundamentalists' view, to become a victim of the historical process, to further what Abdallah Laroui identifies as "historical retardation."[22]

What is Islamic Fundamentalism?

The major problem facing Muslim fundamentalists is not, as Khalid implies, simply one of identity formation. Rather, it is one of professing loyalty *at any cost*. They know their mission: to advocate a moral ideal of Qur'anic purity, a model of history linked to the Prophet and the earliest companions. Fundamentalism is anti-intellectual to the extent that it denies the vigilant *scrutiny* which characterizes aspects of the tradition that has evolved over all the intervening years; it is anti-modernist to the extent that it refuses to allow any durable contribution from either the scientific/technological or the bureaucratic/military achievements of the contemporary era.

The force of fundamentalism is often missed because it is compared to things which it is not, and does not try to be. Hence, there is a sense in which Islamic fundamentalism cannot be a theological system, offering a comprehensive self-consistent integral view of the world and the absolute, scripture, law, and so forth. Rahman laments the general poverty of intellectual content in contemporary fundamentalism; similarly, Shaul Bakhash has noted in a *New York Times* article, "Reformulating Islam,"[23] that the Muslim world needs a new Ghazzali, a contemporary theologian-jurist to formulate the relationship between Islam and modern science.

But to fundamentalists neither the critique of Rahman nor the hope of Bakhash are relevant. In the deepest sense, they are activists with scriptural shibboleths. They espouse an ideology but not a theology, and perhaps one of their enduring values is to force others who use a variety of terms in trying to account for the Muslim world to recognize the chasm that separates theology — a handmaid of philosophy that searches for a cohesive integration of all aspects of life — and ideology — a handmaid of power that looks for ways to authenticate those who have been rendered powerless by forces which they only dimly understand. Fundamentalists are exponents of ideology; they are not theologians. The tensions, ambiguities, and paradoxes that riddle fundamentalist thought and behavior are a direct exemplification of the enormous task that they have set themselves: to be fully authentic Muslims in a world that cares little about religion and less about Islam but whose principal actors nonetheless possess the means to control the one and define the other. Doomed to failure? Of course they are, by any yardstick, whether ideological (such as the theses of Barrington Moore) or political (such as the instrumentalities of current Muslim regimes). Yet they are not unimportant.

In sum, fundamentalism is above all a kind of ideological formation, affirming the modern world not only by opposing it but also by using its means against its purposes. Second, but only second, fundamentalism is a class or generational struggle. The kind of data about Iran that Fischer presents has its counterpart in Saad Eddin Ibrahim's analysis of the militants who opposed and eventually killed Sadat.[24] They are not the disenfranchised, the rural rabble that some social scientists have supposed them to be. They are upwardly mobile, urban transplants from rural settings, with a keen sense of social/cultural/religious disjuncture. It is through a charismatic leader that they are mobilized, and more scholarly attention needs to be paid to the way in which the personas (i.e., the projected images) of particular charismatic leaders enable them to appeal to groups that on any other basis, including traditional Islam, have little in common to bring them together.

There is also a sense in which Islamic fundamentalism is much stronger than any other fundamentalism, because it does not have to struggle with other equally competitive ideologies. Fischer mentions Marxist revolutionaries and religious fundamentalists as being recruited from the same class, yet in numbers and influence fundamentalists are surely greater. Why? Because if our analysis is correct and fundamentalism is a comparatively new phenomenon which looms primarily as active opposition to a radically changed context, then fundamentalist activity is the only means by which dissidents of any sort can express themselves in most Muslim countries. Modernist and communist ideologies have been hampered by the contaminative association with past colonialist powers or present neocolonialist endeavors (the United States in Israel, the Soviet Union in Afghanistan). Islam, as Geertz has observed, was the one area that the colonialist powers could not or would not usurp. ("The only thing the colonial elite was not and, a few ambiguous cases aside, could not become was Muslim."[25]) To the extent that state ideologies of nationalist orientation have replaced the colonial powers they succeeded, their exponents have secularized Islam but not displaced it. The legitimation of nationalist leaders continues to rest in part on their efforts to depict the kind of rule they offer as consonant with the true dictates of Islam. In some cases, for some periods, they prevail, but they cannot eliminate or redefine Islam without attention to scriptural sources, sources which do not naturally or easily justify an authoritarian, ademocratic Muslim state.

Fundamentalists might have remained powerless as well as hopeless anachronisms without the impetus of the Iranian revolution. Instead of being transient, as Haddad imagines, the Khomeini regime illustrates the tenacity of fundamentalism against tremendous odds, both before and since the first visible success of the movement. Mangol Bayat, interestingly, has tried to argue that the Iranian Revolution is not fundamentalist but modernist.[26] She is both right and wrong. Iran's new government is modernist to the extent that Khomeini has manipulated symbols of the past to confer on his own rule a legitimacy that would not be justified from traditional Twelver Shi'i sources. But that manipulation is precisely why he succeeds as a fundamentalist and *not* as a traditional Twelver Shi'i ayatollah. He relies on the instrumentalities of the modern world while rejecting its essential spirit, its progenitors, its allies — internal and external, Iranian and non-Iranian.

The difficulties facing the Iranian revolution are manifold: they extend beyond the war with Iraq, which preoccupies our media-blitzed, religion-obsessed political commentators.[27] From a fundamentalist viewpoint, Iran is the first historical instance in which an oppositional ideology came to power and had to make sense of the contradictions which, because they intensified and abetted its struggle out of power, also precluded its governing successfully once in power. The balancing of the economy, the managing of the bureaucracy, the recruitment and training of the military — all these and other issues do not easily fit in with the objectives of maintaining moral purity as a personal regimen and promoting loyalty to the seventh-century Medinan state as a political ideal.

Yet to dwell on these contradictions, or even to become obsessive about who will replace Khomeini, and what state will evolve after his death, is to miss the most significant point about Islamic fundamentalism in the 1980s: the famous alleged pendulum of rural/ urban, traditional/modern, mystical/scriptural, which Ernest Gellner and some other Middle Eastern anthropologists are fond of swinging,[28] has finally become unhinged (although one may doubt that it ever oscillated with the regularity that its proponents' system-locked minds imagine). What one has instead of a regional, national, or transnational pendulum are a myriad of local situations, each bracketed by a set of variables that determine the issues and actors of the moment. With all due respect to Fischer, however, they are not little islams,[29] all scampering about looking for their special meccas; they are interlocked through a shared perception that Islam, with a capital I and in the singular case, matters more than the several alternate ideologies that compete with it, and more than the several state structures that attempt to define, and so control, it. Because Islamic fundamentalism exists, and will continue to exist, as the only pressure valve in a turbulent, cruel, uncertain world, fundamentalist Muslims will find other successes — some minor, some major, all temporary -- beyond Iran, and also beyond the lifetime of the Ayatollah Khomeini.

Notes

1. Clifford Geertz, "Conjuring with Islam," *New York Review of Books*, May 27, 1982, p. 25.

2. Edward Mortimer, *Faith and Power: The Politics of Islam* (New York: Random House, 1982), p. 249. How ironic it is that among the most laudatory (though heavily qualified) reviews of Mortimer's book is E.R.J. Owen, *Times Literary Supplement*, April 22, 1983, p. 405, titled "Finding Room for Fundamentalism"! Apparently Owen is as comfortable with the concept "fundamentalism" as Mortimer is not. The latter's "militants" or "extremists" become, for Owen as for others, "fundamentalists."

3. Yvonne Haddad, "The Islamic Alternative," *The Link*, XV (September/ October 1982): 1–14. See also her *Contemporary Islam and the Challenge of History* (Albany, NY: State University of New York Press, 1982).

4. Fadwa al-Guindi, "Veiling *Infitah* with Muslim Ethic: Egypt's Contemporary Islamic Movement," *Social Problems*, XXVIII (April 1981): 465–85, but especially pp. 472–74, where she charts the distinction drawn by the Islamists between themselves and nationalists.

5. Reference to "fundamentalism" as a technical term in Arabic and Urdu tends to be derivative from Western press sources. One Pakistani observer even went so far as to suggest that it was Voice of America (VOA) which has been responsible, since 1979, for introducing Urdu neologisms connoting "fundamentalism" through their overseas broadcasts! More difficult to trace or explain is the French term *"intégrisme,"* which enjoys wide currency not only in France but also in Morocco, Tunisia, and Algeria. Its connotations are more amenable to Muslim fundamentalists themselves, and yet it, too, has no plausible English, Arabic, or Urdu equivalent.

6. Ibrahim Abu-Lughod, "Studies on the Islamic Assertion: A Review Essay" (of nine books, beginning with Ajami's *The Arab Predicament*), in *Arab Studies Quarterly*, IV (Spring 1982): 162–63.

7. Fouad Ajami, *The Arab Predicament: Arab Political Thought and Practice Since 1967* (Cambridge, UK: Cambridge University Press, 1981), p. 200.

8. Abu-Lughod, p. 158.

9. Quoted from Barrington Moore, Jr., *Social Origins of Dictatorship and Democracy* (Boston: Beacon Press, 1967), p. 384 in Michael M.J. Fischer, "Islam and the Revolt of the Petite Bourgeoisie," *Daedalus*, III (Winter 1982): 101.

10. Ibid., p. 108.

11. Ibid., p. 125.

12. Ibid., p. 121.

13. Hamid Enayat, *Modern Islamic Political Thought* (London: Macmillan, 1982), p. 69.

14. Ibid., p. 84.

15. Detlev Khalid, "The Phenomenon of Re-Islamization," *Aussenpolitik*, XXIX (Winter 1978): 433–53.

16. Ibid., p. 434.

17. Detlev Khalid, "Islam and the Future of Civilization," *Islam and Civilization*, ed. Mourad Wahba (Cairo: Ain al-Shams University Press, 1982), pp. 127–60.

18. Fazlur Rahman, "Roots of Islamic Neo-Fundamentalism," *Change in the Muslim World*, ed. P.H. Stoddard (Syracuse, NY: Syracuse University Press, 1981), pp. 23–35.

19. Ibid. p. 33.

20. Steven Humphreys outlines his basic argument in his often-quoted article, "Islam and Political Values in Saudi Arabia, Egypt and Syria," *Middle East Journal*, XXXIII (Winter 1979): 1–19, but he refines and develops his ideas in two subsequent articles, equally readable and equally impressive: "The Political Values of Traditional Islam and Their Role in Twentieth Century Egypt," *Self-Views in Historical Perspective in Israel and Egypt*, ed. Shimon Shamir (Tel Aviv: Tel Aviv University, 1981), pp. 25–32, and "The Contemporary Resurgence in the Context of Modern Islam," *Islamic Resurgence in the Arab World*, ed. Ali Dessouki (New York: Praeger, 1982), pp. 67–83.

21. This observation is derived from K. Cragg, *The House of Islam* (Belmont, CA: Dickenson Publishing Co., 1969), p. 97. Though Cragg's reference is only to the Muslims of India who "do not have the context, or the alibi, of the state as an 'obedience context'," the phrase aptly captures the circular legitimating authority of military/tribal rulers in many contemporary Muslim nation-states.

22. Abdallah Laroui, *The Crisis of the Arab Intellectual*, trans. D. Cammell (Berkeley: University of California Press, 1976), *passim* but especially pp. 116, 129–30, and 170–74.

23. Shaul Bakhash, "Reformulating Islam," *The New York Times*, October 27, 1981: 27.

24. Saad Eddin Ibrahim, "Egypt's Islamic Militants," *MERIP Reports* (February 1982): 5–14.

25. Clifford Geertz, *Islam Observed* (Chicago, IL: The University of Chicago Press, 1973), p. 64.

26. Mangol Bayat, "The Iranian Revolution of 1978–79: Fundamentalist or Modern?," *Middle East Journal*, XXXVII (Winter 1983): 30–42.

27. A striking instance of the reductionist identification of Islam with Iran is provided by Stephen R. Grummon, *The Iran-Iraq War: Islam Embattled* ("The Washington Papers," No. 92; New York: Praeger, 1982). The author offers a policy study of macro- and micro-political issues involved in the Gulf war, but with little attention to the conflict's relevance for Islam beyond the alluring subtitle.

28. Fortunately, Gellner's mechanical view of Muslim social forces is now receiving the severe criticism that it fully merits. See especially Geertz, "Conjuring with Islam," pp. 25–26, and also Jon Anderson, "Artful Dodging in the Anthropology of the Near East," forthcoming in the *Annual Review of Anthropology*.

29. On this delicate issue, one must take exception to the arch-empiricist, rank atomist stance of some contemporary anthropologists, Muslim and non-Muslim alike, who find it convenient to avoid the Orientalist search for, or presupposition of, essence (hence, Islam, or Great Tradition of liturgical/literary canon) by stressing diversity and randomness within several societal contexts (hence islams, or little traditions, often lacking either canon or literacy). The most extreme statement of this view is Abdul Hamid El-Zein, "Beyond Ideology and Theology: The Search for the Anthropology of Islam," *Annual Review of Anthropology*, VI (1977): 227–54, but especially his critique of Geertz, pp. 227–32, as an essentialist. A less theoretically informed expression of the same distinction may be found at the conclusion of Mortimer, p. 406: "I believe it is more useful, in politics at any rate, to think about Muslims than to think about Islam." What Mortimer, El-Zein, and a host of others who follow their line of analysis miss is what Owens has rightly pointed out in his critique of the format of Mortimer's *Faith and Power*: the "continuous process of interaction" between Muslim nation-states, or better yet, the need "to find a way of explaining what it is about the history, symbols and central tenets of Islam which continues to exercise such a hold over the peoples of so large a region of the globe" (*Times Literary Supplement*, April 22, 1983, p. 405). One does not have to accept the *umma* at face value to explore the value that it obviously does have, at several levels, among Arabs and Asians and Africans, for minority and majority Muslim communities.

3 THE CONCEPT OF REVIVAL AND THE STUDY OF ISLAM AND POLITICS

Eric Davis

The decade following the 1973 Arab-Israeli war witnessed an outpouring of studies on Islam and politics, particularly Islamic radical movements. While producing a considerable amount of descriptive material, this body of literature has been characterized by a striking absence of theory. Most studies have utilized an implicit conceptual framework that grows out of an earlier tradition of Orientalist writings. A central element of this paradigm is the concept of revival or resurgence which suggests the reappearance of Islamic movements in a cyclical or more or less unchanged form. This concept is linked to the broader notion of "Islamic society" which posits that Islamic norms and values are the key determinants of political behavior and the construction of political community in predominantly Muslim countries. One of the major shortcomings of the concept of revival is its failure to address in a systematic fashion the nature of the socioeconomic changes that have occurred within Islamic political movements during the last century. By uncritically accepting the concept of revival, and failing to make explicit the criteria for its application, Western and non-Western scholars alike have presented a reified, reductionist, and ultimately ideological understanding of the relationship between Islam and politics. An escape from this theoretical *cul-de-sac* requires a historical examination of the articulation of Islamic political movements with the surrounding social structure, state formation, competing ideologies, and exogenous forces such as colonialism and the world market. Only in such manner can a dynamic understanding of the relationship between Islam and politics be achieved and a determination made of what has remained constant and what has changed.

To make the analysis more concrete, two manifestations of Islam and politics in Egypt that have frequently been placed within the context of revival will be examined. These are the Islamic reform movement of the late nineteenth and early twentieth centuries and the Islamic radical movements of the 1970s and the 1980s. The first set of questions to be considered concerns the issue of whether the historical parameters of these two movements can be sharply delineated. Since Islamic revival implies an ebb and flow in the linkage between Islam and politics, it should be possible to ascertain the beginning and end of periods that are characterized by renewed interest in the political uses of Islam. If this were not the case, and the interest in a politicized Islam were more or less constant, it could be argued that it would be more valid to think in terms of continuity, rather than discontinuity, in the relationship between Islam and politics. If the two movements that are being examined were part of a continuous or uninterrupted process, then what logical meaning could be attributed to the concept of revival or resurgence?

A second set of considerations relates to a comparison between the Islamic reform movement and the more recently identified Islamic revival. To what extent are they similar in their social bases and interpretation of Islam and to what extent do they differ? What were the direct stimuli or catalysts for each movement's formation? Who were their supporters and from what social strata were they drawn? How have they constructed their particular understanding of Islam? What was the relationship of each of the movements to the dominant sociopolitical forces in society, particularly the state, the ruling groups and the global economy? By implication, the concept of revival tells us that there should be great similarity between the two movements. Otherwise, in what sense can one speak of revival?

A third set of questions concerns the validity of describing each of the movements as cohesive and unified. Does the application of the concept of revival to the Islamic reform movement of the late nineteenth and early twentieth centuries and to the Islamic radicalism of the 1970s and 1980s suggest a cohesiveness and unity that did not and does not now exist? Obviously, all movements that resort to Islamic symbolism utilize a common referent in some sense. How meaningful is it to treat these movements as part of a unified phenomenon if they are using a common symbolic referent? In other words, how are we to reconcile continuity and change in our study of Islam and politics?

In applying the concept of revival to the Islamic movements of both the late nineteenth century and more recent times, scholars are implicitly arguing that great similarities exist between the two phenomena.[1] Indeed, this assumption of a parallelism between the so-called contemporary Islamic revival or resurgence and the earlier Islamic reform does not just encompass these two movements but extends back to the inception of Islam. That is, scholars, particularly those in the Orientalist tradition, often see the genre of Islamic revival or resurgence as a recurring phenomenon from the establishment of Islam in the seventh century A.D. until the present. The cue for this assumption of parallelism comes from the Qur'an itself. It stems from "the tradition that the Prophet intimated that Islam would need to be revitalized periodically and that in each century Providence would raise up men capable of accomplishing this necessary mission of moral and religious regeneration."[2]

However, the assumption of an isomorphism between the late nineteenth century and the present cannot be sustained under closer scrutiny. The most noticeable difference between the two Islamic political movements is in their respective social bases. The Islamic movements of the 1970s and 1980s enjoy a level of mass support that was lacking during the 1880s, the 1890s, and the first decade of the twentieth century. Furthermore, Islamic reform was much more of a formalized intellectual movement centered around such thinkers as Jamal al-Din al-Afghani, Muhammad 'Abduh, Hifni Nasif, Muhammad Tal'at Harb, Shaykh Hassuna al-Nawawi, and Shaykh Rashid Rida. Unlike the leaders of the Islamic reform movement, the leaders of Islamic radical movements of the 1980s, such as Ahmad Shukri Mustafa and Muhammad 'Abd al-Salam Faraj, are not part of the dominant intellectual paradigm, which is linked to the state, but are considered beyond the law by the government. Their humble backgrounds, their limited education, and their persecution by the state have prevented them from openly producing and distributing anything comparable to the sophisticated body of literature that was the legacy of the Islamic reform movement.

Similarly, it is erroneous to assume that either the Islamic reform movement of the late 1800s or the Islamic radicalism of the contemporary period are as homogeneous as the concept of revival would suggest. The two major proponents of Islamic reform, al-Afghani and 'Abduh, represented very different trends in the movement. Al-Afghani was a déclassé Persian whose writings on Islam were relatively shallow and whose ability to wield influence was largely linked to his relationship with the Ottoman sultan. 'Abduh, on the other hand, was part of a rising Egyptian middle class that was seeking to synthesize Western ideas of economic and technological progress with conservative interpretations of social norms based upon Islam. While al-Afghani was a political activist committed to challenging British imperial interests in the Middle East, 'Abduh was more concerned with working out an accommodation with the

British in Egypt by which the aspiring social class of which he was a part would gradually expand its economic and political influence.[3] Al-Afghani rejected the West; 'Abduh and his colleagues were already partially socialized into its norms. This can be seen by the great lengths to which they went to defend themselves from the attacks of Western Orientalists such as Gabriel Hanoteux. Significantly, many of these defenses were published in European languages, particularly French, showing the extent to which 'Abduh and fellow reformers were concerned with how Europeans, and not just their fellow citizens, viewed Islam as a culture and religion.[4] The radical Islamic organizations that were formed following the 1967 and 1973 Arab-Israeli wars eschewed any effort to legitimate Islam in the eyes of Westerners. Indeed, their ontology explicitly excluded Western culture, science, and technology. While this position suggests considerable problems for economic and scientific development, contemporary Islamic radicals exhibit little of the ambiguity toward Western society that characterized the Islamic reformers of the late nineteenth and early twentieth centuries.

Such differences as existed within the Islamic reform movement find their parallel in the 1970s and 1980s. Although groups such as al-Takfir wa-al-Hijra and al-Jihad trace their origins to the once-powerful Muslim Brotherhood, their creation reflects a profound dissatisfaction with the unwillingness of the Muslim Brotherhood to pose a significant challenge to the power and authority of the Egyptian state. To the more radical Islamic movements, the Muslim Brotherhood is a suspect or even treasonous organization. These more radical and youth-oriented groups view their leader (e.g., Ahmad Shukri Mustafa) as a *mahdi* who will rejuvenate Islam and bring salvation to the masses. Such a messianic outlook has never permeated the Muslim Brotherhood; none of its leaders — Hasan al-Banna, Hasan al-Hudaybi, Sayyid Qutb, or 'Umar al-Tilimsani — have ever made pretenses of being a *mahdi*. The new Islamic groups critical of the Muslim Brotherhood have been characterized by a "withdrawal phenomenon." Members have frequently forsaken traditional occupations to enter into communal living arrangements where begging and peddling have been used to sustain the commune. Although this notion of withdrawal from society due to its thoroughly corrupt nature was influenced by Sayyid Qutb's writings, the Muslim Brotherhood has never been sympathetic to it.[5]

According to Orientalist scholarship, the linkage between the

Islamic reform movement and contemporary Islamic political organizations is centered around Rashid Rida and the Salafiyya movement and their relationship to Hasan al-Banna. In depicting the Islamic reform movement as continuing under the aegis of Rida and Salafiyya, and degenerating into the "fundamentalism" of al-Banna and the Muslim Brotherhood, the traditional Orientalist paradigm creates an intellectual bridge between Islamic reform and the Islamic revival, and suggests the existence of both an isomorphism *and* a historical link between the two eras in question. In other words, this model argues for continuity as well as revival since it presents Islamic radicalism as having persisted over time. Reacting to the challenge of Western values during the nineteenth century, and then again during the 1970s and 1980s, Islam was revived in both instances as a political force. A metaphor appropriate to this type of thinking would be that of volcanic action, with Islamic radicalism seen as always simmering beneath the surface and periodically engaging in violent eruptions. The conceptual difficulty is that this focus fails to distinguish clearly between revival and continuity. How can one speak of revival if Islamic radical movements have been continuous over time?

To challenge this paradigm or model is not to deny that Islam possesses any unitary or homogeneous quality. However, all belief systems, religious or otherwise, are grounded in a human element, and the community of believers that comprises Islam is as socially variegated as any other community of believers. Following Abdallah Laroui, I would argue that the relationship between Islam and politics can be understood only if it is historicized. Islam cannot be discussed as an ideology in abstract terms.[6] Rather, it must be seen as linked to specific individuals or, more importantly, to groups of individuals whose material interests and psychological needs change and develop over time. Although this is not meant to imply linearity — the idea that a society is moving in a teleological sense toward a specific sociopolitical form of organization such as liberalism, secular nationalism, socialism, or a polity based upon Islamic norms — it does mean that ideologies must be linked to changing historical conditions and situated within a well-defined social structure. With these considerations in mind, let me now suggest an alternative approach to understanding the relationship between Islam and politics in modern Egypt.

Islam in Historical Perspective

If we begin with the Islamic reform movement of the late nineteenth century, we find that most scholars have not utilized the type of sociohistorical perspective that has been suggested. Instead the reform movement has been studied almost entirely from the point of view of the history of ideas and the personalities who have expounded them.[7] An important aspect of this approach is its effort to juxtapose Islamic reform to a parallel movement of secular Western liberalism. This juxtaposition is carried out by situating Islamic and Western liberal ideologies within an institutional framework linked to the two major Egyptian political parties of the late nineteenth and early twentieth centuries — the Hizb al-Watani and Hizb al-Umma. It is argued that the first of these parties represented pan-Islamicists supportive of the Ottoman sultan while the latter party represented the rising Anglophile section of the Egyptian upper class linked to the British proconsul, Lord Cromer.

Such a dichotomy is seriously misleading. In reality the bifurcation in thought was less pronounced. First, many prominent writers of the period had close ties to both political tendencies. Second, what differences did exist between the political parties were based more upon kinship and peer networks than upon sharply defined class or ideological differences.[8] For example, the most prominent advocate of Islamic reform, Muhammad 'Abduh, was closely linked to many of the large landowning families that, two years after his death, founded the Hizb al-Umma in 1907. 'Abduh was particularly important to the rising agrarian bourgeoisie because he provided Islamic justification for new financial practices such as government involvements in opening a postal savings bank and the awarding of interest on bank deposits.[9]

Muhammad Tal'at Harb was another prominent member of the emerging Egyptian bourgeoisie. Harb was both a member the Hizb al-Watani and later a founder of the Hizb al-Umma. He wrote extensively on Islam and economic issues. Of particular significance were his attacks on Qasim Amin for advocating the elimination of veiling. In promoting economic reforms, while remaining socially conservative, Harb followed 'Abduh and other prominent figures of the period.[10] It is also significant that Harb was, in the same moment, both an extremely devout and conservative Muslim and the most innovative economic reformer in the history of modern Egypt. This challenges another dichotomy between modernity and tradition, which stems from a reductionist interpretation of Weber, that asserts that devout Muslims are incapable of coming to grips with techniques of modern capitalist enterprise.[11] Just as it is erroneous to argue that ideology led to a sharp dichotomy between political tendencies at the turn of the century in Egypt, so it is invalid to argue that the responses of individuals or groups toward aspects of Western technology and economic development can be differentiated on the basis of ideology. To make the more general point, the excessive focus on ideology by many students of Islam and politics, coupled with a failure to incorporate other elements of social change, tends to lead to predictions about behavior patterns, political affiliations, and responses to the West that often prove to be invalid.

The class dimension of the Islamic reform movement in Egypt becomes clearer if we realize that the intent of these writings was to provide an ideological justification for promoting capital accumulation while sustaining prevailing modes of childhood socialization and hence the reproduction of society according to prevailing norms. In other words, Egyptian intellectuals associated with the reform movement, such as 'Abduh and Harb, sought political and economic change that would correspond to their changing class status. At the same time, they sought to prevent any change in values resulting from the corrosive impact of Western imperialism on the traditional norms or resulting from the upward mobility of members of their social stratum.

Here it is important to recognize the intersection of social class, gender relations, and ideology. Supporters of the Islamic reform movement, such as 'Abduh, Harb, Nasif, al-Nawawi and others were drawn from a class of small to medium landholders or rural petite bourgeoisie. This social stratum experienced considerable trauma during the nineteenth century as the cotton economy expanded and Egypt was integrated into the world market. In many villages, the strength of the extended family gradually eroded as family members were forced to sell their land and migrate to urban areas. Once in urban areas, these migrants often were able to establish a new economic base through education and entry into an expanding government bureaucracy.[12]

Islam and Gender Relations

Although it is difficult to document the psychological dispositions of members of the upwardly mobile petite bourgeoisie at the turn of the twentieth century, it can be argued that the intensity of the debate surrounding questions of gender, particularly as they related to the family, reflected the anxiety of the advocates of reform, all of whom were male, about their own social status during a period of significant social change. By this logic, male members of the petite bourgeoisie felt that Western imperialism not only had the potential to interfere with their accumulation of capital but also threatened their position within the hierarchy of gender relations. Given this anxiety, which is quite evident in the writings of Harb and others, it is understandable why questions of gender should have been so central to the debates of the turn of the century. Power over women became a mechanism whereby urban men could reassert their authority and retain a sense of control over their destiny. Since the family was the most important social institution in the village, the urban kin of the rural petite bourgeoisie sought to maintain its cohesiveness.

Gender relations (in the form of a retention of the traditional family structure), social class, and ideology interacted in three ways. First, it was the vertically and horizontally mobile rural petite bourgeoisie that championed the traditional family, whose key role was the socialization of youth into traditional norms and values. Second, the continuity of the traditional family was not just a means for petit bourgeois males to retain their power within the existing hierarchy of gender relations but also represented a metaphor for achieving status and power within other hierarchies such as the economic and political spheres. Third, the fierce desire to prevent change in the power relations between men and women in the family structure reflected a yearning or nostalgia for a more simple, structured, and stable rural life that was in the process of being transformed.

From Islamic Reform to the Muslim Brotherhood

The Islamic reform movement eventually dissipated as many of its intellectual leaders moved away from their youthful radicalism. Shaykh Muhammad 'Abduh became the Grand Mufti of Egypt, Muhammad Tal'at Harb left the realm of writings on religion and social values to concentrate upon economic issues and the founding of Bank Misr and the Misr Group, while the 'Abd al-Raziq family came to advocate a privatized notion of religion that, in effect, divorced religion and politics. Only Rashid Rida remained as a somewhat iconoclastic figure working to carry on the original aims of Islamic reform.

Although individual leaders may have changed their political outlook, the conditions that originally radicalized members of the rural petite bourgeoisie continued to intensify. It should come as no surprise that this environment stimulated the founding in 1928 of the first mass-based Islamic radical movement, the Society of the Muslim Brothers. Orientalists have viewed the founding of the Muslim Brotherhood as an extension of the Islamic reform movement begun by al-Afghani and 'Abduh. H.A.R. Gibb and others argue that the organization was a logical outgrowth of the efforts of the founders of the Islamic reform movement to discourage excessive exegesis of Islamic texts, thereby promoting a return to the essentials of Islam. According to this view, al-Banna took these efforts to an extreme, thus leading to the fundamentalism that came to characterize the relationship between Islam and politics after the decline of the Islamic reform movement.[13]

What this conceptualization ignores is the differing social context from which the advocates of Islamic reform emerged, as opposed to the circumstances surrounding the rise of Hasan al-Banna and the supporters of the Muslim Brotherhood. While many advocates of Islamic reform had succeeded in entering the ranks of the small agrarian and even smaller industrial bourgeoisie, changes that subsequently occurred in Egyptian society largely eliminated such opportunities for upward mobility by the time of the rise of the Muslim Brotherhood during the 1930s and 1940s. Economic conditions in the Egyptian Delta had deteriorated through increased land fragmentation, exploitation of the peasantry by usurers, neglect of the agricultural sector by the large landowning class, and the failure of economic growth to keep pace with the rise in population.

Members of the Muslim Brotherhood emerged from the lower echelons of the rural petite bourgeoisie, which had become politicized as a result of the worsening economic conditions and an upsurge of nationalism in the wake of the 1919 Revolution. This "second wave" of the petite bourgeoisie was far weaker and more fragile than its predecessors who had supported Islamic reform a half century earlier. Data gathered for the period from the early 1930s to the 1970s indicate that this social stratum was comprised largely of families with small but (in the Egyptian context) not inconsequential amounts of land (i.e., a few feddans), as well as small merchants and village artisans. Extremely conservative, this class despised and feared the middle peasantry (*al-a'yan*) that dominated village life and the absentee landowners who had prospered from the rapid expansion of the cotton economy during the nineteenth century. This marginal sector of the rural petite bourgeoisie likewise feared that it might suffer the fate of the growing ranks of landless peasants who, through their loss of land, had become agrarian wage-laborers.

Members of the petite bourgeoisie brought conservative values with them to urban areas. Since their families had had some material status in the village, their offspring had received an education, usually in a traditional religious school (*kuttab*). Thus, petit bourgeois migrants possessed the skills but not the material resources with which to seek upward mobility. Especially after the 1952 Revolution made higher education more accessible, members of this stratum sought to improve their situation by entering the universities.

The type of ideology characteristic of the Egyptian petite bourgeoisie during the 1930s and 1940s was very specific to the problems faced by a social class that was both geographically mobile and aspired to upward mobility. Its political construction of Islam differed markedly from the manner in which Islam had been cast, decades earlier, by the advocates of a synthesis of Islamic and Western reforms. In expressing a vigorous opposition to big capital, members of the Muslim Brotherhood differed from members of the Islamic reform movement, who ultimately sought reconciliation with foreign capital in the form of a "junior partner" status. In violently attacking Marxism, which was beginning to gain acceptance among some Egyptian intellectuals and political activists during the 1930s and 1940s, the Brotherhood's ideology contained an important element that was absent from the earlier reform movement.

It is true, as Orientalists have argued, that both the Islamic reform movement and the Muslim Brotherhood expressed the notion that the decline of Islam stemmed from the failure of Muslims to follow its true precepts, that they both voiced varying degrees of hostility to the West, and that they emphasized the intrinsic unity of the Muslim community. These similarities should not, however, obscure the significant differences between the two movements. Whereas Islamic reform called for Western imperialism to recognize the influence of the aspiring Egyptian bourgeoisie and give it a role in domestic surplus expropriation, Islamic radicalism of the 1930s and 1940s advocated a corporate unity of Egyptian Muslims in opposition both to the West and to atheist intellectuals and their supporters among the nascent working class. The Muslim Brotherhood also began to speak to issues that were of interest to the emerging working class population, partly due to competition with other emerging mass-based movements such as the Egyptian Communist Party and Misr al-Fatat.

In many respects, the Islamic radicalism of the Muslim Brotherhood reflected more a rupture than a continuity with the earlier efforts at Islamic reform by al-Afghani, 'Abduh, and the Salafiyya of Rashid Rida. Its construction of ideology points to a process, namely the deepening of underdevelopment in Egyptian society and the attendant spread of political consciousness among the lower middle and lower classes, that had not existed during the late nineteenth century. While many symbols of the two movements had surface similarities, their social referents were very different. For reformists, Islamic unity meant unity of the agrarian bourgeoisie and the petite bourgeoisie in their efforts to force British colonial rule to accommodate their needs. For radicals, unity meant the unity of the urban petite bourgeoisie, often in alliance with the working class, in an effort to totally dislodge British economic and political influence from Egypt. Supporters of Islamic reform accepted much of Western culture — having often received a Western education, learned Western languages, and even formed friendships with foreigners — and advocated educational and legal reforms as means for bringing about social change. Advocacy of this type of political perspective indicated that supporters of the Islamic reform movement already considered themselves part of the dominant political and economic system. The Muslim Brothers faced a much more uncertain environment, and their strident politics and vigorous rejection of Western culture reflected a consciousness that accommodation with Western imperialism was neither desirable nor feasible and that only through struggle, often violent, could change occur.

The one area in which there seems to have been some continuity in ideological terms was in the conceptualization of gender relations. Both the Islamic reform movement and the Muslim Brotherhood sought to circumscribe the economic and social freedom of women in Egyptian society. Even so, gender relations reflected the changes that had taken place in a period of three to four decades. Whereas women of the middle and lower middle classes had been firmly under the control of their spouses or male siblings at the turn of the century, this control had weakened somewhat among the urban petite bourgeoisie by the 1930s and 1940s. For one, women from this stratum began to enter the labor market since economic constraints necessitated an expansion of family income. Furthermore, women began to enter the universities in significant numbers which reflected an increased recognition that a university degree was a prerequisite for a position in the expanding state bureaucracy. While it must be emphatically under-lined that gender inequality remained very real, women had become important to men not just for reproduction but also as a source of additional income for the family.

Despite their disapproval, even Islamic radicals were influenced to a limited extent by the ongoing changes in gender relations, as was indicated by the founding of the Society of the Muslim Sisters in 1936. Although always conceived of as an appendage of the Muslim Brotherhood, the participation of women in this organization was significant since it represented the first type of social or political mobilization for many of them. The fact that its members were later to engage in the smuggling of arms and messages to imprisoned Brothers illustrated the sharp differences between them and their politically fragmented sisters of the late nineteenth century.[14] As in the case of the changes in class structure and ideology that have already been discussed, changes in gender relations point to the reductionist fallacy of attempting to force Islamic reform and Islamic radicalism to conform to a simple model of Islamic revival.

Contemporary Islamic Radicalism

One factor that has influenced students of contemporary Islamic radicalism to stress the notion of revival or resurgence is the idea that the Muslim Brotherhood was inactive following its suppression in 1954 and its reappearance along with splinter groups during the early 1970s. Nothing could be further from the truth. The large number of Muslim Brothers imprisoned in 1954 continued to maintain their sense of group solidarity through forming cells in prison. Upon their release between 1959 and 1963, many Brothers immediately began to rebuild the organization throughout Egypt, albeit as a much more fragmented entity. These activities led the government of Gamal Abdel Nasser to arrest over 400 Brothers in 1965 alleging a plot to overthrow the government. Once returned to prison, Brothers reconstituted cells. After having been released during the late 1960s and early 1970s, they began yet again to organize cells throughout urban areas.

The key point here is that even though many of its members were incarcerated between 1954 and the early 1970s, the Brotherhood did not disappear or lose continuity with its past. It seems that, if anything, the Brotherhood and its offshoots had relatively fewer adherents during the 1970s than at the height of the organization's power during the early 1950s when it was estimated to have had almost one million members.[15] In other words, what seems to have remained continuous is the commitment of certain strata of the Egyptian populace to Islamic radical movements, especially urban petit bourgeois youth aspiring to upward mobility. What had changed was the political interpretation of Islam.

These considerations cast serious doubt upon the concept of revival or resurgence. Rather than a new phenomenon, the Islamic radicalism of the 1970s represented a continuity and outgrowth of the Muslim Brotherhood which began to establish its strength during the 1930s. The radicalism of the 1970s had no such revolutionary connections with the Islamic reform movement of the late nineteenth and early twentieth centuries since the two movements differed sharply in terms of social bases, their construction of Islam as a political ideology, and their attitude toward traditional institutions such as gender relations and the family.

Islamic Radicalism under the Infitah

Turning to the so-called Islamic revival of the 1970s itself, many observers have failed to note that the increased strength of Islamic movements was a response in large measure to two factors that had no relationship to Islam *per se*. First, the Egyptian government took an active role in encouraging the legalization and reconstitution of the Muslim Brotherhood. Large numbers of Brothers, who had been imprisoned since 1965, were released following Anwar al-Sadat's "rectification revolution" of May 1971. These policies were part of an effort by the Egyptian government to provide a counter-weight to the left wing of the Nasserite movement, which the Sadat regime saw as the main threat to its rule. Efforts were made to strengthen Islamic norms within society. Secondary school students, especially women, were encouraged to wear Islamic garb (*al-zayy al-shar'i*) and emphasis was placed upon the rule of "science and belief" (*al-'ilm wa-al-iman*). The commitment of

Egypt to pan-Arab nationalism was drastically downplayed while provincial Egyptian nationalism (symbolized in the change of the name of the country from the United Arab Republic to the Arab Republic of Egypt and the name of the national airlines from United Arab Airlines to Egypt Air) came to replace it. To some extent therefore, the "Islamic revival" was orchestrated by the state as part of a larger effort to move the country to the right politically, to prepare for peace with Israel, and by weakening the left, to seek the investment of foreign capital under the "open door" policy (*infitah*).

Second, for some sectors of Egyptian society, the attraction to Islamic ideologies during the 1970s reflected as much a negative reaction to the allegedly socialist policies of the Nasser era as a commitment to Islamic radicalism. The massive defeat by Israel in 1967, as well as the increasing economic decline of large segments of the population, undermined the legitimacy of "socialist" approaches to development. Egyptians no longer believed that the state public sector, which had relied upon central planning and many of whose companies had been built with the aid of the Soviet Union, could solve the nation's massive economic and social problems.

It is unnecessary to look to any inherent characteristic or essence of Islam to find the cause for the increased strength of Islamic political movements during the early 1970s. Rather than speak of resurgence, one could instead argue that these movements had been active during the past three to four decades, but had received more prominence during the 1970s due to state policies and the delegiti- mation of the left. Nevertheless, there also seem to have been dramatic changes in patterns of dress and norms during the 1970s as well as dramatic increases in mosque attendance. Were these phenomena not proof of an Islamic revival?

A distinction needs to be made between religiosity and political Islam. Such changes in patterns of religious observance as the adoption by urban women (mostly from the lower middle class) of Islamic dress or increased mosque attendance in the cities do not necessarily indicate political mobilization. With the increased problems faced by the urban lower middle class in finding employment and housing, and the consequent need to postpone marriage, the existing system of gender relations is undergoing increased stress. Urban areas are extremely crowded and increas- ingly susceptible to sexual stimuli fostered by the spread of Western consumerism. By adopting "Islamic garb," urban petit bourgeois women are responding to pressures placed upon them by men who may question their "honor." As such, these women have made a subtle compact with men. They are attempting to appease male insecurities (arising from economic and psychological vulnerability) in return for economic protection in the form of (eventual) marriage.[16] Increased mosque attendance, on the other hand, could be interpreted as a reflection of anxiety felt by vulnerable strata of Egyptian society caused by economic decline and decreasing faith in the government's ability to cope with this decline as much as a renewed interest in radical Islam.[17]

What changed dramatically during the 1970s for the urban petite bourgeoisie was the decline in prospects for upward mobility.[18] This is reflected in the fact that some of the Islamic radical groups, such as al-Takfir wa-al-Hijra, that have given up the idea of upward mobility altogether. This decision is evident in the "withdrawal phenomenon" whereby youth in secondary schools and the universities have dropped out of the educational system or have left employment to join urban communes. These groups reflect the despair of urban lower middle class youth in contemporary Egyptian society.[19]

Islamic Radicalism, Class Struggle, and Ideological Transformation

What these developments suggest is a very significant transformation of the internal class struggle in Egypt. On the one hand, the contemporary Islamic radical movement has increasingly become comprised of members who defy simple class characterizations since they either lack stable occupations or have consciously rejected efforts to achieve upward mobility. On the other hand, it might be argued that the shrinking opportunities for upward mobility in Egyptian society mean that the Islamic movement will assume more of a class dimension. Since the Egyptian social stratification has become more rigid, individuals will be forced to remain in their social class and thus the lines of conflict will become more sharply defined and acute. Prospects are that violence will increase, but that this violence, as the assassinations and attacks of the past decade indicate, will not be directed toward well-defined ends. This lack of a well-articulated ideology can be attributed to the physical withdrawal of many contemporary Islamic radicals, through failure to enter the occupational structure, as well as a psychological withdrawal represented in the total rejection of existing societal norms. An indeterminate economic status and an aversion to the surrounding society have contributed to the vague understanding by Islamic radicals of their group interests and the larger historical forces shaping their destiny. The recent downturn in the price of oil forcing many Egyptians working abroad to return to an economy ill equipped to absorb them will no doubt exacerbate these trends.

Ideology, in the form of the political construction of Islam, underwent a significant change during the 1970s. As economic conditions for the lower classes have worsened, youthful Islamic radicals (in contrast to the older Muslim Brothers) have felt an increasing need to incorporate a socioeconomic program into their interpretation of Islam. This is evident in the increased impact of socialist ideas, even if not articulated as such, upon radical Islamic doctrine. The emergence of an ideological tendency along the lines of thought of the Iranian thinker 'Ali Shari'ati — one that would attempt to synthesize Islam and certain Marxist tenets — is a distinct possibility in Egypt, and indeed may be already under way.[20] Although gender relations continue to be couched in traditional terms, the exchange of wives among the déclassé members of al-Takfir wa-al-Hijra commune represents an ideologically sanctioned sexual exploitation (by the group's former leader, Ahmad Shukri Mustafa) which has not appeared in modern Islamic radical organizations heretofore.

The Conceptual Poverty of "Islamic Revival"

This synoptic overview of Islamic movements in Egypt from the late nineteenth century to the present suggests that the concept of revival or resurgence is of limited analytic utility. Since the Islamic reform movement, the Muslim Brotherhood, and contemporary Islamic radicalism, both in its more accommodationist and radical forms, have all attributed different political meanings to Islam, the notion of revival suggests a similarity and cohesiveness of thought that does not exist. Furthermore, we have seen that Islamic protest movements, reacting to the deepening of underdevelopment and increased Western influence, and drawn largely from different sectors of the petite bourgeoisie, have existed in continuous form since the late nineteenth century. However, the political and economic options open to each of these protest movements have radically changed. In this context, it makes more sense to speak in terms of the evolution of the political uses of Islam rather than notions of rupture or the cyclical character of Islamic radicalism implied by notions of revival or resurgence. Having made an argument for the need to historicize the study of Islam and politics, let us turn to the treatment of two other theoretical referents mentioned at the beginning of this essay, namely those of social structure and ideology.

While the concept of '*asabiyya* or tribal solidarity is often invoked to explain the solidarity of such diverse groups as the Khawarij, the Wahhabis, and the Sanusiyya, little effort has been made to explain what motivates particular groups of Muslims, and not others, to articulate radical Islamic ideologies at particular points in time. Considerable causal significance is attributed to the role of the leader, such as Muhammad ibn 'Abd al-Wahhab, Jamal al-Din al-Afghani, and Hasan al-Banna, in existing studies of the rise of radical Islamic movements. Were scholars of Islamic movements to take a social structural analysis seriously, they would be required not only to determine the social origins of the movement's membership, but also to try to explain the structure or configuration of conflict within the overall society and to situate Islamic radicals within such a structure. Any systematic analysis of this type would necessitate discarding the notion of Islamic society, since no longer could it be argued that the behavior of all Muslims resonates according to the same norms. It is in this sense that the atomism that characterizes the study of Islamic movements is logically linked to the ahistorical approach discussed earlier. A methodology incorporating both history and social structure would require disaggregating the society under scrutiny and moving beyond such simple dichotomies as traditional or orthodox versus alternative Islam.[21] Such concepts offer no sense of the motion of society, since they cannot theoretically differentiate the seventh from the twentieth century.

The obverse of the neo-Orientalist model is an extreme position that largely denies any causal significance to Islam by reducing it to class. Faced with the strength of Islamic political movements during the last decade, Marxists in particular have been forced to reevaluate this position and to "rediscover Islam."[22] To insinuate that Islam is merely "the opiate of the masses" is to do an injustice not only to the sociopolitical reality of countries in which Islam is a major force but also to the sophistication of much Marxian analysis of ideology and consciousness. Some of the most subtle and nuanced theorizing in this regard is contained in the writing of Antonio Gramsci. Gramsci's notion of hegemony and its derivative concept of the "historic bloc" suggests that ideologies are rarely class-specific. Any portrayal of a secular and Westernized bourgeoisie and laboring class becomes too simplistic.[23] As Gramsci argues, the institutions of civil society always embody the ideology of the hegemonic or would-be hegemonic class or class coalition. Hegemony is a historical process that requires time to become institutionalized as the ruling classes attempt, with each new generation, to mold and "fine-tune" the dominant ideology.[24]

Hegemony implies an acceptance of a fundamental ideology across classes and through this process the potential for creating a historic bloc.[25] To refer to this acceptance or accommodation by the dominated classes as false consciousness would be reductionist since it is often possible for the hegemonic class(es) to offer strata outside the ruling circle material benefits and not just psychological or symbolic palliatives. The Nasserite effort to create hegemony entailed a conjuncture in which an ideology purporting to be socialist expropriated a small landed and industrial bourgeoisie but gave lucrative public sector directorships, and high-level positions in the army and the bureaucracy, to a sizable sector of the upper middle and middle classes while simultaneously extending wage, pension, and educational benefits to the urban petite bourgeoisie and working class. This is but one example of conditions under which a single ideology can permeate large segments of society drawn from different social classes.

In this sense, the critique of the study of Islam and politics cannot simply rest with the negation of a reified or transhistorical concept of Islamic society but rather must seek to understand how the myths and values of the past have come to shape the conflicts of the present. While the concept of Islamic society is unacceptable in its reified form, so too is the reduction of Islam to social class or false consciousness and hence its treatment as epiphenomenon. The challenge becomes one of combining unity and diversity in the analysis of social change: how do we ascertain the contours of political discourse that Islam has provided from the past and how different classes or blocs have come to shape this tradition according to their contemporary material interests and psychological needs?

While focusing upon the construction and maintenance of hegemony Gramsci also sought to elaborate its contradictions. To return to the Egyptian experience, the attempt by Nasserism (and its sister ideologies of Arab socialism in Algeria, Syria, and Iraq) to become hegemonic succumbed to the contradictions of accumulation. Requiring new infusions of capital and access to Western technology, the Egyptian bourgeoisie of the 1970s — created under Nasser but only really flourishing under Sadat — could no longer tolerate the populist corporatism of the late 1950s and 1960s with its heavy social welfare burdens and its egalitarian and anti-imperialist rhetoric. Material conditions impeded the acceptance of a new ideology that sought to combine Western liberal notions fostering accumulation with Islamic norms of political community intended to give the Sadat regime a mass base. Although the regime released large numbers of Islamic radicals from prison and used them to counter the residual influence of Nasserites and their leftist supporters, and was able to offer minor educational and political reforms intended to enhance the regime's "Islamic" credentials, it was unable to reward the classes which it wanted to incorporate into a new historic bloc with significant material benefits either in the form of economic rewards or political power. Thus the Sadat regime's attempt to construct hegemony was even less successful than that of Nasser.

These developments in Egypt during the 1970s point to the double-edged character of the notion of hegemony. In its effort to form a historic bloc, a ruling class will seek to generalize its own interests to other segments of society and, of course, to as large a segment as possible. This creates standards of norms of behavior to which the ruling class often cannot or will not conform. Such was the case for the Egyptian bourgeoisie during the 1970s. Although the political class articulated norms that resonate with the needs and interests of large segments of society, the bourgeoisie's behavior was often so inconsistent with such norms (e.g., the well-known corruption within the Sadat family itself), that the attempt to construct a new hegemonic ideology ultimately failed to take hold among significant sectors of the subordinate classes.

Perhaps the most cogent argument for situating ideologies in a cross-class context is to be found in Marxian theory itself. In those countries in which Islam plays an important role in politics, what Marx refers to as the relations of production have only relatively recently begun the transformation from a precapitalist past. The integration of the countries of the Middle East into the world market began in a significant fashion during the early to mid-nineteenth century. Only during the twentieth century did industrial development take place, with the concomitant development of a small, albeit often radical, working class. Social scientists working in the liberal tradition often view this state of affairs as the persistence of tradition and the corresponding lack of development of modernity. Another way in which they express this relationship is to argue that the values of rural society continue to predominate over those of urban society.

In the Marxian view, however, the weakness of industrial capital signifies that the peasantry is often not sharply differentiated from the urban working class and that members of the urban and rural petite bourgeoisie are often linked to one another by kinship ties as well as to sectors of the laboring classes from which they have only recently been separated. In this context, it is not difficult to understand how large segments of society can share similar ideologies given the lack of class differentiation and the close ties of members of the ruling classes to the mass base of society from which they have only recently emerged. In short, the construction of hegemony in societies like Egypt is problematic. While material conditions may impede the efforts of the dominant classes to construct hegemony, the relative fluidity of the social structure, represented in the persistence of kinship and regional ties that cut across class lines, still provides the opportunity for the creation of sociopolitical coalitions that span broad sectors of society.

To conclude, efforts to gain a deeper understanding of Islamic political movements require a more systematic historical methodology and a more sophisticated understanding of social structure and ideology. The concept of revival or resurgence of Islam, and its attendant notions of fundamentalism and Islamic society, work against such an understanding due to their transhistorical nature. Likewise, mechanistic attempts to link ideology and social class in a one-to-one relationship fail to comprehend many of the subtleties involved in the social mobilization of supporters of Islamic movements and the manner in which the construction of ideologies can serve to promote either hegemony or conflict in society. This essay has examined some of the shortcomings of the genre of literature dealing with the revival of Islam and suggested some possible remedies. Above all, what is needed at present is not ever larger quantities of facts about Islamic radical movements but greater theoretical rigor in their interpretation.

Acknowledgements

I would like to thank Nicolas Gavrielides and Myron Aronoff for comments on an earlier draft of this essay, and the National Fellows Program of the Hoover Institution for a twelve-month research grant which allowed me time to write it.

Notes

1. There is extensive literature on Islamic revival or resurgence during the 1970s and 1980s. For some of the more recent writings, see 'Abd al-Moneim Said Aly and Manfred W. Wenner, "Modern Islamic Reform Movements: The Muslim Brotherhood in Contemporary Egypt," *The Middle East Journal*, 36, no. 3 (Summer 1982): 336–361; Edward Mortimer, *Faith and Power: The Politics of Islam* (New York: Vintage Books, 1982); the special issue of the *Middle East Journal*, 37, no. 1 (Winter 1983) on Islamic revival; John Esposito (ed.), *Islam and Development* (Syracuse, NY: Syracuse University Press, 1980); the perceptive study by Michael Gilsenan, *Recognizing Islam* (New York: Pantheon Books, 1982); and, most recently, Giles Keppel, *The Prophet & Pharaoh: Muslim Extremism in Egypt* (London: Al-Saqi Books, 1985).

2. M.A. Zaki Badawi, *The Reformers of Egypt* (London: Croom Helm, 1978), pp. 74 et passim.

3. E. Van Donzel, B. Lewis, and C.H. Pellet, *The Encyclopedia of Islam* (Leiden: E.G. Brill, 1978), p. 141.

4. See, for example, Muhammad Tal'at Harb's defense of Shaykh Muhammad 'Abduh, *L'Europe et l'Islam: M.G. Hanoteux et le Cheik Mohammed Abdou* (Cairo: Imprimerie Jean Politis, 1905), pp. 3–18, 72–78.

5. Sayyid Qutb, *Ma'alim fi al-tariq* (Cairo: Dar al-Shuruq, n.d.).

6. Abdallah Laroui, *The Crisis of the Arab Intellectual* (Berkeley and Los Angeles: University of California Press, 1976), esp. chapter 4, "Historicism and the Arab Intellectual."

7. The studies of H.A.R. Gibb, *Modern Trends in Islam* (Chicago: University of Chicago Press, 1947); *Islamic Society and the West*, vol. 1, parts I and II (Oxford: Oxford University Press, 1950); and *Whither Islam?* (London: Gollancz, 1932); Malcolm Kerr, *Islamic Reform* (Berkeley and Los Angeles: University of California Press, 1966); and Elie Kedourie, *Afghani and Abduh* (London, 1966).

8. For further details on this point, see my study, *Challenging Colonialism: Bank Misr and Egyptian Industrialization, 1920–1941* (Princeton, NJ: Princeton University Press, 1983), pp. 48–50.

9. Ibid., p. 72.

10. It is interesting to compare the conservatism of Harb's writings on social issues, such as the controversy over the veil and women's roles in Muslim society, and his conservative views on Islam with the innovative, one might even say radical, character of his writings on economic issues. Compare *Al-mar'a wa-al-hijab* (Cairo: al-Turqi Press, 1899), *Fasl al-khitab fi al-mar'a wa-al-hijab* (Cairo: al-Turqi Press, 1901), *L'Europe et l'Islam*, and *Tarikh duwal al-'arab wa-al-Islam*, vol. 1 (Cairo: Jaridat Turk Press, 1905), with *Qanat al-Suways* (Cairo: al-Jarida Press, 1910), and *'Ilaj Misr al-iqtisadi wa mashru' bank al-Misriyyin* (Cairo: al-Jarida Press, 1911) in which he argued for the founding of a national bank to challenge foreign domination of the Egyptian economy.

11. On this issue, see the writings of Maxime Rodinson, *Islam and Capitalism* (Austin, TX and London: University of Texas Press, 1978), pp. 148–152; Alvin W. Goulder, *The Coming Crisis of Western Sociology* (New York: Avon Books, 1970), pp. 178–183; and Bryan Turner, *Weber and Islam* (London: Routledge & Kegan Paul, 1978), esp. pp. 151–70.

12. See my study, "Ideology, Social Class and Islamic Radicalism in Modern Egypt," in S. Arjomand (ed.), *From Nationalism to Revolutionary Islam* (London and Albany, NY: Macmillan and State University of New York Press, 1983), pp. 142–43, which presents data on the social bases of the Muslim Brotherhood and its offshoots between the early 1930s and the 1970s.

13. Gibb, *Modern Trends in Islam*, pp. 109, 119–20.

14. See, for example, 'Abd al-Halim Khafaji, *Hiwar ma'a al-shuyu'iyyin fi aqbiyat al-sujun* (Kuwait: Maktabat al-Falah, 1979).

15. Richard P. Mitchell, *The Society of the Muslim Brothers* (London and New York: Oxford University Press, 1969), P. 328.

16. Of course, this social dynamic underscores the dependent political and economic status of urban lower middle class women in contemporary Egypt.

17. Increased mosque attendance represents yet another of those categories that fails to place Islam in its social context. Have, for example, more upper class Egyptians been attending mosques? The answer is obvious; it is the more economically vulnerable Egyptians who have manifested this behavior.

18. While prospects for upward mobility were enhanced somewhat during the 1970s by the employment of urban lower middle class Egyptians in Libya and the Gulf, the recent decline in oil prices setting in motion a "reverse migration" indicates that the "oil boom" was a temporary phenomenon.

19. Gilsenan, *Recognizing Islam*, pp. 221, 226–28.

20. One example of such a synthesis can be found in the Egyptian journal, *Al-yasar al-Islami* (The Islamic Left), published by the religious and social thinker, Dr. Hasan Hanafi. See also the incipient socialist thinking in Ahmad Shukri Mustafa's critique of contemporary Egyptian society in Keppel, *The Prophet & Pharaoh*, pp. 78–90.

21. See, for example, the distinction between "elitist institutional" and "alternative Islam" in Fadwa El Guindi, "Veiling Infitah with Muslim Ethic: Egypt's Contemporary Islamic Movement," *Social Problems*, vol. 28, no. 4 (April 1981): 465, 473.

22. Among those who have "rediscovered Islam" are such prominent Egyptian leftist intellectuals as 'Adil Husayn, Tariq al-Bishri, and Saad Eddin Ibrahim. Conversation with El Sayed Yassin, Princeton University, May 1983.

23. Even in Iran, which is perhaps the closest approximation of such a model, the bourgeoisie was not unified, being divided between the royalists and the national front; the middle and working classes contained large numbers of secularists and Marxists, and socialist ideologies had strong roots among sectors of the industrial working class, especially the oil workers.

24. Antonio Gramsci, *Prison Notebooks* (London: Lawrence and Wishart, 1971), pp. 5–23, 25–43, 125–205, 210–18.

25. Christine Buci-Glucksmann, *Gramsci and the State* (London: Lawrence and Wishart, 1980), pp. 23–24, 56–58; Martin Carnoy, *The State and Political Theory* (Princeton, NJ: Princeton University Press, 1984), pp. 74–75.

4 ISLAM AND ARAB NATIONALISM

Bassam Tibi

Throughout the modern era, the Middle East has been confronted
with two compelling ideas: secular nationalism and the Islamic
precept calling for the creation of the universal *umma* (community)
of the faithful.[1] A study of this encounter between Islam and secular
ideologies leads automatically to an inquiry into the major concerns
of modern Islam — something which cannot be understood through
an approach based exclusively on a textual analysis of dogmatic
Islamic writings.[2] To be sure, traditional Orientalist scholars and
Islamic fundamentalists would contest the preceding statement by
appealing to the notion of "Islamic essence." They deny the
necessity of studying the historical context in which the Islamic faith
emerged and developed. To Islamic fundamentalists any difference
between the realities of Islam and the contents of traditional or
traditionalist writings is merely a deviation or falling away from the
aforementioned essence,[3] while to some German Orientalist
scholars the study of reality is considered to be the job of social
scientists, of whom these Orientalists habitually speak with
contempt. But since our present purpose in studying the
relationship between Islam and secular ideologies[4] is not exegetic,
the focus here will be on sociopolitical realities. In particular, one
should note that the traditionalist assumption of Islam's immuta-
bility and monolithic universality does not hold up under scrutiny,
for the story of Islam has been marked by both cultural diversity[5]
and historical variation.[6] These characteristics enrich Islam, and
should not be dismissed as deviations from an Islamic essence that
exists only in dogmatic literature.

Our point of departure since the nineteenth century is the
assumption that global interdependence has maintained in
existence a world society linking all nations. This world society is the
end result of the spread of European influence and technology
during the period of colonialism. In the course of this process, the
European market turned into the world market and bourgeois
society into world society. The political units of interaction in this
new setting are the nation-states. The Islamic peoples have been
incorporated (or more precisely forcibly integrated) into this new

structure, which is dominated by the industrialized countries.[7] The social scientist has to deal with two aspects of this world society: its structure and its ideology. First, he has to ask to what extent traditional social structures have been disrupted or transformed, and to inquire whether the notion of a world society implies the global predominance of modern social structures. Second, he has to undertake a "critique of ideology,"[8] by examining how people perceive changing social realities and what devices are employed to legitimize the new social structures.

At present, the world consists exclusively of nation-states that are in both practical and legal terms the actors in world politics.[9] Nevertheless, there exist three political tendencies opposed to the supremacy of the nation-state, and all of them are relevant to the study of Islamic societies. These tendencies are: (1) the plea for universalism beyond the boundaries of the nation-state; (2) the plea of national irredentism, which is similar to universalism in that it challenges the existing boundaries of certain nation-states; and (3) the plea of ethnicity, which sometimes amounts to a call for separatism. The notion of universalism arises in the Islamic context by way of the precept of calling for the creation of a religiously cohesive Islamic *umma*. The notion of national irredentism is manifested in the ideal of Arab unity, though commitment to this goal has receded, with most Arab regimes giving it only lip service.[10] The notion of separatism makes its appearance in connection with ethnic conflicts within the existing nation-states (e.g., the clashes between Berbers and Arabs in Morocco and in Algeria) and the activities of separatist ethnic groups who, though Islamic, long to create their own nation-states (e.g., the Kurds).

We will next examine the concept of ideology, with particular reference to the ideologies of Arab nationalism and of Islamic universalism.[11] This discussion will be followed by an exploration of how the *umma* concept relates to these two ideologies. The chapter will conclude with a look at the implications of the so-called Islamic resurgence.

Ideology and Society

Even among scholars, ideology has become a fuzzy concept. The notion of ideology, and efforts to define it, can be traced back to the end of the eighteenth century, when philosophers began to reflect on the origin of ideas.[12] Since then, the term "ideology" has passed from philosophical and scholarly literature into everyday speech. One could say that the theoretical outline has been lost, because underlying the general notion there remains only a vague memory of the theoretical constructs whereby the now empty concept acquired its meaning. In 1951, Max Horkheimer complained that "very often ideology is used to mean nothing more than any kind of mental association, a theory, a single notion or even everything to do with mind or spirit."[13] The concept is used so loosely that we can, for instance, be informed by Leonard Binder that there has been an ideological revolution in the Middle East.[14]

An outline of that part of the history of ideas concerning the notion of ideology or a discussion of the different definitions assigned to it is beyond the scope of this chapter. It should suffice in this context to note that there is no autonomous world of ideas affecting human action. Ideas are always a part of social realities. They are themselves, as the French sociologist Emile Durkheim has put it, *faits sociaux*.[15] But while I reject idealism (the notion that ideas have an autonomous social power), I also believe that ideas cannot be reduced to nothing but social constraints; in the words of Theodor Adorno, they are "both connected with society and at the same time autonomous."[16] In this connection, I agree with Helmuth Plessner's call for a "stand against [the] severance of the concept of ideology from its original context, and against what one might call its technical transformation into a vague term in empirical research."[17] Idealism and crude materialism both smack of reductionism. Whereas simplistic materialism reduces mind to matter and interprets the latter as social structure, idealism sees society as the product of mind. It should be noted that the latter approach is not just of historical interest, to be associated with, for instance, classical Hegelian idealism.[18] Indeed, a renovated idealism dominates parts of modern U.S. social science. The claim is made that mind (here in the guise of a system of norms and values) shapes society. Underdevelopment, for instance, is considered by these idealists to be the result of cultural tradition.[19] Modernization theory, which plays a predominant role in U.S. social science, is, "like the recent theory of social action to which it refers, characterized by a distinct normative-subjectivist bias."[20]

Ideology is a part of society which we do not divide into infrastructure and superstructure: Ideology and social structure belong to a dialectical and not to a schematic-causal context, so that they are not reducible to an infrastructure or a superstructure.

The point of view advocated above provides the researcher with an analytic framework valid in connection with single societies not exposed to external influences. Our affirmation that ideology always stands in the context of social evolution refers to an indigenous social constellation with its own social dynamic. European history illustrates this case. But Islamic societies (and all other non-Western societies) have been subject to foreign influence since the colonial penetration,[21] and their social formations are no longer the product only of a domestic social dynamic. Thus, no ideology can be found in these societies that is explainable solely in terms of the indigenous social dynamic, not even Islam. Thus, a new approach is imperative for the study of ideologies in Islamic and other non-Western societies. Such an approach cannot be presented in its entirety in this chapter, but some insights can be gained into the nature of the ideologies in these societies.

The disruptive effects of the process of colonial penetration were all-encompassing, and included the phenomenon of acculturation — a process of exogenously induced cultural and political change.[22] According to acculturation theorist Richard Behrendt,[23] when acculturation takes place elements of the penetrating culture may be imitated, adopted, or incorporated into the local structure, which may thereby undergo extensive change. Behrendt considers the most influential of all ideological elements in non-Western societies, namely nationalism, to be an acculturative ideology. Addressing the same context, many U.S. modernization theorists have drawn distinctions between traditional, transitional, and modern ideologies.[24] If the ideology changes, they assume, then the society changes, too. Social revolution is reduced to a change in value and norm systems. Here the "normative-subjectivist bias" is quite clear. Binder's *The Ideological Revolution in the Middle East*[25] and Halpern's *The Politics of Social Change in the Middle East and North Africa*[26] can be cited as classical examples of this approach.

In the light of the preceding theoretical considerations, it is now clear that for the purpose of this chapter we have to regard Islam as an indigenous culture and political ideology and to regard nationalism as an acculturative political ideology. These two ideologies can be studied in three ways. First, they can be looked at abstractly, without reference to a social setting. Second, one can explore their domestic context (but without forgetting the methodological assumption that ideologies are connected with society and at the same time are autonomous). Third, one can try to carry the analysis beyond the domestic level into the international environment (i.e., the world societal setting).

Islam and Arab Nationalism in the Modern Era

History has seen different types of states (e.g., the city-state, the medieval universal state, the dynastic state, and our particular concern, the modern nation-state[27]) and thus different kinds of devices for upholding state legitimacy. "Natural law" constitutes the underlying concept of the nation-state, and its distinctive legitimacy device is the idea of popular sovereignty, i.e., that of the nation.[28] The nation-state system and the idea of nationality became a universal phenomenon as a result of the European penetration and subsequent comprehensive restructuring of the non-Western world.

I have pointed out in the foreword to the English edition of my inquiry on Arab nationalism that the vast majority of the literature on this subject is descriptive rather than analytical. One usually finds either a narrative history of a specific period or a presentation in terms of Hegelian "intellectual history" (Geistesgeschichte). One encounters either a complete lack of effort at conceptualization or a heavily value-laden discussion of the nature of Islam and Arab nationalism. Eric Davis has criticized this literature in the following terms: "It is obvious that writings on Arab nationalism have been affected by the tendency to view ideology in terms of social pathologies. Arab ideologies are seen as irrational and distortive, having transformed Arab history into myth and having twisted the true meaning of Islamic doctrine."[29] The writings of Elie Kedourie and Sylvia Haim are cited by Davis as examples of such an Orientalist approach. The Orientalists ignore the three kinds of analysis discussed earlier which are prerequisites for a proper understanding of Islam and Arab nationalism as political ideologies: critique of ideology, examination in the domestic context, and examination in relation to the international environment.

To carry out the first of these steps, one must refer to the political concepts of Islam and the Arab community. The Arabic translation of the word "nation" is *umma*. Adherents of political Islam and Arab nationalists both use this term. Its use to denote "nation" evolved as a result of European influence; the traditional Islamic notion of *umma* has a completely different meaning and also a different historical background.[30] Prior to Islam, the Arabs were organized in each case as *qawm* (i.e., people in the sense of tribe) within an overwhelmingly tribal setting. The unification of the Arabs within the framework of the Islamic *umma* was, as the research of W.M. Watt[31] has shown, the great achievement of Islam. This *umma* is universal; it is neither ethnic nor national. In Islam, the only criterion for drawing distinctions between Arabs and non-Arabs is piety (*la farq bayn 'Arabi wa 'ajami illa bi-al-taqwa*). The well-known conflicts in Islamic history between Arabs and non-Arab Muslims (*mawali*) are best interpreted as ethnic and not as national conflicts, though they are represented as the latter in contemporary pamphleteering and also in some old sources.[32]

In the contemporary political Islamistic ideology, Islam is perceived as a political identity as well as the framework of an Islamic political community. Furthermore, Islam is interpreted as a political system. To what extent does history show these perceptions and interpretations to be correct?

The Prophet Muhammad first founded a small group of disciples and adherents in Mecca. In 622 (the beginning of the Islamic era) they were forced to emigrate to the nearby town of Medina, where Muhammad founded a city-state which was quite clearly a theocratic, political creation, guided by the religious law of the revealed Qur'an and the deeds and sayings of the Prophet, later handed down in tradition (*hadith*). Muhammad was thus not just a religious leader, but also a clever politician and military strategist. In the words of French sociologist of religion Maxime Rodinson, Muhammed was "a combination of Jesus and Charles the Great."[33] It was only thanks to the mixture of these qualities that an empire could grow out of the theocratic city-state of Medina and a world religion out of Muhammad's small sect. Until its collapse in the thirteenth century, the Arab-Islamic empire contained one of the world's greatest civilizations and cultures.[34] The Ottoman empire founded in the fourteenth century also developed into an Islamic empire, but it was feudal-military and fell behind the bourgeois-democratic culture beginning to flourish in Europe; it was finally disbanded in 1924.

As a result of this past, modern Islam is a defensive culture. The combination of the European colonial penetration, the decay of the Ottoman empire, and the extension of the technologically more advanced European culture all over the world is seen by the Islamic peoples as signifying a real threat. The first reaction was the mobilization of Islam against the foreigners. The leading Islamic thinker of the nineteenth century, Jamal al-Din al-Afghani, understood the recourse to Islam as a weapon in the struggle against Europe. Al-Afghani's U.S. editor and biographer, Nikki Keddie, thus entitles her collection of al-Afghani's works *An Islamic Response to Imperialism.*[35]

Modern Islam can only be understood in the light of the historical background we have briefly outlined. Orientalists, however competent concerning Islam they may be, regularly misinterpret the reactions of the Islamic peoples by relying on the written doctrine and not on the historical process. The rise and decay of Islam can never be derived exclusively from Islamic teachings and sources. Rodinson has shown that there is no such thing as *homo islamicus* and no specifically Islamic mode of development that can be read out of the sources.[36] The idea of *homo islamicus* is an outcome of European romantic and sometimes nonromantic fantasy vis-à-vis the peoples in question.

Let us return to the question of whether there is an Islamic political community distinct from the Arab one, and whether Islam provides the elements for a political system uniting this community. The notion of *nizam* (system) that appears in modern Islamic writings[37] does not exist either in the Qur'an or in the authoritative classical sources:

> This term [*nizam*], however, does not occur in the Qur'an, nor indeed does any word from this root: and there is some reason for wondering whether any Muslim ever used this concept religiously before modern times. The explicit notion that life should be or can be ordered according to a system, even an ideal one, and that it is the business of Islam to provide such a system, seems to be a modern idea.[38]

It is true that the classical Islamic history of ideas included the subject of politics, but the discussion was limited to the issues of the qualifications of the rulers and the limitation of their power within the given boundaries of the *shari'a*. We are familiar with the historical evidence that the *'ulama*, who were virtually the political thinkers in Islam, eventually became legitimizers of political power. Hamid Enayat describes "the absence of independent political thought in Islamic history. Traditionally Muslims rarely studied politics in isolation from related disciplines."[39] According to Enayat, "It was only under the trauma of European military, political, economic and cultural encroachments since the end of the eighteenth century that Muslim elites started to write separate works on specifically political topics."[40]

Efforts to apply the concept of the nation-state to Islam and to the Islamic *umma* are a salient feature of the historically recent Muslim exploration of political issues. Some authors (e.g., 'Abd al-Rahman al-Bazzaz) have tried to combine Islam with nationalism by treating Islam and Arabism (*'uruba*) as an inseparable unity. According to al-Bazzaz, "true nationalism and the genuine Islam cannot go apart and could never be rivals. On the contrary, they go side by side along far paths."[41] Other Muslim authors have adopted the concepts of national sovereignty and consequently of the secular state.[42] An utterly secular position can be found, for example, in the writings of Sati' al-Husri, whose primary doctrine was "*al-din li-Allah wa-al-watan li-al-jami'*" (religion is a matter between the individual and God while the fatherland is the concern of all).[43]

With regard to the domestic context of the political ideologies of both Arabism and Islam, it should be pointed out that controversies over the supposed incompatibility or complementarity of these ideologies have been restricted to the Arab East (Mashriq), where the issues of the Christian minorities and of relations with the Ottoman power, rather than issues pertaining to Islam, were predominant at the birth of Arab nationalism. In the Arab West (Maghrib), which was confronted with European colonialism much earlier and which has had no religiously structured conflicts involving minorities, nationalist ideologies were always shaped Islamically and often manifested themselves under the guise of Salafism (*salafiyya*).[44]

One of the most striking responses to the conflict between Islam and nationalism was the effort of the Egyptian scholar 'Ali 'Abd al-Raziq to interpret Islam as a merely religious system of thought that had repeatedly and inappropriately been employed for political ends. In his important work *Al-Islam wa-usul al-hukm*[45] (Islam and the Forms of Government), published in 1925, he belligerently maintained that Islam was not a political ideology or a form of state. Prior to the publication of his book, 'Abd al-Raziq had been an Islamic judge and had studied Islamic law, the *shari'a*, since his student days at the Islamic al-Azhar University. 'Abd al-Raziq argued that Muhammad was a religious, and not a political leader, and stated that neither the Qur'an nor the Sunna provided any legitimizing support for the alleged forms of government in Islam (the caliphate of the Sunni Muslims and the imamate of the Iranian Shi'i Muslims).

In the wake of 'Abd al-Raziq's book, it was generally thought that the conflict between political-power-seeking Islamic fundamentalists and secularism had finally been settled once and for all in favor of the latter. Throughout the Islamic world, Islam receded into the background, making way for a secular nationalism in which belonging to the nation (not always in terms of citizenship; nation, in this case, is not always nation-state!) was considered the key personal affiliation. The spiritual father of Arab nationalism, Sati' al-Husri, adopted Herder's and Fichte's German concept of nationhood, according to which every nation is a cultural community held together by a common language rather than by a common religion.[46] Arab nationalists attempted to reduce Islam to a cultural phenomenon, arguing that Arab Christians and Muslims are united by a common language and thus constitute a nation, while such peoples as Iranians or Turks, whose only point in common with Arabs is Islam, should be considered foreigners (see my book on Arab nationalism).

Secularization in the Middle East meant not just the separation of state and religion but also the splitting up of the Islamic community, the *umma*, into numerous nations. Under these circumstances, even Islamic scholars, such as 'Abd al-Raziq, interpreted Islam in secular terms, i.e., as merely a religious bond. For a time, it was fashionable to consider Islam as no longer representing a political factor, apart from the case of militant groups, such as the Muslim Brothers, or archaic political systems.

We should now look at the question of whether this splitting up of the Islamic *umma* into several nations is merely an ideological issue or has a deeper significance. Though I disagree with some of Leonard Binder's conclusions, I must concede that there is considerable truth in his statement that the deep psychological and social attachment of Muslims to Islam and the Muslim community "had little political efficacy, that is, it did not determine the limits of the political community . . . The concept of the *umma* served as a referent for the identity resolutions of individual Muslims throughout Islamic history."[47] In this connection, one should recall the terminology once employed by Muhammad al-Mubarak, a former dean of the faculty of *shari'a* at the University of Damascus, who was considered to be an authority on Islam. He used the term *umma* only in the context of what he called the *umma 'arabiyya* (Arab nation), while he used the label *shu'ub islamiyya* to denote the Islamic peoples, with whom he thought the Arabs should cooperate on the level of international relations. But to Arab Muslims and Arab Christians considered as a whole he gave the name *abna' al-'Arabiyya* (sons of Arabism).[48]

Such views seem to have receded since the beginning of the 1970s as Islamic revivalism has intensified. Even some Sunni Muslims (for instance Islamic resurgence groups in Tunisia) see the Shi'i Iranian Revolution as a model to be emulated, thus emphasizing the Islamic link more than the Arab one. To some observers of the political scene in the Middle East this seems to be the prevailing state of affairs with regard to Islam and Arab nationalism. In the next section of this chapter we will see that this assessment needs to be modified.

Implications of Islamic Resurgence

In a recently published paper originally delivered to a seminar on the Middle East at Harvard University, I interpreted the renewed emphasis on Islam as a reintroduction of religious elements into Middle Eastern politics. In the course of political and social transformation in the modern Middle East, Islam was abandoned as a political ideology but not as a belief system. Islamic resurgence is merely the repoliticization of Islam and the use of Islamic symbols in the political realm.[49] As Philip Khoury has put it, Islam "must be seen as the vehicle for political and economic demands, rather than as being itself the 'impulse' behind these demands."[50] To the proponents of Islamic resurgence, "Islam is their most convenient, readily available ideological instrument."[51] Indeed, I have met many adherents of Islamic resurgence who have a very limited knowledge of Islam. Their main concern is articulating their political, social, and economic demands in a politicized Islamic vocabulary. Since the Iranian Revolution, many secularist Arab intellectuals have shifted away from Arab nationalism and in many cases even from Marxism as they have rediscovered Islam as a political ideology of opposition.

The Iranian Revolution was the first one in the Middle East in recent decades carried out (although not led) by the masses and not by army officers.[52] By virtue of its seeming to be a mass movement, the revolution has fascinated Arab intellectuals. For instance, a number of interesting and representative articles concerning the new situation have appeared in the Beirut periodical *Al-fikr al-'arabi al-mu'asir* (edited by the well-known intellectual Mu'ta' Safadi). It is striking that for these authors the rediscovery of Islam as a political ideology of opposition, and even the recognition of the Iranian Revolution as a stimulating example, do not imply a rejection of Arabism. One is reminded of the previously mentioned emphasis of al-Bazzaz on the link between Arabism and Islam. But in the new wave there is somewhat more emphasis on the social critique implicit in some Qur'anic verses than on the habitual nationalist rhetoric. Nevertheless, there is also a focus on the Arabness of Islam and on its having been revealed for the Arabs and in their language. For example, in his article "The Arabs, Islam, and the Iranian Revolution," Dr. Nasif Nassar stresses the link between Islam and Arabism:

> The Arabs . . . cannot feel that they have to accept the Iranian Revolution as a model for their political and civilizational action, though to some extent they sympathize with it . . . Islam is originally Arabic. Some would even say that Islam has an Arab face and an Arab soul. This reality upholds the conviction of the Arabs that those non-Arab peoples who have adopted Islam could never be able to comprehend it, to interpret it, and to apply it in a better way than the Arabs themselves could do.[53]

Safadi himself provides the opening article in the same issue of *Al-fikr al-'arabi al-mu'asir* — an issue devoted to the topic "*Al-'Arab, al-Islam wa-tahaddi al-mustaqbal*" (The Arabs, Islam, and the Challenge of the Future). In his piece, he commits himself to Islam as a political ideology ("revolutionary Islam") without dismissing Arabism; on the contrary, he dismisses Islamic universalism. Safadi compares some neo-fundamentalists with "*mumar-kisun*" ("Marxized") Arab intellectuals who have rejected Arabism in favor of internationalism, and argues:

> The new revolutionary Islam is a feature of well-being which Arabism will gain, in order to seek the resumption of its authentic role. Arabism will bring about the modernization of Islam and will lead the enlightenment of the masses adhering to

Islam. In doing so, Arabism will bring itself closer to the goal of revolution . . .[54]

The above authors are part of an interesting component of Islamic resurgence, but they cannot be considered representative of the whole movement throughout the Arab region.[55] In Egypt and Tunisia, for instance, there are signs of a retreat from Arab nationalism toward regionalism. In all cases, however, any universalist claims made by Islamic revivalists are relatively unconvincing and unappealing. The underlying realities of "the retreat from the secular path"[56] are specific in nature. The erosion of the legitimacy of the secular state reflects a much more fundamental sociopolitical and economic crisis in the Middle East. At the same time, the deepening of the North-South gap – i.e., the intensification of the conflict between the industrialized and nonindustrialized countries — upholds and reinforces every popular anti-Western attitude. Secular ideologies propounded by Western-educated and relatively privileged elites and ultimately stemming from the internationally dominant Western culture can no longer be accepted by peoples rejecting the source of these ideologies. *This great crisis, not Islam, is the real issue.*

Notes

1. See E.I.J. Rosenthal, *Islam in the Modern National State* (Cambridge, UK: Cambridge University Press, 1965).

2. For a discussion of this issue, see the chapter "Islam in Practice" in Dale Eickelman, *The Middle East: An Anthropological Approach* (Englewood Cliffs, NJ: Prentice-Hall, 1981), pp. 201ff.

3. Shakib Arslan, for instance, once raised the question of "Why the Muslims are backward" and said that this was because they do not live in accordance with Islamic precepts. To him there were no structural causes underlying the underdevelopment of the Islamic region. See Shakib Arslan, *Limadha ta'akhkhara al-muslimun wa-taqaddama ghayruhum* (Why Muslims are Backward and Others Developed), first published 1930 (reprinted Beirut: Dar al-Hayat, 1965). For a criticism of this view, see B. Tibi, "Islam and Secularization," in Morad Wahba, ed., *Islam and Civilization: Proceedings of the First International Islamic Philosophy Conference, 19–20 November 1979* (Cairo: Ain Shams University Press, 1982), pp. 65–80, here pp. 72ff.

4. See Abdallah Laroui, *L'idéologie arabe contemporaine* (Paris: Maspero, 1967).

5. For an illustration of cultural variety in Islam see the anthropological comparison between Indonesian and Moroccan Islam provided by Clifford Geertz, *Islam Observed: Religious Development in Morocco and Indonesia* (Chicago, IL: Chicago University Press, 1971).

6. An outstanding account is Marshall G.S. Hodgson, *The Venture of Islam*, 3 vols. (Chicago, IL: Chicago University Press, 1974).

7. This is the conceptual framework of my book on modern Islam: *Die Krise des modernen Islam: Eine vorindustrielle Kultur im wissenschaftlich-technischen Zeitalter* (Munich: Beck Press, 1981). See the review by Barbara Stowasser in *The Middle East Journal*, Vol. XXXVI, No. 2 (1983): 284–86.

8. The approach of "critique of ideology" was developed by the German Frankfurt School of Theodor W. Adorno and Max Horkheimer, who were my academic teachers at the University of Frankfurt. On this school of thought, see Martin Jay's monograph, *The Dialectical Imagination: A History of the Frankfurt School and the Institute of Social Research* (Boston, MA: Little Brown & Co., 1973).

9. See Rupert Emerson, *From Empire to Nation: The Rise of Self-Assertion of Asian and African Peoples*, 3rd ed. (Boston, MA: Beacon Press, 1964). Emerson interprets the claim to be a nation, in the modern sense, as self-assertion.

10. See Michael C. Hudson's highly stimulating book, *Arab Politics: The Search for Legitimacy* (New Haven, CT and London: Yale University Press, 1977).

11. See B. Tibi, "The Social Background of Ideologies in the Arab Middle East," in Gustav Stein and Udo Steinbach, eds., *The Contemporary Middle Eastern Scene: Basic Issues — Major Trends* (Opladen: Leske Press, 1979), pp. 84–93.

12. See Kurt Lenk, ed., *Ideologie, Ideologiekritik und Wissenssoziologie*, 5th ed. (Neuwied: Luchterhand Press, 1971).

13. Max Horkheimer, "Ideologie und Handeln," in Max Horkheimer and Theodor W. Adorno, *Sociologica II*, 3rd ed. (Frankfurt: EVA Press, 1973), pp. 38ff., here p. 38.

14. Leonard Binder, *The Ideological Revolution in the Middle East* (New York: John Wiley & Sons, 1964).

15. Emile Durkheim presented his approach of treating reality as consisting of *faits sociaux* in his outstanding and masterfully written methodological work, *Les règles de la méthode sociologique*, 13th ed. (Paris: Presses Universitaires de France 1895, 1956).

16. Theodor W. Adorno, *Stichworte: Kritische Modelle II*, 2nd ed. (Frankfurt: Suhrkamp Press, 1970), p. 189.

17. Helmuth Plessner, "Abwandlungen des Ideologiegedankens," reprinted in Kurt Lenk, *Ideologie*, pp. 265ff., here p. 281.

18. Adherents of the approach of "intellectual history" are deeply indebted to Hegel, who viewed history as "Geschichte des Geistes." Concerning Hegel and his legacy in this regard, see the outstanding classical work of Karl Löwith, *Von Hegel zu Nietzsche: Der revolutionäre Bruch im Denken des neunzehnten Jahrhunderts*, 5th ed. (Stuttgart: Kohlhammer Press, 1964), especially pp. 44ff.

19. This is the view of Samuel N. Eisenstadt, *Tradition, Change and Modernity* (New York: John Wiley & Sons, 1973); see the critique by B. Tibi, "Unterentwicklung als Kulturelle Traditionalität? Eisenstadts Beitrag zur makrosoziologischen Forschung," *Soziologische Revue*, III, No. 2 (1980): 121–31.

20. Gerhard Brandt, "Industrialisierung, Modernisierung, gesellschaftliche Entwicklung: Anmerkungen zum Stand gesamtgesellschaftlicher Analysen," *Zeitschrift für Soziologie*, I (1972): 5ff., here p. 7.

21. See Samir Amin, *La nation Arabe* (Paris: Editions de Minuit, 1976), translated into English as *The Arab Nation* (London: Zed Press, 1978), especially chapter 2.

22. See my essay "Akkulturation, Modernisierung, Verwestlichung und auswärtige Kulturpolitik," reprinted in my collection of essays, *Internationale Politik und Entwicklungsländer-Forschung* (Frankfurt: Suhrkamp Press, 1979), pp. 176–90.

23. Richard F. Behrendt, *Soziale Strategie für Entwicklungsländer: Entwurf einer Entwicklungssoziologie* (Frankfurt: S. Fischer Press, 1965), p. 116.

24. In this respect, see the introduction to Paul E. Sigmund, ed., *The Ideologies of Developing Nations*, revised 2nd ed. (New York: Praeger Press, 1967).

25. Binder, *The Ideological Revolution in the Middle East*.

72   Bassam Tibi

26. Manfred Halpern, *The Politics of Social Change in the Middle East and North Africa* (Princeton, NJ: Princeton University Press, 1965).

27. See A.F. Pollard, *Factors in Modern History* (London: A. Constable & Co., 1907) and B.C. Shafer, *Nationalism: Myth and Reality* (London and New York: Harcourt Brace, 1955).

28. See the chapter on "The Origins of Nation Formation and Nationalism in Europe" in B. Tibi, *Arab Nationalism: A Critical Inquiry* (New York: St. Martin's Press, 1981), pp. 3ff.

29. Eric Davis-Willard, "Theory and Method in the Study of Arab Nationalism," *Review of Middle East Studies*, 3 (1978): 18–31, here p. 26. Edward Said's *Orientalism* (London: Routledge & Kegan, 1978) should also be consulted.

30. The major Islamic writings concerning Islam and nationalism are documented in part II of John Donohue and John L. Esposito, eds., *Islam in Transition* (Oxford: Oxford University Press, 1982); see my review in *The Middle East Journal*, XXXVI, No. 4 (1982): 614–16.

31. See especially W.M. Watt, *Muhammad at Medina*, 6th ed. (Oxford: Oxford University Press, 1977), pp. 78ff.; see also W.M. Watt, *Muhammad: Prophet and Statesman*, 4th ed. (Oxford: Oxford University Press, 1978).

32. See the chapter of the conflict between Arabs and *mawali* in Werner Ende, *Arabische Nation und islamische Geschichte* (Beirut and Wiesbaden: Steiner Press, 1977), pp. 233ff.

33. Maxime Rodinson, *Mohammed* (Luzern and Frankfurt: Bucher Press, 1975), p. 279.

34. This is the historical judgment of Hodgson in *The Venture of Islam*.

35. Nikki Keddie, ed., *An Islamic Response to Imperialism* (Berkeley and Los Angeles, CA: California University Press, 1968).

36. Maxime Rodinson argues in terms of social and economic history against such an approach in his *Islam et capitalisme* (Paris: Editions de Seuil, 1966). See my review of the German edition of this outstanding work in *Archiv für Rechts-und Sozialphilosophie*, LIX (1973): 155–58.

37. See, for instance, Yusuf al-Qardawi, *Al-hall al-Islami* (The Islamic Solution) (Beirut: Risalah Press, 1974), especially pp. 86ff.; and Husain F. al-Najjar, *Al-Islam wa-al-siyasa* (Islam and Politics) (Cairo: Dar al-Sha'b, 1977), especially pp. 209ff. The *nizam* concept has existed for some decades; it was a major interest of Egypt's Muslim Brothers during the early days of that organization. See Richard P. Mitchell, *The Society of Muslim Brothers*, (Oxford: Oxford University Press, 1969), pp. 234ff.

38. Wilfred C. Smith, *The Meaning and End of Religion*, 2nd ed. (New York: Harper & Row, 1978), p. 117.

39. Hamid Enayat, *Modern Islamic Political Thought* (Austin, TX: Texas University Press, 1982), p. 3.

40. Ibid.

41. 'Abd al-Rahman al-Bazzaz, *Hadhihi qawmiyyatuna* (This is our Nationalism), 2nd ed. (Cairo: Dar al-Qalam, 1964), p. 185.

42. See the classic comprehensive survey of this intellectual history provided by Albert Hourani, *Arabic Thought in the Liberal Age, 1798–1939* (Oxford: Oxford University Press, 1962); see also Hourani's later essay, "Middle Eastern Nationalism Yesterday and Today" in his collection of essays, *The Emergence of the Modern Middle East* (London: Macmillan, 1981), pp. 179–92.

43. See Sati' al-Husri, *Ma hiya al-qawmiyya?* (What is Nationalism?), 2nd ed. (Beirut: Dar al-'Ilm li-al-Malayin, 1963), especially the chapter on "Al-qawmiyya wa-al-din" (Nationalism and Religion), pp. 195ff. On al-Husri, see William C. Cleveland's monograph, *The Making of an Arab Nationalist: Ottomanism and Arabism in the Life and Thought of Sati' al-Husri* (Princeton, NJ: Princeton University Press, 1971), here pp. 148ff., especially p. 155; see also Tibi, *Arab*

Nationalism, pp. 135ff., and the review of it by Cleveland in *The Middle East Journal*, XXXVI, No. 1 (1982): 94–95; and the review by Michael C. Hudson in the *International Journal of Middle East Studies*, Vol. XVII, No. 2 (1985), pp. 292–94.

44. For the case of Algeria, see 'Ali Merad, *Le réformisme Musulman en Algérie de 1925 à 1940* (Paris: Mouton, 1967).

45. Reprinted in Beirut, 1966 (Dar Maktabat al-Hayat Press). The French translation was published in *Revue des Etudes Islamiques*, VII and VIII (1933–34).

46. For a full account of this Arab adoption of the German idea of nationhood, see Tibi, *Arab Nationalism*, pp. 99ff.

47. Binder, *The Ideological Revolution in the Middle East*, p. 131. This thesis leads one to the debate on the relevance of Ibn Khaldun's theory to the new discussion concerning the *umma*. In an extremely interesting appraisal of Ibn Khaldun emanating from a comparison of him with Machiavelli, Barbara Freyer Stowasser draws our attention to the link between *'asabiyya* and religion already stressed in the *Muqaddima* itself. She concludes: "Both Ibn Khaldun and Machiavelli saw personal and collective moral virtue as an important condition for generating and/or encouraging this basic creative political force that engenders solidarity and cohesion . . . If it is to generate, sustain, and guarantee long-term collective morality and virtue, *no political community can do without religion*" (emphasis added). Barbara Freyer Stowasser, *Religion and Political Development: Some Comparative Ideas on Ibn Khaldun and Machiavelli* (Washington DC: Georgetown University, Center for Contemporary Arab Studies, Occasional Papers Series, 1983), p. 20. One should add that, in the view of Ibn Khaldun, religion could only contribute to societal cohesion if combined with *'asabiyya* (group solidarity). In this sense one could say that *'asabiyya* finds its highest expression in a synthesis with religion. If so, Islam cannot be considered universalistic since it is linked with an Arab, Iranian, or other *'asabiyya*. During the height of Arab nationalism, Ibn Khaldun's notion of *'asabiyya* had a revival. Sati' al-Husri published a 655-page volume on Ibn Khaldun — *Dirasat 'an Muqaddimat Ibn Khaldun* (Studies on the *Muqaddima* of Ibn Khaldun), 2nd ed. (Cairo: al-Khanji Press, 1961, previously published as two volumes in 1943–44). On this issue, see the chapter on Ibn Khaldun in Tibi, *Arab Nationalism*, pp. 112ff.

48. Muhammad al-Mubarak, *Al-umma al-'arabiyya fi ma'rakat tahqiq al-dhat* (The Arab Nation in the Struggle for Self-realization) (Damascus: Mu'assasat al-Matbu'at al-'Arabiyya, 1959), especially pp. 139ff.

49. Bassam Tibi, "The Renewed Role of Islam in the Political and Social Development of the Middle East," *The Middle East Journal*, XXXVII, No. 1 (1983): 3–13.

50. Philip S. Khoury, "Islamic Revivalism and the Crisis of the Secular State in the Arab World," in Ibrahim Ibrahim, ed., *Arab Resources: The Transformation of a Society* (Washington, DC and London: Center for Contemporary Arab Studies and Croom Helm Ltd., 1983), pp. 213–36, here p. 215. See also Theodor Hanf, "Arabismus und Islamismus," in H.A. Winkler, ed. *Nationalismus in der Welt von heute* (Göttingen: Vandenhoeck and Ruprecht Press, 1982), pp. 157–76.

51. Khoury, "Islamic Revivalism," p. 215.

52. In the Arab Middle East, opportunities to effect political change have been almost completely monopolized by the military. As I have shown in a comprehensive analysis of the coups d'état in the Arab states, the army officers permit no political change beyond their own seizure of political power. See B. Tibi, *Militär und Sozialismus in der Dritten Welt: Allgemeine Theorien und Regionalstudien über arabische Länder* (Frankfurt: Suhrkamp Press, 1973).

53. Nasif Nassar, "Al-'Arab, al-Islam wa-al-thawra al-iraniyya" (The Arabs, Islam, and the Iranian Revolution), *Al-fikr al-'arabi al-mu'asir* (June, 1980): 12–15, here p. 13.

54. Mu'ta Safadi, "Al-qawmiyya al-'Arabiyya wa-al-Islam al-thawri" (Arab

Nationalism and Revolutionary Islam), *Al-fikr al-'arabi al-mu'asir* (June, 1980): 4–11, here p. 6.

55. The Shi'a character of the Iranian Revolution is pointed out in two presentations written by a Tunisian and an Egyptian university professor and respectively published in Tunis and in Beirut (but not in Cairo!). Neither monograph emphasizes the link between Arabism and Islam. The monographs are: 'Ali al-Shabi, *Al-Shi'a fi Iran* (The Shi'a in Iran) (Tunis: University Press, 1980); and Ibrahim al-Dasouqi-Shita, *Al-thawra al-iraniyya: al-judhur al-idiulujiyya* (The Iranian Revolution: The Ideological Roots) (Beirut: Dar al-Kutub, 1979).

56. Ibrahim Abu-Lughod, "Retreat from the Secular Path? Islamic Dilemmas of Arab Politics," *The Review of Politics*, XXVIII, No. 4 (1966): 447–76.

5 THE ISLAMIC MOVEMENT: ITS CURRENT CONDITION AND FUTURE PROSPECTS

*Richard P. Mitchell**

It has now become the prevailing wisdom to place the beginning of the so-called "Islamic resurgence" at about the time of 1973 and the subsequent rise in oil prices. It is not altogether surprising that this date should be accepted as a beginning of this widely-written-about phenomenon. The ever-increasing volume of literature — journalistic, scholarly, and everything in between — emphasizing its drama, its immediacy, and its ominousness defines the "Islamic resurgence" or "revival" as a function of Saudi Arabia's rise to world prominence. This, in turn, is attributed to the oil price hike of 1973–74. Many who hold this view imply strongly that the recently acquired oil wealth of Saudi Arabia and Libya, in particular, has served to create an Islamic political resurgence as a reflection of the newfound political power of the conservative oil-producing countries.[1]

The following comments are aimed at indicating some of the problems with this periodization and conceptualization of the Islamic movement. They are also intended as a challenge to the vast army of experts that has come to life in the last decade to explain the Islamic resurgence. These experts have typically relied on Orientalist or modernization theory analyses which have often resulted in an obscurantism more deadly than the obscurantism they define as Islamic.

The most authoritative exposition of the view that dates the beginning of the Islamic resurgence in 1973 is the recent widely-applauded study, *The Arab Predicament*, by Fouad Ajami. Ajami approvingly quotes Ali Mazrui's comment that "the 'barrel of oil' and the 'crescent of Islam' were linked, and October 1973 represented a resurrection of Islam."[2] Ajami's book is almost

---

* Because of his untimely illness and death, Dr. Mitchell was not able to make final editorial changes to this manuscript. He requested that Dr. Joel Beinin complete the manuscript. Dr. Beinin used the transcript of Dr. Mitchell's address and his written notes to finalize the manuscript. He relied on his years as a student of Dr. Mitchell and his familiarity with and respect for Dr. Mitchell's scholarship to ensure that the style remained true to Dr. Mitchell's other work. — Editor

mesmerizingly literate, lyrical, poetically sensitive, lucid, and incisive. But this eloquent work is critically flawed by the time frame it adopts. If the Islamic movement is seen as a function of the Arab defeat of 1967 or the oil boom of 1973, it may indeed be a temporary and relatively unimportant phenomenon. If, however, it is seen as an ongoing expression of an alternative framework of identity and political organization in competition with Arab nationalism and Western conceptions of the national state, then the movement's significance is far greater and its origin far earlier than 1973.

The implications of Ajami's ahistorical approach are profound. In the context of my own career, let me point out that about three decades ago, in 1953, I was in Egypt attempting to understand the Society of the Muslim Brothers. Already by 1948–49 this movement had reached such massive political proportions as to undermine the claim of the rulers of the time to speak for the Egyptian people. The government's decision to crush the movement in 1949 was presumably taken because of the organization's potential threat to the existing political order. However real the threat may have been, the regime believed in it. Does my concern with the Muslim Brothers make me a student of the "preresurgence?" Or is the Society of the Muslim Brothers a movement of the neo-*jahiliyya*?

If the beginning of the Islamic resurgence is a function of Arab oil wealth, how can one account for the revival of the Society of Muslim Brothers in the years 1951–54? How should one explain the movement's reappearance in 1965–66, after it had suffered massive repression by the Nasser regime in 1954? Does oil wealth account for the emergence of Sayyid Qutb and his challenge to the political quiescence that characterizes the consensus of Sunni political theory? The publication of his seminal work, *Ma'alim fi al-tariq*, was a significant factor in the decision of the Nasser regime to hang the author in 1966. All of this happened even before the Arab political disaster of 1967 in the war with Israel, another commonly accepted landmark for the beginning of the upheaval in the Arab world now called the "Islamic resurgence."

Does the notion of the 1973 benchmark, which makes Saudi Arabia the standard bearer of fundamentalism, prepare one for the Iranian Revolution of 1978–79 and the emergence of another, or from the Iranian point of view the sole, standard bearer of "true Islam?" And to add to the analyst's confusion and dismay, how can one explain, using the oil wealth theory of Islamic resurgence, the almost immediate conflict between the Islamic leaders of Iran and

Saudi Arabia over which of them represented the correct version of Islam, and the reserve of many Muslims, transcending Sunni-Shi'i distinctions, about the validity of both claims?[3]

Furthermore, aside from the Muslim Brotherhood and the Iranian Revolution (the most prominent cases which contradict the oil theory of the Islamic resurgence), this theory is also useless as a tool for understanding the pre-Khomeini phenomenon of Navab Safavi and his *Fada'iyan-i Islam* established in 1946 or the *mullah* political activism which has been an important factor in Iranian political life since the late eighteenth century. Some may wish to discount the tradition of Islamic political activism in Iran as a fair case for comparison, since the Iranians are Shi'a. But then what of the Sunnis in India and the drive for Muslim self-assertion throughout the 1930s and 1940s culminating in the partition of the subcontinent and the creation of the Islamic state of Pakistan? Does not Abu al-'Ala' al-Mawdudi of Pakistan, one of the most prolific Islamic political thinkers of the twentieth century, count as a proponent of political Islam? In short, one is justified in wondering of what those asserting the oil theory of Islamic resurgence speak.

As Eric Davis notes in his chapter on "The Concept of Revival and the Study of Islam and Politics" when we use the terms "revival" and "resurgence" we refer to a broad appreciation of Muslim efforts, organized and unorganized, lay and *'ulama*, to respond to the transformations occurring in Muslim countries, directly or indirectly touched by the colonial encounter with the technologically and militarily superior West. If the terms "resurgence" and "revival" must be used at all, they must be considered in this extended time frame. Thus, the events of 1967 and 1973 should be seen as moments intensifying a long-term ongoing historic process. It does not make analytical sense to regard the events in the Middle East commonly referred to as the Islamic resurgence as a response to crises so narrowly defined as the 1967 defeat or, paradoxically, the "victory" of 1973.

The true crisis is as monumentally large as its response. It is the more than a century-long reminder on a daily basis by foreigners and their client local elites that Muslims are no longer in charge of either their destiny or even the definition of that destiny. It is the realization that efforts to modernize and reform from within brought not strength, but more weakness and intensified domination by the West. It is the realization that protection of social cohesion and individual sanity requires a serious reexamination of the Muslim heritage (*turath*) as a potential mode of action.

That such a choice, a reexamination of the *turath*, was acceptable to masses of believers, was due in great measure to the precedent for reexamination well-established in Islamic history, where believers had periodically been called to return from the abyss. We can see Islamic resurgences in this sense during the eras of Ibn Taymiyya, the eighteenth-century Wahhabis, and the pan-Islamic movement of the late nineteenth century. The acceptability of the strategy of reexamining the *turath* is also due to the fact that many of the institutions and ideas that challenged Muslims (constitutions, parliaments, presidents) were not essentially incompatible with the Islamic *turath*.

The most critical issue in the reexamination of the *turath*, however, has proven to be a concept that is entirely incompatible with Islam as it has been lived since the time of the Prophet. This is the concept of secularism. Coming from a secular liberal tradition myself, I would not personally feel comfortable in any other cultural framework. However, my years of trying to understand Muslims have taught me to respect their disdain and horror of even considering secularism as an option.

We all know that the Christian West resolved the issue of secularism in the formula, "Render unto Caesar that which belongs to Caesar, and unto God that which belongs to God." Nevertheless, there remains a lively tension and a certain degree of ambivalence among all major Christian sects from the fundamentalists of the Moral Majority to the Roman Catholic Church about the notion of secularism. The Moral Majority's rise to prominence in the current U.S. political scene is a reflection of that tension. The conflict within the Roman Catholic Church between the traditional hierarchy and priests of Latin America practicing what they call liberation theology is perhaps the most dramatic current expression of this tension in the Christian context. Liberation theology resembles Islam more than any other variety of Christianity because of the extraordinary range of its views on a plethora of issues which cannot narrowly be defined as religious.

Secularism will remain *the* major issue in the Muslim world, and it will probably never be wholly resolved, as it has not been in the Roman Catholic Church, for there is no ambiguity in any significant Muslim self-analysis or reevaluation about the meaning of the doctrine of *tawhid* (the unity of life). Even modern liberal Muslim ideologies like 'Ali Shari'ati in Iran and Hasan Hanafi in Egypt, who also use the concept for other purposes, accept its classical meaning that nothing in the world is intrinsically Caesar's and that everything belongs to God.

In this sense, whatever its temporal and worldly views and its program, the search for an Islamic meaning in the modern world is not only a test of the viability of an Islamic order in that world, but also a test of the very validity of the revelation. Neither Christianity nor Judaism has so unrelenting and stark a problem to address as Islam on this level. The problem can and will be bypassed by the Muslim community in historic time. But for the present, it is important to underscore this dilemma because it is pivotal to understanding the parameters and the passions of both the Islamic movement and its Western analysts, who are largely critics.

For many Western intellectuals (and some Easterners) to understand that man may act in the mundane world as though God were alive and well requires almost a transcendental act of will and thought process transfer. So deeply ingrained is secularism as to make even the most sympathetic observers cynics floundering for meaning in simplistic explanations such as "Mahdism," "Messianism," "religious obscurantism," "fanaticism," "nativism," "cover for power grab," etc. All of these things exist in the Islamic movement. But it would not be a serious movement worthy of our attention were it not, above all, an idea and a personal commitment honestly felt.

As Hasan Turabi, leader of the Sudanese Muslim Brothers, put it, "We are now searching for our *qibla* [direction]."[4] This is not a fundamentally different notion than Edmund Burke's suggestion, approvingly quoted by Ajami, that "a society wrenched away from its past and its roots may be a society without a future."[5]

The issue of secularism is what gives substance to the description of the movement as "fundamentalist," although we should note as an aside that there is no real Arabic equivalent for that term. Bruce Lawrence has dealt with the word and its meaning in his contribution to this book, "Muslim Fundamentalist Movements: Reflections Toward A New Approach." I agree with him that it is better as a descriptive term than Yvonne Haddad's suggestion of "neo-normative," which seems to imply a specific program or set of rules.

Here we will use the word fundamentalist to suggest not a program, though most who are called Muslim fundamentalists would deny that their movement lacks a program, but a *style* and, above all, a mood. The preoccupation of critics of the Islamic movement, with programs and solutions that leave the movement open to somewhat justifiable accusations of naïveté and deception, is misplaced. Even the most benighted rulers, whether Muslim or not, will usually respond to pragmatic concerns.

Whatever one might think about Islamic government, the heritage of 'Ali, Hasan, and Husayn, the *shari'a*, and Shi'i-Sunni theological conflicts, it remains true that Ayatollah Khomeini and those around him are running a functioning state. They are fighting a war, buying arms, selling oil, and doing all those things against immense odds, including isolation and general hostility from most quarters, including many Muslims. The fact that the Iranian leaders are animated by Islamic convictions does not seem to be leading to the downfall of the state. Nor has the Islamic character of the state transformed Iran into a beacon of light for other Muslims or non-Muslims. Ajami, in one of his most lucid and important statements about fundamentalism (which contrasts sharply with the dominant spirit of his text) says, "The hopes among those of the faithful who sense that a civilization broken and defeated several centuries ago is on the verge of resurrection and the fears of those who see in Islam's resurgence some great revolt against modernity are both mistaken."[6]

Let us now explicitly consider the question of the future prospects of the Islamic movement. This author has no inside track, no special knowledge, no hard data, only informed impressions. The Islamic movement, I think, is alive, flourishing, and experiencing serious intellectual ferment. (Professor Isma'il Al-Faruqi's contribution to this book, "The Islamic Critique of the Status Quo of Muslim Society," reminds us of the volume and fluidity of contemporary Muslim writing and certainly underscores the vitality of the movement.) The Iranian Revolution, although it did not begin as such, became an Islamic revolution. It must be regarded as the most important Islamic event in modern times, akin in impact to the Wahhabi movement, which had reverberations from Morocco to Indonesia. The remainder of this paper will therefore concentrate on issues which the Iranian Revolution has brought to prominence within the Islamic movement.

The Iranian-Islamic victory has, among other things, shifted the Islamic movement from the realm of a theoretical outline of goals to the practical level of application. As in all revolutionary situations, this fact has raised the level and the quality of debate about *means* as well as *ends*. Real political power transforms many things, including the nature of the questions asked and the interpretations of the consequences (both anticipated and unanticipated) of specific actions. Nowhere is the debate about the meaning of the Iranian Revolution more lively than in the Sunni Arab world as it watches the unfolding of the Shi'i version of the Islamic state.

The central political question for the Islamic movement which has emerged from the Iranian experience is one asked of Professor Faruqi during the 1983 CCAS annual symposium, of which this book is a product, namely the issue of the legitimacy and authority in the Iranian Revolution encapsulated in the Khomeini doctrine of *wilayat al-faqih* (governance, or guardianship of the jurist). This doctrine is opposed even by some Iranian Shi'i leaders (notably Ayatollah Shari'at Madari) as unjustified by Shi'i *fiqh*, or jurisprudence. The doctrine has raised large theological questions, but even larger political questions about the nature and purpose of Islamic government. On the theological level, the debate has to do with the historic Sunni-Shi'i division over the nature of the succession to the Prophet — *imama* vs. *khalifa*. On that level, establishment *'ulama* in the Arab world can describe the Iranian Revolution as just another Shi'i/Persian heresy.

For Arab Muslims committed to the Islamic movement of revitalization (and other non-Arab Muslims) the issue of legitimacy and authority has a populist dimension as well. Fundamentalism, after all, is not only to be defined in terms of resistance to the West. It is also a reassertion of purity inside the community as the most important weapon in the defense against the West. Such a demand for purification inevitably targets the local elites who are clients of the West.

For the Islamic movement as a whole, however, theological hair-splitting about imams and caliphs would gladly be put aside were there not a deeper question of political participation in the modern sense. The issue is not usually acrimoniously or even publicly discussed. In effect one hears, "We will avert our eyes from the concept of *wilayat al-faqih* because it is temporary; and in any case it is necessary to assure the preservation of the Islamic Republic."[7] Or one hears that it may be permissible for this imam (Khomeini) only.[8]

The "but" implied and sometimes explicit in these formulations has to do with the vision of representative government in Islam. (I avoid the word democracy deliberately.) There are two questions here. One is the succession to the Prophet, *khalifa* or *imama*. Who is the leader of the Islamic movement? The second is *how* the imam or caliph becomes leader. If any of the literature of the Islamic movement on political theory is to be taken seriously, and it should be, far more important than whether a leader is called imam or caliph is the means of accession, the *shura* (consultation). This should be understood in both its simplest and most complex sense as the political participation of the community in that choice and how the leader governs.

The Islamic movement has been multifaceted in inspiration. The insistence on ideological and spiritual purity is real. No less real, in fact most important, are the issues of the exclusion of the mass of Muslims in the world from meaningful participation and of mundane economic and social inequities. Anyone who thinks that the Islamic movement is other worldy should look again at Iran.

There is real reservation and fear in some quarters of the Islamic movement about arbitrary, authoritarian, even dictatorial government, however "Islamic," in Iran. 'Adnan Sa'd al-Din, the self-described spokesman for the Syrian Muslim Brotherhood, was recently quoted as saying, "I do not want to be an ayatollah. I want to be an ordinary citizen [*muwatin*] in a democratic state which respects Islamic values."[9] He goes on to attack the Islamicness of the leaders of Iran's revolution because of their close relations with the governments of Syria and South Yemen, both enemies of Islam in Sa'd al-Din's opinion.

The explicit denunciation of the political process in Iran by some in the Islamic movement is coupled with an implicit denunciation of reversion by Iranian Muslims to policies primarily serving Iranian national state interests. These include the purchase of arms from Israel, the war against Iraq, and the alliance with Syria. The Iran-Iraq war is frowned on despite the general hostility of the Islamic movement to the Ba'thist regime of Iraq. The alliance of Ayatollah Khomeini and the "Alawite regime" of Hafiz al-Asad is the biggest enigma of all for the Islamic movement.

Another political issue facing the Islamic movement is the important and universal question of how representative government, even with the divinely ordained precept of *shura*, operates in a setting which supposes a limited democracy, or a divinely inspired set of social and legal parameters which allow no debate and no freedom for correcting error.

The Islamic movement must also contend with the reality of

plural and conflicting peoples and non-Muslim versions of the truth. Put in Western terms, this is the issue of national integration of multiethnic religious and social groups. How do non-Muslims live in an Islamic society and how do Muslim minorities live coherent lives in non-Muslim-controlled societies?

In addition to bringing specific issues to prominence, the Iranian Revolution has affected other developments in the Islamic movement whose origins precede the Iranian events, but which were all heightened by it. These developments reflect a sharpened sensitivity to questions relating to politics and power. We will now briefly outline some of the more salient of those developments.

First, there is a tendency, especially in Egypt, toward a more activist assertion of the Islamic movement. This phenomenon of splinter groups with names like al-Takfir wa-al-Hijra, Jihad, and Jund Allah has already been noted by many observers, including Eric Davis, Saad Eddin Ibrahim, and Halida Sufi. For these activist groups the execution of Sayyid Qutb in 1966 may be a more important symbol than the assassination of Hasan al-Banna in 1949. Qutb had become the spokesman for those unwilling to work from within the system, this refusal having been more or less the traditional position of the Muslim Brothers. Qutb's insistence on the incompatibility of Islamic and *jahili* societies intensified a significant dimension in the political thought of the leadership of the Muslim Brotherhood about which it had remained and still remains ambivalent: the need for real power to implement the Islamic message by force if necessary.

Another development, less dramatic and less widespread, represents activism of a reformist rather than a revolutionary character. This is the refinement of the reformist argument that the Islamization of Muslims is a gradual process that must be patiently pursued, even to the extent of overcoming the traditional reluctance of the Muslim Brotherhood to participate in national governments and to bear responsibility for "un-Islamic" policies. The leader of the Sundanese Muslim Brothers, Hasan Turabi, has become a public advocate of this strategy.[10]

Beyond these visible developments — the revolution in Iran, the acceleration of Muslim activism in Egypt, and low-key political participation in the Sudan — the Islamic movement in its broadest sense does not weaken. Its future prospects are not to be defined in terms of concrete successes or failures. So long as Muslims respond to its appeal it can be said to be a viable option. No government in a society with a substantial Muslim population now or in the foreseeable future can ignore its appeal, despite the diversity of the motives for believers' response to this appeal. As suggested above, these motives include justifiable indignation and political desperation in the face of economic and social inequity. They also include the political and military impotence of the Muslim world in the face of Western civilization and what is regarded as its most aggressive expression in the Middle East, Israel.

This may be the appropriate place to note that Zionism, whatever its founders intended, has contributed greatly to the Islamic movement and shares a certain spirit in common with it. Zionism can, of course, be seen in many ways, but not the least significant of these is as the political affirmation of religious Judaism and, paradoxically, a justification for political Islamic reaffirmation. This aspect of Zionism became more pronounced during the Begin era. So long as Israel poses its claims in terms of God's gift to the Chosen People (rather than the more constructivist and pragmatic argument of "making the desert bloom"), Arabs are that much more inclined to pursue the Islamic option as a solution to the Palestine question. So long as it is a contest of gods, it is a test, not only of the power of those gods, but of the validity of their revelations. In the context of the ongoing debate about the viability of an Islamic society in the modern world, this issue will fester, while the Arab-Israeli conflict may become only secondarily a question of territory and ultimately a question of the meaning and intention of God. In the end, of course, for the resolution of this question as well as all the others addressed in this paper, even God will not suffice. The Islamic movement recognizes this, as is apparent in the frequent reference to the following Qur'anic passage: "God does not change the situation of a people until they change it themselves."

The question of how to regain Palestine is, of course, only a small part of the great debate between Arab nationalists and those who wish to reaffirm the Islamic view of the world. Whether Muslims respond to the Islamic message on the material level of class and social interest groups or the ideal level of spirit and mind (and the response is variable and complex), nothing suggests that the crisis which inspires that message is near an end. For this reason it is most useful to view the Islamic movement not as a narrow and specific programmatic entity with discrete beginning and ending points, but as a broad endeavor which Muslims are pursuing — a search for authenticity, a search for "roots," so to speak — as a necessary aspect of contending with the Muslim situation in the contemporary world. This purpose — the obscurantist analyses of Orientalists, modernization theorists, and political scientists notwithstanding — should not be minimized.

The Islamic movement, like all civilizational movements, will be erratic in direction and purpose, never clear in meaning and destiny, ineffable, and unpredictable. It will have themes with more emphasis here than there, at this time more than that time. It will not be different from the West in process — ever changing in expression, but searching always to remain true to whatever is defined as relevant or authentic by those participating in the process.

In this context the common Western revulsion at the Iranian Revolution deserves a comment. Without making a rigid parallel, it should be recalled that the French Revolution, whose outcome laid the basis for modern Europe, was a bloody, violent, and criminal affair in the eyes of its victims and many contemporary observers. There is no doubt — this is the character of revolution.

We should not expect the Islamic movement to provide us with a clear set of final answers about itself or its objectives. The movement will never be completed or successful in a narrow sense. As Ajami has noted, "There is no happy conclusion . . ."[11] We are likely to see the emergence of a variety of Islams, just as there is a multiplicity and variety of religious expression in the West, or in any other civilization. In the end, Islam will be what Muslims say it is; and that is all that really matters.

Note on the Author

On September 12, 1983, while on leave from the University of Michigan, Dr. Richard P. Mitchell passed away. He died in Egypt, a country he loved. He was intensely engaged with its people, their past and their future. Everything Mitchell taught was rooted in his deep appreciation for the fundamental humanity of the Egyptian people and his ability to appreciate the broadest range of their experience. This was the source of his greatness as a teacher. Mitchell's insight and wisdom had the immediacy and authority that comes from a lifetime of personal commitment, not simply to an academic discipline, but to the real people whose past and present he studied. — Joel Beinin

Notes

1. These have been frequent themes in Daniel Pipes' journalistic articles. His arguments are now available in book form; see *In the Path of God* (New York: Basic Books, 1983).

2. Fouad Ajami, *The Arab Predicament: Arab Political Thought and Practice Since 1967* (New York: Cambridge University Press, 1981), p. 173. The thrust of my comments is here directed against Ajami, but they may just as well be taken to apply to Pipes and many others.

3. Ajami's work is most problematic in the context of discussions of the Islamic movement because it emphasizes what is accurate but misleading, that Saudi Arabia is, in fact, the leader of "fundamentalism" in some important senses. But he nowhere deals with the very real distinction between Saudi Arabia's "Muslim" views of the world and those of such movements as the Muslim Brothers who, while occasionally benefiting from Saudi funding, would most often emphatically deny Saudi Arabia's legitimacy as the leader of any significant Islamic movement in the sense intended on the current world scene.

4. This quote is from a transcript of remarks made by Turabi. The transcript was found among Professor Mitchell's effects with no indication of the occasion of the remarks.

5. Ajami, *The Arab Predicament*, p. 193.

6. Ibid., p. 139.

7. This was implied by Professor Isma'il Al-Faruqi, who answered the question about legitimacy put to him during the 1983 CCAS annual symposium by saying, among other things, that the "success of the revolution against its enemies" conferred a measure of legitimacy.

8. For example, see the comments of Sadiq al-Mahdi, the former prime minister of Sudan, in *Arabia*, February 1983, p. 29.

9. *Al-Sharq al-Awsat*, March 26, 1983.

10. Fathi Osman, "The Radical Islamists in National Governments," *Arabia*, February 1983, p. 11.

11. Ajami, *The Arab Predicament*, p. 193.

6 ISLAMIC RESPONSES TO THE CAPITALIST PENETRATION OF THE MIDDLE EAST

Joel Beinin

I

In his now classic work, *Islam and Capitalism*, Maxime Rodinson has most convincingly argued that, contrary to the assertions of Max Weber and many others, Islam did not in the least inhibit the development of protocapitalist economic activity during the Umayyad, Abbasid, and Fatimid caliphates. He cites numerous cases in which the Qur'an, the Hadith, and the development of *fiqh* (in particular the use of *hiyal* or legal fictions) positively encouraged petty commodity production and mercantile capitalism. Turning to the modern period, Rodinson says that "the Muslim religion has influenced significantly neither the structure nor the functioning of the capitalist sector in the countries of Islam."[1]

Rodinson's basic thesis, with which this author wholeheartedly concurs, is that the ideology of Islam, despite the existence of certain Qur'anic injunctions and other texts traditionally considered inimical to capitalist development, was less powerful than the social reality in which it was imbedded.[2] In the long run, this social reality and the outcome of its internal struggles for power imposed itself on the religious texts of Islam, forcing a reinterpretation or circumvention (by *hiyal*) of those texts.

As Rodinson's work clearly indicates, there is no single, unequivocal, and clearly definable Islamic attitude toward capitalism. There exists a large body of texts, interpretations, and concrete practices that has served to substantiate opposing points of view within a common Islamic framework. This discussion of Islamic responses to capitalism is not at all concerned with discovering or proving the "true" Islamic position vis-à-vis capitalism. While this question is undoubtedly an urgent problem for many believing Muslims, here we will confine ourselves to a more restricted task: to show how Islam has been used as a framework and validating principle for a broad range of anti-capitalist sentiments in the twentieth-century Middle East. (Such a discussion should not at all be taken as a suggestion that Islam is therefore inherently anti-capitalist.)

The recent popularity of this particular interpretation of Islam is related to the fact that the development of capitalism in the Middle East and the incorporation of that region into the world capitalist market, a process which has been under way since at least the middle of the eighteenth century, has meant simultaneously the military conquest, colonization, regional fracturing, and neocolonial domination of the Middle Eastern countries by the capitalist West. Resistance to this process has taken a variety of forms — compromise and conciliation on the part of large landowners and local minorities, who often served as agents for European commercial enterprises; authoritarian and liberal varieties of nationalism promoted by, e.g., Kemal Atatürk and the Egyptian Wafd; and the radical nationalism or "Arab socialism" of Nasser, the Ba'th, and the Algerian National Liberation Front. All of these are now regarded as disappointingly inadequate to the challenge that Western domination has posed.

There has long been a critique and response to Western capitalist domination framed in Islamic terms. Perhaps the best known early popularizer of this trend of thought was the pan-Islamic anti-imperialist, Jamal al-Din al-Afghani. The world view and sentiments articulated by al-Afghani never ceased to be an influential element in Muslim popular social consciousness in the modern Middle East. Many local intellectuals and Westerners have, however, considered his ideas to be outmoded and superseded by varieties of secular nationalism or socialism. Now, in the light of what is commonly perceived as the failure of the ideological alternatives and the "success" of the "Islamic Revolution" in Iran, there is increased interest, among both Westerners and Muslims, in exploring Islam's potential as a framework for articulating and mobilizing anti-capitalist and anti-imperialist sentiment.

II

Muhammad 'Abduh (1849–1905) was both a disciple of al-Afghani and, in his later years, an advocate of cooperation with the British occupation of Egypt. He was a friend of Lord Cromer, who regarded the members of the intellectual current that 'Abduh represented to be "the natural allies of the European reformer."[3] Despite his willingness to cooperate with the British, 'Abduh maintained a clear position of criticism of certain capitalist practices. As reported by his disciple Rashid Rida, 'Abduh argued that the excessive accumulation of money and wealth and the widespread practice of *riba* (usurious interest) results in the eclipse of the role of religion in society and the diminution of compassion and mercy. Consequently, the poor die of hunger. A social problem (*mas'ala ijtima'iyya*) is created. This is manifested in a variety of social conflicts including labor unrest and strikes, which are the result of owners of enterprises paying workers less than the wages they deserve. Workers, therefore, seek an upheaval (*inqilab*) of the existing order.[4]

'Abduh was, however, ambivalent in his attitude toward capitalism. This should not surprise us since this parallels the contradictory tendencies that coexist throughout the body of his thought. 'Abduh distinguishes between two kinds of *riba*: *riba al-nasi'a*, which is absolutely forbidden, and *riba al-fadl*, which may only have been forbidden by jurists because it was considered to be a means (*dhari'a*) to *riba al-nasi'a*. If *riba al-fadl* is necessary for economic growth, it may therefore be permissible if approved through consultation (*shura*) with *'ulama*, teachers, judges, engineers, doctors, large landowners, and merchants.[5]

It was apparently on the basis of this distinction that 'Abduh issued a *fatwa* in 1903 authorizing the deposit of funds in the Egyptian Post Office Savings Bank where they would earn a "dividend" of 2.5 percent.[6] J. Jomier, who was the first to point out the existence of this *fatwa* (the text of which unfortunately has not survived), insists that despite this sanctioning of interest, "it seems . . . absolutely certain that the Master did not intend to legitimize the capitalist structure of modern society."[7] However, this judgment may well reflect Jomier's own sentiments more than 'Abduh's, because there is nothing in the texts on which it is based that condemns capitalism as a whole, beyond the question of *riba*. On the other hand, it may be argued that 'Abduh employed *riba* as a metaphor for capitalism as a whole.

It is of no importance to this discussion that Muhammad 'Abduh was not the first to make a distinction between the two types of *riba*. What is significant is that this view of *riba* appeared in Egypt at this particular time, and that it was adopted by the circle around Muhammad 'Abduh. 'Abduh can be considered one of the intellectual representatives of the rising agrarian bourgeoisie in Egypt. His ambivalence toward capitalist development meshed closely with the concerns and internal debates within this class. A fraction of this class subsequently emerged as the leading force in the formation of Bank Misr, the centerpiece of the attempt to develop Egyptian national industrial capitalism.

Eric Davis has argued that the establishment of the Post Office Savings Bank and the acceptance of the legitimacy of interest prepared the ground for the subsequent establishment of Bank Misr.[8] Bank Misr's founder, Muhammad Tal'at Harb, was close to Muhammad 'Abduh and strongly influenced by his thought. Harb admiringly quoted 'Abduh on the title page of his book on the appropriate social role of Egyptian women, *Fasl al-khitab 'an al-mar'a wa-al-hijab* (Cairo, 1901), and he translated into French a series of 'Abduh's articles which had originally appeared in the Egyptian daily *al-Mu'ayyad*; these were published in *L'Europe et l'Islam: M.G. Hanoteux et le Cheik Mohammed Abdou* (Cairo, 1905). The same volume contains a reprint of Tal'at Harb's obituary of 'Abduh first published in *L'Egypte* (July 13, 1905).[9]

Muhammad 'Abduh's legacy on the question of the relationship between Islam and capitalism developed in two contradictory directions. On the one hand, he clearly foresaw the "social problem" that the spread of capitalism was bound to create in Egypt. On the other hand, among his disciples and associates were some of the largest landowners in Egypt who were closely linked to British capitalism, and later to Bank Misr, and Tal'at Harb himself, the father of Egyptian industrial capitalism.

III

By the end of World War II, hardly anyone in Egypt continued to display the ambivalence toward capitalism that characterized Muhammad 'Abduh's thought. Industrial capitalism in Egypt grew rapidly during the 1930s and especially during the war. A large number of new enterprises were established to supply material for the Allied war effort. Many former peasants crowded into urban centers seeking employment. At the end of the war, the sudden cutbacks in many of the war-related industries resulted in large-scale unemployment. There was widespread public debate about the "labor question" and how to resolve it. The social problems created by the development of capitalism were, in the public consciousness, inextricably linked to the continuing British military occupation and political domination of Egypt. This is because, despite the existence and growth of Egyptian-owned industry (Bank Misr and its associated enterprises, the 'Abbud complex, and other firms), foreign capital played a dominant role in the capitalist sector of the Egyptian economy until the 1960s.

The postwar period in Egypt is also marked by the rapid spread of Marxist concepts among the intelligentsia and the establishment of several communist organizations. These communist groups, in alliance with the left wing of the Wafd, the Wafdist Vanguard, played a major role in the massive upsurge in the nationalist movement in late 1945 and early 1946. The Marxist critique of capitalism was popularized by the communist organizations themselves in their press and by the left-wing Wafd intellectuals who had access to a number of magazines and journals, including the popular daily *Al-Wafd al-Misri*.

In this atmosphere of widespread dissatisfaction with the results of capitalist economic development and the popular feeling that capitalism and British political domination were two aspects of the same phenomenon, it is not surprising to find the emergence of critiques of capitalism framed in Islamic terms. These critiques do not, however, represent a unified Islamic perspective. At least three distinct trends of criticism can be identified: (1) an Islamic modernist trend that essentially embraced the secular socialist critique of capitalism and the advocacy of socialism as an alternative, and argued that socialism is sanctioned by Islam; (2) a conservative Islamic trend that argued that many of the practices of capitalism in Egypt contradicted the requirements of Islam, placed responsibility for this entirely at the feet of the British occupiers, and engaged in only minimal criticism of Egyptian Muslim capitalists; the leadership of this trend was generally unwilling to mobilize the public for a struggle against the prevailing social order because this would exacerbate social tensions and encourage the spread of communist ideas; (3) a revolutionary Islamic trend that proceeded from the same premise as the conservative Islamic trend, but concluded that it was necessary to struggle against both foreign and Muslim Egyptian capitalists and to bring about a completely new Islamic social order.

The Islamic modernist trend was represented by Shaykh Khalid Muhammad Khalid and his book, *From Here We Start (Min huna nabda')*. The economic program that Khalid advocated was European social democracy justified in plainly utilitarian terms: "The whole civilized world has now agreed that socialism is the regime in which social utility reaches its utmost realization."[10] The program of socialism was also supported by a reference to a statement attributed to the quintessential Islamic socialist figure, Abu Dharr al-Ghifari, a companion of Muhammad who distributed all his property to the needy. Abu Dharr is reported to have said, "I wonder how the person who does not find food in his home can refrain from attacking others with his sword."[11]

Khalid did not want to see the hungry going about with drawn swords and he claimed that this could only be avoided by implementing a "comprehensive and clear socialist program."[12] Khalid apparently had a very mild form of socialism in mind and he approvingly referred to measures taken by the Labour Party in Great Britain and to suggestions made by Eric Johnston, president of the American Chamber of Commerce.[13] Although it was perhaps not as revolutionary as many other calls for socialism issued in Egypt at the time, Khalid's platform had the merit of being programmatically concrete. He demanded a fifty-feddan limit on land ownership, a legal maximum for agricultural rents, nationalization of natural resources and the means of production, and enactment of protective legislation for workers.[14] He also clearly advocated the implementation of birth control as a necessary corollary to a socialist program.[15]

Khalid Muhammad Khalid was unusual among *'ulama* in his willingness to embrace an economic program originating in the West and to claim that it was sanctioned by Islam. A much more common approach was to criticize both capitalism and the socialist/communist alternatives and to advocate an economic order based on Islam. This was the approach of both the conservative and the revolutionary Islamic trends.

The conservative Islamic trend was represented by the Muslim Brotherhood in the period up to the dissolution of the Society in December 1948 and the assassination of its General Guide, Hasan al-Banna, in February 1949. The Brothers had been, to a limited extent, involved in trade union activity since the late 1930s, and a Social Affairs Section of the Society was established in 1942. In 1942 and 1943 several articles on "social reform" appeared in the Society's semimonthly magazine, *Al-Ikhwan al-Muslimun*. These were generally theoretical expositions of the Islamic view of social organization rather than efforts to elaborate a programmatic alternative to the existing social order. In January 1944 this magazine temporarily ceased publication. During the hiatus, the antagonism between the Muslim Brothers and the Wafd sharpened. As a result of the need to present a clear alternative to the Wafd, and especially to its left wing, *Al-Ikhwan al-Muslimun* adopted a much more popular tone and became more pointedly political when it resumed publication in December 1944. It was also in 1944 that the Society established a Workers' Section. This arm of the Society was one of the main vehicles for the popularization and implementation of its economic program. Its formation marks a sharp increase in the Society's activity in the trade union movement.

There were two principal reasons for the intensification of the Society's activities in the trade union movement and its increasing attention to social questions. The first was the extent of the social crisis created by massive unemployment at the end of the war. Equally important was the ideological challenge posed by the spread of Marxist ideas, the appearance of communist organizations with significant influence among some sectors of the working class (particularly the textile workers of the Cairo suburb of Shubra al-Khayma), and the emergence of the Wafdist Vanguard-communist coalition at the head of the nationalist movement. Muhammad Sharif, the head of the Workers' Section of the Society of Muslim Brothers from 1944 to 1948, has stated clearly that the principal objectives of the Society's activity among workers were to propagate the call of Islam and to fight the spread of communism.[16] The Society's activities during the period 1944–48 were motivated as much by the perceived ideological threat posed by communism as they were by the desire to expel the British from Egypt and establish an Islamic order.

In opposition to the communists' theory that divided society into contending classes with mutually contradictory interests, the Muslim Brothers counterposed the ideal of an organically interdependent social unity. Relations between the various social strata (functionally differentiated groups rather than classes) were to be governed by the principle of "mutual social responsibility" (*takaful ijtima'i*). The application of this principle to relations between employers and employees has been succinctly summarized by Richard Mitchell in his path-breaking study of the Muslim Brothers as follows:

> Islam has established certain rights and duties for the worker. His relationship with his employer is governed by the principle governing all human relations — "a mutuality of duties and

rights" based on mutual "respect and sympathy" and ordered by the "spirit of brotherhood." He has the right to a healthy and clean home, wages adequate to provide the needs of life and "punctually" paid, and limited hours of work. The worker is forbidden to "allocate any part of his wages" to his leaders. In return for these rights he shall "perform his work faithfully," thus respecting the rights of management and fulfilling his own responsibilities.[17]

The Brothers also insisted that society must provide each of its members with a certain degree of social security. A properly functioning Islamic state should achieve this by organizing mutual social responsibility that provides for the needs of all. The principal method of providing for the poor and needy was to be the traditional Islamic practice of giving alms (*zakat*) regulated and directed by the state, which could tax the wealthy to support the poor when necessary. Particularly important in the context of massive postwar unemployment was the Society's view that an individual's right to work must be guaranteed by the state. If work was unavailable or wages were insufficient to support a worker and his family, the state must supplement incomes through alms.[18] The Society was very sensitive to the general economic crisis of postwar Egyptian society and the insecurities it created. It was especially concerned with the issue of unemployment and articles on the "problem of the unemployed" and a variety of proposed solutions appeared regularly in the pages of *Al-Ikhwan al-Muslimun*.

The concept of mutual social responsibility stands in stark contradiction to the capitalist notion that workers can be hired and fired according to the fluctuating requirements of production and profitability. The Brothers rejected the notion that no one was responsible for workers after they were dismissed. Most often the Brothers appealed to the Egyptian state to remedy the unemployment problem. They considered that the government was morally bound to find work for the unemployed because it had taken them from their villages to work in the war industries.[19]

Although the Brothers upheld an individual's right to hold private property as a basic human impulse, they opposed the materialist values and greed that, they argued, capitalism promoted. Foreign-owned enterprises bore the brunt of the Brothers' attacks on capitalism. The Brothers saw these firms as imperialistic companies exercising an economic occupation of

Egypt, "exploiting its national wealth, humiliating its labor force
. . . and the spirit of its people."[20] In the period 1944–48, Egyptian-
owned capitalist enterprises were very rarely criticized. M.T.
Audsley, labor attaché in the British embassy in Cairo, noted that
"Hasan al-Banna was willing to support workers against foreign
employers, but not against Moslem ones."[21] The restriction of the
Society's criticism of capitalism to foreign-owned enterprises during
the middle 1940s allowed this criticism to merge easily with the
general upsurge in the postwar nationalist movement. Among the
most frequent complaints that the Society raised against foreign-
owned companies were firing Egyptian workers, replacing them
with foreigners, and paying foreign workers higher wages than
Egyptians performing the same work.[22] These issues were especially
sharp at the Suez Canal Company and the Suez Refinery of the Shell
Oil Company and its subsidiary Anglo-Egyptian Oil Fields. It is
therefore no accident that the unions in these enterprises, and
throughout the Suez Canal zone generally, were the strongest
centers of the Muslim Brothers' strength in the Egyptian trade
union movement.

The Muslim Brothers' attack on foreign capitalists and their
vision of an economic and social order governed by principles of
Islamic brotherhood and mutual responsibility corresponded with a
widely shared, if imprecisely articulated, popular and traditional
definition of social justice in Egypt. A large number of Egyptians
identified with the Islamic idiom of the Brothers (despite the
novelty of many of their interpretations of Islam) much more easily
than with the theoretical concepts and style of the communists or
the Wafdist Vanguard. The Brothers' criticism of foreign economic
domination of Egypt and the impersonal and materialistic values
and practices of the large foreign monopoly corporations, particularly the firing of workers during periods of recession, resonated
with many Egyptians' sense of what was wrong with the postwar
Egyptian society and economy. In this sense the Brothers' vision of
a just Islamic society bears a great similarity to the concept of a
"moral economy" that E.P. Thompson has used to describe the
social consciousness of the eighteenth-century English crowd.[23]
This vision held a strong attraction for many former peasants
recently arrived in Cairo, the canal zone, or other urban centers,
wrenched from their rural and pre-industrial social solidarity
networks and confronted with the harsh regime of industrial
discipline dominated by what appeared to be specifically European

rather than simply capitalist values and norms. This vision also appealed to small independent artisans and craftsmen whose markets and very livelihood were under constant attack from commodities produced by large-scale capitalist methods.

The Muslim Brothers' world view was articulated in conservative Islamic terms calling for the restoration of an ideal society of the distant past. Yet this conservatively couched appeal had a profoundly radical effect, since it denied the moral legitimacy of both British imperial domination of Egypt and the secular nationalist movement that arose to challenge that domination. Some of the leaders of the Muslim Brothers were interested only in the conservative aspects of the Society's message. However, many of the Society's rank and file members who had been attracted by the Brothers' social solidarity and mutual aid, their nationalism and their vision of a "moral economy," were quite open to the radical interpretations of the Society's doctrine, which began to gain influence and widespread attention even outside the ranks of the Muslim Brothers. Some Brothers were propelled by their radicalism into the ranks of the communist movement. In early 1949 Prime Minister 'Abd al-Hadi was reported to have said that half of the Brothers who had been sent by the Society's leadership to spy on the communist organizations had been recruited to membership in those organizations.[24] When the Society was dissolved, many Brothers were rounded up and placed in detention camps together with communists, many of whom had been interned since the declaration of martial law at the start of the Palestine war. This experience, too, seems to have had a radicalizing effect on many of the Brothers. A number of communist veterans of these detention camps recall that some of the Brothers were deeply impressed by the egalitarian social relations among the communist prisoners.

The death of Hasan al-Banna led to sharp factional disputes among the remaining leaders of the Society when it emerged from underground following the electoral victory of the Wafd in January 1950. Previously, doctrinal and programmatic disputes had been resolved by the fiat of the General Guide. Now no decisive and final authority was universally recognized by the membership. One consequence of Hasan al-Banna's death was that many of the potentially radical and even revolutionary tendencies in the Brothers' world view began to develop and become explicitly articulated. Thus, from May 1, 1951, when the Wafd government restored legal recognition to the Society, it is possible to see the emergence of a revolutionary Islamic tendency whose views were most comprehensively articulated in an official publication of the Workers' Section, al-Bahi al-Khuli's *Al-Islam . . . la shuyu'iyya wa-la ra'smaliyya* (Islam . . . Not Communism and Not Capitalism) and in some of the articles in the "workers' page" *al-Da'wa* (The Call), the weekly magazine of what may loosely be termed the left wing of the Society of Muslim Brothers during the period 1951–54.

As an official publication of the Workers' Section, al-Khuli's book represents the fullest official theoretical exposition of the Brothers' critique of the existing capitalist social order and their programme for an economic and social system based on Islam. The bulk of the book reiterates and amplifies the basic views of the Muslim Brothers on mutual social responsibility explicated previously and repeats criticisms of the Egyptian government's labor policy. Both communism and capitalism are attacked as materialistic ideologies emanating from the West in opposition to which it is necessary to uphold and affirm the Islamic heritage. The novel and revolutionary implications of al-Khuli's exposition are contained in the final sections of the book. He relates a *hadith* attributed to the Caliph 'Umar according to which an employer complained to 'Umar that his workers stole from him. 'Umar replied that if the workers repeated this offense the employer's hands would be cut off. 'Umar reasoned that the workers had stolen because the employer's wages were insufficient. The employer, therefore, bore the responsibility for the workers' crime and he should receive the appropriate punishment.[25] Al-Khuli goes on to argue that those who do not work have no right to a share of the wealth of society. But, he notes, in contemporary Egypt the rich and idle are systematically oppressing those who work. Exploitative monopoly companies and big landowners are held responsible for this situation.[26] Both foreign and Egyptian companies are attacked for their treatment of workers.[27] The conclusion of the section of the book devoted to urban labor contains an appeal to improve workers' conditions based on the concepts of "human rights" and "natural rights." Al-Khuli warns that if these rights are not secured, the result will be a violent and destructive social upheaval. This is not the outcome which he desires. Therefore he urges workers to retain their self-control and rally round Islam.[28] This call seems to rescind the directives implied in the oral tradition attributed to 'Umar. It may have been inserted in order to satisfy more conservative members of the Society's leadership or the requirements of government censorship. It is also possible that at the very last moment al-Khuli was unable to embrace the ultimate conclusions of his own argument or to break completely with the Brothers' long-standing aversion to exacerbating social tensions.

Expressions of militant anti-capitalist sentiment in the pages of *Al-Da'wa* were less ambiguous. Muhammad al-Fuli, a labor lawyer who served as counselor for several unions in the Alexandria area, contributed a regular column offering legal advice to workers and expounding the Islamic point of view on labor questions. His opposition to capitalism was unequivocal, and rather than calling on workers to restrain themselves, he urged them to unite and struggle against the capitalists, not only around day-to-day economic issues in the factories, but for a workers' ideology (*fikra 'ummaliyya*).[29] He warned the capitalists against the righteous wrath of the workers:

> Oh tyrannical capitalists . . . the sword of justice is unsheathed against you. Either you grant the workers their rights or justice will conquer. And the day that it will triumph you will have neither existence nor power.[30]

The radicalization of a section of the Muslim Brothers made possible the establishment of a limited, sporadic, and unstable national united front including some elements of the Society and the largest of the communist organizations, the Democratic Movement for National Liberation (DMNL). This united front functioned briefly in the second half of 1951 in opposition to the increasingly discredited Wafd regime and again in 1953 after the Wafd, the DMNL, and some of the Brothers turned against the military regime of the Free Officers.

Although it was the largest organized expression of the revolutionary Islamic tendency, the left wing of the Muslim Brothers was not the only, nor in the long run the most effective, exponent of this position. Sayyid Qutb, in two works written before he joined the Society, produced the most powerful, cogent, and long-lived arguments for this position.[31] The impact of these works, *Al-'adala al-ijtima'iyya fi al-Islam* (Social Justice in Islam) and *Ma'rakat al-Islam wa-al-ra'smaliyya* (Islam's Struggle Against Capitalism), is still strongly felt in contemporary Islamic revivalist movements.

Social Justice in Islam, written in 1948 and first published in 1949, is the more cerebral and subtle of the two works. The text is replete with Qur'anic quotations, reflecting Qutb's own struggling evolution toward a comprehensive Islamic intellectual framework. The critique of capitalism is limited and largely inferential. According to Qutb, Islam forbids the establishment of monopolies trading in the necessities of life, and, of course, all forms of interest are prohibited.[32] But capital and the accumulation of capital *per se* are not condemned so long as they remain within the limits prescribed by Islam. Abu Dharr is praised in connection with his opposition to the excessive accumulation of wealth permitted by the Caliph 'Uthman and the Umayyad dynasty. But the modern relevance of Abu Dharr's actions is not clearly stated.[33] Qutb's Islamic economic program is based on government collection of alms (*zakat*); establishment of mutual social responsibility; the levying of additional taxes on the rich to provide for public services, education, and health care; nationalization of natural resources, public services, and transport; the abolition of extremes of wealth and poverty; equal provision of health care and education for all; worker participation in the ownership of enterprises; and prohibition of gambling, prostitution, and alcohol.[34]

Certain passages in *Social Justice in Islam* prefigure the more clearly revolutionary stand that Qutb adopts in *Ma'rakat al-Islam wa-al-ra'smaliyya* and in his later work, *Ma'alim fi al-tariq* (Milestones). Contemporary Egypt is criticized as an ignorant pre-Islamic (*jahili*) society.[35] The implication is that it is the duty of Muslims to wage *jihad* against such a society. Qutb concludes the book with a call for the establishment of a third camp — neither capitalist nor communist, but Islamic.[36] This is Qutb's point of departure in *Ma'rakat al-Islam wa-al-ra'smaliyya*.

This book was written while Qutb was in the United States during the years 1948 to 1950 and first published in February 1951. Qutb's dislike of the crass consumerism and moral degeneracy that he felt characterized U.S. society are evident throughout the book. It is probable that it appeared several months before al-Khuli's *Al-Islam . . . la shuyu'iyya wa-la ra'smaliyya*. Many of Qutb's themes appear in that work.

In *Ma'rakat al-Islam wa-al-ra'smaliyya* Qutb's condemnation of the prevailing social order in Egypt is unequivocal. He repeatedly invokes, in the opening chapter, the clarion call, "I indict these current social conditions," and boldly asserts that they cannot persist.[37] He specifically attacks the Egyptian Muslim magnate

'Abbud for breaking the union of his employees at the Hawamdiyya sugar refinery because they went on strike to demand that he grant them the increased cost of living allowance that the government had decreed.[38] Qutb gives unqualified support to trade unions and other struggling organizations (*hay'at mukafiha*).[39] He repeatedly refers to Islamic legal opinions upholding the view that workers are entitled to half the profit derived from capital because the only legitimate source of private property in Islam is labor, and ownership of capital in and of itself is not a legitimate source of gain.[40] Qutb is sharply critical of the privileges of Egypt's aristocratic elite and condemns all forms of social inequality and class society.[41]

The right of private property is severely restricted by Qutb's proclamation of society's "absolute right" to seize all and redistribute it to avoid catastrophe.[42] This extreme measure is not justified by reference to the Qur'an or any other traditional authority. In this passage, and indeed throughout the book, Qutb's willingness to embrace a clearly revolutionary program seems motivated principally by his horror as the Egyptian monarchy and its social order tottered on the edge of collapse.

The economic program that Qutb advances is essentially an elaboration of the positions taken in *Social Justice in Islam*, but in *Ma'rakat al-Islam wa-al-ra'smaliyya* his proposals are much more concrete, clear, and immediate. He specifically condemns existing monopolies on sugar, alcohol, and cement and the monopolistic concessions given to foreign capitalists to operate the Suez Canal and the tramway, electricity, and water systems of Cairo and Alexandria. Nationalization of these enterprises is advocated because "nationalization of public utilities is a basic principle of Islam."[43]

Qutb is acutely conscious of the link between capitalism and British imperialism and denounces the alliance between Egypt's "dictatorial ruling class" and imperialism.[44] The Egyptian ruling class, he says, is merely a curtain veiling imperialist rule.[45] Qutb predicts that all of the political parties in Egypt — the Wafd, the Sa'dists, and the Constitutional Liberals — will stand shoulder to shoulder in defense of the interests of capitalism against the interests of the masses should the masses ever pose any threat to capitalist interests.[46] All these political parties are natural allies of imperialism and will therefore oppose the anti-imperialist struggle of the masses.[47] Qutb's condemnation of the Egyptian capitalist ruling class even includes a denunciation of the major daily newspapers, which are attacked as hirelings of the large capitalist firms that advertise in them.[48]

Qutb's analysis of the nature of the Egyptian ruling class, its institutions, and its alliance with imperialism has much in common with the Marxist analysis of these questions that was widespread and popular in Egypt at this time. However, Qutb is just as opposed to communism as he is to capitalism, and he once again puts forward the call for the formation of a third bloc — an Islamic bloc — because Islam is the most unifying rallying cry behind which the Egyptian people can be united to struggle against imperialism and defeat it, not only on the material, but also on the spiritual level.[49] Islam alone can provide the basis for both the material and the spiritual reconstruction of society.

Qutb joined the Society of Muslim Brothers after the autumn of 1951 because he was impressed by their dedicated participation in the guerrilla struggle against the British bases on the Suez Canal. He rose quickly to a position of responsibility within the Society and his inspiration is apparent, not only in al-Bahi al-Khuli's work, but also in the pages of *Al-Da'wa*. In December 1954, after being accused of masterminding an unsuccessful assassination attempt on the life of Gamal Abdel Nasser, the Society of Muslim Brothers was once again banned. Six of its members were hanged and many were imprisoned. Although he had no connection with those accused of the attempted assassination, Qutb was among those imprisoned as part of the regime's general crackdown on the Society.

IV

The dissolution of the Muslim Brothers did not reduce the potency of the Islamic critique of capitalism. On the contrary, as the Egyptian regime moved toward the policies that eventually became known as "Arab socialism," a house-broken variety of Islam was pressed into service by the government to legitimize its policies both in Egypt and in the broader Arab world. A number of works on the general theme of "Islamic socialism" were published by the government-supervised publishing houses of Egypt. Among the titles were Ahmad Farraj, *Al-Islam din al-ishtirakiyya* (Islam, the Religion of Socialism, Cairo, n.d.), and Mahmud Shalabi's series of hagiographies of early Islamic figures which found in their lives early Islamic endorsement of socialist principles — *Ishtirakiyyat Muhammad* (The Socialism of Muhammad, Cairo, 1962), *Ishtirakiyyat Abi Bakr* (The Socialism of Abu Bakr, Cairo, 1963), and *Ishtirakiyyat 'Umar* (The Socialism of 'Umar, Cairo, 1964).

The regime was aided in its attempt to press Islam into the service of Arab socialism by the high degree of factionalism which persisted in the Society of Muslim Brothers. One element of the society adopted a "realist" position that supported the regime, the establishment of the United Arab Republic (U.A.R.), and the policies of Arab socialism. This element was wholeheartedly embraced by the Egyptian government.

Mustafa al-Siba'i, dean of the Faculty of Islamic Jurisprudence and the School of Law at the University of Damascus, was, from 1945 to 1961, the leader of the Syrian branch of the Society of Muslim Brothers known as the Islamic Socialist Front.[50] In 1958 al-Siba'i formally dissolved the Syrian branch of the Muslim Brotherhood, yielding to Nasser's demand that all Syrian political parties be dissolved as a condition for the establishment of the United Arab Republic.[51] He remained the head of the organization until it emerged from underground following Syria's secession from the U.A.R. in 1961.

In 1959 al-Siba'i published a work called *Ishtirakiyyat al-Islam* (The Socialism of Islam). Its central argument is that Islam is not antagonistic to socialism and that there is complete harmony between the two sets of principles. This book was reprinted several times in Egypt and enthusiastically endorsed by many government spokespersons. Two scholars who have paid particular attention to the emergence of Arab socialism in Egypt have commented about al-Siba'i's book: "We are assured from authoritative sources that [al-Siba'i's book] is considered to be of the utmost importance in providing form, direction, and legitimacy to the social system emerging in present-day Egypt. It is considered to be, in brief, a major statement of ideology for Egyptian socialism."[52]

While al-Siba'i's theories were being promoted to support the policies of the Egyptian regime, Sayyid Qutb and many others from the anti-government faction of the Egyptian Muslim Brotherhood were languishing in jail.

In Syria, on the other hand, by 1961, just as al-Siba'i's work was becoming popular in Egypt, the Syrian Muslim Brothers eliminated "Islamic socialism" from their lexicon and chose a new leader, 'Isam al-'Attar.[53] By the middle 1960s, the Syrian Brothers had adopted a new economic program reflecting "the outlook and interests of the urban Sunni trading and manufacturing middle and lower middle classes."[54] Thus, from a position of endorsing "Islamic socialism" and a clear critique of capitalism, the Syrian Brothers shifted to the advocacy of competitive capitalism and protection of the rights of small capitalists and merchants in opposition to the Syrian state, the Ba'th Party, and its "socialist" principles.

Of course, the ideology of Arab socialism was never thoroughly anti-capitalist. It can perhaps best be understood as an ideology of opposition to foreign monopoly capitalism. This limitation on the extent of Arab socialism's anti-capitalism may have made it easier for the Syrian Muslim Brothers to adopt the positions that they now hold. It is nonetheless clear that a significant shift in economic policy occurred within the organization in a rather short time. This should serve as additional confirmation of Maxime Rodinson's thesis that the social milieu in which Islam finds itself in the end has the largest influence on what Islam actually is.

Sayyid Qutb did not approve of the term "Islamic socialism." For him, as he stated most clearly in *Milestones* and in *Social Justice in Islam*, there were only two ideological alternatives: Islam or pre-Islamic ignorance (*jahiliyya*). Qutb considered capitalism, socialism, and communism alike as manifestations of *jahiliyya* thought and refused any concession to their world outlooks that would be implied by linking Islam with them.[55] Qutb remained relentless in his opposition to capitalism; but his refusal to lend any legitimacy to the Arab socialism of the Egyptian regime and his implication that Muslims were obliged to wage *jihad* against the *jahiliyya* of contemporary Egyptian society cost him his life. He and several other Muslim Brothers were tried for conspiracy against the state and executed in 1966.

As the regime began its roundup of the Muslim Brothers in the summer of 1965, it became engaged in a debate over whether socialism is sanctioned by Islam. The second conference of the Muslim World League was held in Mecca in the spring of 1965, and it denounced the Egyptian regime. The government then counter-attacked, defending its position that Islam and socialism are one and the same.[56] This period also saw the publication by the ardent Nasserist, 'Ismat Sayf al-Dawla, of a work reiterating the Islamic sanctions for socialism — *Usus ishtirakiyyat al-Islam* (The Foundations of the Socialism of Islam, Cairo, 1965). A year later Kamal al-Din Rif'at, Secretary for Propaganda and Thought of the Arab

Socialist Union, wrote in the religion supplement of the official daily *Al-Jumhuriyya*, "there is no contradiction at all between Islam and socialism . . . socialism is one of the principles of Islam."[57]

Thus, during this period in Egypt the Islamic critique of capitalism was transformed from a revolutionary indictment of the old regime into one of the ideological pillars supporting Nasserism. Those who refused to acquiesce to this transformation, such as Sayyid Qutb, paid a very high price.

Notes

1. Maxime Rodinson, *Islam and Capitalism* (Austin, TX: University of Texas Press, 1978), p. 168.

2. Ibid., p. 157.

3. Earl of Cromer, *Modern Egypt*, 2 vols. (New York: Macmillan, 1908), Vol. 2, p. 180.

4. Rashid Rida, *Tafsir al-Qur'an al-karim*, 12 vols. (Cairo: Dar al-Manar, 1367 A.H.), Vol. 3, pp. 107–9.

5. Ibid., Vol. 4, pp. 128–31.

6. Rodinson, *Islam and Capitalism*, p. 148; Eric Davis, *Challenging Colonialism; Bank Misr and Egyptian Industrialization, 1920–1941* (Princeton, NJ: Princeton University Press, 1983), p. 72.

7. J. Jomier, *Le Commentaire Coranique du Manar* (Paris: G.P. Maisonneuve, 1954), p. 225.

8. Davis, *Challenging Colonialism*, p. 73.

9. Ibid., pp. 100–101.

10. Khalid Muhammad Khalid, *Min huna nabda'* (Cairo, 1950). All references are to the English translation: *From Here We Start* (Washington, DC: American Council of Learned Societies, 1953), p. 96.

11. Ibid., p. 75.

12. Ibid.

13. Ibid., pp. 96–97, 107, 109.

14. Ibid., pp. 103, 104, 107–9.

15. Ibid., pp. 109ff.

16. Personal interview, October 28, 1980.

17. Richard P. Mitchell, *The Society of Muslim Brothers* (London: Oxford University Press, 1969), p. 253.

18. Ibid., p. 274.

19. *Al-Ikhwan al-Muslimun*, May 7, 1946.

20. Ibid., December 6, 1948.

21. Foreign Office (Great Britain), FO 371/73474/J3567 (1949).

22. *Al-Ikhwan al-Muslimun*, June 17, August 15, December 13, 1946; August 12, 1947.

23. E.P. Thompson, "The Moral Economy of the English Crowd in the Eighteenth Century," *Past and Present*, No. 50 (1971): 76–136.

24. Foreign Office (Great Britain), FO 371/73476/J1937; and FO 371/73476/J3502 (1949).

25. Al-Bahi al-Khuli, *Al-Islam . . . la shuyu'iyya wa-la ra'smaliyya* (Cairo: Al-Ikhwan al-Muslimun, Qism al-'Ummal, 1951), p. 106.

26. Ibid., pp. 107–8.

27. Ibid., pp. 110–11ff.

28. Ibid., pp. 117–18.

29. *Al-Da'wa*, October 2, 1951.

30. Ibid., August 21, 1951.

31. I am indebted to Adnan Musallam for the details concerning the timing of the publication of these two works. His arguments are available in his Ph.D. thesis, "The Formative Stages of Sayyid Qutb's Intellectual Career and his Emergence as an Islamic *Da'iya*, 1906–1952" (Ann Arbor, MI: University of Michigan, 1983).

32. Sayyid Qutb, *Al-'adala al-ijtima'iyya fi al-Islam* (Cairo: Maktabat Misr, 1949). All references are to the English translation: *Social Justice in Islam* (New York: Octagon Books, 1970) p. 118.

33. Ibid., pp. 214–18.

34. Ibid., pp. 267ff.

35. Ibid., p. 227.

36. Ibid., pp. 277ff.

37. Sayyid Qutb, *Ma'rakat al-Islam wa-al-ra'smaliyya* (Cairo: Dar al-Kitab al-'Arabi, 1951). All references are to the fifth edition (Beirut: Dar al-Shuruq, 1978), pp. 8, 23.

38. Ibid., p. 21.

39. Ibid., p. 23.

40. Ibid., pp. 40–41.

41. Ibid., pp. 47, 49.

42. Ibid., pp. 43–44.

43. Ibid., p. 47.

44. Ibid., p. 101.

45. Ibid., p. 120.

46. Ibid., pp. 114–15.

47. Ibid., p. 117.

48. Ibid., p. 118.

49. Ibid., pp. 25–26, 36.

50. Hamid Enayat, *Modern Islamic Political Thought* (London: Macmillan, 1982), p. 144; Hanna Batatu, "Syria's Muslim Brethren," *MERIP Reports*, no. 110 (November-December 1982): 14.

51. Batatu, "Syria's Muslim Brethren," p. 18.

52. George H. Gardner and Sami A. Hanna, "Islamic Socialism," *The Muslim World* 46, no. 2 (April 1966): 73.

53. Batatu, "Syria's Muslim Brethren," pp. 12, 18.

54. Ibid., p. 14.

55. Sayyid Qutb, *Ma'alim fi al-tariq* (Cairo: n.d.). References are to the English translation: *Milestones* (Beirut: Dar al-Qur'an al-Karim, 1978); pp. 14–17, 173ff.; Sayyid Qutb, *Social Justice in Islam*, pp. 87ff.

56. Yvonne Yazbeck Haddad, *Contemporary Islam and the Challenge of History* (Albany, NY: State University of New York Press, 1982), p. 30.

57. *Al-Jumhuriyya*, July 1, 1966, quoted in Haddad, *Contemporary Islam*, p. 31.

7 ISLAMIC MARXISM IN COMPARATIVE HISTORY: THE CASE OF LEBANON, REFLECTIONS ON THE RECENT BOOK OF HUSAYN MURUWAH

Peter Gran

This essay explores why Lebanon, a country generally known in recent times for its liberal capitalist culture among the Arab countries, has seen the most profound attempt at the integration of Marxism and Islam. The question "Why Lebanon?" is approached as a problem in comparative history in which Lebanon is taken to be a hinterland of Syria, and Beirut a financial entrepôt within that hinterland. Through a general consideration of the varying relationships of states, hinterlands, and financial entrepôts, abstracted from modern Third World history generally, one can start to develop a line of analysis to explain the relative success of fusion movements of the sort represented by Islam and Marxism in Lebanon, differentiating them from the popular front-type of Islam and Marxism common enough in Syria or in Egypt. Husayn Muruwah, a Lebanese writer, is a convenient figure to dwell on as he has recently written a formidable interpretation of rationalism through Islamic history, a subtle work integrating Islam and Marxism, which has no parallel in Egypt or Syria; he plays a role in politics as well. On a more general level, Lebanon is an urgent subject on which to focus because of the continuing devastation there. The hope is always that a comparative approach can shed some new light on the specific features of Lebanese culture and politics that the more localized focus of other approaches may have missed.

In the Middle East, religious Marxism exists not merely in Lebanon, but in Syria, Turkey, Iraq, Iran, Egypt, and elsewhere. Of course it exists outside the Middle East and the Muslim world as well as in parts of the East Bloc, Latin America, the United States, India, etc. A first step in pursuing this subject is to construct some hypotheses to guide this and future research, in other words, to state what one would accept to work with and what one would tend to refuse. At this point, many scholars would have to refuse a theory of Islamic exceptionalism as too Orientalist, or a hypothesis of a *sui generis* religious revival as simply begging the question.

A general feature of a hinterland is fluidity; its political and cultural tendencies are marked by at least surface discontinuity. This is the case both for internal reasons as well as a result of the pressures exerted by the neighbouring state. For the scholar studying the history of a hinterland, it is important to use appropriate methods and not to rely on a genre like institutional history as one would in the case of a state. The variability of hinterlands, or their fluidity, helps to explain our hypothesis that new fusion movements, such as Islam and Marxism, can progress there in a relatively unimpeded fashion. The various component parts (Islam, Marxism, ethnicism) are not imbedded so deeply in powerful institutions which have to be accommodated, as is the case in states. Depending on the political situation, one can begin from scratch. Then again depending on politics, the new movement may develop relations with the state and gain legitimacy or it may bring down repressive measures as was often the case in the recent history of Lebanon. Clearly in the Lebanese case, repression comes to mind whether one thinks of Israel or Syria or whether one thinks of the various alliances of the Lebanese National Movement, the communists, the Palestinians, the Maronites, or, more recently, Amal. Our hypothesis is that Lebanon has suffered repression far more than have other hinterlands such as those of the Sahara, or the Horn of Africa, because the states of the Middle East have solidified their position moving to the right. They have been able to dramatize the cataclysmic possibilities inherent in local rivalries as a way to procure foreign aid while at the same time to collaborate with each other increasingly against their own and neighboring people. Much of the aid and military support which they have received has come at a time when the West's need for Middle East oil is actually declining. Movements which are predominantly located in the hinterlands like the Palestinians have suffered disproportionately. Some of their leaders want to escape into statehood at any cost. Of course, others reach quite the opposite conclusion that all these unpopular governments are bound to be ripe for revolution. Still others decided that there is no escape but to function as Jordanian, Syrian, or Israeli proxies. Splits in the Druze communities in Israel and Lebanon and among the Shi'a of Lebanon provide other examples of small groups following these strategies. On a slightly less pronounced level, the influence of the Libyans, Iraqis, and Egyptians was always noticeable in Lebanon as well. As I write, the local newspaper reports overtures by Lebanese Maronites to their "Arab brothers" in Damascus; even if they abandon Israel, they cannot abandon life as a proxy. The strong states like Israel appear to find the new trend to the right most congenial while the weak states like Jordan appear most anxious to quiet the hinterland movements. King Hussein, who once tried to massacre the PLO, now extols the moderate qualities of Yasser Arafat to any American who will listen, and given what the Middle East is costing the United States, there are definitely people listening.

We now turn to consider the particular features of Lebanese history which appear to explain why it is only in the past few years that Lebanon has been converted into the "slaughter house of nations." It is not the presence or activities of the PLO, one unassimilated group among many, but rather the economic decline of Beirut which created a context for the political and military disasters of the past few years. The decline of the economy of Beirut crippled the Lebanese government and brought to the foreground military proxy struggles and external invasions by neighboring armies. As the most independent group, the Palestinians are fair game for everyone else; but Lebanese politics would not change much even if all Palestinians left tomorrow.

Lebanon was formed, as many hinterlands have been, by its amputation from a country to which it previously was joined, and from a set of relationships of which it was traditionally part. Lebanon was amputated from Syria by French colonialism, but its florescence as a region was based in recent years on the dominance of Beirut, one of the world's main financial entrepôts. Over a long period of time, Beirut, like Hong Kong and Nairobi, produced a cosmopolitan culture linked as much to France or the United States as to a national or regional culture. But, with the decline of Beirut's banking and insurance businesses, and with the rise of the Arab Gulf as a rival business center before and during the Lebanese civil war, one witnesses the birth of contemporary Lebanon. New forces emerge reflecting the regional as opposed to the international character of Lebanon: first, the Lebanese National Movement, second, the Phalange, and third, Amal. The relative importance of these developments can be judged by the tacit acceptance of the Israeli invasion by most of the other surrounding states. It is this hinterland context, in what previously appeared to be a modern independent state, which gave rise to writers like Husayn Muruwah.

Despite wide differences, nation-states, the old Lebanon included, share in common a divide-and-rule strategy, under which they tend to promote religious and secular culture as separate and also as rival forces. In times of crisis, the nation-state looks to short-term national unity coalitions like the popular front, which combines a range of religious and secular forces in alliance. But when normalcy returns, no government would want these coalitions to remain. When there is a fairly permanent state of social, economic, and cultural crisis, however, segments of the religious intelligentsia ally themselves with Marxist movements first in tactics and subsequently in ideology. This happened gradually in Brazil; it happened later but more rapidly in Lebanon when the very weak state apparatus in a hinterland context tried to assert Maronite claims as a style of domination. How did the divide-and-rule strategy fail?

In the first part of the twentieth century, the solution to social, economic, and cultural problems was less problematic than today; it was universally found in the form of the nation-state. In this matter, the Third World of the twentieth century emulated Europe of the nineteenth century. Even for countries which were nominally independent in the nineteenth century, the project of creating a nation-state had high priority. Like the countries of nineteenth-century Europe, few countries in the Arab world or elsewhere were homogeneous in social or cultural terms. The local intelligentsia sought to overcome the social divisions through a new universalist ideology; they championed secular nationalism. On the other hand, the colonial powers and their local allies, which were mainly the feudal elements, relied heavily on a policy of promoting religious cleavages to maintain their position. Secularism was more than a tactic, however; it was a foundation for the development of a modern culture. This meant fighting Europe, but adopting the principles found in Europe, on which science and social science could proceed. Secularism played an additional and crucial role for the minorities of the Third World who feared being totally marginalized if a communalist movement came to the fore. This was true among the Christian Arab nationalists of the Levant from the early part of the century; it was true for the Arab communists of the 1940s and thereafter. It is a common observation that the membership of the communists and other secularist movements contained a disproportionate number of Christians and Jews. Finally, secular progress or developmentalism was a large part of the ideology of most of the intelligentsia as they placed all their hope in the growth of the economies and the states which they served.

It certainly cannot be argued that during the same first half of the twentieth century religion died in the face of secularism and that therefore a revival is now under way. Rather, several schools of thought manifested themselves and they can be well understood in their context. The best known and best studied in the West is religious modernism. The modernists, who included segments of the upper classes in Third World countries as well as missionaries working within the colonial administrations, maintained that the religion of the local natives had decayed and must be revived and brought into line with the assumptions of the modern West. What Islam needed was a reformation, a Martin Luther. Such ideas found their way into Arabic through the writings of Muhammad 'Abduh and his followers in Egypt, e.g., Mustafa 'Abd al-Raziq. The Egyptian school influenced Ibn Badis in Algeria, as well as Muslims from remote states, such as Indonesia. Muhammad 'Abduh and a small handful of like-minded individuals sought to provide a textual basis for a historical and developmental religion. Among Christian writers who were his contemporaries, especially in Lebanon and Syria, religious modernists emphasized the Golden Age of Islam (a period of ethnic tolerance and the high point of cultural achievement among the Arabs) more than the reformation of Islam, which was from a political point of view more ambiguous.

A second main trend was that of the Muslim Brotherhood. Its origins lie in the Sufi resistance movements which had long been simmering openly or covertly among provincial merchants and various segments of the urban class structure. Officially, the Brotherhood "began" in the interwar period as a result of the teachings of Hasan al-Banna in Egypt. It might be more precise to claim that it represented before and after in both ideological and sociopolitical terms much that was swept under the rug in the euphoria of the nationalist movement. Hasan al-Banna attacked secularism; he recognized that secularism meant that the state was governed by an impersonal statutory law, which the individual believer had no way of influencing; law was in the hands of politicians. States could do what they wanted to because they were not obliged to base themselves on the Qur'an. Since Islam was not the religion of the state, or was only nominally so, individuals could treat Islam as a matter of private conscience. This meant in effect that many abandoned religion altogether, or in all but name, and there were no sanctions against such behavior. Al-Banna further observed that this was particularly the case with the rulers and people of influence. He realized that in the early Islamic states such a situation would have called for *fitna* (revolt), while in the present states there was no longer a juridical basis for revolution. Islam, he and many after him argued, covered all aspects of society (in contrast to Protestant Christianity). A second point which al-Banna made was that the period of the *nahda* (Western-sponsored revival) benefited the minorities. Christians and Jews rose in social and economic status very rapidly at the expense of the Muslim majorities through service to the state or through commerce. Al-Banna attributed this to the failings of the Muslim rulers and to imperialism. Further, he opposed the idea, common among the modernists, that the members of the major religions were People of the Book and argued that they had abandoned God, who subsequently chose new prophets. All this lends support to our claim that the basis of al-Banna's following was precisely from those groups who were not benefiting from the rise of the nation-state and from the nationalism of the period. This explains the strength of the movement until today in the disadvantaged secondary towns and among the merchants generally. It also explains the images of struggle against the great and powerful often evoked, and the ultra-conservatism in matters relating to women and marriage.

In most countries in the Arab world, the balance of forces through the 1950s favored the modernists. The liberation struggles were unresolved and a growing industrial proletariat was forming in the cities. The industrial proletariat was invariably organized in trade union movements and supported radical but secular ideas of change and progress. The state thus had a fairly wide social basis; it included some capitalist farmers, some industrialists, and a large number of petit bourgeois clerks and trade union officials. By the 1960s, however, the Western economic structure underwent important modifications and this had drastic effects on the states of the Arab world. Western economies confronted higher costs in their industrial production and increasing competition from each other, and on occasion from the less developed countries. Increasingly, corporations in the developed countries sought to form new relationships with public sector corporations and private capital in the Third World to farm out their labor-intensive production and to encourage export agriculture. The impact of Western economic policies on Third World states gradually led to a shift in internal emphases within Third World states. An increasing number of them abandoned autocentric development and sought to engage in multilateral relations with Western corporations. The incentives to do so were numerous; they ranged from the price of fuel, to the availability of weapons and industrial spare parts, to the hope of political gains in ongoing conflicts like that between the Arabs and Israel.

The foregoing should not be taken to mean that Western pressure was decisive in the Third World; usually internal dynamics were. What occurred internally was a slow development in a stagnant domestic market. In some of the Arab countries, industrial production was subsidized by oil revenues, and in others, like Egypt, by agricultural exports. Subsidy was necessary because of the lack of a domestic market; however, this was not merely an economic fact, but rather more a consequence of political alliances, specifically the alignment of the state bourgeoisie with semifeudal elements in the countryside, who had products to market. In many states this alliance created starving rural masses, as well as large numbers of people who fled to urban slums looking for work, groups scarcely capable of serving as a market for the products of local industry. Thus, in all the countries of the Arab world, the politically motivated state bourgeois-semifeudalist alliance served to sabotage economic development. The capitalist class had no choice but to go into uneven partnerships abroad or risk social revolution at home. Pressures from agricultural interests, as well as from wide segments of the society that did not benefit from the support of industry, forced a de-emphasis of industrial self-reliance, i.e., an "open door," and an end to state socialism.

Lebanon in particular suffered in a very dramatic way from the global economic changes of recent decades, now called the New World Economic Order, although it had no great productive capacity and its population was quite small. Since the late 1950s, petrodollars had begun to flood into the leading Lebanese banks and this in turn began to exacerbate internal social and economic problems. The new wealth resulted in a high rate of inflation which had a very uneven impact on Lebanese society. Maronites who owned the largest banks and controlled the drug trade emanating from the Biqa' Valley were, of course, prime beneficiaries. Less prosperous parts of the ruling political alliance, however, like the Shi'i landlords who owned large tracts in the south but who lived in Beirut, began to suffer, as did the salaried populations in the cities. Inflation led the landlords to try to raise rents. A violent reaction to rising ground rent was noticeable in the south and elsewhere; for example, the late Imam Musa Sadr became in the eyes of some observers "a Maoist" on land questions.[1] Nonetheless, many peasants had to abandon the land; they flocked to the slums along the rim of Beirut.[2] The predominantly Sunni and Christian Orthodox urban middle class in the cities felt their position erode and they turned away from their traditional political leaders, the notables of towns like Tripoli. The Druze mountain people also felt the impact of inflation and their leader, Kamal Jumblat, underwent an evolution toward socialism. Thus, the changes in Lebanon affected the traditional people of the commercial cities — Sunnis and Orthodox, the peasantry, the Shi'a, and the mountain people like the Druze, pulling them toward radicalism or radical populism.

By the mid-1970s, many of the traditional Lebanese politicians who had been in and out of lists for a generation sought to avoid politics. A collision was coming between the super wealthy Maronite elite on the one hand and the Lebanese National Movement (LNM) on the other. Suffice it to say that the collision never developed as many had predicted; other factors intervened. The Syrians and Israelis invaded to keep the peace, each in their own way. For the Israelis, the Palestinian presence in South Lebanon was a factor, but the violent, indiscriminate attacks that Israel made against West Beirut and the verbal onslaughts against Muslim opponents left no doubt that the scope of Israeli concerns was much wider. The invasions were rendered easier by the internal divisions in Lebanon. By allying itself to the PLO and to the Iraqi cause in the Iran-Iraq war, the Lebanese left created severe conflicts with the Shi'i southerners. Following the assassination of Musa Sadr, probably at the hands of the (Sunni) Libyans, yet another blow was struck at the popular front approach which Jumblat was employing. Jumblat's own death created a void which could scarcely be filled by his youthful son. By the late 1970s, it was clear that the collapse of the popular movement was the result of a lack of organization and ideology as much as the intervention of outside forces. There had only been the most diffuse conceptualization of the LNM during the Jumblat period; reliance on the leader greatly overshadowed organizational development.

Official Culture and Popular Culture

From the nineteenth century, Lebanon, defined by the power of its entrepôt, Beirut, was marked by its openness to the West, its large number of Christians, and its lack of a conventional Islamic cultural concentration in the sense commonly understood in Damascus, Cairo, Baghdad, Istanbul, and so forth. Yet it is equally true that Lebanon has produced numerous systematic leftist writers as well as works of religious thought; its publishing houses print much of what is produced in Arabic religious thought. Beirut, even in its entrepôt days, was more than simply a place of commerce in the wares of others; there is a difference between the books produced through the famous publishing houses in Beirut and those of comparable establishments in Cairo or Damascus. What is noticeable is the number of books that develop a clear ideological position either of the left or the right. What accounts for this diversity, intensity, and clarity of expression in Lebanon?

The answer would seem to lie in the nature of the state. Lebanon, as a hinterland forced to try to be a state, is unique in the formation of its political apparatus, and in the character of its petite bourgeoisie. The state functions with a minuscule bureaucracy, through an alliance of Beirut merchants, bankers, and feudalists. Most states in the Third World are characterized by large bureaucracies, which support and depend on a petit bourgeois intelligentsia. In such states, the intellectual production has a vocational cast; it has a large textbook component, and such original work as takes place is often of an empirical or fact-gathering nature. This would characterize much of the writing of a country like Egypt, where the state in the period since 1952 has often been both the sponsor and the publisher, as well as the validator through its reviews and even its censorship. Of course, Egypt is so large that alternative presses and other cultural worlds exist, but it is nevertheless very different in this respect from Lebanon, where the petite bourgeoisie is a congeries of small groups employed by a myriad of little institutions. The fragmentation of the society and the growing conflict of the various groups permits or even encourages development in ideology and philosophy. There is little attempt at state control and indeed the weak political elite might well wish that the various extreme views might simply cancel each other out.

The most coherent explanation in popular Lebanese thought for what went wrong and what can be done is religious in nature. To understand this one must always remember that secularism, Marxism, and liberalism were controlled by the apparatus of centralized states. For example, the classical Marxism of the communist parties was geared to the needs of the trade union movement. With the victory of the national movements and the commitment of the new states to national industrial programs, there also came considerable benefits to the industrial workers, who formed one of the pillars of the state. Quite quickly, the communist parties of the Arab world on the official level became virtual parties of the status quo. They defended the rights of workers, but they did so in a reformist or economistic way since the workers had much to lose, given the extreme poverty of the majority of the population. The communists did not try to reach into the slums with their recruitment, in contrast to the street imams and the traditional preachers, who did and do. Liberalism was even more limited in its appeals and drew its followers from among the wealthy, who could be concerned with individual liberties. The first major eruption reflecting the rising power of the new forces was Iran, and since 1978 the Iranian Revolution has served as a prototype for many Arabs — among them certain Syrians and the followers in Lebanon of the Amal movement, e.g., Husayn al-Musawi.

A few analysts appear to have overcome on a conceptual level some of the problems of integration of the religious and the secular that continue to plague the parties on a practical level. Husayn Muruwah is a Lebanese leftist and author of an immense work in two volumes entitled *Materialist Trends in Arab Islamic Philosophy*.[3] The principal issue examined in this unique book is the Islamic heritage and its role in the modern period. He correctly sees this as an essentially political issue and in the conclusion to the second volume (pages 713ff) he argues that there is a link between the medieval struggles for liberty waged by the middle class rationalist philosophical tradition against Caliphal autocracy and the struggle today against the reactionary Arab bourgeois powers tied to world imperialism.

In recent times, the issue of heritage (*turath*) has been a hotly-contested one, usually between the conservative right and the state, with the traditional left adopting the position of the state. In essence, the state position has been to encourage the ministry of culture to sponsor studies of the Islamic past as part of the national patrimony, which in one way or another might be inspirational. The use of the term heritage, however, reveals that states consider it to be remote and not modern although not necessarily entirely in conflict with what is modern. It is a layer of the present identity, but not the one which animates present-day affairs, or one which is in a position to judge the details of the contemporary world. The position of the state is utilitarian and modernist and it stands against romantic conceptions of the past Golden Age of Islam. These rules of course do not apply across the board; they apply only to the quintessentially modern subjects, the rational ones. As for literature and the wider domain of imagination, a considerable tolerance exists for the idea of the relevance of classical Arabic literature for the modern world. The opposite is true, however, in a field like the history of science, where the Arabs made considerable contributions. The left, while traditionally serving the state, has viewed heritage as part of the feudal or pre-capitalist phase. Relatively few books of a Marxist sort examine the history of medieval culture. Most that touch the period at all speak only of its economic or political structures. Among the Muslim Brothers the concept of heritage has always been rejected out of hand. Islam never declined; Muslims always confronted the issues of their day. If Islam has suffered it is only in the modern period when some Muslims have been persuaded by European influence to abandon or distort the true essence of their religion. The Muslim Brothers were not interested in the European attempts to portray a Golden Age of the Arab world. To them, the Golden Age idea was in reality a part of Europe's own cultural problematic.

In *Materialist Trends*, Muruwah begins his long opening chapter on methodology by noting his debt to the well-known contemporary Islamic writers, but he proceeds in a way distinct from theirs (or, to my knowledge, that of any previous author in Arabic) to review the extensive contributions of the Soviet Orientalists to the study of Arab philosophy. Much of what he stresses about the struggle of Arab-Islamic philosophy against Platonic idealism appears to come from them, while at the same time he rejects the mechanistic materialism which sometimes marred their overall view of history, cutting off the past from the present in too total a way. Broadly speaking, Muruwah sets out to demonstrate at great length that there was a rationalist climate in the Arab world before Islam among the *hukama'* (rulers), that it further developed in Mecca and Medina at the time of the Prophet, when class formation brought on the debates about *tawhid* (the doctrine of unity), and that it continued to develop in the intellectual struggles surrounding the Kharijites and the early Shi'i revolts. Muruwah studies the social context of the rise of early feudal landownership under the Umayyads as well as the intellectual struggle against feudalism. This rationalist struggle reached an apogee during the Abbasid caliphate when the translation movement took place; it struggled on for many centuries thereafter in the form of *kalam* (speculative theology). His treatment of the Abbasid period almost entirely stresses the objective social and cultural forces which induced the choices and the concerns of the translation movement, which he does not view as simply some automatic response to the prestige of Greek learning. In the conclusion to Volume II (pp. 705–10), he raises a point that has eluded previous writers, namely that Islamic society was more nearly of the feudal and commercial type, whereas the Greek society, which had produced the original Peripatetic philosophy, was a slave-owning one. From this comes his argument that Muslim thinkers in what he calls the Arab-Islamic phase of rationalism (hence that part of the book's title) place a greater emphasis on man's relationship to and control over nature and are less concerned with idealism than was the case for Plato, whose society was purely tributary. Furthermore, when Europe received this rational philosophic inheritance through its own translation movement, it was not structurally prepared to benefit from it. Muruwah here relates his explanation to Marx's distinctions between the Asiatic mode of production and European feudalism, but with a new twist. In the Arab world of the caliphate which permitted rationalist critical thought to flourish, religion and state were fused. Religion was not separate from society, and religious issues interpenetrated with other matters of practical concern. In Europe, on the other hand, there was a bifurcation for many centuries between the Vatican (which was the initial European locus of interest in Greek thought) and the various states. This explains why European scholasticism exhibited such a single-minded preoccupation with abstract issues like the nature of God, the trinity, and God's creation of the earth, while science was pursued elsewhere. This of course is not an absolute distinction, Muruwah maintains, since the Islamic religious structure had its reactionary spokesmen who produced such doctrines as that of *jabariyya* (predestination), according to which man's actions mean little.

The crux of this part of the argument is that the middle classes were the bearers of a rationalist protest stimulated by their technical and scientific educations, which were needed by the state during its phase of expansion. With the breakdown of the caliphate and the rise of the imarate system, the same classes struggled on against bureaucratic and military elements that had grown stronger and that denied them much of their patronage. The religious outer covering of *kalam* was simply a necessary concession which the rationalist forces had to make to carry on their struggle. The affinity between the Islamic Marxists and the *mutakallimun* is striking. The reactionary forces Muruwah saw had as their great ally al-Ghazzali, who argued that received knowledge and tradition could serve as a framework for Islam.[4]

Muruwah holds Europeans at fault for perpetuating many misunderstandings about these Arab-Islamic writers from the Middle Ages onward. In the first instance, Europeans have ignored the class dimension (hence the title wording "Materialist Tendencies"); second, they have tended in the case of both Ibn Sina and Ibn Rushd to impose on them a confused religio-philosophical identity that was alien to them. Muruwah claims that the decisive grounds for arguing his position that these two thinkers were pure philosophers lies in the nature of their theories of truth. Ibn Sina defined the relationship of the universal to the particular in three ways, which conflicted with a Christological understanding of the origins of true knowledge. He maintained that the universal existed before it was concretized in a material object, that the universal was part of the essence of the object, and that the universal existed after its manifestation. Only in the European Age of Enlightenment of the eighteenth century did scholasticism get displaced adequately so that the doctrine of the eternity of matter could emerge. For Muruwah and for other writers like Hasan Hanafi, the Western Renaissance figures, like Giordano Bruno, who paid with their lives for their naturalist ideologies, were true followers of Ibn Rushd in a society which did not appreciate them.

Some Hypotheses about the Relationship of Muruwah's Book to Contemporary Society: Literary Sources and the Study of Islam and Marxism

One is struck by the extent to which Muruwah's long methodological introduction follows the tradition set by French theoretical writings. Terms are defined, sources are identified, debts are acknowledged, and so on. However, some epistemological contradictions do crop up. For example, how can Muruwah claim that Aristotelian rationalism was the revolutionary antecedent of dialectical materialism? Numerous writers have shown that the whole dialectical tradition was always in opposition to the Peripatetics.[5] What one ultimately uncovers is a range of interesting questions from his study that come as much from Lebanese politics as from texts. Did Muruwah encounter a Stalinist Marxism that is essentially taxonomic and hence like Aristotle? If so, he appears to try to reject it. The five-stage approach to history does not really accommodate the continuity of intellectual struggle for the heritage, which is the main subject of the book (Volume I, p. 20), or even his analysis of the antecedents of the Greek translation movements in the Arab world. Muruwah clearly opposes the notion (common in Russian and Western Orientalism) that the rational heritage came from the books that were translated; he argues for an internal continuity of rationality emerging back in the tribal past. A purely textual approach to his work would tend to miss the incredibly contradictory nature of the political and economic situation that gave rise to this type of historical construction. But given this situation, it seems fair to ask about the role of Christians and Christian heritage in an Islamic Lebanon. Muruwah does not develop Christian rationalism in his analysis of *turath*.

Conclusion

Islamic Marxists are perhaps the first in the Middle East to try to translate the impact of the New World Economic Order into the language of opposition politics. Books like Muruwah's, therefore, must be seen as straddling the two worlds of academics and politics. In this essay, I tried to lay some of the groundwork for an analysis of Islamic Marxism which could fit into a larger comparative historical framework. For this reason, I chose to emphasize the tension between state, hinterland, and entrepôt. Such a beginning does not prove the desirability of this approach over more traditional ones emphasizing the purely Islamic or Arabic character of Muruwah. A range of further steps are necessary even to raise seriously such a question. It would certainly be necessary to show how Muruwah differs from other important Shi'i writers in the major states of Iraq and Iran like Muhammad Baqir al-Sadr or 'Ali Shari'ati. In addition, it would be necessary to show that individual categories used here, like financial entrepôt, permit fruitful comparisons for example of entrepôt cultures like those of Singapore and Beirut. Would the critique of Singapore intellectuals that one finds in the works of Hussein Alatas serve to characterize as well the Beirut intellectuals up to the civil war? Finally, can one compare religious Marxists on a world scale and comment on how their works are integrated? Would the writings of the Mexican Marxist priest José Porfirio Miranda serve? Answers to these questions — which are not necessarily easier or more difficult than others that we usually pose for ourselves — would permit students of Islam to speak to a wider audience concerned about the direction of contemporary history and culture.[6]

Notes

1. This interpretation is based on Selim Nasr's suggestive essay and other contributions in *MERIP Reports*, No. 73 (1978), on the crisis of Lebanese capitalism.

2. A discussion of the economic aspects of this theme is found in Chris Gerry and Ray Bromley, eds., *Casual Work and Poverty in Third World Cities* (New York: John Wiley & Sons, 1979).

3. Husayn Muruwah, *Al-naza'at al-maddiyya fi al-falsafa al-'Arabiyya al-Islamiyya*, 2 vols. (Beirut, 1979). The literal translation of "Materialist Trends . . ." might better be rendered "A Materialist Interpretation of Arabo-Islamic Philosophy"; the main review article until now is Na'if Balluz, "*Waqfa ma'a al-naza'at al-maddiyya fi al-falsafa al-'Arabiyya al-Islamiyya*," Dirasat 'Arabiyya XV, No. 4 (1979): 23–65.

4. Muruwah promises to extend his work to a possible third volume to carry this struggle to North Africa up to the time of Ibn Khaldun.

5. Leszek Kolakowski, *Main Currents of Marxism* (Oxford: Oxford University Press, 1981), Volume I, Chapter 1.

6. Muhsin S. Mahdi, *The Political Orientation of Islamic Philosophy*, (Washington, DC: Center for Contemporary Arab Studies, Georgetown University, 1982) raises this theme in a general way.

8 RELIGION AND POLITICS UNDER NASSER AND SADAT, 1952–1981

Ibrahim Ibrahim

Since the fall of the Shah and the rise of the Islamic republic in Iran much attention has been focused in the West on the role of Islam in the political process. The assassination of President Anwar al-Sadat by Muslim militants has led to speculation that Egypt might experience the same sort of revolutionary religious upheaval as took place in Iran. Indeed, we are often reminded of the deeply religious nature of the Egyptian masses; as Hasan Hanafi puts it, "Religion has always been identified with the Egyptian. Religion was his science, art, philosophy, literature, belief-system, values . . ."[1]

Islamic resurgence in the Arab world, as indeed in all other Islamic countries, surfaces at times of crisis, when the welfare and unity of the body politic are seriously threatened. That is, Islamic movements emerge in reaction to the state's inability to assimilate and integrate the body politic; its exclusion of the masses from the political process; its failure to eliminate inequality or its toleration of social injustice; and, finally, its impotence in defending the nation, its national honor, and dignity. At this point, the crisis may be defined as a decline in the status and power of the ruling class, which results in lessening its claim to legitimacy.

This is exactly what happened in Egypt in the late 1940s. Although al-Ikhwan al-Muslimun (the Muslim Brothers) was founded in 1928, it remained on the periphery of Egyptian politics until then. From the beginning of the 1940s signs of domestic instability were apparent in Egyptian society. At that time, failures in the operation of the political system and frustration over the severe economic crisis, which was intensified by World War II, brought about disenchantment with the existing social and political structure.

Solving the problem of earning an adequate livelihood, especially in that time of crisis, was a question of utmost importance to the lower classes in particular. Yet, for all Egyptians, the issue of achieving full independence was the major national concern; the continued British presence in the country was a living denial of Egyptian independence and a constant reminder of the inferior status of the state and the impotence of its rulers.

It was in this postwar environment that the Muslim Brothers grew rapidly and developed into a militant mass movement. They came to play an important role in Egyptian politics in the wake of World War II, when the old political parties had lost their hegemony and standing, and were no longer able to control the rising body of radical students, workers, and the masses of city dwellers. Beginning in the autumn of 1945, newly radical student and worker committees were organized for political action. Despite the fact that these organizations were led by Marxist and communist groups, their effect on the program of al-Ikhwan was considerable. Because of its size, its organization, and the discipline of its members, al-Ikhwan emerged as the most militant and powerful political force in the country. Its members initiated a campaign of violence and terror against their opponents, Wafdists and Marxists on university campuses, as well as against government institutions, officials, and politicians. The Muslim Brothers accelerated their activities during and after the Palestine war of 1948, in which they participated; on December 28, 1948 one of their members assassinated Mahmud Fahmi al-Nuqrashi, the prime minister, whereupon the government dissolved the organization. On February 12, 1949, Shaykh Hasan al-Banna, founder and charismatic leader of the movement, was assassinated, allegedly by agents of the palace.[2]

Immediately after the revolution of 1952, the Muslim Brothers hoped to turn the new political and social circumstances to their advantage. On July 26 they issued a declaration of support for Gamal Abdel Nasser's revolution, which they termed "the blessed movement" for liberating Egypt. Even at the outset of the revolution, however, al-Ikhwan repeatedly proclaimed the need for basing the new government on Islam.[3] But Nasser and his fellow officers were opposed both to the party system and to Islamic fundamentalism. Muhammad Naguib, the first president of the republic, while exalting the teachings of Islam, denied its validity in the modern world. Thus, he rejected the Muslim Brothers "who wanted to go back to the days of the Sultan Salah al-Din when Egypt was a theocratic state." For him, "the rebirth of Egypt depended on the continuous modernization of its social, political and economic institutions."[4]

Nevertheless, when Nasser pronounced the dissolution of all parties on January 16, 1953, he excluded al-Ikhwan al-Muslimun because the movement was identified as an organization rather than as a party.[5] The fact is, however, that Nasser was still working hard to consolidate his leadership in the complex struggle against some of his fellow officers (particularly General Naguib) who were counting on the Muslim Brothers, the last well-organized political force in the country, and therefore he did not want to risk alienating them. Despite this, in 1954, when the Muslim Brothers challenged Nasser's leadership and tried to assassinate him, he ruthlessly suppressed them. Six members of the movement were executed and thousands were imprisoned without trial.

After suppressing al-Ikhwan (and with them the Marxist groups), Nasser's government vigorously pursued a policy of secularization; all religious institutions were made subject to state control. The land reform of 1952 abolished *awqaf ahliyya* (the religious personal endowments) and thus brought this important Muslim institution under secular state control. In 1955 the government abolished all religious courts — those of the minorities as well as those of the Muslims (the *shari'a* çourts); as of January 7, 1956, these courts were absorbed into the state's secular adjudication system. Henceforth, the court system administered a uniform code of law applicable to all citizens throughout the land. The once-powerful *shari'a* system was relegated to the backstage, restricted to lesser matters such as personal status and inheritance questions.

Al-Azhar, the famous center of theological learning which during the interwar period had successfully resisted attempts by the Wafd to end its autonomy,[6] could not now escape reform; its longstanding independence was finally breached when it was brought under government control in 1961. This reform placed al-Azhar's various administrations under the secular government, reformed its curriculum, and reduced the rector, Shaykh al-Azhar, to the position of a figurehead.[7] With this measure the conservative *'ulama* lost their only remaining autonomous institution[8] and with it their political prowess. "In a word, al-Azhar has been 'nationalized'."[9]

Nasser's success in suppressing the Muslim Brothers without encountering any resistance from the Egyptian masses can be attributed to many factors. First of all, most of his aims were consistent with a broad national consensus. Indeed, Nasser was able to gain popular support because he embraced a policy that embodied two feelings that were widespread throughout Egypt.

The first of these was a concern for the welfare of the peasant class from which most of the military officers had come. In conjunction with this, Nasser's plans for the improvement of social conditions in the countryside and his industrialization and urbanization schemes bolstered his popularity among the masses.[10] For these people, positioned below the upper echelon and deprived by the corrupt landowning classes of participation in the social and political life of the time, Nasser was an inspired hero.

In almost every walk of life he instigated a revolution: in land reform, in industrialization, and in the expansion of social services in the countryside. He had inaugurated the nationalization process in 1961; by 1964 almost all big companies of any kind had been nationalized. In agriculture, however, Nasser did not envisage public ownership of land, but rather an increase in the number of farmers and an extension of the cooperative system. By 1965, successive agrarian reform laws and other government measures had made some 1,250,000 acres (about twenty percent of the cultivable area in 1952) available for redistribution.[11] Thus, large sections of the rural population profited to some extent from the expansion of social services in the countryside.

Nasser's energies, also, were visible in his policies on education. As new schools were built at the rate of one a day, the number of children attending primary school increased from 1,300,000 in 1952 to 3,400,000 (1,300,000 of them girls) in 1966.[12] The successful and rapid expansion of education must be cited as one of Nasser's most positive achievements.

The second national longing which Nasser embodied lay in the field of foreign policy. Here he eloquently expressed the sentiments of the majority of Egyptians (and other Arabs as well) through his insistence on decolonization and neutrality. During the 1950s and 1960s Nasser was able to gain popular support due to his determined struggle against Egypt's historical masters.

His stand against British and French colonialism (as seen in the Suez War of 1956 and the Algerian revolution) and his embrace of pan-Arabism were expressions of the demands of the rising intelligentsia, the new "middle class," and the masses. Each had an interest in shaking off colonial control; all of them were seized by the spirit of Afro-Asian independence and wished to increase Egypt's strength in the world by heightening its influence in the Arab countries, where Britain in the Arab East and France in the Maghrib would be its chief rivals.[13]

Nasser's pan-Arabism was therefore dictated by the Egyptian *raison d'état*; its vibrant energies were marshaled by a consideration of Egypt's strategic interests, and by the needs of the rising intellectual elites, including those of the Muslim Brothers who deepened Egypt's involvement in pan-Arab issues, particularly the Palestine question.

In other words, Nasser created a broad national consensus in support of his economic and foreign policy by broadening the regime's social base domestically while capitalizing on his image as the preeminent leader of the larger Arab world in its common struggle for independence. Notwithstanding this broad Arab consensus, however, the defeat of the Muslim Brothers in the 1950s and in 1965–66[14] can also be attributed to Nasser's total domination of the efficient apparatus of the state.[15] Although the regime was drawn from or acted in the interests of the petite bourgeoisie and the rural middle class, it proved fully capable of sidestepping their concerns when expedient by exerting state control in order to achieve its more immediate ends. Suppression of al-Ikhwan al-Muslimun is one prominent example of the regime's successful domination of the body politic.

Nasser appeared at a time when political parties, particularly the Wafd, were entering a phase of decline and the era of "mass politics" was coming to the fore. By destroying the party system and replacing parliamentary democracy with the referendum, he brought the Egyptian (and Arab) masses into play. He was able to silence the opposition by placing decolonization and development on top of the national agenda.

The turning point for Nasserism was the stunning defeat of June 1967, which represented a challenge to what Nasser symbolized for Arabs and Egyptians and consequently was a setback for the secular revolutionary nationalist spirit.[16] Nevertheless, Islamic movements in Egypt could not rise up against Nasser in the wake of that defeat; what secured his position then was not only his charisma and his power of manipulation, but also his record of social reforms — industrialization, education, land reform, and the expansion of social services to the countryside — and his benevolent use of all the resources of the state machinery to promote social programs and national independence.[17]

Nonetheless, following the June defeat and the economic crisis that had been developing since 1965, resentment of Nasser began to spread. Although the student-worker riots of February 1968 shook his grip on power, religious activist groups were not able to rise; this would happen under Sadat, who inherited a republic plagued by economic difficulties and the defeat of 1967.

Generally speaking, there were no substantial differences between Sadat's political outlook and that of his predecessor. As with Nasser, Sadat's government initially took a secular stand on religion in the state; religion and politics were seen as separate matters. However, anticipating political opposition from the left (Marxists, Nasserites, and radical students), which was alleg.·!lv behind the disturbances of 1972 and 1973, Sadat unleashed the forces of religion. At the beginning of his presidency, he took a series of steps to help promote and reintegrate these religious forces into national life. In 1975 he authorized the Muslim Brothers' publication of two journals, *Al-Da'wa* and *Al-I'tisam*, which soon captured a broad audience.[18]

Feeling itself to be in a vacuum and without a popular base, the new regime needed a legitimating motive, and the process of de-Nasserization needed an ideological justification. Nasserites, as the major opposition force, had been discredited in the eyes of the masses as Marxists, atheists, and agents of the Soviet Union. Still, Sadat needed al-Ikhwan to purge the last waves of Nasserite students from the campuses. To reward them for their services, the regime released the last of the Muslim Brothers imprisoned by Nasser and encouraged them to revive their activities under a newly formed Islamic umbrella group, Jama'at al-Islamiyya.

Sadat turned also to the official religious leaders for support; this move was of great political importance in that they were in daily contact with a dramatically increasing number of people who were swelling the cities. For the most part, Sadat was successful in wooing these leaders; during most of his reign, the religious establishment gave him full support. During the strikes of 1974 and 1975, for example, the leaders of al-Azhar urged the populace to rally around Sadat. Other national institutions were called upon to lend credibility to his personal religiosity; he instructed the media to portray him as *al-ra'is al-mu'min* (the pious president). Sadat was no doubt trying to use religion and manipulate the Muslim Brothers to gain the upper hand in his struggle with his opponents, whom he termed "the adventurous left."

Moreover, external factors influenced the government's policy toward Islamic movements and institutions. The ascendancy in the 1970s of the Gulf oil-producing states, in particular Saudi Arabia, aided the cause of Islamic groups.[19] The new orientation toward Saudi patronage after the October 1973 war merely opened the way to Muslim influence of a more conservative kind. For example, Shaykh al-Azhar, Dr. 'Abd al-Halim Mahmud, a firm opponent of the liberalization of the personal status law, an enemy of socialism and the left, and a man to whom the Saudis allegedly had easy access, supported the regime vehemently. Disparities in wealth, he argued, are accepted by Islam; he termed "Crypto-Communists" "all those who advocated state intervention to promote egalitarian redistribution."[20] His book, *Fatawa 'an al-shuyu'iyya (Fatwas* on Communism), published in 1976, undoubtedly reflected the views of Sadat's government and the conservative Saudi regime. "Communism is a heresy, for, among other things, it attacks private property, whereas Islam sanctions property and opens before the individual the path to wealth and property." According to the Shaykh, communism is a form of *jahiliyya* (paganism) and therefore "cannot meet on the same soil"[21] with Islam. In 1975 some legislators began to lobby energetically for making the *shari'a* the sole source of law in the country. More concretely, in that same year, perhaps to please Saudi Arabia whose financial support he needed badly, Sadat authorized the full, legal resumption of the Brothers' activities.

However, the seemingly sound relations between Sadat's regime and the Muslim Brothers did not prevent the rise of far more dangerous militant Islamic movements, a phenomenon through which Sadat met his demise. In April 1974, the Islamic Liberation Organization, known interchangeably as Shabab Muhammad (Muhammad's Youth), became the first Islamic militant movement to stage an attempted coup d'état against the government. In July 1977 another militant group, al-Takfir wa-al-Hijra (Repentence and Holy Flight), kidnaped and murdered a former member of the cabinet, the minister for religious endowments. But the most disturbing moment for the regime was the massive popular uprising in January 1977 against a government decision to eliminate basic food subsidies. For two full days Egypt was in revolt. Intense riots took place all over the country; police stations and policemen were the primary targets. By the official count, 80 deaths occurred, 560 people were wounded, and 1,200 were arrested. Of course, the regime put the blame on the usual scapegoats: the Soviet Union, Libya, and the Egyptian left. President Sadat dubbed the riots *thawrat al-haramiyya* (the revolt of thieves), but they are better remembered as "the bread riots." Even *Al-Iqtisadi*, an establishment publication, saw the riots as a genuine expression of popular protest against Sadat's economic policy.

Regrettably, the majority of the Egyptian people has come to feel no confidence in Egypt in light of the new consumer society, but they believe — and this feeling was expressed in numerous debates with the observers of the operations of sabotage — that they live in the shadow of a system of economic apartheid, that is, economic discrimination that prevents the majority from the fundamentals of life and gives fabulous gains and fabulous advantages to groups newly added to the society, whether this new group is that of parasitic incomes, or members of a new class in Egyptian society, or the Arab tourists who come to Egypt with dreadful buying power, dismembering and destroying Egyptian society with it.[22]

It is not difficult to ascertain that these popular uprisings and occasions of spontaneous dissent were related to the larger and very severe crisis resulting from social and economic policies that dated back to Nasser's era but which were also accelerated by Sadat himself.

For example, Egypt in the 1970s experienced an acute, continuing crisis in the agricultural field, the origins of which can be traced back to political decisions made during the Nasserist era. Nasser's land reform had allowed the new ruling elite to destroy the economic base of the old landowning classes, but it had not fully benefited the mass of peasants; the land reform instead came to benefit primarily the rural middle class from which the Free Officers sprang, thus resulting in an increase in the numbers of landless peasantry. (According to one estimate, thirty to forty percent of the rural population is landless.)[23]

Further to its detriment, in 1974 for the first time in its history, Egypt became a net importer of agricultural commodities, while at the same time the rate of growth of land yields for some of Egypt's most important crops (for example, cereal, cotton, and sugar cane) stagnated or even declined.[24] Coupled with this, the cost of agricultural imports grew from $209.6 million in 1975 to $2 billion in 1977[25] while rural inflation rose to thirty percent per year. This led to a large rural-to-urban migration, which caused severe problems for the government. At that time serious housing shortages became apparent; at least an additional 300,000 units per year were required to begin to cope with this most pressing need.

In addition, Egypt since 1970 had lost almost one-sixth of its cultivated land to nonagricultural uses; little had been done by the state in the meantime to prevent the loss of valuable agricultural land to commercial and residential construction.[26] Under these circumstances, in the absence of state policies to counteract these trends, or to propose alternate means of earning a livelihood, landless peasants began to migrate to the cities, swelling the ranks of the urban unemployed.

Sadat's *infitah* (opening) economic policy failed to ease the economic crisis and came instead to benefit a new comprador class, with rampant inflation sweeping the country as a result. A further direct outcome of the *infitah* was a new pattern of income distribution, with the income share of the poor falling as that of the rich rose. This was compounded by the return of some leading figures from the old families of pre-1952 Egypt and by the spread of corruption among some members of Sadat's inner circle, his relatives, and the *munfatihun* (the beneficiaries and/or supporters of the *infitah*).

In the wake of the *infitah*, militant Islamic groups intensified their denunciation of social injustice and their attacks on the excessive enrichment and corruption among the privileged few. Unlike the traditional leaders of the Muslim Brothers, such as 'Umar al-Tilimsani, editor of *Al-Da'wa*, the young militants deplored the *infitah* (and Sadat's Saudi connection) with all of its attendant corruption. Concern about social justice is, after all, at the very heart of religious militant movements; after the fall of the Shah and the rise of Khomeini, militant Islamic youth were more inclined to accept the Shi'i revolutionary interpretation of Islam than that of the Sunni *'ulama*.[27]

Rapid urbanization without the creation of adequate industrial centers and the expansion of education without credible employment opportunities can lead to economic dislocation, alienation, and even revolt. While all of these factors hampered Egypt's development, the most serious problem facing the Sadat regime in the late 1970s was the unprecedented demographic explosion which exacerbated the entire spectrum of national concerns. During the mass migration from the countryside to the cities in the 1970s, Cairo, for instance, grew rapidly: from four million in 1960 to more than eight million in 1979. This doubling of the Cairene population in twenty years' time naturally yielded grave economic, social, and political consequences and eventually overloaded the system.

The influx of cheap labor from the countryside depressed employment and lowered living standards among the unskilled masses. It involved the uprooting, socially and psychologically, of large sections of the population from the guardianship of the closely-knit village society. In the appallingly crowded city quarters, the collectivity that once existed had broken down completely, and the social guidance that the village had provided vanished. These conditions of deprivation provided the revolutionary base for action, as indeed was the case with al-Takfir wa-al-Hijra, whose leaders and rank-and-file are of rural origin; they joined the movement as recent arrivals in the big cities. For newcomers to the huge "impersonal city," Muslim groups provide a sense of communion, a sense of all-togetherness (*Zusammengehörigkeit*) and "soft landing."[28] Nevertheless, these people remain on the periphery, and feel marginal and extremely alienated.

No one could better describe this alienation from the economically distressed and unorganic city than the four Qutb siblings, Sayyid, Muhammad, Amina, and Hamida, who experienced similar societal and personal upheaval in an earlier era. In *Al-atyaf al-arba'a* (The Four Spirits), their literary autobiography, they explain their love for the countryside and their hatred for Cairo, the symbol of corruption. Cairo for them is the New Society, the new home which could never become theirs. In it they feel mental discomfort, anguish, and "lostness." Thus, when addressing his recently deceased mother, Sayyid likens himself and his siblings to a tree which, once uprooted, could not take root in new soil (Cairo).

> We today are *ghuraba'*, exiles; we are the small branches whose roots have withered after their estrangement from their native soil. And how far are the branches from establishing themselves in the foreign soil![29]

This resentment of the exile is even more clearly expressed by his sister, Hamida:

> I felt the bitterness of exile in every part of this environment [Cairo], and I felt it because I am not part of it and I shall never be absorbed by it . . .[30] I feel a stranger to every part of the Wide Creation with the exception of what was in the recent past. Here is this great ghoulish spectacle [Cairo], oppressing my soul . . .[31] For the first time I realized that I had no place in this great noisy city; and that everything in it was foreign to me and that I shall remain a stranger to it.[32]

Her real home is far away from Cairo, in the countryside:

> There I found my home, wherein I feel close to everything, to everyone. It is the countryside, that soft haven, whose soft air mingled with my flesh and blood from my early years.[33]

Throughout the 1970s, the massive rural migration worked against the assimilation of the growing numbers of city dwellers to the new sociocultural and political patterns drawn by modernizing ruling elites. As a result, Cairo and other cities were "ruralized" and Islam reemerged as the sole ideology.

This is understandable, for the idea of the Muslim *umma* and the virtuous Muslim society is still alive in the popular mind, and inherent in this popular Islam is an ideal of revolutionary justice. As Albert Hourani so eloquently puts it:

> For rural immigrants, seeking security, employment, or wealth in the city, cut off from the ties of kinship or neighbourliness which made life in the village bearable, victims of urban processes that they can neither understand nor control and living in a society of which the external signs are strange to them — for these, the religious community may provide the only kind of world to which they can belong. Its spokesmen use a language which is known and appeals to moral values deeply rooted in their hearts, its rituals and ceremonies are familiar, its shrines are already known to rural visitors as places where prayer has been valid: Sayyida Zaynab in Cairo, Muhyi al-Din Ibn al-'Arabi in Damascus, Mawlay Idris in Fez. If they do not find what they need in the city, they bring it with them from the countryside; if rural migrants have become city-dwellers, the cities, or at least the immigrant quarters, have been 'ruralized'.[34]

By the late 1970s and early 1980s, the state had begun to show serious signs of strain in its effort to integrate the body politic; at the same time, it was not able to withstand pressure from the West and from Israel.[35] Most dangerous, however, was Sadat's retreat from pan-Arab commitments, notably the Palestine question. Throughout the "Muslim world" Palestine has been sacrocanct; Sadat's visit to Jerusalem and later the conclusion of the Camp David Accords and the signature of a peace treaty with Israel brought him under attack from militant Islamic groups like al-Ikhwan and the Nasserites. "Palestine is an Islamic question," declared *Al-Da'wa*; therefore Sadat had no right to give or offer concessions, since he could not legitimately speak for Islam.[36] Sadat's actions in this sphere were bound to incite a Muslim backlash and inflame popular sentiment against the government and its connection to the United States and Israel.

Islamic militant movements, as indeed all dissident movements in many countries of the Third World, are the by-product of the socioeconomic crisis but stem, above all, from deficiencies in the political system. The very fact that Sadat's Egypt was more of "a Presidential monarchy"[37] than a republic encouraged the rise of militant Islamic activists. Living in the age of "mass politics" and at a time of fervent Islamic militancy (e.g., the Iranian Islamic revolution), Sadat and his ruling associates had misread reality and were not able to appraise accurately the dimensions of the crisis. From the late 1970s onward, Egypt was becoming a nation of two nations: one comprised of the depressed masses, the other of the middle and managerial class.

Some twenty years ago, the prominent American sociologist Edward Shils foresaw the serious effects on political legitimacy of the growing gap between the elite and the masses in Third World countries. He wrote:

A modern society is not just a complex of modern institutions. It is a mode of integration of the whole society. It is a mode of relationship between the center and the periphery of the society. Modern society entails the inclusion of the mass of the population into the society in the sense that both elite and mass regard themselves as members of the society and, as such, as of approximately equal dignity. It involves a greater participation by the masses in the values of the society, a more active role in the making of society-wide decisions, and a greater prominence in the consideration of the elite.[38]

It is clear that Sadat and his ruling elite failed to understand the seriousness of excluding the periphery from the consideration of the elite at the center.

It can be concluded that militant Muslim and other opposition forces will continue to rise in Egypt, as indeed in other "Muslim" and Third World countries, as long as vast numbers of the body politic remain on the political and economic periphery of society.

The absence of social and economic justice and political participation, as well as the excesses of coercion, all contribute to instability. Thus, under these circumstances, it does seem possible that Islamic movements will continue to be visible, albeit in the form of clandestine organizations; but for them to be able to seize power from the present ruling elite in Egypt is rather unlikely. This is not only because the elite is shielded by a powerful security apparatus and the army, backed by the "silent majority" of the middle class and the intelligentsia, but also because of the absence of strong, cohesive, and autonomous religious institutions that could assume popular leadership; neither the *'ulama* nor al-Azhar can perform this role since both stand under the firm control of the secular state.

Notes

1. Hasan Hanafi, "The Relevance of the Islamic Alternative in Egypt," in Ibrahim Abu-Lughod, ed., "The Islamic Alternative," *Arab Studies Quarterly*, IV (Spring 1982): 54.

2. See Tariq al-Bishri, *Al-harakat al-siyasiyya fi Misr, 1945–1952* (Political Movements in Egypt, 1945–1952) (Cairo: Al-Hay'a al-Misriyya al-'Amma li al-Kitab, 1972), pp. 268ff. This work is the most informative account of the events leading up to the 1952 revolution.

3. Richard P. Mitchell, *The Society of the Muslim Brothers* (London: Oxford University Press, 1969), pp. 107–8.

4. Muhammad Naguib, *Egypt's Destiny* (London: Gollancz, 1955), p. 150.

5. See Maxime Rodinson, "The Political System," in A.J.P. Vatikiotis, ed., *Egypt Since the Revolution* (London and New York: Praeger, 1968), pp. 98–99.

6. In the interwar period there had been a constant duel between the king and the Wafd over the control of al-Azhar. See F. Al-Zawahiri, *Al-siyasa wa-al-Azhar* (Cairo: Al-I'timad Press, 1945), pp. 32ff.; and S.G. Haim, "State and University in Egypt," in *Universitaet und moderne Gesellschaft* (Frankfurt: 1959), pp. 99ff.

7. Daniel Crecelius, "Al-Azhar in the Revolution," *The Middle East Journal*, XX (Winter 1966): 44.

8. A. al-Moneim, S. Aly, and M.W. Wenner, "Modern Islamic Reform Movements: The Muslim Brotherhood in Contemporary Egypt," *The Middle East Journal*, XXXVI (Summer 1982): 343–44.

9. D. Crecelius, "Al-Azhar in the Revolution," p. 44.

10. Albert Hourani, *Arabic Thought in the Liberal Age* (London: Oxford University Press, 1970), pp. 358ff.

11. R. Stephens, *Nasser: A Political Biography* (London: Penguin Press, 1971), pp. 365ff.

12. Ibid., pp. 375 and 377.

13. Albert Hourani, *A Vision of History* (Beirut: Khayyats, 1961), p. 132.

14. In 1965 the Muslim Brothers were accused of plotting to overthrow Nasser; many were arrested and, in late August 1966, three of their leaders were hanged.

15. See John Waterbury, *The Egypt of Nasser and Sadat: The Political Economy of Two Regimes* (Princeton, NJ: Princeton University Press, 1983), p. 425.

16. See also Ali E.H. Dessouki, "The Resurgence of Islamic Organisations in

Egypt: An Interpretation," in A.S. Cudsi and A.E.H. Dessouki, eds., *Islam and Power* (Baltimore, MD: The Johns Hopkins University Press, 1981), pp. 113–14.

17. R. Stephens, *Nasser: A Political Biography*, p. 578.

18. J. Waterbury, *The Egypt of Nasser and Sadat*, pp. 359 and 362.

19. M.E. Yapp, "Contemporary Islamic Revivalism," *Asian Affairs*, XI, Part II (June 1980): 181.

20. J. Waterbury, *The Egypt of Nasser and Sadat*, p. 361.

21. Fouad Ajami, "In the Pharaoh's Shadow: Religion and Authority in Egypt," in J.P. Piscatori, ed., *Islam in the Political Process* (Cambridge: Cambridge University Press, 1983), pp. 14–15.

22. Cited in Mark N. Cooper, *The Transformation of Egypt* (Baltimore, MD: The Johns Hopkins University Press, 1982), p. 238.

23. Alan Richards, "Egypt's Agriculture in Trouble," *MERIP Reports*, No. 84 (January 1980): 7.

24. *Ibid.*, p. 3.

25. Roger Owen, "The Arab Economies in the 1970s," *MERIP Reports*, No. 100/101 (October-December 1981): 8.

26. Ibid., pp. 9–10.

27. Eric Rouleau, "Who Killed Sadat?" *MERIP Reports*, No. 103 (February 1982): 3–5.

28. Saad Eddin Ibrahim, "Egypt's Islamic Militants," *MERIP Reports*, No. 103 (February 1982): 5–18.

29. *Al-Atyaf al-Arba'a* (Cairo: n.p., 1945), p. 163.

30. Ibid., p. 16.

31. Ibid., p. 21.

32. Ibid., p. 23.

33. Ibid.

34. Albert Hourani, "Conclusion," in James P. Piscatori, ed., *Islam in the Political Process*, p. 227.

35. Philip S. Khoury, "Islamic Revival and the Crisis of the Secular State in the Arab World: An Historical Appraisal," in Ibrahim Ibrahim, ed., *Arab Resources: The Transformation of Society* (Washington and London: Center for Contemporary Arab Studies and Croom Helm Ltd., 1983), p. 221.

36. Cited in A. al-Moneim, S. Aly, and M.W. Wenner, "Modern Islamic Reform Movements," p. 356.

37. David Apter, "Political Religion in the New Nations," in Clifford Geertz, ed., *Old Societies and New States: The Quest for Modernity in Asia and Africa* (New York: Free Press of Glencoe, 1963), pp. 57–105.

38. Edward Shils, "On the Comparative Study of the New States," in Geertz, *Old Societies and New States*, p. 21.

9 OFFICIAL ISLAM AND POLITICAL LEGITIMATION IN THE ARAB COUNTRIES

Ali E. Hillal Dessouki

One shortcoming of many studies on Islam is a tendency to approach the religion as a unitary object or monolithic phenomenon that acts on or reacts to an equally unitary phenomenon, namely modernization. Therefore, my previous work has included a plea to contextualize, to appreciate the variety, subtleties, intricacies, and complexity of historical and contemporary Islamic sociopolitical experiences, which include official Islam and popular or folk Islam, Islam of the status quo and of revolutionary change.[1]

This chapter deals with one aspect of the Islamic experience: the role of official institutionalized Islam in Arab political systems. That role is viewed in the context of Arab political development, a situation characterized by recent statehood and the dominance of mostly Western-educated and secular-oriented elites.

The relationship between Islamic institutions and governments in most Arab and indeed most Islamic states can be analyzed in terms of two processes: the increasing subordination and loss of autonomy of religious institutions, and the provision of religious legitimation to the policies of the state.

Subordination

In most Arab countries, religious institutions have been "nationalized" and "officialized" by the state[2] — that is, penetrated by the state and subordinated to its will. In its attempts to establish a new national identity, new bonds of social cohesion, and a homogeneous socialization process, the state has increasingly diminished, and in some cases destroyed altogether, the financial and administrative autonomy of religious institutions. This subordination to governmental policies explains the critical and hostile posture taken by dissident Islamic groups toward official Islam.[3]

Four methods of subordination can be identified:

1. The elimination of independent sources of finance through the takeover of *awqaf* or *hubus* (endowments for religious

135

purposes). In the absence of their traditional sources of financial support, religious institutions become dependent on budgets and resources allocated by the state.

2. Control through administrative reorganization and structural change. For instance, two important religious educational institutions, al-Azhar University in Egypt and al-Zaytuna University in Tunisia, were reorganized to allow more governmental say in their affairs.[4] In Morocco, the role of the Higher Council of *'ulama* was weakened. In many cases, prominent religious positions are filled through royal or presidential decrees.

3. Integration and absorption of religious schools (*kuttab* and *madrasa*) into national governmental systems of education. Governments further established alternative institutions to compete with the religious ones. In Egypt, the government established the college of Dar al-'Ulum in 1873 "to train the *'ulama* in a more practical modern way by teaching some modern sciences in addition to the sciences taught at al-Azhar."[5] In Algeria, the government controls the schools that train the preachers in mosques (*imams*) and in 1977 most of the Qur'anic schools were integrated into the national education system.

4. Abolition of the *shari'a* (Islamic law) courts and the integration of their jurisdiction into a unified court system.[6]

Legitimation

In almost every Muslim country, the constitution declares Islam to be "the official religion of the state." In some countries, the *shari'a* is referred to as a source, or the source, of legislation in society (see the Syrian constitution of 1964 and the Egyptian constitution of 1971). The preamble of the Tunisian constitution states that the purpose of the state is to "adhere to the teachings of Islam." The Iraqi constitution of 1964 states that the republic derives its democratic and socialist principles from "the Arab heritage and the Islamic spirit" (Article 1).[7] Furthermore, official documents and public speeches are usually prefaced by the Islamic salutation "in the name of God, the Compassionate, the Merciful."

In practice, however, most of these governments pay only lip-service to the teachings of Islam. They emphasize their own Islamic credentials in order to ward off attack rather than using Islam as a source of policies or a guide for action. Governments are in the habit of giving an Islamic character and justification to their ideas and policies, even when the former are of foreign origin or the latter dictated by pragmatic considerations.

Muslim political regimes resort to Islamic legitimation to make their policies acceptable to the masses. This is the more so when they are on the defensive or lacking in legitimacy. For instance, in the early 1960s Egypt's Gamal Abdel Nasser increasingly invoked Islamic symbolism as he faced growing problems in the Arab world. Confronted with Saudi Arabian, Jordanian, and Yemeni criticism of his policies as being communist and atheist, he argued that socialism was the essence of Islam.[8] Scores of books were published to demonstrate that Islam is the true religion of socialism and that the Prophet Muhammad was a socialist. A book entitled *The Socialism of Islam* written by Mustafa al-Siba'i, a Syrian Muslim Brother, was required reading in high schools.[9]

Examination of Islamic journals published in Egypt during the early 1960s reveals their role as apologists for the regime's policy. In 1961–62, for instance, *al-Azhar* magazine published a number of essays on Islam and socialism. One issue reported on a meeting headed by Shaykh al-Azhar to discuss the National Charter. A statement issued at the meeting concluded that "the National Charter is in conformity with the principles of Islam"[10] and thanked the president for issuing it. Other publications such as the *Islamic Forum, Islamic Youth*, and *Islamic Affairs* took the same line.

Sadat also employed Islam as a legitimizing device, but in a much more direct and frequent way. His speeches were full of religious words, symbols, statements, and quotations from the Qur'an.[11] According to him, society is based on two pillars: *al-'ilm wa-al-iman*, science and faith.[12] Meanwhile, Sadat encouraged Islamic groups in the universities as a counterweight to Nasserite and Marxist ones. He released from prison members of the Muslim Brothers and gave them de facto recognition by allowing their monthly, *Al-Da'wa*, to resume publication.[13]

A striking example of the legitimating role of Islam is provided by the position of official *'ulama* in different Arab countries on the Camp David treaties and peace with Israel. In Syria and Iraq, the treaties were condemned as a betrayal of true Islamic principles, while in Egypt the precedent of al-Hudaybiyya (when the Prophet made a settlement with the Jews of Medina) was invoked and the treaties were justified in the light of the Qur'an and the Sunna. A declaration (*bayan*) published on May 10, 1979 in the name of all the organs of al-Azhar University (which include the Council of Islamic Research, the Higher Council of al-Azhar, the *Fatwa* Committee, the Azharite Institutes, and the general Department of *Al-Da'wa* and Guidance) stated that affairs of war and peace are the responsibility of the ruler (*wali al-amr*), that the Qur'an ordered us to make *sulh* (to end a dispute or conflict) with the enemy if the imam considered this to be in accord with Muslim interests, and that the Egyptian-Israeli treaty is within Islamic bounds.[14] Less than a month later the Mufti issued another *bayan* emphasizing the same points and arguing that other Arab rulers should have supported the treaties.[15] (It should be noted that some fifteen years previously, al-Azhar had issued a *fatwa* stating that any *sulh* that recognizes the state of Israel is not Islamically permissible, and condemning cooperation with states that support Israel as not permissible.)

Bargaining

Another main component of the relation between states and official Islamic institutions is that consisting of alliance, appeasement, and accommodation. As we have seen, religious institutions perform an important role in the political legitimation of most Arab regimes. So that they can fulfill that role, these religious institutions are rewarded, deferred to in certain spheres (particularly civil status issues), and accorded prestigious public positions.

The position and behavior of official *'ulama* differ from one country to another. In some cases, religious officials seek to make a deal with the government whereby they provide political support in exchange for being allowed to keep their jurisdiction in civil affairs and religious education (Nasser's Egypt).[16] On other occasions, religious officials have criticized regime policies and have become involved in confrontations (Syria and Somalia in the early 1970s).[17] In still other instances, they may use their relationship with the regime to advocate implementation of the *shari'a*, thus giving more impetus to Islamic groups (Sadat's Egypt in the mid-1970s).[18] Sometimes the regime is based on a historical alliance between men of politics and men of religion (e.g., Saudi Arabia),[19] or the regime may derive its legitimacy from certain religious roots (Morocco,[20] and to a lesser degree Jordan[21]). In all cases, official Islam is not a monolithic actor, nor does it deal with one adversary at a time. It has to engage in debates and/or fights with a number of other actors, e.g., the government, secular and Western-oriented groups, and other religious, dissident, or revolutionary groups.

The role of official Islam is constrained by the nature of its political environment. It makes a great difference whether the state considers itself an embodiment of reform Islam (Algeria[22]), the custodian of puritan orthodox principles (Saudi Arabia), anti-religious or at least not sympathetic to religion (South Yemen), or ready to resort to Islam in a pragmatic, instrumental way.

Consider, for example, the role of Egypt's al-Azhar University. It would be incorrect to argue either that al-Azhar has always been a bastion for popular agitation against oppression and injustice or that it has always been at the service of the country's rulers. Its role has differed from one period to another, and its *'ulama* have passed different judgments on the same issue. At one point during Napoleon's expedition to Egypt, the Egyptian historian 'Abd al-Rahman al-Jabarti states, al-Azhar was the core of resistance and anti-French sentiment. The French became so exasperated that they bombarded the University for a whole day, after which French cavalrymen invaded it, destroyed most of its furniture, and threw copies of the Qur'an on the ground. During the same period, Shaykh al-Sharqawi, a prominent *'alim*, refused to wear the symbol of the French Revolution that was awarded to him by Napoleon. At a later stage, however, the French were able to divide the *'ulama*, play them off against each other, and through the use of carrot-and-stick tactics make them issue a *fatwa* requesting the Egyptians to calm down and accept their authority.[23]

Detailed historical accounts exist of clashes between prominent members of the *'ulama* and the rulers of Egypt. Muhammad 'Ali clashed with a number of prominent religious personalities, including 'Umar Makram (who was exiled to Damietta), Shaykh Ahmad al-Tahtawi, and Shaykh al-Azhar al-Sharqawi (who was put under house arrest). Similar clashes took place between Khedive Ismail and Shaykh Muhammad 'Abduh, and between King Faruq and Shaykh 'Abd al-Majid Salim.[24] When the government announced plans for a new law of civil affairs in 1980, a number of prominent official *'ulama* objected to it in public. Thus, it was al-Azhar which produced those who challenged the government as well as those who supported its policies.

To conclude, official Islam plays different roles in different milieus. The role varies depending on the ideological orientation of

140   *Ali E. Hillal Dessouki*

the ruling regime, the sectarian or communal makeup of the society, the nature of social and ethnic cleavages, and the social origin and dominant orientation of the *'ulama*. In sum, the role of official Islam in a given country depends on the societal context of politics and the balance of political and social forces. A crucial factor here is the congruence, or lack of it, between the *'ulama* and the ruling regime's policies in terms of material interests and religious priorities. As long as Muslim societies have not achieved a broad-based and widely accepted consensus, the relation between state and faith will remain flexible and open to major alterations.

Notes

1. Ali E. Hillal Dessouki, "The Islamic Resurgence: Sources, Dynamics and Implications," in Ali E. Hillal Dessouki, ed., *Islamic Resurgence in the Arab World* (New York: Praeger, 1982), pp. 4–9.
2. For a general treatment, see E.I.J. Rosenthal, *Islam in the Modern National State* (London: Cambridge University Press, 1965).
3. Saad Eddin Ibrahim, "Anatomy of Egypt's Militant Groups," *International Journal of Middle Eastern Studies*, XII (1981): 432–53.
4. The case of al-Azhar is telling. Under the British occupation, a law was issued in 1911 according to which al-Azhar was to be administered by a council whose majority were non-Azharite civil servants. In 1961, another law reorganizing al-Azhar abolished the Higher Council for the *'ulama*. For details, see Assem al-Dessouki, *Dawr 'ulama al-Azhar fi al-mujtama' al-misri* (The Role of al-Azhar *'ulama* in Egyptian Society) (Cairo: Dar al-Thaqafa al-Jadida, n.d.).
5. Charles C. Adams, *Islam and Modernism in Egypt* (London: Oxford University Press, 1933), p. 45.
6. On this process, see N. Coulson, *A History of Islamic Law* (Edinburgh: Edinburgh University Press, 1964).
7. In revolutionary Iraq, the birthday of Husayn (grandson of the Prophet) was declared a national holiday and the government actively participated in organizing religious ceremonies.
8. Nasser's May 1962 ideological document, the National Charter, states that, "all religions contain a message of progress . . . in their essence, all divine revelations constituted human revolutions which aimed at man's dignity and his happiness" (Chapter 7). See also his speech of April 23, 1964, where he addressed in more details the link between Islam and socialism.
9. On Islam and socialism, see Sami Hanna and George H. Gardner, *Arab Socialism* (Leiden: E.J. Brill, 1969), pp. 64–79, 149–71; and Hamid Enayat, *Modern Islamic Political Thought* (Austin, TX: University of Texas Press, 1982), pp. 111–59.
10. *Al-Azhar*, XXXIV (July 1962): 132–36. See also *Al-Ahram*, June 14, 1962.
11. On October 7, 1970, for example, President-designate Sadat made a speech to the People's Assembly that concluded as follows: "Our Lord, do not punish us if we forget or err. Our Lord, do not lay on us a burden as Thou didst lay on those before us. Our Lord, do not impose upon us that which we have not the strength to bear, and forgive us, and pardon us, and have mercy on us. Thou art our protector. So help us against the nonbelievers." *Al-Ahram*, October 8, 1970.
12. Raphael Israeli, *The Public Diary of President Sadat: The Road to War*

(Leiden: E.J. Brill, 1978), pp. 15, 251; and Raphael Israeli, "The Role of Islam in President Sadat's Thought," *The Jerusalem Journal of International Relations*, IV (1980): 1–12.

13. For more details on how Sadat used Islam and Islamic groups as a legitimizing device, see Ali E. Hillal Dessouki, "The Resurgence of Islamic Organizations in Egypt: An Interpretation," in Alexander S. Cudsi and Ali E. Hillal Dessouki, eds., *Islam and Power* (London: Croom Helm, 1981), pp. 107–18; and Ali E. Hillal Dessouki, "The Limits of Instrumentalism: Islam in Egypt's Foreign Policy," in Adeed Dawisha, ed., *Islam in Foreign Policy* (London: Cambridge University Press, 1983), pp. 89–95. It is a real irony that Sadat was assassinated by a force whose return to the foreground of Egyptian politics he actively fostered.

14. *Al-Ahram*, May 10, 1979.

15. *Al-Ahram*, June 14, 1979. Pope Shenuda III, patriarch of the Coptic Orthodox Church, sent a telegram in the name of all the Christian communities in Egypt supporting President Anwar al-Sadat's efforts for peace. *Al-Ahram*, January 31, 1978.

16. On the Egyptian situation, see Louis J. Cantori, "Religion and Politics in Egypt," in Michael Curtis, ed., *Religion and Politics in the Middle East* (Boulder, CO: Westview Press, 1981), pp. 77–89; and Gabriel R. Warburg, "Islam and Politics in Egypt, 1952–1980," *Middle Eastern Studies*, XVIII (1982): 131–57.

17. See Raymond A. Hinnebusch, "The Islamic Movement in Syria: Sectarian Conflict and Urban Rebellion in an Authoritarian Populist Regime," in Dessouki, ed., *Islamic Resurgence*, pp. 157–65.

18. The role of 'Abd al-Halim Mahmud Shaykh al-Azhar is a case in point. For example, see his anti-communist articles in the daily newspaper *Al-Akhbar*, February 1, August 20, 24, 27, 1975. See also Fouad Ajami, "In the Pharaoh's Shadows: Religion and Authority in Egypt," in James P. Piscatori, ed., *Islam in the Political Process* (London: Oxford University Press, 1983), pp. 14–19.

19. The foundation of the Saudi state rests on a historical alliance between the pen and the sword, the house of Muhammad Ibn 'Abd al-Wahhab (*al-shaykh*) and the house of Saud. The first provides the raison d'être and the moral justification of the regime and the latter the military power, financial resources, and political leadership. See James P. Piscatori, "The Roles of Islam in Saudi Arabia's Political Development," in John L. Esposito, ed., *Islam and Development* (Syracuse, NY: Syracuse University Press, 1980), pp. 123–39; and James P. Piscatori, "The Formation of the Saudi Identity: A Case Study of the Use of Transnationalism," in John F. Stack, Jr., ed., *Ethnic Identities in a Transnational World* (Westport, CT: Greenwood Press, 1981), pp. 105–140. See also Edward Mortimer, *Faith and Power* (New York: Vintage Books, 1982), pp. 139–85.

20. Article 14 of the 1962 constitution states: "the King, commander of the faithful [*amir al-mu'minin*], symbol of the unity of the nation, guarantor of the permanence and the continuity of the state, watches over the observance of Islam and the constitution." Thus, projecting an image of monarch-saint, the Moroccan king combines the traditional authority of commander of the faithful and the modern one of a strong Third World political leader.

21. The full name of the state — the Hashemite Kingdom of Jordan — is illustrative of this.

22. The Algerian government has been strongly influenced by the ideas of the 'ulama association and 'Abd al-Hamid ibn Badis. This is reflected in all major political documents, including the Tripoli programs of 1962 and 1963 and the National Charter of 1976. See Jean Claude Vatin, "Religious Resistance and State Power in Algeria," in Cudsi and Dessouki, eds., *Islam and Power*, pp. 119–57.

23. Details in Assem al-Dessouki, *Dawr 'ulama al-Azhar*.

24. Ibid.

10 ISLAM AND POLITICS IN MODERN TURKEY: THE CASE OF THE NATIONAL SALVATION PARTY

Ergun Özbudun

Islam and Secularism in Turkey

Among all Islamic Middle Eastern countries, Turkey remains the only one whose legal and constitutional systems have been completely secularized. In contrast to even most secular Arab states such as Syria, Iraq, Egypt, and Tunisia, the Turkish constitutions of the last half century (those of 1924 as amended in 1928 and 1937; 1961; and 1982) declared secularism to be one of the fundamental organizational principles of the state, did not recognize Islamic law as a source of legislation, did not require the chief of state to be a Muslim, and specifically forbade any discrimination on the basis of religion.[1] Furthermore, Turkey is the only Islamic country where the entire legal system (including such areas as personal status, family, and inheritance law), which in other Islamic societies has proven highly resistant to secularizing trends, has been completely secularized. Perhaps the most telling manifestation of radical Kemalist secularism is that the constitution (and other laws) prohibits, under penal sanctions, the use of religion for political purposes, and political and associational activity with the aim of establishing a political, economic, social, or legal order based even partially on religious principles. Finally, religious functions are performed not by autonomous community organizations but by a special governmental agency, the Directorate of Religious Affairs, linked to the office of the prime minister. The last feature has led many critics of Kemalist secularism to describe the Turkish case not as a genuine example of secularism in the sense of a strict separation between religion and the state, but instead as a case of state control over religion.[2] Those critics further argue that even religious freedoms, guaranteed as they are by the constitution, are incomplete since Sufi orders remain outlawed and religious education by private bodies is subject to state control and supervision.

Against this background of radical secularism, manifestations of religiosity in Turkey, and in particular its political implications, always arouse a keen interest among Turkish and foreign observers. Thus, the relaxation or modification of certain restrictions on religious activities during the transition to competitive party politics in the late 1940s and the period of Democratic Party rule between 1950 and 1960 led to a series of articles on the "revival of Islam" in Turkey.[3] Among these changes one may cite the introduction of religious courses in the curriculum of primary schools (on a voluntary basis), the opening of Prayer Leader and Preacher Schools (*Imam-Hatip Okullari*) and of the Faculty of Theology at Ankara University, the reopening of sacred tombs (*türbe*) to visits, making foreign exchange available for the pilgrimage to Mecca, and permitting the recital of *ezan* (the call to prayer) in Arabic. In the following decades, the number of private Qur'an schools, as well as of the official *Imam-Hatip* schools, increased substantially. Another significant change was the rapid rise in the number of private religious associations, most of which were formed with the aims of constructing mosques, starting Qur'an courses, or providing aid to religious functionaries. Such associations constituted almost one-third of all Turkish associations in the 1960s.[4]

How can these changes be reconciled with the Kemalist secularist background? Should one simply conclude that Kemalism failed in its basic aim of creating a modern, secular, positivist, rationalist society? Should one go even further and describe it as an artificial effort from above to impose an alien and enforced secularization upon an Islamic society, an effort that was bound to fail because it isolated itself from the cultural heritage of the people and therefore failed to mobilize its energy?[5] Are some of the problems faced by present-day Turkey the outcome of an identity crisis which, in turn, was the result of the Kemalist attempt to replace the traditional religious identity with a secularist-nationalist identity? If these questions are pertinent, should one expect a militant Islamic revival in Turkey, perhaps even a popular explosion similar to the Iranian Revolution?

In fact, these questions are often asked, sometimes reflecting wishful thinking, sometimes originating from an insufficient knowledge of Turkish society. Clearly, such changes and relaxations as those mentioned above affected neither the secular character of the Turkish state nor the essentially secular nature of political discourse in Turkey. By the same token, it would be a mistake to describe them as signs of a religious revival, for the simple reason that religion has always been alive in Turkish society.

The only change was in the official attitudes on secularism, and that has to be seen as the inevitable outcome of the transition to competitive politics.[6] A sociologically much more significant change, however, was the steady secularization (in the sense of privatization) of Islam itself in Turkey. This trend had its origins in the de facto separation of worldly and religious spheres in the Ottoman Empire. In the words of Binnaz Toprak,

> . . . in practice . . . the boundaries between the functions of the religious hierarchy and the state were clearly drawn. The *'ulama* were concerned with the integration of society — or rather, with the integration of the Muslim population — into a unified community of believers. Hence, the functions of the *'ulama* covered those areas of social life that could be manipulated for effective socialization: the family, educational institutions, and the law. The state, on the other hand, took responsibility in administrative, military, and economic fields. The distribution of functions allowed little confusion as to the respective powers of the state and the religious institution . . . In any case, there was no question of a complete merging of religion and the state as the term *din-u-devlet* may imply.[7]

In this light, the Tanzimat (as the Ottoman reform period of 1839–76 came to be called) reforms can be seen as an enlargement of the secular sphere, as more and more areas of social life came to be regulated by secular legislation. The Young Turk movement significantly contributed to this trend as, in the dominant thought of Ziya Gökalp, the proper sphere of religion (or the sacred) was limited to matters of faith and religious rituals, and the two most important religious institutions, the pious foundations (*evkaf*) and the *shari'a* courts, were brought under the jurisdiction of secular authorities.[8] The much-emphasized revolutionary aspect of Kemalism consisted of its sudden and total elimination of all vestiges of Islamic influences and symbols from the governmental sphere. Its less revolutionary, albeit no less significant, contribution to the development of secularism in Turkey rested in its continuation and intensification of the already existing trend toward the secularization, or privatization, of Islam. In this sense, high levels of religiosity and religious observance in Turkey are no longer incompatible with the secular state, nor do they threaten it. It appears that a great majority of believing and practicing Turkish Muslims today keep the two spheres separate and do not make their political choices on the basis of their religious beliefs and values. If this observation is correct, then the ultimate aim of Kemalism seems to have been accomplished.

This paper intends to look at one particular aspect of the broader problem outlined above, namely the National Salvation Party (NSP). Obviously, the political influence of the religious factor in Turkey cannot be reduced to this party alone. Since the NSP has been the most important manifestation of "political Islam" in modern Turkey, however, an analysis of its ideology, appeal, leadership, social bases, and governmental performance will hopefully shed light on the overall influence of Islam in contemporary Turkish politics.

The Emergence of the NSP

The NSP is a direct heir of the short-lived National Order Party (NOP), itself established in January 1970 under the leadership of Professor Necmettim Erbakan. The NOP was banned by the Constitutional Court on May 20, 1971, following the military intervention of March 12, 1971, on the grounds that it sought to restore a theocratic order in Turkey. The NSP was founded on October 11, 1972; many of its founders had previously been involved in the NOP. At first, Erbakan prudently refrained from taking a formal position in the new party, which was led by Süleyman Arif Emre. Erbakan assumed the leadership of the NSP only after the October 14, 1973 elections assured transition to full civilian rule.[9] The NSP participated in two general National Assembly elections. In 1973, it gained 11.8 percent of the total valid votes cast and forty-eight Assembly sets out of 450. In 1977, it received only 8.6 percent of the vote and twenty-four Assembly seats. In both elections, the NSP emerged as the third largest party, in terms of the size of its parliamentary delegation, although it was far behind the two major parties, the Justice Party (JP) and the Republican People's Party (RPP).

The NSP was suppressed once again, together with all other political parties, following the military takeover of September 12, 1980, by a decree of the ruling National Security Council. Erbakan and other party leaders were tried at a military court for having conspired against the secular nature of the state and received prison sentences ranging from two to four years. Between 1973 and 1980, however, the NSP played an important role in Turkish politics, one probably out of proportion to its numerical strength. The peculiar parliamentary arithmetic of the decade made the NSP a key party in all governmental coalitions. Thus, the NSP remained in power during most of the period under discussion and joined coalitions headed by Bülent Evecit's RPP or Süleyman Demirel's JP.

Ideology

The NSP's ideology is an interesting mixture of religious and nonreligious themes. On the religious side, the NSP, operating under legal rules explicitly forbidding the use of religion for political purposes, prudently refrained from a frontal attack on secularism or an explicitly Islamic appeal. But throughout its program, election platforms, and leadership statements, the NSP consistently stressed a "national outlook" and "national and moral values," which were commonly and correctly understood as Islamic. The NSP maintained that material progress was impossible without "moral progress." Moral progress, in turn, could be attained only by thoroughly respecting freedom of conscience and by instilling a moral and virtuous outlook.[10]

The NSP sharply criticized both the JP and the RPP on ideological grounds even when it was part of a coalition government including one of these parties. In the NSP view, both major parties represented alien and materialistic ideologies derived from a blind imitation of the West. Thus, the JP's liberal conservatism was branded as a "colorless" ideology, an imitation of Western capitalism, while the RPP's social democracy was characterized as an equally alien and materialistic imitation of Western socialism. The salvation was said to be in the national outlook, which the NSP claimed was the only one based on Turkish national values and national heritage.

The NSP's own ideology seems to have aimed at a synthesis of Islam and Turkish nationalism. Frequent references were made to the glorious history and heritage of the Turks. In particular, the glories of the Ottoman Empire were emphasized. The Turks had lost their power and influence because they had alienated themselves from their own cultural heritage and had fallen under the influence of foreign (i.e., Western) cultures.[11] Consequently, the NSP leaders criticized Demirel's slogan of "Great Turkey" and suggested that it should be rephrased as "Great Turkey Once Again," or "Recreating Great Turkey."

The religious aspect of the NSP ideology can be seen in the party's opposition to pornography, alcohol, gambling, and birth control, and in its advocacy of more modest dress for women. Perhaps more important, the party advocated a much larger role for religion in education. It saw the lack of religious instruction as the main cause of violence and lawlessness among the youth, and maintained that the present "materialistic" education could be expected to breed such anarchists. Therefore, education should combine proper instruction in religion and morals with the teaching of the positive sciences. The NSP was also in favor of the removal of legal restrictions on religious propaganda, particularly Article 163 of the Penal Code which made such propaganda a punishable offense. On this last point, the NSP's stand found some support among leftists who saw a parallel between Article 163 and Article 142 of the same code which similarly penalized communist propaganda.

Finally, the influence of Islamic values upon the NSP program was reflected in the party's advocacy of the abolition of lending money at interest. Interest was seen as a means of exploitation. This stand was often justified on secular grounds by the assertion that high interest rates led to high production costs and high prices which, in turn, exploited and caused misery for the consumer. Even though few people doubted that the party's position against interest derived from religious considerations, the fact that it was supported by secular arguments was significant in itself. It indicated the extent to which political discourse had been secularized in Turkey.

In the field of foreign policy, the NSP's Islamic outlook led the party to a strong advocacy of closer relations with other Muslim countries — in the words of its 1977 election platform, "with nations with which we have geographical, cultural, and historical affinity." The party hoped for the eventual creation of a Muslim United Nations, a Muslim Economic Community with an Islamic Dinar as a common unit of currency, and a Muslim version of the North Atlantic Treaty Organization.[12] Understandably, the NSP was vigorously against Turkey's association with the European Community (EC), which it saw as an organization of Christian states. Again, this opposition was justified partly on religious and partly on secular grounds. On the one hand, it was maintained that Turkish national, moral, cultural, and ethical values would degenerate as a result of such close contact with the Europeans. On the other hand, it was argued that association with the EC would crush Turkey's nascent industry and, after the political integration phase, would reduce Turkey to a mere province of Europe.[13]

Many other items in the NSP program and platforms, however, had no clear or explicit Islamic origin. Particularly important among these was the party's strong emphasis on rapid industrialization. The NSP criticized the industrialization policies of the DP (Democratic Party, predecessor of the JP) and JP governments as having been oriented toward light consumer goods industries ("coca-cola" or "gaseuse" industries, as the NSP leaders liked to call them). Indeed, the NSP stressed heavy industrialization "almost with a religious zeal."[14] Rapid development of heavy industry was seen as the surest way for Turkey to regain its historical power and influence in the world. The NSP also favored a more balanced distribution of industrial plants throughout the country and criticized their heavy concentration in western Turkey under the DP-JP governments. Erbakan's motto of "a factory for each province" may have seemed like a demagogic promise to his opponents, but it indicated the NSP's commitment to reducing regional imbalances in industrialization.

Another major point in the NSP program was a concern for social justice. The party favored a more equitable distribution of income both in regional and social group terms. It criticized the social democratic doctrine of the RPP for sacrificing the interests of the individual in the name of the society and for being unable to achieve economic growth. At the same time, it attacked the liberal-capitalist doctrine of the JP for having led to the exploitation of the masses by a small group. The NSP claimed that its own approach would combine rapid economic development with a just distribution of income, but it was not too specific about how it would achieve this goal. The party's 1977 election platform included such planks as exemption of minimum wages for taxation, workers' participation in the management of the enterprises and a share of the profits, and introduction of unemployment insurance. On the other hand, it is clear that the NSP was not an anti-business party. It did not support land reform and nationalization of private enterprise. Most of the policies advocated by the NSP favored small businessmen, merchants, and artisans; these groups appeared to have formed the backbone of its support.

Although the constitutional-legal restrictions under which the

NSP operated make it difficult to locate the party's ideology among various contemporary Islamic political movements, one is tempted to conclude that it represented the tradition of "Islamic modernism" rather than either pure and simple traditionalism or militant revolutionary radicalism. While it was against Western cultural influence in matters of morals, ethics, and social customs, the NSP had a positive attitude toward modern science and technology. According to Erbakan, the West had heavily borrowed the scientific knowledge accumulated by Muslims and had "erroneously claimed to have been the originators of many scientific principles which Muslims had previously developed."[15] The NSP's insistence on the need to develop Turkish heavy industry, even if it sometimes reached unrealistic proportions, indicated an awareness of the requirements of a modern society.

Party Leadership

Three different analyses (by Jacob M. Landau, Frank Tachau, and Binnaz Toprak) of the social background of the NSP parliamentary contingent elected in 1973 give somewhat conflicting pictures (see Table 10.1).

These differences appear to have been caused by different methods of classification. For example, Tachau[16] classifies religious educators (that is, teachers in religious schools or teachers of religious subjects in general schools) in the religious category, while the other two authors include them among officials. Again, Tachau lists engineers and medical and health practitioners as professionals, even if they are government employees, as many of them are. Taking Tachau's figures as a basis for comparison with other parties, one finds that the main difference between the NSP parliamentary group and those of the other parties was the higher proportion of religious functionaries and religious educators in the

Table 10.1: Occupations of the NSP Parliamentarians, 1973 (in percentages)

	Landau	Tachau	Toprak
All Professionals	27.1	44.9	55.8
All Officials	47.9	12.2	20.7
Business-Commercial	10.4	18.3	10.4
Religion	12.6	24.4	12.5

NSP, which is what one would expect. The business and commerce contingent (18.3 percent) was slightly lower than in the JP (20 percent) but higher than in the RPP (11.8 percent) and the Democratic Party (14.3 percent). The NSP parliamentary group included a smaller percentage of government officials (12.2 percent) than did the parliamentary groups of either of the two major parties. According to Landau's[17] much broader definition, however, government officials comprised almost half of the entire NSP parliamentary delegation. Professionals (lawyers, doctors, engineers, etc.), no matter which definition is adopted, constituted a large proportion of the NSP parliamentarians, and in this respect there were no significant differences between the NSP and the other parties. Almost two-thirds (65.2 percent) of the NSP parliamentarians were university graduates, slightly worse than the RPP (70.4 percent) and the Democratic Party (69.7 percent) but somewhat better than the JP (64 percent). The average age of the deputies was lowest in the NSP (42.1), compared to 47.7 for the JP, 46.7 for the Democratic Party, and 43.8 for the RPP. Finally, the NSP parliamentary group contained the lowest percentage of deputies born in the province they represented in the National Assembly: 63.3 percent, compared to 78 percent for the JP, 76.3 percent for the RPP, and 67.4 percent for the Democratic Party.[18] This last point does not lend support to the view that the NSP was led by people who had strong local connections and who represented local religious conservatism.

These social characteristics of parliamentarians, whatever their descriptive and analytical value may be with respect to the party as a whole, do not suggest that the NSP, at least at the leadership level, was based predominantly on the traditional strata of Turkish society, or on marginal economic groups (such as the men of the bazaar) adversely affected by modernization, or on those social groups driven out of the state apparatus, the "modernist center," under the secular republic. On the contrary, as Toprak[19] rightly concludes, they show "a group of people who are, on the whole, well-educated, professionally successful, presumably of middle or upper-middle class income, and relatively young." The relatively high proportion of professionals and government officials among the NSP parliamentarians indicates that

the elite culture is no longer as monolithic as it was for the past four and a half decades since the establishment of the Turkish

Republic. For the first time in the history of the Republic, there has emerged a counter-elite with a different cultural orientation than that of Kemalist Westernists. In other words, the elite-mass gap is being supplemented by an elite-elite gap.

Voters

Clearly, social background data on parliamentarians do not tell us anything about the characteristics of party voters or supporters, and in the absence of survey data, it is impossible to reach firm conclusions in this regard. Some tentative observations can be made, however, based on ecological analyses of the NSP vote.

Turkish election statistics allow us to differentiate directly between urban (defined here as all settlements with a population of more than 10,000, plus the two provincial capitals which did not satisfy the numerical criterion) and rural votes. The NSP obtained 10.8 percent of the urban and 12.4 percent of the rural vote in the 1973 National Assembly elections (its national percentage of votes was 11.8).[20] This does not support the view that the NSP did significantly better in the villages than in urban centers, although, since a majority of Turkish voters still live in rural areas, some two-thirds (67.2 percent) of the NSP vote came from such areas.[21] The relatively narrow gap between the percentages of rural and urban voters choosing the NSP suggests that religious conservatism in Turkey is not peculiar to rural areas. A second measure of the relationship between the type of settlement and the degree of support for the NSP is the correlation between the degree of provincial urbanization (the percentage of provincial population living in communities with more than 10,000 inhabitants) and the percentage of the NSP vote; this correlation was found to be only very weakly negative ($r = -0.158$).[22]

When we further differentiate among different sizes of urban communities, some interesting findings emerge. The NSP performed rather poorly, compared to its own national and urban average, in the three largest cities (population over 500,000), namely Istanbul, Ankara, and Izmir. The party's average percentage of votes in these three major metropolitan centers was 8.1. On the other hand, the NSP showed its best performance in the category immediately below (cities with a population between 100,000 and 500,000) with an impressive 17.2 percent of the total valid votes cast. One suspects, however, that what is involved here is a regional or developmental phenomenon, rather than the impact of community size. In other words, the NSP's particular strength in this category was due to its extremely high percentage of votes in certain cities, most of which were in the less developed north-eastern, southeastern, and east central regions. Thus, the NSP obtained 43.5 percent of the vote in the city of Urfa, 41.1 percent of the vote in Kahraman Maras, 38.2 percent in Sivas, 34.2 percent in Erzurum, 31.8 percent in Malatya, 26.6 percent in Elazig, and 19.5 percent in Diyarbakir. The NSP strength in smaller cities and towns was closer to its overall urban average, and no clear patterns emerged in these categories.[23]

What can one make of the NSP's urban voting profile? The party's good showing in the medium-large cities of the less developed (i.e., less industrialized) regions seems to lend support to the view that the NSP supporters in urban areas came predominantly from the more traditional sectors of the urban middle classes, namely small businessmen, merchants, and artisans. It stands to reason that these groups, being more traditional in their outlook and feeling insecure and threatened by industrialization, responded in greater numbers to the NSP appeal. On the other hand, the party was not nearly as successful in the cities of the more highly developed regions, which suggests that it was unable to make deep inroads into more modern urban groups, namely industrial workers, white-collar workers, and urban professionals.[24]

As for the relationship between the NSP vote and the indices of provincial socioeconomic development, such correlations were negative, but not strongly so. The strongest negative correlation obtained was with the rate of literacy (-0.342), thus indicating that the NSP received greater, but not predominant, support from less developed provinces in 1973.[25] One wonders, therefore, whether the greater NSP strength in the less developed eastern regions was due to developmental variables or to the greater strength of some Sufi orders (particularly the Nakşibendi and Nurcu) in these regions. In the complete absence of data on Sufi orders, there is no way to answer such questions with any degree of accuracy. The regional analysis of the NSP vote (Table 10.2)[26] suggests, however, that regional influences might be at work, perhaps to some degree independently of the impact of developmental variables.

The NSP's voting profile showed significant changes in the 1977 elections. Not only did the party lose about one quarter of its

Table 10.2: Regional NSP Vote Percentages, 1973

Marmara	8.9
Aegean	5.9
Mediterranean	9.7
North Central	13.1
South Central	15.8
Black Sea	11.7
East Central	20.9
Northeast	16.9
Southeast	13.9

percentage of the national vote, which went down from 11.8 to 8.6 percent, and exactly half of its National Assembly seats (down from 48 to 24), but it also became a more pronouncedly regional party. The NSP's losses were mainly in western and central Turkey and in the Black Sea region. Thus, it lost its single seats in Afyon, Amasya, Balikesir, Bolu, Bursa, Kayseri, Kocaeli, Manisa, Nevşehir, Rize, Sakarya, Samsun, Tokat, and Zonguldak; it also lost both of its seats in Çorum, two of its three seats in Sivas, and one of its two seats in Ankara; and it did not gain any new seats in these regions. In the eastern and southeastern regions, on the other hand, it generally held its own (with such exceptions as Agri, Bingöl, Elazig, Erzurum, Gaziantep,and Gümüşhane) or even gained a new seat (Bitlis, Mardin, Siirt, Van). As a result, more than half (13 out of 24) of the NSP deputies elected in 1977 were from the eastern provinces.[27]

These changes seem significant for a number of reasons. First of all, the NSP's partnership in all coalition governments in the 1973–77 period and its consequent control of important sources of patronage did not enable the party to increase its vote; on the contrary, its vote declined significantly. Secondly, as noted above, the NSP was reduced to a party of much more regional character, with its pockets of strength mainly in the least developed eastern regions. In other words, the NSP did not appear as a party which represented the future of Turkish politics. Third, a preliminary analysis of the 1977 election results suggests that the most likely beneficiary from the NSP losses in central and east central Turkey was the Nationalist Action Party (NAP) of Alparslan Türkes.[28] In these regions, where the cleavages between Sunnis and Alevis (Shi'a) were exacerbated by increasing political polarization and violence, the NAP appeared to have capitalized more successfully on the conservative Sunni reactions against the more leftist Alevis. Translated into socioeconomic terms, the same trend may mean that parts of the traditional middle class, which had supported the NSP in 1973, switched to the militantly nationalist, neo-fascist right in the face of what they perceived as a growing threat from the left. Indeed, this is consistent with the events in some European countries between the two world wars. Whatever the explanation, which has to remain only tentative and impressionistic, this trend indicates a significant degree of "softness" in the NSP's support except in the least developed eastern provinces.

Conclusion

The NSP, during its relatively brief life, constituted an entirely novel phenomenon in modern Turkish politics, and played an important role in coalition governments due to its position as a key party in coalition formation. In terms of parliamentary and governmental performance, the NSP can be compared with the National Religious Party in Israel, in the sense that the NSP could form coalitions with either the center-left or center-right parties in exchange for concessions on issues relating to religion. In terms of both its ideology and its leadership, the NSP appeared as a moderate Islamic party, prudently refraining from a direct attack on the secular state, but trying to increase the influence of Islam in Turkish society and politics. Its leadership correctly judged that the party's fortunes were closely tied to those of the democratic regime. Indeed, the two military interventions in 1971 and 1980 quickly led to the dissolution of the NSP and its predecessor, the NOP (National Order Party). Perhaps with this realization, the NSP strove to preserve the democratic consensus and the competitive party system in a period of increasing political polarization and violence. It is to the credit of the NSP that its members and supporters did not take part in the violent clashes and terrorist actions of the late 1970s. Also to its credit is the fact that the NSP leadership kept the channels of communication and dialogue open with the other parties when such dialogue between the two major parties was at a bare minimum.

The NSP leaders did not seem to realize, however, that their reluctance to endorse openly and explicitly the secular framework of the state would at least indirectly contribute to the undermining of the democratic consensus. In my opinion, the facts of Turkish politics are such that an Islamic party can play a role and be accepted as truly legitimate by some other important political force, notably the military, only to the extent that it is willing to operate within the parameters of the secular Kemalist republic. This would still leave a fairly broad area for such a party to promote the moral and ethical values of Islam without being seen as an actual or potential threat to the secular state.

Notes

1. For comparisons, see Jean-François Ryox and Gilles Blanchi, "Références à l'Islam dans le droit public positif en pays arabes," *Pouvoirs* No. 12 (1980): 57–70.

2. For example, see Ali Fuad Basgil, *Din ve Laiklik* (Istanbul: Yagmur Yayinevi, 1977).

3. Bernard Lewis, "Islamic Revival in Turkey," *International Affairs* XXVIII (1952): 38–48; Howard A. Reed, "Revival of Islam in Secular Turkey," *The Middle East Journal* VII (Summer 1954): 267–82; Howard A. Reed, "Turkey's New Imam-Hatip Schools," *Die Welt Des Islams* IV (1956): 150–63; Lewis V. Thomas, "Recent Developments in Turkish Islam," *The Middle East Journal* VI (Winter 1952): 22–40; Lewis V. Thomas, "Turkish Islam," *The Muslim World* XLIV (July-October 1954): 181–85.

4. Ahmet N. Yücekök, *Türkiye'de Örgütlenmis Dinin Sosyo-Ekonomik Tabani* (Ankara: S.B.F. Yayinlari, 1971).

5. See, for example, Hichem Djait, *L'Europe et L'Islam* (Paris: Editions du Seuil, 1978).

6. For the same view, see Thomas, "Recent Developments in Turkish Islam"; and Binnaz Toprak, *Islam and Political Development in Turkey* (Leiden: E.J. Brill, 1981), p. 88.

7. Toprak, *Islam and Political Development*, p. 31.

8. Ergun Özbudun, "Antecedents of Kemalist Secularism: Some Thoughts on the Young Turk Period," in Ahmet Evin, ed., *Modern Turkey: Continuity and Change* (Opladen: Leske, 1984), pp. 25–44.

9. Jacob M. Landau, "The National Salvation Party in Turkey," *Asian and African Studies* XI, No. 1 (1976): 1–57.

10. On the NSP ideology in general, see Landau, pp. 8–11; Toprak, pp. 98–104; and Dogu Ergil, "Electoral Issues: Turkey," in Jacob M. Landau, Ergun Özbudun, and Frank Tachau, eds., *Electoral Politics in the Middle East: Issues, Voters and Elites* (London and Stanford, CA: Croom Helm-Hoover Institution Press, 1980), pp. 11–38.

11. Toprak, *Islam and Political Development*, pp. 100–101.

12. Ibid., p. 104.

13. Ergil, p. 31.

14. Toprak, *Islam and Political Development*, p. 102.

15. Landau, "The National Salvation Party," p. 33; Toprak, *Islam and Political Development*, p. 100.

16. Frank Tachau, "Parliamentary Elites: Turkey," in Landau, Özbudun, and Tachau, eds., *Electoral Politics in the Middle East*, pp. 205–42.

17. Landau, "The National Salvation Party," p. 30.

18. Tachau, "Parliamentary Elites," pp. 230–35.

19. Toprak, *Islam and Political Development*, pp. 107–8.

20. Ergun Özbudun, "Voting Behaviour: Turkey," in Landau, Özbudun, and Tachau, eds., *Electoral Politics in the Middle East*, pp. 107–43.

21. Toprak, *Islam and Political Development*, pp. 110–12.

22. Özbudun, "Voting Behaviour: Turkey," pp. 126–27.

23. Ibid., pp. 116 and 119.

24. See also Landau, "The National Salvation Party," pp. 22–25; Tevfik Cavdar, "Seçim Sonuçlarinin Getirdigi Ön Bulgular," *Özgür Insan*, June 18, 1974, pp. 75–79.

25. Özbudun, "Voting Behaviour: Turkey," pp. 125–28.

26. Table 10.2 is based on Ergun Özbudun and Frank Tachau, "Social Change and Electoral Behavior in Turkey: Toward a 'Critical Realignment'?" *International Journal of Middle East Studies* VI (October 1975): 460–80. For a list of provinces included in each region, see Ergun Özbudun, *Social Change and Political Participation in Turkey* (Princeton, NJ: Princeton University Press, 1975), p. 98.

27. See also Toprak, pp. 111–21.

28. On the NAP, see Jacob M. Landau, "The Nationalist Action Party in Turkey," *Journal of Contemporary History* XVII (1982): 587–606.

11 HOW THE CLERGY GAINED POWER IN IRAN

Mansour Farhang

I

This essay will try to show that politics as an independent force played a significant role in Iran's post-revolutionary development. While acknowledging the structural and historical limitations of political action, the analysis is based on the assumption that real choices concerning issues of power/authority were made by competing actors in the crucial year following the fall of the Shah in February 1979. The time period is distinguished because it was clearly marked by the existence of nonviolent struggle for power among the ideologically diverse forces whose functional coalition produced the revolutionary success. By the spring of 1980 the fundamentalists were in firm control of the state and open political competition had come to a virtual halt.

The sudden collapse of the Pahlavi regime was a surprise not only to foreign specialists but also to native revolutionaries themselves. One could make a convincing case that Iran's rapid political disintegration in 1978 was primarily due to the lack of even a minimal capacity on the part of the ruling elite to contain or accommodate a peaceful popular challenge. Indeed, the Pahlavi state proved to be much weaker than universally expected, not only in its relations with the society at large but, more important, within itself.[1] The surrender of the Shah and his security apparatus was so rapid that most of the participants in the revolution were unprepared to utilize the fruits of their own victory. The arbitrary rule of one family could no longer be maintained in the face of new socioeconomic realities that, beside causing cross-class disaffection, entailed a massive increase in the urban poor population as well as the growth of a service sector whose members had no loyalty to the state or ruling family.

The spontaneous mass movement that forced the Shah into exile did not have a platform for post-monarchy Iran. Some isolated leaders and groups subscribed to certain theories about what had to be done, but there were no concrete political expressions of such abstract views in the public perception. In short, the revolutionary upheaval was a delegitimizing rather than a legitimizing movement. For a variety of sociohistorical reasons, the vast majority of Iranians had come to believe that the fall of the monarchy would *necessarily* produce an improvement in their lives. Thus the *kind* or the *degree* of this supposed gain was not a matter of serious concern.

Between the fall of Prime Minister Sharif Emami on November 6, 1978 and the succumbing of the military on February 11, 1979 there was no political authority in Iran. Ayatollah Ruhollah Khomeini represented the moral power of the revolution and the military was the only force capable of delaying the victory of the revolutionaries. Schools, universities, government bureaucracies, public agencies, shops, factories, and export facilities were all shut down. Khomeini had asked the oil workers to produce enough gasoline and kerosene for domestic consumption. Voluntary business transactions were limited to basic necessities. Under such circumstances, that is to say in the total absence of political order, there could be no serious attempt at a military coup against the revolutionary movement.

President Carter's envoy to Iran, General Robert Huyser, had an accurate understanding of the situation. His hope was to keep the military intact in the face of the revolution's seemingly inevitable success. If the revolutionaries took over the government while the armed forces remained under the control of the same commanders, then a coup d'état to reestablish a modified version of the Shah's regime could be a realistic possibility. This evaluation compelled General Huyser to urge the Iranian military leaders to come to terms with the revolutionary forces.[2] Khomeini played his hand with precision to reinforce Huyser's perception of the situation.

In the crucial days between the departure of the Shah on January 16 and the collapse of the military on February 11, Ayatollah Muhammad Beheshti was Khomeini's trusted negotiator with both the U.S. envoys and the Iranian military leaders. On behalf of Khomeini, Beheshti guaranteed the safe departure of U.S. personnel from the country and pledged to General Abbas Gharabaghi, the chairman of the joint chiefs of staff, to respect his freedom in exchange for his cooperation.[3] After the armed forces announced their neutrality, Khomeini encouraged raids on the military barracks and headquarters. The People's Mojahedin and the People's Fadayan took the initiative in raids on the army depots. That is why immediately after the collapse of the military Khomeini issued a plea to these guerrilla organizations to turn in their looted weapons to his representatives at collection points set up at mosques.

The summary trial and execution of the Shah's generals and the appointment of *mullahs* as military prosecutors were designed to bring about the disintegration of the armed forces. The military commanders had expressed their neutrality, but Khomeini sought not only to destroy their fighting capability but to humiliate them psychologically as well. Yet he rejected the proposal of the Mojahedin and Fadayan to form a People's Revolutionary Army, for he correctly maintained that the Shah's military could be transformed to serve the Islamic republic. The missing element in both General Huyser's hope of saving the military intact and the guerrilla groups' design of becoming part of a revolutionary army was Khomeini's alertness to their potential danger to the new regime.

II

At the time of the Shah's departure in January 1979, the political forces on the scene could be divided into four groupings: 1. the Islamic fundamentalists under clerical leadership; 2. the liberal-left forces, ranging from progressive religious elements to social democrats and democratic Marxists (in the immediate post-revolutionary period the principal groups representing these persuasions were the Iran Freedom Movement, the National Front, and the National Democratic Front); 3. the Marxist-Leninists, mainly the Tudeh Party and the People's Fadayan Organization; and 4. the People's Mojahedin Organization of Iran (PMOI), a devout and radical Islamic sociopolitical formation.

These political formations had little organized support at the time of the revolutionary takeover in February 1979. During the 1970s SAVAK, the government security agency, had been quite successful in neutralizing both the political activities of the liberal-left and the armed struggle of the Mojahedin and Fadayan guerrilla movements. Thus after the fall of the Shah each group had to develop a new strategy for organizing and building coalitions in pursuit of its own objectives. It was evident at the time that sociopolitical conflicts were brewing beneath the surface of the joyous public atmosphere. The period of making moral or theoretical claims was over; the time for concrete political competition and interest articulation had come.

Five of the six founders of the Islamic Republican Party (IRP), which came to represent the fundamentalists, were Muhammad Beheshti, 'Ali Akbar Hashemi Rafsanjani, Javad Bahounar, Abdol-Karim Musavi Ardebili, and 'Ali Khamenei.[4] These clerics had been closely associated with Ayatollah Khomeini since the early 1960s. The sixth, Hassan Ayat, a non-cleric, had been a follower of Ayatollah Abol-Qasem Kashani, who broke with Mossadeq in 1952 and supported the 1953 coup d'état against him. The IRP also contained many young men with modern education, including a significant number of Iranians who had graduated from U.S. universities. These individuals, who later came to function as the technocrats of the fundamentalist power structure, had been active members of the Muslim Students Association in the United States or in Western European countries in the 1970s.

The liberal-left forces, while differing on some socioeconomic issues, were all inspired by the legacy of Mossadeq. They were committed to the idea of a pluralistic political order but ignored the question of whether such an order was feasible or practical under the existing conditions. For twenty-five years prior to the revolution the liberal-left personalities had lived with the memory of Mossadeq and had never missed an opportunity to condemn his overthrow. But during all those years the liberal-left activists and thinkers, whether living at home or abroad, did not publish a single article dealing with the question of why the CIA-engineered coup succeeded so easily and cheaply. They made no effort to analyze the weaknesses and shortcomings of the Mossadeq experience.

Thus the liberal-left forces entered the competition for power in the post-revolutionary period without having learned any lessons from their previous defeats. For example, a principal reason for the quick defeat of the National Front in 1953 was a total lack of preparedness to confront the predictable onslaught of the pro-Shah opposition against the Mossadeq government. Yet in 1979 the liberal-left elite were incapable of building a coalition or popular organization. They remained loose associations of men who had come to prominence through their struggle against the Shah. They knew how to attempt to negate or delegitimize the holders of power, but they had no strategy to take power or to legitimize a new system of authority. The liberal-left tendencies probably had the widest base among the middle-class sector of the population, but the activation of this popular base rarely went beyond verbal and sentimental expressions. The vast majority of Iranians who identified with the liberal-left persuasions in the post-revolutionary period were unwilling to engage in a sustained collective undertaking. In short, they were the most fragmented and atomized elements on the political scene.[5]

At the time of the revolutionary takeover in February 1979 the People's Mojahedin Organization of Iran enjoyed considerable national popularity but its membership and organizational strength were at their lowest level. The sympathetic public recognition of the PMOI was largely the product of its highly publicized armed struggle against the Pahlavi regime, while its actual weakness was due to the effective work of SAVAK in suppressing the guerrilla movements of the 1970s. For example, the top leaders of the PMOI, including Masud Rajavi and Musa Khiabani, were in prison until the departure of the Shah in January 1979.[6] The PMOI gradually built a nationwide network of underground cells, including militia units, but in the first fateful year of the post-Shah power struggle the Mojahedin lacked the capacity to influence significantly the course of events. Even though Khomeini's initial popularity compelled the Mojahedin to be respectful of his authority at the beginning, Khomeini never trusted them because he perceived their radical interpretation of religious doctrines as a dangerous deviation from Islam.

Furthermore, the Mojahedin's radicalism prevented them from taking a conciliatory position toward the provisional government of Mehdi Bazargan, which was under attack by the fundamentalists, the Marxist-Leninists, and most of the liberal-left elements. In general, for about a year the positions of the Mojahedin on various sociopolitical issues were much closer to those of the Fadayan than to those of the liberal-left forces which seemed to be their logical allies at the time. For example, it took the Mojahedin nearly a month to separate themselves from the Marxist-Leninists in regard to the hostage-taking at the U.S. embassy in Tehran. It must be said, however, that they quickly realized how Khomeini and his lieutenants were using the hostage crisis to weaken or discredit the opponents of the emerging fundamentalist rule.

As was indicated earlier, most of the Marxist-Leninists were in one of two groups — the Soviet-controlled Tudeh Party and the independent People's Fadayan Organization. There were also a number of other Marxist-Leninist groups, including some Maoist and Trotskyite formations, but they were too small to have any influence on the power struggle among the revolutionary forces.

The actual social base of the Tudeh and the Fadayan was limited to a tiny segment of the middle class but, given their effective organizations and devoted full-time cadres, their impact on the political situation was quite significant.[7] This is particularly the case with respect to the Tudeh Party. With its experienced, disciplined, Soviet-trained leadership, the Tudeh Party had a very disproportionate impact on the timing, content, and outcome of the public debates among the revolutionary forces. From the very beginning, the Tudeh pursued a calculated strategy of supporting the most passionately anti-Western, especially anti-American, political elements. This strategy played into the hands of the fundamentalists because they believed the greatest threat facing them emanated from the liberal cultural values that had penetrated the lives of the professional-bureaucratic intelligentsia and the civil service sector whose members largely subscribed to liberal-left persuasions.

Thus, even though the anti-Americanism of the fundamentalists was regressive and reactionary, the Tudeh became their ally against the liberal-left forces. This functional alliance was not a coincidence, for in the post-revolutionary period, the Tudeh Party perceived the Mojahedin and the liberal-left elements as the principal obstacles to its long-term objectives. Marxist-Leninists could not conceive of the fundamentalist *mullahs* becoming the new rulers of Iran. Therefore, the Tudeh Party's support for the fundamentalists (the Islamic Republican Party) against all other contenders for power or influence was a tactic which, supplemented by the Tudeh infiltration of the newly established institutions of the Islamic republic, was supposed to pave the way for the eventual domination of the revolution by the Tudeh Party.

Unlike the Tudeh Party, the Fadayan had a sentimental image, particularly among middle-class youth, during the 1978–79 uprisings. Their armed struggle in the 1970s had earned them considerable political respect among the anti-Shah forces, but at the time of the revolutionary takeover they were organizationally weak and had little public support. The Fadayan regarded themselves as the only legitimate defender of the needs and aspirations of the lower classes, but their sociocultural outlook and the very language of their discourse prevented them from even communicating with their theoretical constituencies. In early 1979 the Fadayan assisted the Kurdish rebellion against the central government but after a brief period of frustration they chose to limit themselves to legally permitted political work.

By the end of 1979 there was a split in the leadership as well as the ranks of the Fadayan. The Tudeh Party was the beneficiary of the division, for the majority (*aksarriat*) faction joined the Tudeh in accommodating the fundamentalists. The minority (*aqalliat*) faction continued the original categorical opposition of their organization to the Islamic republic. Yet even the *aqalliat* followed the Tudeh line in regarding the liberal-left forces as the main threat to the "true" path of the revolution. Thus, even though the various Marxist-Leninist groups were constantly squabbling among themselves during the first year after the revolution, they were all in functional agreement that the liberal-left forces should be defeated in their competition with the fundamentalists. The Tudeh was the principal pursuer of this strategy and its tactics included classic totalitarian propaganda techniques. The early phase of the hostage episode at the U.S. embassy in Tehran provided the Tudeh with a fruitful opportunity to engage in character assassination and dissemination of false information against those (virtually all liberal-left personalities) who opposed the holding of the hostages. There is no question that the Tudeh leaders functioned as mentors to the fundamentalists in their campaign against the Mojahedin and the liberal-left forces.[8]

III

Disagreements between and sometimes within the above groupings were so basic that calls for compromise invariably fell on deaf ears. Disputed issues included the name of the republic, the structure of authority, the nature of the new economic order, the origin of political legitimacy, women's rights, the role of the state in the national economy, and the extent of autonomy for the national minorities, including the Kurds. In the midst of this multifaceted clash of ideas and viewpoints, Khomeini remained the ultimate source of power and legitimacy. In the beginning he pretended to be above politics and factional rivalries, but as time went on his close ties with the fundamentalists became clear.

The fundamentalists were determined to transform Iran, but they had no concrete ideas concerning the nature or forms of the institutions of the Islamic state. Even Khomeini, whose writings were more political and specific than those of any other theoretician of the revolution, merely assigned to the government the traditional duties of protecting Islam, defending the frontiers, administering justice, and collecting taxes. Yet history is not made out of plain cloth. In the post-revolutionary power struggle the following givens favored the fundamentalists: 1. the general public's newly romanticized view of Islam as an ideology (a reaction to the sociocultural crisis produced by two decades of uneven growth and relative deprivation); 2. Khomeini's uncontestable position of spiritual leadership; 3. the fundamentalist clergy's control over the passions and sensibilities of the mobilized urban poor; 4. the fragmentation and confusion of the liberal-left forces; 5. the sectarian behavior of the Marxist-Leninists, in addition to the more sinister role of the Tudeh Party; and 6. cross-class anti-Western sentiment, the result of the Shah's blind Westernization policies in the realm of sociocultural mores and values.[9]

The popular personalities of the liberal-left and the People's Mojahedin Organization (Ayatollah Mahmoud Taleghani, Karim Sanjabi, Mehdi Bazargan, Hedayatollah Matindaftari, Abolhassan Bani-Sadr, Masud Rajavi, Musa Khiabani, 'Ali-Asghar Haj Sayd Javadi, Shokrollah Paknejad, Kazem Sami, and many others) had the potential to form a broadly based coalition embracing large sectors of the population. Such a progressive coalition in the early days of the revolutionary victory could have become a formidable contender for power. The failure to pursue this option was primarily due to the failure of the potential coalition's constituent elements to see the need for political and ideological compromise in the interest of their common aspirations. For all practical purposes, they lacked the capacity to relate to each other as equals or to subject their abstract objectives to pragmatic considerations.

The participation of the Mojahedin in this coalition would have been indispensable because they had a unique and effective appeal to the frustrated urban youth. In 1979 more than two-thirds of Iranians were twenty-five or younger. Nearly ninety-five percent of those gunned down in the streets of Iran in 1978 were teenagers from urban slums. Yet the older statesmen of the National Front and the Freedom Movement seemed resentful of the Mojahedin's radicalism on economic issues and thus made no serious effort to work with them. Mehdi Bazargan's socioeconomic conservatism was a major reason for the cold relationship between the Mojahedin and the Freedom Movement.

The viability of the potential coalition was further sapped when, just as the National Front was trying to make a political comeback from the damage done by a quarter century of repression and dramatic changes in the country's demographic composition,[10] Shahpour Bakhtiar, a member of the Front's central committee, defied his colleagues and accepted the Shah's offer to become his last prime minister. Bakhtiar's gamble was doomed to fail from the outset but his naiveté helped the fundamentalists by badly damaging the anti-regime image of the National Front, particularly among the youth.[11]

IV

During the 1960s and 1970s the Shah forced opposition politics into the religious idiom by successfully suppressing secular democratic criticism of his regime. The religious-left writers such as Bazargan, Taleghani, Bani-Sadr, and 'Ali Shari'ati were far more effective than their fundamentalist counterparts in promoting rebellious consciousness among the literate sectors of the population. But once the revolutionary demonstrations of 1978 began to attract urban masses, the fundamentalist *mullahs* proved better equipped to sustain and control the momentum of the movement.

Since there was no national organization to manage the affairs of the revolution, the fundamentalists took the lead in forming hundreds of local committees across the nation which performed public tasks ranging from aiding striking workers to caring for the wounded. By September 1978, every neighborhood mosque had become a revolutionary headquarters as well as a place of worship and public speaking. As the fall of the regime neared, the fundamentalist *mullahs* came to dominate the network of mosque-centered committees throughout the country. The centralization of this network under the hegemonic leadership of Khomeini was a significant aspect of the fundamentalists' evolving capacity to establish a theocratic state.

Three weeks after the fall of the Shah, Khomeini returned to Qum, but instead of resuming his teaching, as he had said while in Paris he wished to do, he set out to consolidate his hold on the main instruments of rule in revolutionary Iran, namely the *Sepah-e Pasdarad* (Revolutionary Guards), the *Komitehs* (Revolutionary Committees) , the *Dadgahhaye Enghelab* (Revolutionary Courts), the *Bonyad-e Shahid* (Martyr Foundation), the *Sazman-e Jahad-e Sazandegi* (Organization of the Crusade for Construction), and the

Setad-e Namaz-e Jumeh (Friday-prayer Headquarters).[12] These institutions, taken together, came to constitute a centrally controlled system of national security, patronage, mass mobilization, and propaganda. Before the revolution, there were 1.2 million government employees in Iran. Today the total number of people on the public payroll exceeds 2 million, even though 300,000 have been fired or retired since February 1979.

From the very beginning, Khomeini reserved for himself the appointment of Friday-prayer imams, religious judges, and revolutionary prosecutors. (So far he has appointed about 200 Friday-prayer leaders for cities and towns across the country.) The Friday-imams, the religious judges, the revolutionary prosecutors, and the revolutionary guards became the real wielders of power in the provinces shortly after Khomeini's assumption of absolute rule. There soon developed rivalries among the various appointees of the "Imam" and it was Khomeini himself who had to settle the major disputes.

The Islamic Republican Party was able to become a national mass organization because it could rely on the network of Friday-imams to represent its interests and objectives throughout the nation. Even though the Friday-imams were supposedly nonpartisan, they were functional allies of the IRP from the very beginning. Soon after the foundation of the party, the IRP cadres began to form lumpen elements into gangs of club-wielders, later to be known as *hezbollahis* (the party of God people), to harass competing groups or activities. The IRP also recruited organizers and administrators to work with clerical leaders in the provinces. It is true that no other party had the same initial opportunities as the IRP, but it is also the case that no other party worked as vigorously and systematically. While the secular forces (except the Mojahedin and the Tudeh) were confused and fragmented, the IRP under the leadership of Beheshti was proceeding with a coherent strategy to gain power.

To understand the surprising character of the Islamic fundamentalist hegemony in revolutionary Iran, it is helpful to keep in mind that until 1978 no one even imagined that an ayatollah could become a national leader or that Iran could become a theocratic state. For fifty years following the 1906 Constitutional Revolution, the most influential politicians, intellectuals, writers, poets, popular historians, and journalists were secularists. It seemed completely natural in the post-World War II period that the nationalists and the leftists should lead the movement against the British domination of the country. Even though some religious elements under the leadership of the Ayatollahs Abol-Qasem Kashani and Muhammad Behbahani participated in the plot to overthrow the National Front government, the actual beneficiaries of the 1953 coup were right-wing secularists. The Shah and his first post-coup prime minister, General Fazlollah Zahedi, had no tolerance for religious interference in the affairs of the state. Even the leading religious thinkers and activists during the half century following the Constitutional Revolution did not express fundamentalist or theocratic views. They emphasized the need for purifying Islam of superstitious practices and gave primacy to socioeconomic issues over the celestial ones. Such highly respected Shi'i clerics as Sayed Hassan Modarress and Muhammad Khiabani stressed the compatibility of Islam with democratic government.[13]

The emergence of Shi'i Islam as the dominant ideology of opposition during the 1970s was in part a social reaction to the blind pursuit of Westernization by the Pahlavi regime. Many among the nonreligious intelligentsia viewed the new interest in Islam as a positive development in combating the Western cultural penetration of the society. As late as March 31, 1979, when a national referendum was held on changing the name of the country to the Islamic Republic of Iran, most elements of the liberal left voted for the change, even though they had serious reservations about the implications of the "Islamic" designation. The affirmative vote was in part rationalized on the basis of cultural and populistic considerations.

V

Khomeini had made his views clear in his 1970 treatise, *The Islamic Government*, where he asserted the right of the Shi'i clerics to establish a theocracy.[14] But such political doctrines were not perceived by the anti-Shah forces as a threat to the democratic aspirations of the revolution. Until the election of the *Majlis-a Khebregan* (Assembly of Experts) in the summer of 1979, hardly anyone took seriously the possibility of a formal theocratic state.

The chain of events that led to the formation of the Assembly of Experts began soon after the fall of the Shah, when a group of Iranian lawyers and political thinkers started work on a draft constitution for the new republic. The provisional government of

Mehdi Bazargan planned to hold a national election to form a 250-member constituent assembly. This elected body was to review and amend the draft constitution, which would then be voted on in a national referendum. When the document was submitted to Khomeini for his approval, however, he advised Bazargan to bypass the constituent assembly and instead submit the draft directly to a plebiscite. Khomeini was concerned about the delay in institutionalizing the authority of the revolutionary regime. He was afraid that an elected body of 250 members would so prolong and sensationalize the debate on the draft that the revolution itself could be endangered.

In the draft constitution, Shi'ism was acknowledged as the state religion but the government was structured according to the principle of the separation of executive, legislative, and judicial powers. The draft also recognized the inalienability of popular sovereignty and looked to political equality and majority rule as the general means of determining the preference of the people. The procedures of the draft were democratic and its principles and provisions were egalitarian in substance.

The divergence in the views of Bazargan and Khomeini concerning the method of finalizing the constitution was at last resolved by Ayatollah Taleghani's proposal to form a popularly elected seventy-five-member Assembly of Experts to review and approve the draft document before putting it to a plebiscite.[15] As it turned out, Taleghani's idea could not have been more beneficial to the Islamic Republican Party, because the independently fundamentalist or IRP-affiliated *mullahs* who had gained local popularity during 1978 by leading the anti-Shah demonstrations were in a favorable position to present themselves as the best and most legitimate "experts" on formulating a constitution for the Islamic republic.

It is a historic irony that Khomeini and some of his top clerical associates were originally opposed to the review of the draft constitution by a constituent assembly.[16] The liberal-left forces could not foresee that the establishment of such an elected body would enable the fundamentalists to discover the extent of their own untapped popular support, and the advantage it gave them relative to their confused and unorganized opponents. 'Ali-Akbar Hashemi Rafsanjani, the present speaker of the *Majlis*, expressed his initial opposition to the creation of a constituent assembly when he remarked to Bani-Sadr, "who do you think will be elected to the constituent assembly? A fistful of ignorant fanatics who will do such damage that you will regret ever having convened them."[17]

The debate over the draft constitution involved all political formations. The National Democratic Front presented a highly idealistic critique of the document and demanded that the Universal Declaration of Human Rights be integrated into the Iranian constitution. The Mojahedin proposed a more radical version of the NDF recommendations. The leftist Kurdish groups claimed that Iran was a "multinational" country and demanded that the new constitution be based on the rights of the "nations" of Iran. The Fadayan simply viewed the constitution as an instrument of capitalist exploitation and dismissed the proposed elections as a sham.

Khomeini reacted to these attacks on the draft constitution by urging his followers to review the document "from an Islamic perspective," rather than allowing "others" to rewrite the document. The fundamentalists' response to Khomeini's call was overwhelming. When the election for the Assembly of Experts was held, a coalition of ten Islamic organizations led by the Islamic Republican Party won fifty-five of the seventy-five seats. A number of well-known liberal-left personalities were elected to the Assembly, but they were unable to contain the determination of the fundamentalists to transform the draft constitution into a theocratic document.

The Islamic Republican Party and other fundamentalist groups were vigorous and united in pursuing their objectives. In contrast, the secular forces were fragmented, disorganized, and incoherent in their analysis of the situation. They simply substituted moral assertions and ideological claims for a realistic assessment of the political reality at hand. Virtually every secular group saw the other secular groups as a primary threat to its own position and aspirations, while regarding the fundamentalists as "ultimately" irrelevant. Such a mode of perception seemed so built into the secularists' mindset that its consistent defiance of empirical experience could not produce a reexamination of their views and analyses. It is undeniable that the fundamentalists tremendously benefited from the immaturity and incoherence of their political opponents. In fact, they systematically exploited the secularists' fragmentation and gradually neutralized them all.

The capacity of the fundamentalists to emerge as the hegemonic force in post-revolutionary Iran has to be understood in the context of the Iranian political culture, in which the rule of the strong man has been a constant. Historically, the difference between effective and ineffective leadership in Iran has often been a matter of life and death. Contrary to the hope it generated, the revolution simply made the stakes more deadly. Khomeini proved to be quite astute in manipulating the political attitudes and expectations associated with this tradition. His decisive personality and his capacity to alternate between pragmatic and crusading behavior helped him to disarm or discredit his many opponents within the revolutionary movement.

Admission of the Shah to the United States in late October 1979 was the final act of unintended U.S. assistance to the fundamentalists' drive to consolidate their power. There is no question that the ensuing hostage crisis presented a crucial political advantage to the fundamentalists in the internal struggle for power. Khomeini used the hostage-taking to put the secularists, particularly the Marxist-Leninist groups, on the defensive and to gain the time needed for their elimination. The liberal-left forces were critical of the hostage-taking, but given the history of U.S.-Iranian relations and the general public's perception of the Shah's admission to the United States as a threat to the revolution, they were incapable of facing the issue openly. The Fadayan were paralyzed by the hostage crisis, Bazargan was gone, and they could no longer accuse the government of pursuing an accommodationist policy toward the United States. Since anti-Americanism had the highest priority for the Fadayan, Khomeini's sensational confrontation with the United States robbed the Fadayan of their supposedly vanguard position. The Fadayan's disorientation in the face of Khomeini's militant anti-Americanism was a major cause of their previously mentioned split into majority and minority factions.

President Jimmy Carter tells us in his memoirs, *Keeping Faith*, that he decided to let the Shah into the United States for medical and humanitarian reasons. Yet soon after the seizure of the U.S. Embassy in Tehran, he confined the Shah to a Texas air force base hospital while Hamilton Jordan was trying to find him a new country. Carter's virtual expulsion of the Shah from the United States lent support to Khomeini's claims that intransigence was the only way to deal with the United States.

VI

Of the four groupings competing for power or influence in post-revolutionary Iran, only the Islamic forces succeeded in building an effective coalition. This achievement would not have been possible, however, without the strong and undisputed leadership of Ayatollah Khomeini. In other words, the fundamentalists had the advantage of operating within the native political culture. The Mojahedin were able to expand the popular base of their organization and thus proved to be the most formidable opponents of the regime, but when their inevitable armed confrontation with the fundamentalists came, they were no match for the security apparatus of the Islamic republic, which had been vastly enlarged after the Iraqi invasion of Iran in September 1980. The liberal-left elements lacked an uncontested leader and were incapable of creating a sustained coalition movement under collective leadership. As political actors, the liberal-left forces suffered from the fact that their concrete behavior militated against their ideals and aspirations. In order to become influential, the liberal-left elements had to work together in spite of the divisive characteristics of the native political culture. In this sense, they represented a truly revolutionary tendency within the national political tradition.

The Marxist-Leninists suffered from analytic confusion within themselves and alienation from the society at large. Yet they never ceased to substitute their alien thoughts for empirical sociopolitical analysis. Thus, their irrelevancy grew and their fragmentation multiplied with time. The Tudeh and the majority faction of the Fadayan remained at the disposal of the Islamic Republican Party until their violent elimination in early 1982.[18] The minority Fadayan bravely fought against the regime and they were finally subjected to the same kind of repressive treatment as the Mojahedin and the liberal-left elements.

Nevertheless, in 1979 there were no compelling structural-material reasons for the clergy's hegemonic control of the Iranian state and society. The emphasis is on the term *hegemonic*, because given the sociohistorical causes of the Iranian Revolution it was inevitable that the active clergy were going to play a principal role in the course of the revolutionary movement. Such a position for the clergy, however, did not have to lead to the establishment of a theocracy or the elimination of other revolutionary forces. It was the failure of the alternative tendencies to seize the space between the clergy's firm position of leadership and their potential to gain monopoly control of the state that enabled the fundamentalists to establish their hegemonic rule. The analytic weakness and the destructive behavior of the secularists served the fundamentalist clergy well. Yet Islamic fundamentalism was not alone in its desire for hegemonic domination of the revolution. Most of the organized political forces of the period had similar potentials. For example, while Prime Minister Bazargan in the immediate post-revolutionary period was condemning the work of the clergy-dominated revolutionary tribunals as shameful, most of the active secularists were demanding more executions without any analysis of how such vengeful punishment could serve their own political objectives or strategies.

The sociopsychological factors contributing to the emergence of the theocratic state in post-revolutionary Iran are rooted in the country's political culture. Iran has no precedent of peaceful succession to authority in its long history. Perception of politics as a zero-sum game is what most Iranian political formations, regardless of their ideology or class origins, have in common. Centuries of invasion from without and oppression from within have conditioned the Iranians to perceive politics as an interplay between peril and refuge from peril. The Iranian Revolution was an authentic and popular effort to resolve this paradox, but it ended up by ushering in a new form of peril and an unprecedented manifestation of insecurity in the refuge. Under the traditional form of peril like that of the Shah, politics was merely one component of life; it did not interfere with the very thoughts and life-styles of the citizens. Under Khomeini's theocracy, however, politics is the method as well as the substance of constructing a supposedly organic society in which every aspect of life is to be integrated with the basic purpose of the state, and the way this purpose is defined by official theocrats, no citizen is allowed to stand aside.

The Iranian political order has traditionally been a coercive monopoly of power by one man. All other levels of the political hierarchy derive their authority from the absolute ruler's arbitrary power. One manifestation of such personal authoritarianism and insecurity in Iranian politics is the equation of criticism with animosity. In all social classes, discussion of issues and ideas, no matter how distant or irrelevant, often breaks into attacks by each speaker on the other's character or motives. This historically conditioned but nevertheless internalized characteristic of Iranian political culture has created a mind-set within which every unpleasant problem or upheaval in the society is perceived as the work of foreign conspiracies,[19] traitors, or official corruption — usually a combination of all three. This habitual way of "making sense" out of sociopolitical problems or dilemmas is equally pervasive among rich and poor, educated and illiterate. The notion of rational and humane disagreement on substantive issues is rarely taken seriously by the activist groups. It is exceptional for Iranians genuinely to believe that there can be well-intentioned men and women with diverse political views and thus dissimilar prescriptions for social change. Recognition of the legitimacy and permanency of such diversities in Iran is a precondition for coalition building, without which consensus politics and civil society cannot begin to emerge.

Politics in Iran immediately after the 1979 revolution can be characterized as the politics of fragmentation, exclusion, and imposition. Nearly all political formations on the scene, whether by action or inaction, contributed to the final outcome. The truth is that for the third time in this century (once in the Constitutional Revolution and again in the Mossadeq era), Iranians, after a successful struggle against despotism, failed to rise above their repressive political culture and thus ended up with a new and more brutal form of despotic rule. The irony, as well as the challenge, of the situation appears when one considers the fact that the ideology of the elite of the new order has deep roots in the popular tradition of Iran. Indeed, Iranians can no longer hold the intruding "other" responsible for what has happened in their country. This could be a priceless lesson for a people who have been conditioned to blame foreigners for their own flaws and failings.

Notes

1. Robert Graham, *Iran: The Illusion of Power* (London: Croom, Helm, 1979); and Mansour Abdul Kasim, "The Crisis in Iran," *Armed Forces Journal*, January 1979, pp. 26–33, provide valuable analyses concerning the internal weaknesses of the Shah's regime.

2. An account of the Huyser mission is presented in Michael A. Ledeen and William H. Lewis, *Debacle: The American Failure in Iran* (New York: Alfred A. Knopf, 1981). Also see Sepehr Zabih, *Iran Since the Revolution* (London: Croom Helm, 1982), Chapter 1.

3. William Sullivan, *Mission to Iran* (New York: Norton, 1981).

4. For an account of the Islamic Republican Party's internal politics see Gregory Rose, "Factional Alignments in the Central Committee of the IRP," *The Iranian Revolution and the Islamic Republic*, eds. Nikki R. Keddie and Eric Hooglund (Washington, DC: Middle East Institute, 1982), p. 45–55.

5. For information and analysis concerning the character and development of the National Front see Richard Cottam, *Nationalism in Iran* (Pittsburg, PA: University of Pittsburgh, 1979); and Sepehr Zabih, *The Mossadegh Era: Roots of the Iranian Revolution* (Chicago, IL: Lake View Press, 1981).

6. *Massoud Rajavi: A People's Mojahed* (Union of Moslem Iranian Students Societies Outside Iran, 1982) provides useful information on the background of the Mojahedin.

7. For an informative analysis of the activities of the Marxist-Leninists see Sepehr Zabih, *Iran Since the Revolution*.

8. See Sepehr Zabih, *The Communist Movement in Iran* (Berkeley, CA: University of California Press, 1966) and Chapter 6 in *Iran Since the Revolution*.

9. See Michael M.J. Fischer, "Islam and the Revolt of the Petite Bourgeoisie," *Daedalus* (Winter 1982): 101–25.

10. See Homayoun Katouzian, *The Political Economy of Modern Iran* (New York: New York University Press, 1980); and Nikki Keddie, *Iran: Roots of Revolution* (New Haven, CT: Yale University Press, 1982).

11. William Sullivan in *Mission to Iran* and the late Shah in *Answer to History* (New York: Stein and Day Publishers, 1980) both treat Bakhtiar's premiership as a desperate attempt that was doomed to fail.

12. Descriptions of the revolutionary institutions can be found in Kalim Siddiqi (ed.), *The Islamic Revolution in Iran* (London: The Open Press in association with the Muslim Institute, 1980).

13. See Nikki Keddie, "The Origins of the Religious-Radical Alliance in Iran," *Past and Present* XXXIV (1966): 70–80.

14. Imam Khomeini, *Islam and Revolution: Writings and Declarations of Imam Khomeini* (Berkeley, CA: Mizan Press, 1981), translated by Hamid Algar.

15. I heard this from both Bazargan and Taleghani.

16. I learned about Khomeini's view of the original draft constitution from Mehdi Bazargan.

17. Abolhassan Bani-Sadr, *L'Espérance trahie* (Paris: Papyrus Editions, 1982), p. 70.

18. The Tudeh Party and the majority faction of the Fadayan were the last of the secular groups to be suppressed. Some of their leaders are presently in jail; others were executed after being convicted of espionage.

19. In his book *Answer to History*, the Shah actually accuses the CIA and the U.S. oil companies of having engineered his downfall.

12 KEY VARIABLES AFFECTING MUSLIM LOCAL-LEVEL RELIGIOUS LEADERSHIP IN IRAN AND JORDAN[1]

Richard T. Antoun

In the Muslim Middle East, joining a religious group or reactivating a religious affiliation has for more than one thousand years been a means of expressing political opposition. To note the activities of the Muslim Brothers in Egypt and Syria, or an Islamic *tariqa* in the Caucasus today, or the symbolism of Muharram processions in the recent Iranian Revolution — with white shrouds, the blood of Husayn, and the sword of 'Ali — is to note that this tradition is alive and well toward the end of the twentieth century. Joining a religious group intensifies social interaction at the local level and thereby collectivizes opposition and allows for its expression at regular intervals (the riots that punctuated the end of every forty-day mourning period in Iran during the long year of 1978 constitute a dramatic example). Of course, the political history of the Middle East contains many instances of urban demonstrations that began in the central square outside the main mosque after the Friday congregational prayers. But joining a religious group or simply performing one's individual ritual obligations can do something more than express individual opposition or collectivize that opposition. It localizes that opposition, gives it a spatial focus and an institutional base — the mosque, the shrine, the *takiyya*, the *husayniyya*. And it provides leadership — regular leadership at the local level. This essay will describe some key variables that affect that local-level leadership not only in revolutionary situations but also in calmer times and over the long run.

The first set of variables is broadly social structural and relates to the formality of the overarching religious hierarchy, its degree of centralization, and the range, function, and intensity of the social network that comprehends it. Generally speaking, there is a lack of formal hierarchy either laterally or lineally. For instance, in Jordan there is no organization that comprehends or would bring together on a regular basis such members of the religious institution as the judge (*qadi*) of the religious court, the shaykh of a mystic order (*tariqa*), and members of the Muslim Brothers. Moreover, although

175

a village preacher (*khatib*) in Jordan may come into contact with many of the above, he is not beholden to them and does not receive orders from them or report back to them unless he so chooses. For that matter, although the village preacher in Jordan is today substantially supported by the Ministry of Religious Endowments he is not in any formal sense one of its members or obliged to carry out its edicts. In Iran there is a proliferation of ranked, somewhat labile, religious titles granted on the basis of scholarly achievement and piety, and confirmed and given political significance by the development of a popular following and adulation among a group of devotees: e.g., *ayatollah al-'uzma, ayatollah, hujjat al-Islam, mullah*. And there is no doubt that individual Muslims, say at the village level, profess loyalty to a particular *ayatollah* based on the blessing and mediation he is believed to confer, that they seek his counsel either directly or (more frequently) through the local prayer leader (*pishnamaz*) or preacher (*akhond*), and that through the same intermediaries they present to him the alms tax (*zakat*) and the portion of the descendants of the Prophet (*khums*). The *ayatollah*, on his part, imparts blessing, distributes largesse in the form of contributions for mosques, hospitals, schools, and social welfare, and upon solicitation recommends for appointment particular preachers and prayer leaders at the local level. The religious institution in Iran, then, can be described as a wide-ranging social network that functions as a redistributive system and as a disseminator of information such that all parts of the network become aware of the critical problems facing the majority and of its dominant moods.

Although the religious institution in Iran does provide a system for the rapid dissemination of information and for the redistribution of economic resources, it remains an informal and noncentralized institution. Its informality is attested to by the mode of training and employment of its seminary students. They study a number of subjects such as Islamic law, the Qur'an, the Traditions of the Prophet, theology, philosophy, logic, and Qur'anic commentary over a period of from ten to fifteen years at the famous seminaries of Qum or Meshhed. At a middle point in their studies they begin to serve as temporary resident preachers in various villages around the country during vacations and the commemoration of the holy months of Ramadan and Muharram. At some point their main professor indicates that they have mastered their studies. Long before this they will have donned the distinctive religious headdress of the scholar and have been referred to by the title "shaykh" by the populace. At no point do they officially "graduate," and the only certificate at all resembling an educational degree that they receive comes long after they have left the seminary. They travel to Najaf in Iraq or to Qum and after an informal examination receive a kind of honorary degree which does not, however, refer to any specialty. After they have left the seminary they do not necessarily consult in a hierarchical manner with their former professors on particular points of interpretation. On an important point of interpretation they would write directly to the *ayatollahs* at Najaf or Qum. Their method of employment is also extremely informal and non-hierarchical. After terminating his seminary studies, the scholar is free to contract with any village the terms of his preachership. Often the happenstance of his temporary preacherships while still at seminary will have made him known in several different areas of the country (temporary preaching often goes on for eight years or more), and the notables of particular villages will solicit his services even before he terminates his formal studies.

Since there are a number of *ayatollahs*, each of whom commands a personal following, and this characteristic (of personal following) holds for every other level of the religious structure down to the level of the village preacher, the religious structure can be characterized as polycephalous and decentralized as well as informal.

The polycephalous, decentralized, and informal character of the religious institution assumes special importance during times of trouble, particularly when the religious institution opposes state policy and/or challenges its legitimacy. This polycephalous, informal character assures a constant supply of leaders, protects the identity of many, limits the efficiency of intelligence-gathering by the state, and disarms the adversary with the appearance of weakness. At the same time, during both revolutionary and more stable periods it allows for the rapid dissemination of information and economic redistribution throughout a wide-ranging network and thereby the recruitment of followers across class and cultural boundaries.

If the degrees of polycephaly, decentralization, and informality are key variables affecting the anatomy of local-level religious leadership, certain indices allow some degree of measurement of their range and importance. Among them is source of income. In Jordan in 1960 the annual income of the village preacher (*khatib*) of Kufr al-Ma' was $378, of which $270 was provided in kind by the inhabitants of the village annually on the threshing ground and the remaining $108 was provided by the Ministry of Religious Endowments in the form of a monthly stipend.[2] By 1966 the preacher's annual income was $861, of which $105 was still in kind from the village, $180 was from the village improvement fund (local taxes paid by villagers), and the remainder, $576, was from the Ministry of Religious Endowments either as a monthly stipend or as a salary for the preacher's taking on the additional position of marriage officer (*ma'dhun*). By 1979, the preacher's income was $3,618, of which only $360 was from the village. The remainder was from the Ministry of Religious Endowments or other government departments: $2,628 in the form of a direct monthly stipend, $180 as remuneration for services as marriage officer, and $450 as remuneration for acting as a pilgrim guide to Mecca. In the space of twenty years the *khatib*'s income had moved from being paid largely by villagers in kind to being paid largely by government departments in cash — certainly an indicator of greater centralization and formalization of the religious institution. This social structural trend had been accompanied by substantial economic and occupational mobility on the part of the *khatib* (even if one takes into account the impact of oil money and inflation on the Jordanian economy) as he successively became preacher, marriage officer, and pilgrim guide (never relinquishing any previous occupation with the addition of each new one).

A certain Iranian village religious specialist provides an interesting contrast. He became prayer leader of a large village in northeastern Iran in 1954 and acted simultaneously as a teacher, teaching the Qur'an, arithmetic, handwriting, and the rudiments of Shi'i history and theology for the more advanced primary school pupils. At that time his total annual income was approximately $1,650, most of it in kind in rice from land given to him by the landlords of the village (in return for serving the village); in addition, he received payments in cash and kind from individual villagers for his services as teacher and narrative chanter (*rozekhan*) during Ramadan and Muharram as well as during mourning and commemorative ceremonies for the deceased of particular families. In 1962 a secular primary school was established in the village; it drew the prayer-leader's students away from him and gradually reduced his income to a low of approximately $700 by 1970. In 1972 he recontracted with the village for a salary of $570, to be paid in installments four times a year; in addition, he earned $430 from individual villagers for his services as narrative chanter, for a total annual income of $1,000. In his particular case there was no evidence of an increase in either the formalization or centralization of the religious institution over an eighteen-year period at the local level. However, in 1972 the village did hire a second and more accomplished prayer-leader who had studied at the seminary in Meshhed for fifteen years.[3]

This brings us to a discussion of a second important variable affecting local-level religious leadership — the relationship between the religious leader and the local power structure. In the Iranian case discussed above, the religious leader was brought to the village by the dominant family of landlords in the village, and the major part of his income was provided by a land grant from them; by 1972 the landlords, though still influential, had been reduced in influence (largely by the Iranian Land Reform Act of 1962) and the salary of the prayer-leader was provided mainly by the village council (collected in taxes) and by individual villagers for particular services rendered. Thus, while the relationship to the national religious institution had not changed appreciably in terms of increasing centralization and control, the relationship to the local power structure had changed substantially. The negotiations with the new and more influential prayer-leader hired in 1972 were conducted entirely by freehold villagers and not the landlords, and his salary was drawn entirely from the former source. It is important to note that in the Iranian case (in contrast to the Jordanian one) at no point did the state provide any part of the income of the local-level religious leader. In the Jordanian case, although there are many landless villagers, no landed gentry has dominated the political and economic structure of the village since the founding of the kindgom in the 1920s. Landowners are freehold owners, and it is they who have always negotiated with the *khatib* the terms of his annual contract; therefore, in terms of the local power structure, the *khatib* is relatively autonomous. His autonomy was enhanced until the early 1970s by the shortage of trained *khatibs* — he could and often did threaten to go elsewhere unless the villagers agreed to a reasonable salary and kept their promises. As the *khatib*'s income came more and more from central government sources, the possibility of asserting his autonomy vis-à-vis the local power structure — in this case the elders of the village and its younger successful entrepreneurs — was enhanced.

An aspect of the variable centralization/decentralization

operating specifically at the local level is the strength and dispersion of the secular system of education. The spread of this system to the village level in the Iranian case mentioned above led to the downward economic mobility of the first prayer leader, a loss of prestige, and a narrowing of his occupational opportunities. On the other hand, in the Jordanian case the spread of the secular educational system (from a primary school for girls through the third grade and for boys through the sixth grade in 1960, to schools for both boys and girls through the ninth grade in 1979) has not adversely affected the income or status of the *khatib* (indeed, his income and status have increased over the last twenty years) nor has it precluded teaching activity on his part (he opened a Qur'an school for all ages in 1977 whose classes begin in the afternoon a half hour after the secular school's sessions terminate).

It should be pointed out that we have discussed three rather different types of centralization. The first is centralization entirely within the religious institution itself, e.g., the assertion of control by higher-ranked clerics over lower-ranked clerics in Iran. The second is centralization entirely within the state apparatus, e.g., the extension of the secular education system to the village level in both Iran and Jordan. And the third is the bureaucratization of religious leaders at different levels of the social structure by the state, e.g., the co-opting of village preachers with a formerly independent economic base as marriage officials and pilgrimage leaders.

Another important and often overlooked variable affecting local-level religious leadership is the geographic origin of the preacher/scholar/teacher. The Iranian preacher referred to above had lived in the village for eighteen years, but he complained of being a "stranger" (*gharib*). He was not born and bred in the village, was not considered one of the "home-towners" (*ahle deh*) or "people of the same wall" (*as yek divar*). Strangers do not have the same freedom as home-towners and are subject to special social constraints. One longtime migrant in the village who had lived there for more than twenty years said that if he were involved in a dispute with a home-towner and the dispute was arbitrated by the village council, he would be told: "You ought to mind your own business. Why are you always fighting? Remember, you are a stranger (*gharib*) here." One way for the religious leader to reduce such constraints and cancel the "stranger" status is for him or one of his family to marry within the village, thereby creating kinship ties. On the other hand, the home-town *khatib*, the "son of the village" (*ibn al-balad*) as he is known in Jordan, enjoys many social advantages but suffers under the brand of familiarity. In years of drought when the grain crop is reduced, often villagers will not pay their full promised share to the *khatib*, and this is more likely to happen if he is a "son of the village." Sometimes, the *khatib* is forced to go from household to household asking for his promised share — something he certainly would not have to do if he were a "stranger." But the sermon of the "son of the village" can be more effective in relating Islamic law and ethics to the day-to-day events of the village since he is personally familiar with the foibles of its inhabitants.

A final variable affecting local-level religious leadership is the career achievement pattern of the preacher/scholar/teacher and the concomitant presence or absence of psychological struggle. In the case of the two Iranian leaders, the narrative chanter/teacher and the younger seminary scholar, career achievement seemed to be relatively smooth and without psychological struggle. In both cases their fathers had been religious scholars or *mullahs*, and the sons had begun their religious education under the direction of family members, the mother's brother in the first case, the father in the second. And both had been encouraged and supported through subsequent years of education by family members and friends. The career pattern of the Jordanian preacher was quite different. His father was a well-to-do peasant by village standards, that is, he had enough land to provide a decent subsistence for his family. Moreover, he had served for a time as the mayor (*mukhtar*) of the village, the governing attribute of the mayorship before 1960 being the elder's having sufficient wealth (and willingness) to extend hospitality to villagers and visiting officials. But he was illiterate, and he not only failed to encourage his son to carry on his education but actively discouraged him. At the end of the third grade he expected his son to take his place alongside his brothers as ploughman on the family land. Only the remonstrations of the boy's teacher convinced the father to allow his son to finish six years of primary school. At the end of that time the father terminated the son's education, although the son had indicated beyond doubt that he was an excellent student. The son continued to pursue his religious studies privately and clandestinely with a scholar in the next town, all the while carrying on his agricultural duties. Instead of spending his evenings in the guest houses of the village as was the men's custom, he spent them in his room reading or in silent meditation clicking the beads of his rosary. His father believed he was going mad. The final confrontation between father and son came during the month of Ramadan in the year 1948 when the fast month coincided with the wheat harvest. The father ordered his son to carry on the harvesting with his brothers in the Jordan Valley. The son, on the other hand, consented but insisted on fasting at the same time. At the end of the harvest period, to terminate what from the father's point of view was a long period of filial disobedience, the son was ejected from the household. He carried on as a part-time assistant of the scholar in the next town, teaching children the recitation of the Qur'an, and a few years later, at the age of twenty-four, he was finally selected as village preacher and prayer leader over all competitors on the basis of his clear superiority in scholarship and homiletics.[4] But up until this final moment of career achievement not only his own father but also the village in general was unsympathetic to his aspirations. On the contrary, most thought him to be foolish in persisting in his vocational training, since in a peasant village the bread of the *khatib* is hard to come by and his prestige among his parishioners is not high, particularly when he has been born and bred among them. Perhaps because of this career struggle waged against his own family and the consensus of his own community, this *khatib* had an unusually strong commitment not only to religion but also to education — the subject of some of his strongest sermons. It might also explain the fact that the *khatib* was the only one who answered in the affirmative when I asked twenty villagers of different occupations and ages the question, "If you were in a public meeting and a citizen arose to defend a point of view that you and the majority of the assembled considered contrary to the interest of the country and the people, do you believe that he has the right to be heard?" The career achievement pattern and its social psychological concomitants, then, may leave an impact not only on the character of the leader but on certain ideological positions he may hold.

Notes

1. An earlier version of this paper appears in Fuad Khuri, ed., *Leadership and Development in Arab Society* (Beirut: American University of Beirut, 1981).

2. The data on the village preacher (*khatib*) in Jordan were collected during field work in Kufr al-Ma', Jordan, during the years 1959, 1960, 1966, 1967, and 1979.

3. The data on the two prayer leaders in Iran were collected during field work in 1972. The village is located in the northeastern part of the country in the province of Gorgan:

4. A fuller account of the life cycle of this prayer leader and his career achievement pattern is found in Richard T. Antoun, "Social Organization and the Life Cycle in an Arab Village," *Ethnology* VI, No. 3 (July 1967).

13 COMMUNALISM AND NATIONAL COOPERATION IN LEBANON

Iliya Harik

The Cultural Perspective

The affinity between communalism and nationalism in Middle Eastern societies is quite paradoxical: on the one hand, the two tendencies are intricately related, and on the other, they are in conflict. They both draw on the cultural, religious, and ethnic characteristics of a group.

In a sense, nationalism may be viewed as a glorified form of communalism. Communalism, however, is a term that has more often been associated with one cultural factor: religious affiliation of a collective nature. A person's location in the social fabric is most effectively defined in terms of his communal affiliations. This affiliation may be at variance with a person's actual faith. An atheist, for example, would still be defined socially by the religious group in which he was born, i.e., the religion of his parents.

Still, communalism is less in conflict with religion that it is with nationalism. While nationalism draws from the same cultural sources as communalism, it has generally been the case in the Middle East that nationalism tends to stress secularism and integration of particular groups into the larger society. Indeed, in certain modern secularist-nationalist movements that were particularly rife from the 1940s to the late 1960s, obliterating communalism from national life was an avowed objective.

Since then, two opposing traditional forces have shown a powerful resurgence and threatened the very fabric of the modern secular nationalist state. These are religious fundamentalism, which lends strength to a supranational commonwealth, and religious sectarianism (affiliated with enthnicity), which lends strength to particularistic separatist groups. Both tendencies undermine the nationalist-secular ideology and state. Nationalist setbacks and religious revivalism have spilled over and tainted the ephemeral secularist trends in the modern Arab state system. Nationalists, whether Arab or Lebanese, are now less reluctant to declare the preeminence of Islam or Christianity in their nationalist perspectives. This tendency is not unnatural, since both nationalisms draw much of their cultural substance from Arab Islam and from the history of the Christian community in Lebanon, respectively.

Thus, the resurgence of universalism and its opposite, particularism, have cut deeply into the delicate Lebanese state system. While Islamic revivalism has led to an emphasis on the universalistic principle in many Arab countries, in Lebanon it has led to emphasis on sectarian particularism.

The communal strains in Arab and Lebanese nationalisms stem from the cultural backdrop of the Muslim and Christian communities in Lebanon. Critics may see in nationalism in Lebanon a sublimation of Muslim and Christian communalism. It is important, however, to recognize that while Arab and Lebanese nationalisms rest on a communal background, they go beyond its limitations. Muslims in Lebanon in tune with their natural Arab affinities take a strong integrative stand by which they seek to bring Arab Christians into the Arab nationalist fold on a secular basis. Christian Lebanese tend to suspect that this proposed broad political framework would favor the country's Muslims, and themselves seek integration of the Lebanese Muslims into a Lebanese secular nationalism within the confines of Lebanon. While neither side is willing to compromise on its major goals, each sometimes offers concessions to the claims of the other. During the independence period, Arab Lebanon as an independent state became a reality for Lebanese Muslims, while Arab unity has been viewed as a long-range objective. For the Christians, Arab nationalism has been a cultural synonym for an Arab world to which they realize they belong, and with which they wish to live in conciliation and as much harmony as possible. Recent Muslim revivalism in the region and the conflict in Lebanon have set back trends toward reconciliation and underlined religious sectarianism once again.

In Lebanon, however, it is not religious revivalism as witnessed in the world today that defines the difference. It is rather religion as a sociocultural system that provides its followers with attachments and mundane prescriptions. The cultural precepts that religion provides to the community pertain to the community's place in society, pride, solidarity, and political orientation. When one looks at the political orientation of the Maronites, for instance, one encounters a nationalism rooted in the Christian heritage of the community and its historical experiences in Lebanon. The product is Lebanese nationalism, which Muslims and Arab nationalists conveniently describe as sectarianism. Similarly, the orientation of the Lebanese Muslims draws on a religious heritage conveyed through an Arabic language laden with religious and historical overtones reaching far beyond Lebanon's borders. The result is an Arab nationalist orientation which the Christians conveniently refer to as Muslim sectarianism. In a way, both are right; but if one ignores the symbiosis in the concepts of communalism, nationalism, and religion, one will find it very difficult to understand the social and political meaning of communalism in Lebanon. It should also be noted that this symbiosis is the product of dynamic forces that pertain to our modern era and are predicated on the revolution in communications.

Other aspects of Arab culture that are conceptually possible to segregate from religion (such as language, literature, poetry, and science) bridge the gap between Christian Arabs and Muslim Arabs. Herein lay the gradual growth in Lebanon of a conciliation between the two communities that served as a basis for their accommodation over thirty years of independence. It was also their social heritage and traditional attachment to freedom and self-determination that provided the new state with a burgeoning culture of its own that had the effect of moderating differences.

In short, it is clear that the political culture of Lebanon is one characterized by dynamism based on a peculiar mix of proximity and distance. Such a situation carries with it the seeds of integration and of conflict at the same time. The way events unfold thus depends to a large extent on the stimuli that provoke them. The stimuli could be accidental and external or they could be internal to society.

This author believes that the recent conflict in Lebanon, which seemed to correspond to sectarian divisions, was provoked by regional forces. It was not necessarily a natural outcome of the communally pluralist nature of Lebanese society.

Analysts often have tended to assume that when a society is composed of communal groups, these groups could be subject to severe conflict and to social disintegration. Social and political pluralism are not synonymous with social disintegration; all societies have social and political cleavages. The effect of such cleavages on the social and political order depends largely on their extent and depth, and the way stimuli stemming from other causes affect them. We shall trace here the relations of Muslims and Christians in Lebanon with a view to illustrating how communalism, religion, and nationalism functioned to produce integration at times and conflict at other times.

The Historical Perspective

A. Integration of the Christians

The Christians of the Middle East held on to their church and faith under more than a millennium of Muslim dominion. In Lebanon they are remnants of a once flourishing Christian-Aramaic population and culture. Their survival is a testimony to Muslim tolerance toward people of the revealed religions (*ahl al-kitab*), and their reduced number is an indication of the tendency of populations to conform to the dominant culture superimposed on them.

Traditional political systems in the Middle East have shown considerable tolerance toward religious communities, so long as those communities respected higher authority and refrained from espousing a competing political ideology and/or political organization. Thus, the Christians have enjoyed equality with Muslim subjects in terms of rights to life and property and freedom of religious practice provided by the imperium. They were not on an equal level with the Muslim population in political rights, such as existed at the time, nor in the right to assume military and judicial offices. Socially, they were considered inferior and often were required to wear attire that signified their special status.

The Maronites of Lebanon lived in such an environment until the seventeenth century, yet with a sense of grievance and unwillingness to accept the legitimacy of this state of affairs. Insubordination, it seems, landed them in trouble quite often, and this led to their withdrawal from the coastline to more distant mountain abodes. The rugged mountains of Lebanon provided them with relative security and isolation, thereby enabling them to avoid complete submission to Muslim authority. Unlike the Orthodox and Catholics, they did not enjoy recognition by higher Ottoman authorities, nor did they seek it; indeed, they avoided it and in later years resisted pressures to accept *millet* status, like other Christians.

From the start, the Maronites were a proud and self-centered community. Several factors helped to develop their nationalism in contravention to the general principles of Muslim domination represented in Ottoman authority. Their community was small and isolated. Furthermore, they were given considerable political freedom and protection by local Muslim chiefs whose core following came from a heterodox Muslim sect, the Druze. These chiefs, mainly the Maanids and their Shihabi successors, found in minorities, such as the Maronites, devout followers whose loyalties were not adulterated by adherence to the Ottoman rulers. By virtue of their distinctive communal character, the Maronites and Druze were able to create an autonomous feudal principality of their own (Mount Lebanon) which, while formally paying allegiance to the Ottomans, could occasionally stand them off and maintain an adversary relationship with Ottoman governors in the region.

The principality of Mount Lebanon was built on the loyal support of the Druze and Maronites for the *iqta‘* system, upon which it was based.[1] It was carved out of several Ottoman administrative provinces (*vilayets*), not being itself in any way a distinctive Ottoman administrative unit. The origin of the Lebanese state, which was entrusted to the French mandate in 1922 and became independent in 1943, lay in the principality of Mount Lebanon. It started in the early sixteenth century as a small region in the Shuf area of the southern mountain range of Lebanon, one almost exclusively inhabited then by Druze under Sunni amirs. Then the principality expanded north to include adjacent Christian-inhabited areas by the seventeenth century, and by the middle of the eighteenth century, it had expanded farther north to include the heartland of the Maronite community. The political unity of Mount Lebanon as a feudal principality based mainly on the Druze and Maronites was realized in the middle of the eighteenth century.

This historical event is significant for understanding the political relations among Lebanese sects, but most important for understanding the Maronites' political position in Lebanon. Unlike any other Christian community in the Middle East, they developed and dominated a state, a situation now being challenged by rival nationalisms.

Two factors were especially important in the development of a Maronite dominated polity in the midst of a Muslim world: Maronite integration into the ruling class of the feudal principality, and the freedom given to their church (which was also the custodian of their national culture). The Sunni Maanids (1515–1697) and their Shihabi successors (1697–1841) bequeathed noble titles on some of their Maronite aides, thus converting them into hereditary aristocrats with land and subjects. The Shihabis also recognized the local Maronite chiefs of the north after they were incorporated. Druze feudal chiefs accepted the noble status of Maronite leaders, but continued to enjoy greater weight in the political affairs of the principality.

The integration of Maronite Christians into the ruling class of the principality was in contravention of the *dhimmi* status of Christians in a Muslim commonwealth, which confined Christians to the status of subjects. Thus Maronites could ride horses, rule over the population, and fight wars, often on the side of the amir against Ottoman governors (*valis*). This high political status generated a sense of political pride in the community and of self-determination and equality with others.

The church protected by the amirs and the Maronite aristocracy was able to establish ties and religious allegiance to the universal church of Rome and to develop Maronite culture and eventually nationality. By the late eighteenth century, Maronite nationalism was already an articulated expression of the community's self-image — it expressed their distinctive communal identity, origins, and political status in Lebanon. By the first half of the nineteenth century, Maronite political ideology started to envisage the Shihabi principality as an aspect of Maronite polity. Maronite polity meant a dominant position in an autonomous political system including other communities such as the Druze. (Other religious communities did not have political power then.) Despite their small numbers, the Druze had always considered themselves as the politically dominant group. However, the increasing numbers, wealth, and foreign connections of the Maronites posed a definite challenge to Druze power by the early nineteenth century, a fact symbolized by the conversion of many Shihabis and Abillama' amirs to Christianity.

The Maronite challenge to Druze power was to shatter the centuries-old integrated principality. The situation was made acute by the fact that the Maronite challenge was two-pronged: a claim of superior status in the amir's government and a peasant revolt against feudal privileges. The peasants led the revolt against feudal lords, thus alienating the Druze and dividing their own community. The church, on the other hand, led the bid for a superior political position for the Maronites in the amir's government. The result was a protracted and bloody conflict which in 1860 resulted in diminution of Druze power and in the autonomy of Mount Lebanon under a new statute. Other significant results were: 1. the internationalization of the Lebanese question; 2. the abolition of the feudal system; 3. the creation of an autonomous Lebanese polity with increased Ottoman authority and recognition of Lebanon by the great European powers; and 4. the beginning of formalized communal pluralism in the Lebanese political system. The Maronites had the lion's share in the new system compared to other communities, which included Sunnis, Shi'a, Melkite Catholics, and Melkite Orthodox, in addition to the Druze.

Another feature of this historic period is the hostility toward the Muslim Shi'a on the part of the Druze and Maronites. The mountain chiefs had little politically to do with the Sunni population of the coastal towns since relations with urban centers were regulated by Ottoman officials. The Shi'a, however, like the Druze and Maronites, had their own feudal chiefs and lived in the mountains contiguously with those groups. Before the sixteenth century, most of the territory around the Druze principality was inhabited or controlled by the Shi'a. Subsequently, the feudal principality of the Druze expanded into Shi'i territory, pushing the latter farther and farther into the fringes of the mountains. The struggle with the Shi'a continued until the latter part of the eighteenth century. The Maronites, many of whom were under Shi'i chiefs, rebelled and were assisted by the Shihabis in driving off the Shi'i lords. As early as the sixteenth century, the amirs of the Shuf encouraged the Maronites to settle in territory evacuated by the Shi'a. Thus, many Maronites gradually moved south, living among both the Druze and Shi'a. Some territories became completely settled by the Maronites.

The settlement pattern of the modern period is the legacy of these historical developments. Basically, there was a communal division of land, with different groups concentrated in different regions. The population mix in the Druze region included a large number of Maronites and other Christians. The Shi'a constituted a belt around the Shihabi principality stretching from the southwest to the east and northeast. The northern half of the mountain was inhabited by Christians.

By the beginning of this century, the three main sects of the mountain had known very cooperative and friendly relations as well as very hostile ones. The Druze and Maronites experienced three centuries of integration as participants in one commonwealth. Revolution turned them against each other during the middle of the nineteenth century. After 1860, only the memories of civil war remained, while political issues were settled and the two peoples lived in peace again, though not without reserve and even caution.

With the end of dynastic rule in the mountain principality in the middle of the nineteenth century, relations with the Shi'a improved, although the Shi'a basically remained outside the autonomous province of the mountains.

B. Integration of the Muslims

The modern state starts with the end of Ottoman rule and the beginning of the French mandate in 1922. The coming of the French, traditional friends of the Maronites, both confirmed the political primacy of the Maronites and seriously undermined their political position. The French recognized the communal system, in which the Maronites played a predominant role. The Maronites responded favorably and cooperated with the French.

The threat to the Maronite position came with the incorporation of the Sunni Muslim coastal towns and the Shi'i mountain fringes in the new state of Lebanon. At that time the Maronites still constituted the largest sect, and the Christians on the whole had a numerical edge over all the Muslims put together. This situation changed rapidly for three reasons: 1. significant Christian outmigration; 2. higher Muslim fertility rates; and 3. the influx later of Palestinian refugees. The Palestinians, although most remained without Lebanese nationality, gradually became part of the social, economic, and political life of the Lebanese Muslim communities.

Thus, Lebanon started its modern history with a precarious and unstable demographic problem. It had to integrate very large Sunni and Shi'i communities, which remained aloof from the French. The Muslims' reserved attitude toward the French mandate left the field open for the Christians, who filled most state positions.

If a fair measure of integration did occur during this century, as I believe to be the case, the main reason is a unifying cultural factor — all parties being Arabs of similar social traditions. A second factor is the urban tradition of the Sunnis (basically an urban business community), and a third is the political skills and experience of the Maronites and Druze in self-government, and the political formula they devised to manage political diversity.

The Muslims who were integrated into the state of Lebanon initially resented being attached to the mountain, which they always felt was dominated by Christians and Druze. They had more affinity to Muslim Syria. The major Muslim reconciliation to the notion of a united Lebanon came in 1943 when the Christians and Muslims joined forces against the French in a major effort to secure the independence of the country. After independence, democracy, political stability, and economic prosperity helped win the adherence of the Muslim leaders and population to the Lebanese state. Ideological differences remained visible because the Muslims saw Lebanon as having a strong Arab character and the Christians emphasized its unique national character first. None of these aspects, however, were considered intense or exclusive, as is sometimes suggested.

The ingenious arrangement that made all this possible was the National Pact of 1943, in which Muslim and Christian leaders expressed their commitment to an independent Arab Lebanon and distributed state positions on a fixed basis to the various communities, with a preponderant share going to the Maronites, followed by the Sunnis. Thus, Lebanon from 1943 to 1975 was really a Maronite-Sunni concordat replacing an earlier Maronite-Druze concordat. Discontent among other sects was contained by giving each community a share of power relative to its demographic strength. One should be careful not to perceive the communities as corporate bodies. The arrangement specified that positions be filled by members of each sect by means of electoral contest based on communally mixed electorates.

Under this arrangement, Lebanon was the only constitutional, democratic, stable, and prosperous country in the Arab world. Empirical evidence also shows significant strides in elite and popular integration as well. Before we discuss the reasons for the recent war and disintegration, let us document and explain the integration that occurred during the early post-independence period.

In the first place, surveys in the early 1970s show considerable agreement in the attitudes and views of Muslims and Christians on domestic issues. They also show a growing convergence of views on the national identity of Lebanon, with more Muslims committed to the Lebanese identity and more Christians committed to the Arab character of the country. In short, an agreement on an Arab Lebanon was taking shape.

Moreover, one is struck by the alignment of leaders in parliament and in the cabinet based on political rather than sectarian criteria. Coalitions in parliament, for instance, were almost always nonsectarian, with deputies from both religious communities. Some political parties had communally integrated representation in parliament. For instance, the National Liberal Party was represented by deputies from the following sects: Maronites, Druze, Shi'a, Sunnis, and Orthodox Christians. Its head is Camille Chamoun, the former Maronite president who tried to confront Nasserism at its zenith, and who is now a strong member of the Lebanese Front. Indeed, many members of parliament and politicians from Muslim sects continued to visit and consult with him during and after the civil war.

Similarly, the Progressive Socialist Party was represented in parliament by Druze, Maronites, Catholics, a Protestant, and Sunnis. Its head was Kamal Jumblat, who later led forces of the Lebanese National Movement against the Maronites. He continued to meet with Christian deputies and politicians even during the war.

In parliamentary voting one rarely finds votes distributed along religious lines. It was almost always Christians and Muslims lining up against another group of Muslims and Christians.

Elite relations, it should be mentioned, showed a higher degree of integration than relations among ordinary citizens. For instance, while the leaders of the parties discussed above were a composite of different sects, party members were primarily from one sect. Chamoun's party members were mostly Christians and Jumblat's party members were mainly Druze, though their voting public was mixed.

Another feature of elite integration was reflected in the electoral process. In many constituencies, the population was religiously mixed and the law called for a mixed representation. Since these were multiple-seat constituencies, candidates from different sects joined together and formed electoral slates. The leader of the slate could be Muslim or Christian, depending on his strength. A regionally strong candidate like Catholic Joseph Skaff in the Biqa' could be seen leading Shi'i and Sunni candidates who would give him their support in parliament once elected. Similarly, a strong Shi'i leader like Kamil al-As'ad was responsible for the electoral success of Sunni, Christian Orthodox, and Shi'i deputies from his region. The cooperation among the elite was almost totally political and not religious.

The way the electoral law functioned also contributed to influences that cut across religious lines. A voter was allowed by law to vote for as many candidates as there were seats assigned to his constituency, regardless of the candidates' religious affiliations. Thus, a Sunni voter would often find himself voting for a Maronite candidate, a Shi'i candidate, or other non-Sunni candidates. This practice had the effect of generating solidarity between voters and leaders across sectarian lines. Moreover, it discouraged communalism. Candidates from mixed constituencies tried to be moderate on sectarian issues in order to attract voters from other communities.

The electoral arrangement, based on the quota principle and multiple-sect constituency, reduced sectarian tensions and promoted integration. Candidates had to compete against others from their own sects although they received votes from voters of different religions. For example, Kamal Jumblat could be defeated in an election only if two other Druze candidates in his constituency received more votes than he did. The number of votes received by the Maronite candidates in that constituency did not affect him; his score was counted against candidates of his own community. This gave community members security against being excluded by stronger communities or by voters from other sects aligning against them.

The Roots of Conflict

The problem with the quota system was that a group might no longer be satisfied with its share of seats in the government. The Lebanese Muslims' dissatisfaction in the late 1960s and 1970s tested the survival of this arrangement.

How did Lebanon's fixed quota system respond to rising Muslim aspirations? The laws concerning the electoral process did not change and the quotas remained the same. In practice, however, an interesting development occurred. Since 1943, the quota arrangement provided that for every five Muslim deputies the Christians would have six deputies. Thus the parliament, which consisted of ninety-nine deputies, was composed of fifty-four Christian and forty-five Muslim deputies. In the election of 1972, for instance, thirteen Christian deputies were elected to parliament under the sponsorship of Muslim leaders and five Muslims were elected under the sponsorship of Christian leaders. Since those sponsored deputies followed their slate leader in parliament, the effective sectarian distribution of seats was no longer the same as in the law. If one considered a Christian-sponsored Muslim deputy as voting with his Christian leader, then he should really be considered as a member of the Christian deputies and vice versa. Therefore, the actual distribution of seats in parliament was forty-six "Christian" to fifty-three "Muslim" deputies.

The number of deputies, however, was never the real bone of contention for the Muslims in Lebanon. Nor, for that matter, was the number of officials and army officers. These numbers adjusted remarkably well to change. In the civil service parity was achieved; in the army Christians had more high ranking officers while Muslims were more numerous among the lower ranks and enlisted men.

The main issue for the Muslims was to win Christian recognition of the fact that they had become demographically the majority and deserved to occupy the top echelons of power. In short, they believed that the presidency or the chief executive office should be occupied by a Muslim. This meant the reversal of roles from Christian to Muslim primacy in the state. The Muslim demand was an entirely legitimate claim on the basis of democratic philosophy; it had no visible connection to the Islamic religion as such. Had the Lebanese Muslims been, say, Buddhists and found themselves in the same demographic situation, they would have been equally justified in asking for change. Being Muslim did not prevent them from living in the Lebanese system with less power but in peace and cooperation with their Christian compatriots for thirty years of independence. Indeed, the spokesman of the Lebanese Higher Muslim Council openly stated that Muslims finding themselves in a predominantly non-Muslim state would not find that situation a violation of their religious principles. This was possible to say because in a democracy Muslims are participants rather than subjects. Besides, in Lebanon religious laws govern personal matters and Muslims have not been subjected to laws they do not recognize.

In seeking to hold out on the issue of the presidency, the Christians, like any other group in their situation, were unwilling to give up power gently. They perceived their role in Lebanon as synonymous with a predominant Maronite presence. They countered the Muslim argument, which is based on the democratic principle of numerical majority, with another democratic principle, namely corporate communal representation, known in modern Western thought as consociationalism after the pluralist systems of the Dutch, the Belgians, and the Swiss.

The community rights issue, even as it involved the presidency, is not, however, what led to the explosion of 1975. The political gap separating the two communities was not that wide or insurmountable. It can in no way explain the vicious violence and political stalemate of the past decade. The Muslims had no reason to think that their demands would not eventually be met. Moreover, accession to the presidency by the Muslims was not a taboo. Indeed, Muslim leaders had twice presented themselves as candidates in the 1960s and 1970s. They had also been gaining power in the state councils since independence. The office of prime minister, for instance, was a minor office traditionally occupied by a Muslim, and the constitution attached less power to it than to that of a minister; this explains why prime ministers used to hold a ministerial portfolio in addition to being premiers. By 1974, however, the office had gained so much power that it was nearly equal in importance to the presidency. Indeed, a major problem of the Lebanese state since the 1960s was that it had become a two-headed institution, with each head having veto power over the other.

Lebanon's Muslim leaders, like their Christian counterparts, were committed to peaceful democratic change and would not do anything to destroy the system. They were middle class citizens and notables whose power had been stable over the years. The Sunnis in particular were not about to wreck the Sunni-Maronite concordat; they wanted precedence, not domination. They had, moreover, a keen interest in containing the growing political challenge from the Shi'a and the ambitions of Kamal Jumblat.

The crisis of 1975 was the result of converging forces mostly external to the domestic political game and led to an intractable confrontation among the Lebanese. These forces proved to act against Muslim leaders as much as against Christian leaders with one exception: the Christian population rallied behind its veteran leaders because it perceived a challenge directed against the Christians' political position. On the other hand, the Muslim population turned against its leaders in office and gave its allegiance to newcomers who were not committed to the National Pact of 1943. In short, what happened was nothing less than a revolution within the Muslim political community. Veteran Muslim leaders were left with no choice but to toe the line of the new forces.

The new Muslim forces comprised fragmented organizations and marginal political parties backed and supported by the Palestine Liberation Organization (PLO) in Lebanon. Except for the Druze party of Kamal Jumblat, they were mostly insecure elements outside the system who professed an Arab nationalist ideology. Some were communists and others Syrian nationalists; these two parties were of mixed sectarian composition and secular in ideology. They all had failed to gain prominence under the parliamentary system. A dozen of them raised to parliament only two deputies in 1972; two other deputies belonged to the secularist groups in that front.

Why were the small groups — i.e., the political have-nots — able so suddenly to undermine the established veteran Sunni leadership? They did not achieve this result on their own, but rather as proxies. The emergence of the PLO as a mighty force on the Lebanese scene changed the complexion of Lebanese domestic politics. The PLO backed the small estranged groups with all its political and military might; the Palestinian factor had an effect similar to that of Israeli activities in Lebanon. The Israelis provoked both Muslims and Christians and humiliated the hand-tied Lebanese government. Israel's violation of Lebanon's sovereign territory and its use of violence against Lebanese civilians undermined the authority of the Lebanese government. It was glaringly clear to the Lebanese people that their government could neither control the Palestinians and the Israelis, nor protect the population from actions by these two forces. Once the authority of the central government was undermined and weakened, pretenders and challengers gained disproportionate stature and factionalism became rife. It should be remembered that uncontrollable factionalism is not a function of social cleavages but of decline in central power.

The momentous events that destabilized the Lebanese system beginning in 1969 were the mounting Palestinian-Israeli struggle on Lebanese soil and the outcome of the Jordanian-PLO war in 1970. As it unfolded over Lebanese soil, the Israeli-Palestinian conflict directly affected the Lebanese and forced them to take positions on the matter. The Christians wanted to put an end to the conflict, fearing both an Israeli invasion and the growing power of the PLO over Lebanese groups. They called for containing the PLO and its attacks on Israel from Lebanese territory. This was also the position of the Lebanese government, which had the responsibility of protecting its citizens and land. This position was shared by the Christian leaders in government and by many Muslim leaders, including Kamal Jumblat, who as minister of the interior successfully negotiated a short-lived arrangement with the PLO to halt its activities. When the Lebanese army turned its guns against the PLO in 1969, the Sunni prime minister was content to register a symbolic protest: he resigned his office but continued to conduct affairs as caretaker for six months. The Shi'i speaker of parliament went along with the government.

Neither the Lebanese army nor any other force was able to stop the Palestinian-Israeli war on Lebanese soil. Especially after it had been expelled from Jordan in 1971, the PLO grew too big in Lebanon to be controlled. It was well armed and supported by 400,000 Palestinian refugees living in Lebanon, and it started to spread its influence over many Lebanese political groups (mainly the radicals who had not succeeded in the parliamentary game), arming and training them. Even more important, the appeal of the Palestinian cause was irresistible to Lebanon's Muslims, and the Palestine issue evoked sympathy among some Christians as well. Meanwhile, the communists and the Syrian nationalists were turning ideologically toward an accommodation with the Arab nationalists. They found in the PLO a welcome protection against the Lebanese regimes that had subordinated them for such a long time.

The established Sunni politicians were neither radical nor eager to share power with the PLO. They could ill-afford to stand up to it, however, since their constituency was strongly pro-PLO. The result was a docile conformity to PLO demands; this created a chasm with the Sunni leadership's Christian counterparts and a serious rift in the Maronite-Sunni concordat. The Christian leaders, realizing the inability of the veteran Muslim leaders in government to act freely, ruled out cooperation with them. This prevented reliance on the government, since no Lebanese government could make major decisions without the concurrence of both sides. The conclusion they reached was to prepare for self-defense by relying on their own communal resources.

Muslim leaders lost not only the trust of their Christian colleagues but also their own supporters who were co-opted and recruited by the PLO and its Lebanese protégé parties — the Nasserite groups, the communists, the Syrian nationalists, and a newly rising Shi'i power organized by Imam Musa Sadr. A new Shi'i militia, called Amal, was started, trained, and armed by the PLO and supported by Syria.

The small radical groups were never a party to the National Pact, on which Lebanese political pluralism rested. They were not particularly concerned about it, and had no real idea of what its replacement should be. They were driven by the military might of the PLO and the passionate mass support for it. Veteran Muslim leaders were pushed to the sidelines and did not actually participate in the fighting, with the exception of Druze leader Jumblat. Shi'i involvement in the fighting in the early stages of the conflict occurred for the most part under the banner of non-Shi'i leaders.

Realizing that in order to act freely in Lebanon they had to overcome the Christian opposition and weaken the government, the Palestinians played the sectarian game. Doing away with Christian opposition, however, was tantamount to staging a coup, which would have put a Muslim Lebanese in the executive office. The Palestinians and their Muslim client groups pushed the issue of Muslim rights in Lebanon to the forefront, but once that issue was brought out into the open it became explosive and hard to contain again.

Traditional Muslim leaders were not indifferent to Muslim rights; they simply dealt with the issue at the elite level. By choosing a frontal attack strategy, the PLO and the Lebanese National Movement forced the hands of both Christian and Muslim leaders, putting them publicly on opposite sides. This did not end all cooperation between them, but reduced the opportunity for it. As the National Movement has started to fragment and weaken in the last few years, the veteran leaders cautiously and reluctantly have moved to assume leadership of the Muslim community again, with the exception of Amal.

The Palestinian strategy was based on the following considerations. By 1970 most Lebanese Muslims wanted to see a Muslim in the country's executive office. The PLO could not, of course, overthrow a regime on the pretext that it was not supportive of the Palestinian revolution, but through its clients the PLO could advocate Muslim political primacy, which was possible and would amount to the same thing. Such a course of action would have the presumed effect of ending the Christian presidency and undermining veteran Muslim leaders. Indeed, the Muslim leaders had no choice in 1975 but to call for political change and declare the end of the National Pact era.

Transition in Lebanon would have been possible in due course by peaceful means, but it was not possible under the threat of force. The Christians felt that giving up power under force would pose a serious threat to their survival. Yet Muslims seemed to think change would be possible because of the tremendous striking force of their Palestinian allies. All this was done in the name of secularization, since an explicit demand for a Muslim president would have made them look sectarian; they wanted to project a nationalist and progressive image in the Nasserist tradition. Secularization became a code word for ending Christian privileges and replacing them by Muslim primacy.

Only Kamal Jumblat (along with minor groups like the communists and Syrian nationalists) took the secularist argument seriously. Jumblat, a prominent leader with a strong and stable base and with some international recognition to boost his spirits, was not willing to be kept out of supreme authority simply because he represented a small sect. When he saw the balance of power shifting in favor of the Palestinians and their allies, he joined in and developed a patronizing position toward the small have-not parties and directed them to the line of the PLO. He became the head of this force, allied it formally with the PLO, and challenged the veteran Muslim leaders as well as the Christian position. Jumblat had already begun to challenge the Sunni leaders by spreading his and the Palestinians' influence over their constituency through small militant Sunni parties.

It seemed as if the Lebanese Muslims were fighting for their political rights, but this was far from the truth. The Lebanese Sunnis had nothing to win from such a struggle; indeed, they turned out to be the greatest losers. The forces emerging from the rubble were the PLO, the Shi'a, and the Christian Kata'ib Party, all under some sort of Syrian or Israeli sufferance. The fighting forces consisted of a Palestinian element that varied between 20,000 and 30,000 men, and around 20,000 Christians, 15,000 of whom were fighting under the Kata'ib banner. Only 1,000 non-Palestinian Muslim fighters and 2,000 Jumblat followers were involved. The latter restricted their activities to their home area, which was not attacked.

The above figures clearly point to one thing: the war was between the PLO (supported and abetted by Lebanese Muslims) and the Kata'ib (supported and abetted by Lebanese Christians). The situation before the Israeli invasion in June 1982 was one in which Lebanon was controlled by the Kata'ib, the PLO, the Syrians, and the Israelis, and each had its own exclusive domain. The Shi'i Amal movement was struggling for space but had not yet found it, its natural domain being controlled by Palestinians and Israelis who gave no quarter.

Conclusion

If not contained quickly, a conflict tends to expand beyond the original parties or participants. The protagonists themselves seek such expansion and try to involve others by provocative acts; and in a communal situation, familial and other relations bring into the fray others who were not involved from the start. Conflict also tends to intensify the emotional involvement of participants far beyond the original grievances. Thus it becomes more difficult to contain the conflict, particularly in pluralist societies, even if the causes and provocateurs disappear. In addition, power becomes so fragmented that the sheer number of actors becomes an obstacle to resolution, and the prospect of reaching a common ground of agreement becomes dim. The atmosphere of violence tends to permit a single group to veto an agreement by all the others unless the majority strongly supports the agreement. This, however, is rarely the case.

In the 1960s and 1970s, Lebanese politics reflected a disagreement between Christians and Muslims over distribution of power. The difference, however, was not very great and could not be considered intense enough to lead to a serious armed conflict. It was being resolved gradually in favor of the Muslims through peaceful political measures. Experience had shown Lebanese leaders that their communities could cooperate and secure political needs by working together, regardless of whether a Muslim or a Christian was president. In practice, the situation was moving in the direction of a weakened Christian president and a strong Muslim premier. Eventually, this process would have put the Muslims in the saddle and resulted in a change from a presidential to a cabinet system.

Regional disturbances created for the Lebanese a confrontation that diverted them from this course. The intensification of the Palestinian-Israeli conflict on Lebanese territory created a tragic situation of great dimensions for everyone involved. The armed Palestinian presence in Lebanon augmented Muslim power, mobilized the Muslim masses, and threatened the position of the Christians and the whole democratic system in which they found security. To carry out their struggle against Israel, the Palestinians felt it was necessary to have as much freedom of action in Lebanon as possible, regardless of who was in power. Since Christian masses were not willing to give the Palestinian cause primacy over Lebanese integrity, an inevitable confrontation developed that destroyed the fragile political system. Arab nationalism, which fired the spirits of Muslim Lebanese, bolstered the Palestinians' objective; however, it suffered a serious moral and political setback on Lebanese soil.

One cannot say that on a certain day a confrontation developed and the guns bellowed. The conflict in Lebanon developed over a number of years during which clashes with the Palestinians created mounting tension and drew others into the fray. Gradually, the situation became uncontrollable. The constant friction between Palestinian guerrillas and their Lebanese allies on the one hand, and the Christian Lebanese militias on the other, expanded the conflict and polarized forces on the Lebanese scene.

Islam was only tangentially relevant to the conflict, for Islam is a community (*umma*) only in the spiritual sense. Politically, it has been fragmented into many states and nations for nearly a millennium, during which time Muslims adjusted to international divisions and coexistence with other communities. However, Islam has given an additional dimension to the conflict among communities in Lebanon for a number of reasons. First, as a political and social culture, Islam is associated with Arab nationalism, providing it with substance and constituting an element of solidarity among its following. (Arab nationalism is more pronounced among Muslims than Christians, although they both share the heritage of the Arabic language.) Second, Islam created linkages between Lebanon's Muslims and the incoming Palestinians, whereas the Christians' relations with the latter were strained.

In effect, one witnesses a situation in Lebanon where a civil culture developed whose main orientation was loyalty to the political system with deep attachment to the land. It has shown that Arab and Lebanese nationalisms are not necessarily irreconcilable. The difference in political orientation on the identity question is not by itself a source of severe conflict; rather, it constitutes a potential for conflict that, under certain conditions, might cause discord. Except for specific short periods, the Lebanese lived peacefully and cooperated in all spheres of life. While religious revivalism has shown a high degree of social segregation, traditional communalism and nationalism have proved more amenable to coexistence under the framework of a pluralist polity.

Lebanon's historical experience over several hundred years shows that Christian-Muslim political coexistence in a single commonwealth is possible, regardless of the way power is distributed. Episodes of armed conflict have been very brief and caused by nonreligious factors (often due to the coincidence of domestic changes with the intrusion of external forces). It would be a mistake to view these short-lived conflicts as evidence that Christians and Muslims are unable to coexist. For peaceful cooperation and coexistence to be restored in Lebanon, the regional combatants must be disentangled from the Lebanese scene and the Lebanese must be allowed to fulfill their strong desire for national reconstruction without outside interference.

Notes

1. *Iqta'* in Lebanon was a political system in which authority was distributed among autonomous and hereditary chiefs subordinate in a certain political respect to a common overlord.

14 IRAQ'S SHI'A, THEIR POLITICAL ROLE, AND THE PROCESS OF THEIR INTEGRATION INTO SOCIETY

Hanna Batatu

When the modern Iraqi state was formed in 1921, Iraq's Shi'a did not constitute a closely knit body of people. Though sharing similar traits, they were split up, like the other inhabitants of Iraq, into numerous distinct, self-involved communities. In most instances, they did not identify themselves primarily as Shi'a. Their first and foremost loyalty was to the tribe and the clan. This was especially true in the villages and the *salafs* (clusters of rural dwellings).

But even at Najaf, which was the principal center of Shi'i learning, the feeling for the tribe, or the *mahalla* (city quarter), was in a political sense stronger than the tie of Shi'i sentiment. In 1915 the people of Najaf rose against the Turks and expelled them from the city. They became politically free and continued in that condition until they were subdued by the English in 1917. In the interval Najaf was not transformed into a Shi'i or Islamic city-state. Rather, each of its four quarters became independent. The constitution of one of the quarters, that of Buraq, has been preserved. "We, the inhabitants of Buraq quarter," reads its principal paragraph, ". . . have assembled ourselves and become united and of one blood and follow one another should anything happen to our quarter from other quarters."[1] The other paragraphs indicate clearly that the social organization of the quarter was based on the tribe and that its values were fundamentally tribal. Power was vested in the headman of the quarter. The constitution assigned no political role to the *marji'iyya* (the highest Shi'i authority) and indeed made no mention whatever of this institution which is at the very heart of any authentic Shi'i polity.

Of course, the inhabitants of Najaf were conscious that they were Shi'a. Their Shi'ism, however, was not of the dynamic kind, at least politically. In other words, they did not feel impelled to give it an active political expression. This applied with greater force to the Shi'i peasants who constituted the overwhelming majority of Shi'a. The notion of a political Shi'ism or of an Islamic state supervised by a *marji'* deputizing for the Absent Imam existed merely as an undefined vision of idealist *'ulama*.

It should not be inferred from the foregoing observations that the *maraji'* — the most authoritative Shi'i jurists — were without political influence over the faithful. Indeed, some of them took a leading part in precipitating the 1920 uprising against the English of the Shi'i tribesmen of the mid-Euphrates. But it should be kept in mind that this region, being contiguous to the holy cities of Najaf and Karbala, was hospitable to the wishes of the *maraji'* and had, in addition, special reasons to be aggrieved.[2] The *fatawa* for a holy war against the occupiers issued by the *maraji'* at that time received scarcely any response from the more distant Shi'a of the Tigris or the Gharraf or Shatt al-'Arab.

The feeble influence that the *maraji'* exercised over the Shi'i peasants of these river valleys stemmed from the fact that in most of their villages there were scarcely any traces of organized religion. For example, as late as 1947 there was not a single religious institution in the Shi'i rural districts of the Tigris or the Gharraf,[3] that is, not a single mosque or religious school or *husayniyya*.[4] In some villages, however, resident tribal *sada* (claimants of descent from the Prophet) used their guest-house as a kind of mosque or *husayniyya*. To other villages itinerant preachers came from nearby towns. But many of these preachers and *sada* were unauthorized by the *maraji'* and not infrequently dealt in superstition. To the paucity of mosques and religious schools among the peasant-tribesmen may be linked their unfamiliarity with the basic ideas of conventional Shi'ism and their observable laxity about their prayers and the other precepts of the faith.

The tenuous authority of the *maraji'* over the bulk of the Shi'i peasants was also connected with the fact that, unlike the peasants, most of the Shi'i *'ulama* and students of religion in Iraq were non-Arabs. This is a fact that is freely admitted by Shi'i fundamentalists and strongly deplored by them.[5] Iraqis still remember an anecdote from 1920 about Abu al-Qasim al-Kashani, one of the prominent religious leaders of the day. He had been sent from Karbala' to a district in the mid-Euphrates to persuade its tribal chiefs to rise up in arms, but his Arabic was so poor that no one present could make out what he intended. In the end his vivid gestures put his point through.

All the aforementioned factors made for a feeble sense of Shi'i identity and a lack of communal cohesion among the greater number of Shi'i peasants, which, together with their social and economic disadvantages and their physical dispersion in isolated or tenuously linked rural districts, contributed to their palpable political ineffectiveness.

If the urban Shi'a had stronger Shi'i feelings, they were numerically insignificant, in a comparative sense, especially where it mattered politically — in Baghdad. Here, prior to World War I, the Jews enjoyed a plurality, accounting probably for as many as 53,000 of the estimated total population of 150,000 and, more than that, dominated the trade of the city.[6] But politically the Sunnis were of first importance. They formed the backbone of the landed class and preponderated in the state administration. The Shi'a added up to less than one-fifth of the city's inhabitants and, on the whole, belonged to the poorest of its poor. They lived in separate quarters and led their own separate lives, seldom mixing with the Sunnis or intermarrying with them.

From the standpoint of the sociopolitical integration of Sunnis and Shi'a, the English invasion of 1914–1918, or rather the resistance that it provoked and that attained its highest point in the armed uprising of 1920, forms a landmark in the modern history of Iraq. For the first time in many centuries, Shi'a and Sunnis pulled together and acted in concert. Unheard-of joint Shi'i-Sunni celebrations were held at Baghdad in all the Shi'i and Sunni mosques in turn: special *mawalid* (Sunni observances in honor of the Prophet's birthday) were succeeded by *ta'azi* (Shi'i lamentations for the martyred Husayn). With the bond, however tender, that was thus created between Sunnis and Shi'a, a new process set in: the difficult, now imperceptible, now fitful growth of an Iraqi national community.

The coming together of Shi'a and Sunnis at that historic juncture was to be inferred from the situation that arose out of the English conquest, but the credit for consciously bringing it about belongs primarily to Ja'far Abu al-Timman, a Shi'i trader from Baghdad. To turn this temporary closing of ranks into a lasting political fact became a persistent burden of his thought. In his view, there was no other way to break English influence. Often Shi'i politicians sought to draw him toward sectarian politics but he invariably gave them the cold shoulder. Toward the two interconnected goals of Shi'i-Sunni union and the elimination of English power, Ja'far Abu al-Timman steered the chief efforts of the National Party, which played an active role in the 1920s and the first half of the 1930s in promoting an Iraqi national consciousness.[7]

The Hashemite monarchy, which was founded in 1921, also made a significant contribution to this process. Though a creation of the English, the monarchy, by choice or from necessity, directly or indirectly, through processes it initiated or through processes in which it became involved, did much to link Shi'a and Sunnis and to integrate the Shi'a into the body politic.

Owing to the initial, intimate interweaving of its dynastic interests with the fortunes of the pan-Arab movement, the basic instinct of the monarchy in the first two decades of its life was to further (to the extent that its status of dependence permitted) the work of nation-building in Iraq. With this in mind, but also in order to meet its administrative needs, it added considerably to the existing educational facilities in Sunni and Shi'i districts. It also systematically nurtured in the schools the passion of patriotism and a lively sympathy for the pan-Arab ideal. Faysal I, who occupied the throne from 1921 to 1933, was as sensitive as Abu al-Timman to the need for cultivating among Iraq's diverse elements enduring ties of common feeling and common purpose. Realizing how much depended on winning the confidence of the Shi'a and clearly troubled by the half-truth that "the taxes are on the Shi'a, death is on the Shi'a, and the posts are for the Sunnis" — which he heard "thousands of times," as he confided in a secret memorandum[8] — he took special pains to associate the Shi'a with the new state and to ease their admission into the government service. Among other things, he put promising young members of this sect through an accelerated program of training and afforded them the chance to rise rapidly to positions of responsibility. Moreover, Faysal (who regarded the army as "the spinal column for nation-forming"[9]) fought hard for the principle of national military service, partly to reduce the state's financial burden, but also in the hope of turning the armed forces into an effective means for the intermingling of Shi'a with Sunnis and tribesmen with townsmen, thus loosening the communities from their sectarian moorings, undermining the power of the tribal shaykhs over their peasants, and breaking down the hard and fast line between the tribes — a necessary precondition for their integration in national life.

In brief, initially the monarch formally stood and in practice worked for the ideal of an integral community — one Iraqi people.

After 1941, however, the political orientation of the monarchy changed. The Hashemite house sided with the English in the Anglo-Iraqi war of that year and thus vitiated itself as a symbol of the nation in the eyes of the nationalists and the urban populace. Alienated from the bulk of the townsmen, the crown tied its fortunes more closely to those of the English and the tribal shaykhs and thus developed a living interest in the continuance not only of the English connection but also of the tribal order. Moreover, the crown allowed more and more of the customary tribal land and of the best state land to pass into the exclusive possession of the shaykhs. By thus increasing their essentially nonproductive grasp over agriculture and at the same time keeping their villages barren of governmental controls, the monarchy enabled the shaykhs to weigh more and more heavily on the peasantry. The shaykhs began to symbolize the extreme economic inequality that, by the last decade of the monarchy, was hindering, even more than tribalism, the integration of the community and the inclusion of the Shi'i and Sunni peasants within the purview of national life.

In other words, the monarchy ceased in effect to play a unifying social role, even though it continued, through the sharp increase in oil production, the proliferation of roads, the building of dams and reservoirs, and the expansion of the security services and the governmental apparatus, to add to the material factors making for a consolidated and more powerful state.

Under the monarchy there were other significant developments which, irrespective of the crown's own intentions, had the cumulative effect of enhancing the potential importance of the Shi'a and simultaneously decreasing their religious sense and assisting the process of their incorporation into society.

For one thing, Shi'i urban and tribal families in the upper income brackets amassed considerable economic power. Related to this was the rise of the Shi'i merchants to first place in the trade of Baghdad after the exodus of the Jews in 1949. In fiscal 1935 the Shi'i merchants had only two out of the eighteen seats on the Administrative Committee of the Baghdad Chamber of Commerce, but in fiscal 1957 fourteen out of the eighteen seats belonged to them.[10] Access to state offices having been on the whole, at least in the past, comparatively more difficult for them than for urban Sunnis, many urban Shi'a had vigorously applied themselves to trade and thus came to excel in the art of buying and selling. Their material advance led to the enhancement of the role of their co-religionists in state affairs, which is, however, also explicable by their now higher educational qualifications. Thus, while in the first decade of the monarchy only 17.7 percent of the ministerial appointments went to the Shi'a, in the last decade of the monarchy their portion came to 34.7 percent.[11] But their role in the government was never conclusive.

One other development needs to be highlighted: the Shi'a who had been a majority in the country as a whole, became by the time of the 1958 Revolution a majority also in Baghdad (and are still preponderant there, if one does not count the 700,000 or so Egyptian laborers who have flowed into the capital and its outlying areas since 1973). The ascent of the Shi'a to a numerical superiority in Baghdad was the result of unprecedented migrations of peasant-tribesmen from the countryside, caused by the new attractions of city life, the wide income differentials between agricultural and urban laborers, the oppressiveness of the shaykhly system in the Shi'i provinces of Kut and 'Amara, and the drying up of river branches in the lower Tigris by dint of the rapid pump development in the regions of Kut and Baghdad.

These large-scale movements of peasants and the concomitant inflationary currents (generated by the scarcities of World War II and the oil boom of the 1950s) affected deeply the poorer urban laborers and brought them, along with a large number of the migrants, under the moral influence of the communists, who grew rapidly in numbers in the late 1940s and 1950s and penetrated so deeply among the Shi'a that numerous cells thrived in their name even in the holy city of Najaf, alarming the conservative Shi'i *'ulama*. Through their positions in the Communist Party, the Shi'a came to play a conspicuous role in the history of Iraq. In the revolutionary years 1958–59, when the communists were at the pinnacle of their influence, the Shi'a filled most of the crucial places in the party apparatus, including the office of first secretary and the posts of secretaries of Baghdad, the Mid-Euphrates Zone, the Peasants' Bureau, and the Military Organization of the party. Of course, the communist Shi'a acted as communists, but while they had become communists, they did not entirely cease to be Shi'a.

The weight of the Shi'a in the Ba'th Party was also considerable in the period from the founding of the party's Iraqi branch in 1952 to the collapse of the first Ba'th regime in November 1963. Out of the total of 52 members of the top Ba'th command in that period, 53.8 percent were Shi'a,[12] including Fu'ad al-Rikabi, the party's secretary from 1952 to 1959, and 'Ali Salih al-Sa'di, its secretary from 1960 to 1963. Incidentally, the latter is of Fayli extraction, Fayli being the appellation attached to Kurds who are Shi'a.

The spread of communist and Ba'thist secular values and ideas among the educated Shi'a and segments of the urban Shi'i populace naturally weakened the hold upon them of the old Shi'i beliefs and decreased their reverence for traditional usages and norms.

The 1958 Revolution initially reinforced this trend. It also advanced the process of the integration of the Shi'a into the body politic. First it brought peasants and townsmen — Shi'i and Sunni — under the same laws. Prior to 1958, the bulk of the country people came under the Tribal Disputes Regulations which had been promulgated by the English in 1918 and, on English insistence, made law of the land in the monarchic period. By abolishing the Tribal Disputes Regulations, the revolution brought the Shi'i and Sunni countryside within the purview of the national law. Moreover, the revolution strengthened the prospects of the meaningful association of Shi'i and Sunni peasants with the larger community by transforming many of them into landowners, aiding them, even if inadequately, with their cultivation, extending educational, electric, and health services to many of their villages, and breaking the social power of their paramount shaykhs.

But the revolution also signified the political dominance of army officers, which in effect meant the eventual rise to an advantaged position of the families from which most of the army officers stemmed — middle-class families who live in the Arab Sunni northern and northwestern provincial towns or who have relatively recently moved to Baghdad from these towns. But it was only after 1963 and the destruction of the regime of General 'Abd al-Karim Qasim that these families came to provide the main recruiting ground for the holders of positions of responsibility in the government and the army.

General Qasim was in a class of his own. He hailed from the south and was of mixed Sunni-Shi'i parentage, his father being Sunni Arab and his mother Fayli Kurd. He did not derive his support from the northern and northwestern officers but prevailed for a time by counterpoising against them and their nationalist allies the forces of the communists, relying primarily on the common soldiers, particularly in his own brigade, who by and large came from the ranks of the Shi'i poor.

The year 1963 was important for two other reasons. In that year much of the old cadre of the Communist Party was decimated by the Ba'thists. This led to its sharp decline which, in a sense, implied a decreased political role for the Shi'a. In the same year the Shi'a also lost their weight in the Ba'th Party, which previously had to a considerable extent the earmark of an authentic partnership between the Sunni and Shi'i "pan-Arab" youth. The proportion of Shi'a among the members of the Ba'th Command, which had been as high as 53.8 percent in the period 1952–63, dropped to as low as 5.7 percent in the period 1963–70.[13]

One of the causes of this remarkable decline was the severing from the Ba'th Party of many Shi'i Ba'thists because of the support they gave in November 1963 to the Ba'thist leader 'Ali Salih al-Sa'di in his dispute with the party's military wing. But the principal reason for the decline in the significance of the Shi'i Ba'thists lay in the discriminatory practices of the political police. After the 1963 coup by 'Abd al-Salam 'Arif, they were on the whole more harassed than their Sunni comrades and, when captured, treated with harshness, whereas the latter frequently received light sentences. This enabled Sunnis to take the helm in the Ba'th underground. The explanation for the behavior of the police is to be sought not so much in sectarian prejudice as in the fact that Sunni Ba'thists were often from the same town or province or tribe as the members of the police, for the departments of interior and security teemed with functionaries from the northern and northwestern provinces from which many of the Sunni Ba'thists also hailed.

All these happenings increased the susceptibility of disadvantaged Shi'a to the ideas of the Da'wa, a fundamentalist Shi'i party that became active in the late 1960s. Led by Shi'i *ulama* of intermediate rank, the Da'wa gathered strength during the drought that struck Shi'i areas in the mid-1970s in the wake of the building of the Syrian dam at Tabqa and the attendant reduction of the flow of the Euphrates River. The drought ruined fruit orchards and the rice crop, affecting hundreds of thousands of Shi'i peasants. The Iranian Revolution of 1978–79 gave the Da'wa a further impetus and radicalized its methods of struggle.[14]

The Ba'th government, which came to power in 1968, reacted swiftly and forcefully to the Da'wa's militancy. Its chief figure, Saddam Husayn, pursued two tactics. With one hand he violently suppressed the followers of the Da'wa, and with the other offered rewards to the Shi'i *ulama*, spending millions of dinars on shrines, mosques, and other affairs of religion. By the time of the outbreak of hostilities between Iraq and Iran, he had succeeded in decisively weakening the Da'wa.

Moreover, Saddam Husayn, who does not think in sectarian

terms, went out of his way to recruit Shi'a into the Ba'th Party and to associate them with his regime. In fact, there are now many Shi'a in the party's lower and middle ranks. But they are thinly represented where it matters. From 1968 to 1977 there was not a single Shi'i member of the Revolutionary Command Council, which is the highest policy-making body. From 1977 to 1979 only three Shi'a sat on the council, which then counted twenty-two members. At present there are two Shi'a out of a total of nine members. Out of the fifteen members of the Ba'th Party Command, however, four are Shi'a. But it must be emphasized that, unlike the Shi'i Ba'thists of the pre-1963 period, the Shi'a now prominent in the regime and the party have no power base of their own. Their influence is not fundamental but springs from their relationship or loyalty to Saddam Husayn. This is, however, also true of the Sunni members of the Revolutionary Command Council and the Party Command. In other words, the lack of any genuine participation by Shi'a in the political process is a consequence of the absolute power of Saddam Husayn.

This carries the seeds of potential trouble for Iraq's ruler and might lead to a revival of the Da'wa Party and of political Shi'ism, if Iraq suffers a decisive defeat at the hands of Iran or if the continuing military impasse between the two countries weakens qualitatively the economic and political capacities of the regime.

Notes

1. For the text of the constitution, see Great Britain, *Reports of Administration for 1918 of Divisions and Districts of the Occupied Territories of Mesopotamia* (1919), 1:111. For excerpts from the constitution, consult Hanna Batatu, *The Social Classes and the Revolutionary Movements of Iraq* (Princeton, NJ: Princeton University Press, 1978), pp. 19–20.

2. Batatu, *The Old Social Classes*, pp. 174–75.

3. For this and for the factors accounting for the paucity of religious institutions in the Shi'i countryside, see Hanna Batatu, "Iraq's Underground Shi'i Movements: Characteristics, Causes, and Prospects," *The Middle East Journal* XXXV, No. 4 (Autumn 1981): 582–84.

4. The *husayniyya* is the place where Shi'a gather, especially in the month of Muharram, to commemorate and lament the martyrdom of Husayn.

5. See Ahmad al-Katib, *Tajribat al-thawra al-Islamiyya fi al-'Iraq* (The Experience of the Islamic Revolution in Iraq) (Teheran: 1981), pp. 100–101.

6. See Batatu, *The Old Social Classes*, pp. 244ff.

7. Ibid., pp. 294–97.

8. For the text of the memorandum, which was written in March 1933, see 'Abd al-Razzaq al-Hasani, *Tarikh al-wizarat al-'Iraqiyya* (The History of the Iraqi Cabinets) (Sidon: 1953), 3: 286–93.

9. Ibid., p. 290.
10. Batatu, *The Old Social Classes*, p. 271.
11. Ibid., p. 47.
12. Ibid., p. 1080.
13. Ibid.
14. For a detailed treatment of the Da'wa, see Batatu, "Iraq's Underground Shi'i Movements," pp. 578–94.

PART II: NORMATIVE AND REFORMIST ANALYSES

15 ISLAM FINDS ITSELF

Habib Chatty

Over the past few years, the West has been surprised and somewhat disturbed to discover the importance of Islam in today's world. On the ideological level, Islam has proven to be a strong mobilizing force. Suddenly, the searchlights of the Western media focused on "the awakening of Islam" and there was much talk about the effects of this awakening on the world balance of power. Old fears buried in the collective subconscious of the West suddenly emerged, and old recipes were brought out to ward them off. Trivial events of limited regional scope would be used by the media as the basis for attacks on the entire body of Islam, as though excesses and flaws existed nowhere else. Thus, the entrance of Islam on the political scene, not only as a powerful demographic entity liberated from colonial shackles but also as a system of original thought capable of meeting the challenges and aspirations of modern times, got a mixed reception. To understand this phenomenon, we must first examine the past.

Ebb and Flow

From the eighth to the twelfth century, the civilization most brilliant in all fields of science, letters, and art drew on Islam for its inspiration and dynamism. Many of the world's major population, economic, and intellectual centers were then to be found on Islamic land: e.g., Baghdad, Damascus, Cairo, Kairouan, Fez, Cordoba, and Toledo. Later, Europe drew on the Islamic heritage for certain elements of its Renaissance to an extent that is not yet sufficiently known or acknowledged, notwithstanding good contemporary studies by such Western authors as Joseph Schacht, C.E. Bosworth, and W. Montgomery Watt. Roger Garaudy has underscored the West's unwillingness to acknowledge this debt. "The West," he wrote, "for thirteen centuries, has refused this third heritage, i.e. the Arab-Islamic heritage."[1] Such refusal has deprived our two civilizations of a bridge that could have been a privileged place for communication and rapprochement.

One of the reasons for this refusal lies in the triumphant attitude of the West in the face of Islamic civilization's gradual decline. After being for a long time the main source of enrichment for world civilization thanks to its countless scientists and thinkers, the Islamic world became worn out by endless internal quarrels, a lack of political leadership, and a steady loss of interest in learning and science. Having lost their passion for research and *ijtihad* (interpretation and exegesis of Qur'anic precepts) and having been weakened by devastating Mongol attacks from the East and by the Crusades from the West, Muslims slid more and more into the depths of ritualism, and huddled together in a kind of hibernation, something which contributed to ignorance of each other on the part of the Islamic peoples and the rest of the world. Then came the colonial phenomenon, with the sharing out of the spoils of Islam. How, in this context, could a certain overpositivistic and overscientific Western erudition resist the temptation to belittle Islamic civilization?

An uncompromising spokesman for this point of view was Ernest Renan. In his inaugural lecture at the College de France in 1862, he decreed: "Islam is fanaticism . . ., Islam is the contempt of science, the abolition of civil society, it is the appalling simplicity of the Semitic mind, which shrinks the human brain and closes it to every refined idea, every delicate feeling, every rational research, in order to put it in the service of the perpetual tautology: God is God." Renan went on to predict the end of Islam "when the last son of Ismael has died of destitution or is banished by terror to the bottom of the desert."[2] Renan repeated the same themes in his famous 1883 lecture at the Sorbonne on "Islamism and Science." But this prediction, which a certain policy had tried to make a reality, did not materialize. Islam has been able to take up the challenge. However, let us not take offense. The quotation is only meant to show the abysmal depth to which Islam had been pushed just a century ago.

What Renan did not say is that Islam, as a religion and a model for society and human relations, cannot be blamed for the Muslims' decline, for if it was responsible for the decline, to what could one attribute the extraordinary cultural splendor that had formerly prevailed in the Arab-Islamic world at a time when the West was plunged into the darkness of ignorance? Therefore, the long lethargy of the Islamic world must be attributed not to Islam as such but to Muslims themselves, to their rifts and their departure from the stimulating model of Islam, as well as to the external factors outlined above.

Islam Under Colonialism

The final end of the colonial period did not come until the middle of this century. To a greater or lesser extent, all Islamic countries were subjected to foreign occupation and to humiliation. To territorial aggression was added a more subtle and more pernicious type of aggression whose purpose was to alienate colonized peoples through deculturization. The Muslim religion, as the most powerful element of identification, was among the favorite targets.

At the close of the first quarter of the twentieth century, the Swedish writer Tor Andrae, whose book was translated into French under the title *Les origines de l'Islam et le Christianisme* (Islam's Origins and Christianity)[3] used the paraphernalia of modern scientism to prove that Islam is but a borrowing from Eastern Christian tradition, or indeed a crude or deceitful plagiarism. What he carefully avoided saying was that Islam cannot fail to include the principal Christian and Judaic traditions since it is both the synthesis and the last of the revealed religions in the lineage of Abraham. Thus, similarities that are natural signs of the continuity and unity of the message of Abraham were misrepresented as indications of plagiarism. David Sidersky's book, *The Origins of Islamic Legends in the Qur'an and in the Lives of the Prophets*, published in Paris in 1933, is written in the same vein. More recently still, Father Gabriel Théry, who used the pseudonym Hanna Zacharias, in four volumes entitled *From Moses to Mohammad*, tried to make the reader discover in Islam a Jewish undertaking. His disciple, Father Joseph Bertuel, took up the same theme in a quite recent book prefaced by Admiral Gabriel Adrien Joseph (Paul) Auphan and written for a large readership: *Islam, Its True Origins*. Similar notions inspired two celebrated Soviet Orientalists, S.P. Tolstov and E.A. Belayev. Many more examples may be quoted. A title which needs no comment is *Hagarism, the Making of the Islamic World*, by Patricia Crone and Michael Cook. Let us finally quote these few lines which serve as a conclusion to a book by an eminent modern Orientalist, Dominique Sourdel, who wonders "whether there is or not an Islamic thought, an Islamic culture, an Islamic art, an Islamic social order, an Islamic political order, an Islamic economy, an Islamic civilization"![4]

Thus, by downgrading Islam and giving it a sense of guilt and an inferiority complex, scientism helped justify and complete in-depth colonization. Such was the situation of Islam until the middle of this century and, even now, such notions persist in some current and very scholarly written words and, naturally enough, in the Western media. Edith Delamare wrote in frustration in *Rivarol*: "The resurgence of Islam is one of the phenomena of our time. In France, it is, numerically, the second religion. In Africa, it is gradually supplanting Christianity. In Asia, and particularly in India, it is gradually gaining ground on traditional religions. Everywhere, it tends to destabilize states thus benefiting Moscow."[5] The dynamism and growing importance of Islam on the political scene are thus perceived as a threat.

We will not dwell on the accusation that Islam serves Moscow's interests because it is so remote from reality. The fact that Islam is supplanting Christianity in some parts of the world and gaining ground on traditional religions cannot be construed as a subversive factor. People in the Third World are attracted to Islam, whose advance is not due to force but to spontaneous conversion. In this regard, should we consider Christian missionary activities in Africa, Asia, and in Islamic countries as subversive? If they are not, how could the accusation be leveled at Islam, which does not have such an organized movement as the missionaries? Indeed, we should not mistake the awakening of a community of a billion people (which had long been dominated and humiliated and which is recovering its identity, its rights, and its position among other world communities) for warlike intentions against the rest of the world. Such groundless charges are inadmissible in our age when the quest for truth and justice is shared by all those who intend to work for peace among the peoples of the globe. But the existence of these denunciations must be taken into account if one is to understand the reactions currently evolving in Islamic countries that have just come out of the alienating hegemony of the West.

Islam's Resurgence

The Islamic renaissance began in the seventeenth century, and the nineteenth century witnessed an increasingly active movement specifically aimed at the modernization of political institutions, the reorganization of armies, the restructuring of economies, and, above all, the reassertion of the value of the Arab-Islamic culture as the main guarantee against depersonalization. Among the best-known architects of the recovery were Jamal al-Din al-Afghani, Muhammad 'Abduh, Rashid Rida, the Indian scholar Sayyid Ahmad Khan, Khayr al-Din of Tunisia, Ibn Badis of Algeria, Muhammad Iqbal of Pakistan, and Taha Husayn of Egypt. Thanks to the return to basic traditional values advocated by Salafi reformism as well as the modernism of Western-educated academics, Islam succeeded in escaping the disaster and death that had been cheerfully predicted by some of its detractors. Today it is finding its dynamism again and no longer suffers from an inferiority complex.

It should be emphasized that no overall judgment can be passed on Orientalism; its work was very often positive and greatly contributed (in many ways, including its critical approach) to the resurgence of Islamic civilization. Among the architects of the *nahda*, many were trained in the school of Orientalism. One example will suffice. In the list of works about Ibn Khaldun, which contains hundreds of titles,[6] works in Western languages constitute a very clear majority; such books conveyed the genius of Islamic civilization to the rest of the world.

We do not dispute the freedom of interpretation, including the freedom to commit honest mistakes, for freedom is a necessary condition for any sincere and serious research. Bernard Lewis[7] correctly observes that Islam, like Hellenism, belongs to universal civilization and, not being the exclusive property of its followers, constitutes a field of study open to everyone. Furthermore, epistemological diversity is necessary and enriching. We only claim the same freedom for ourselves, including the freedom to contest certain results and certain postulates of Orientalism. Islam is no longer what it was in the nineteenth century. It is no longer a passive object of study. Henceforth, it is a full-fledged partner. In this context, *Orientalism*, by the Palestinian scholar Edward W. Said, which caused a storm of praise and refutation, must be understood, beyond its shortcomings and its often unsubtle, abrupt, and polemic tone, as an attempt to break "this fabric which racism, cultural stereotypes, political imperialism and dehumanizing ideology are continually weaving around the Arab or the Muslim person: a stifling fabric that Palestinians in particular feel as their own expiatory destiny."[8]

Henceforth, on the cultural plane and in all other fields, Islam means to assume fully its civilization and its destiny. This was very well perceived by P.E. Kemp, who wrote: "Over the past three or four decades, Orientalists — among others — had to get used to the idea that Orientals demanded participation in the determination of their own destiny. And over the past few years, Orientalists — among others — have had to put up with an even more traumatizing upheaval which consists in realizing that 'Oriental' researchers want to contribute to the modelling of their own past."[9] Thus, thanks to its cultural recovery, based on its numerous elites in all fields of learning and often in high quality universities, Islam, consistent with its age-old tradition, is today fully able to play its role, as Mohammad Arkoun put it, "in the redistribution of ethical and cognitive values."[10]

A recovery has also begun on the economic plane, but Islam still faces struggles in this area. Islam is not self-sufficient in terms of food products nor has it adequately mastered a technology that is rapidly changing and increasingly complex. However, Islam is not without assets. It possesses raw materials — capital and brains as well as oil. It also realizes the importance of the challenges it faces and, notwithstanding some internal tremors, it is organizing itself accordingly. The next stage of its recovery on the international scene will necessarily involve the development of its economic potentialities, which are real and which represent an element of hope for the future.

On the political level, Islam benefits from the progress achieved in the sociocultural and economic fields, and is engaged in the same battle as the rest of the Third World — a battle for dignity, peace, and justice for everyone. The Islamic countries, about forty in number, actively participate in all international organizations and sometimes constitute a key factor in the decision-making process, although major choices are still the exclusive responsibility of a few nations which, alone, possess more than half the world's resources. Beyond any shadow of doubt, this serious imbalance constitutes the gravest threat to mankind. There will be no peace or security for anyone as long as entire peoples are living below minimum acceptable standards.

All the efforts of Islam are directed toward a reduction of disparities and a better distribution of responsibilities within a new and more equitable world order, the only true guarantee of stability and progress for all.

To live up to these principles, Islam can use its demographic weight and the increasingly favorable reception accorded to its message and ethical values thanks to its ongoing revival. Indeed, Islam today is constantly progressing, which proves its attraction and dynamism, and is gaining ground even among Western intellectuals. With regard to demographic growth (which is not problem-free) the number of Muslims has increased from an estimated 365 million in 1954[11] to an estimated 800 million at present. Of these, forty million are Chinese and fifty million are Soviet citizens. On the latter, who are often forgotten, Michel Lelong has very rightly commented:

> Right inside the border of the vast Soviet Union, Islam is a human, cultural, and spiritual reality with which the U.S.S.R.'s leaders must reckon more and more both at present and in the future. There are currently 50 million Muslims in Soviet Russia and they will soon be 80 million. Their coherent bloc unites more than one-fifth of the country's total population within a community which certainly intends to abide by its faith, history, culture, and traditions. In the Daghestan as in Tashkent, whether in the city or in the country, Muslims are asserting themselves as such.[12]

This Islam, which intends to remain faithful to its traditions so as better to convey its message and values and thus provide a possible alternative to the challenges of modern times and to the crises of certain ideologies, is organizing itself through a number of institutions which serve as a forum for reflection, concentration, and awakening of the masses to their cultural Islamic identity. These include the Arab League (established in 1945), the World Islamic Congress (established in 1926), the World Islamic League (established in 1962), and the Organization of the Islamic Conference (OIC), which was established in 1969 following the criminal arson of Al-Aqsa Mosque which brought home to all the Islamic countries the extent of the peril to which their most sacred heritage is exposed. The OIC, whose secretary-general I have the honor to be, performs its activities on both the national Islamic and the international scenes. Accordingly, while its priority objective is to develop solidarity between Islamic peoples with a view to reinforcing their ranks and their potentialities, it attaches no lesser importance to its international activities whose object is to develop friendly and cooperative relations with other world communities. Thus, we are anxious to open a fruitful dialogue with all those working for friendship and cooperation between peoples as well as for world peace.

One of our main objectives is to liberate occupied Arab territories and to seek a solution that would restore peace in the Middle East and would necessarily include a settlement of the Palestinian problem and the safeguarding of Jerusalem as the common heritage of Jews, Christians, Muslims, and indeed of the entire world. Wounded by the Palestinian tragedy, which is hampering its efforts for advancement and development, Islam has long appealed to the international community to work for a peaceful settlement to this painful conflict. Such a solution, based on dialogue and the respect of the legitimate rights of all concerned, would release all available resources for peaceful and productive uses.

The growing importance of Islam in the cultural, ethical, economic, social, and political fields is one of the most positive developments of our time. It restores to humanity an essential dimension and in doing so constitutes a further guarantee of success for the planetary effort now taking place before our eyes to define "a new human project." Since Vatican II, Islam has been conducting a constructive and fraternal dialogue with Christianity in order to substitute for the old sterile and outdated polemics (even if these are draped into the majestic folds of an arrogant scientism that does not fool anybody) a healthy and fruitful competition in the service of justice and peace.

Decolonized, renovated, and complex-free, Islam is today in a position to play its thousand-year-old role and also to be more appreciated and better understood. Within two decades, the world is expected to contain more than six billion people. In this era of computer science, satellites, space shuttles, and teleconferencing, will there still be separate destinies? We are all aboard a space vessel, a vessel that sometimes pitches and tosses dangerously. Let us watch out! If it capsizes, we shall all sink. There will be no survivors. Thus, parochialism and systematic denigration will no longer pay. On our vessel, no civilization will be dismissed as second-rate. An African politician who is both wise and sensible has warned us that "twentieth century humanism can only be the civilization of the universal and [that] it would grow poorer if it were deprived of a single value from one people, from one race, from one continent."[13]

Notes

1. Roger Garaudy, *Promesse de l'Islam* (The Promise of Islam) (Paris: Seuil, 1981), p. 17.

2. Quotation borrowed from L. Gardet and Mohammad Arkoun, *L'Islam, Hier, Demain* (Islam, Today, Tomorrow) (Paris: Editions Buchet Chastel, 1978), pp. 95–96; see also V. Monteil, *Clefs pour la pensée arabe* (Keys to Arab Thought) (Paris: Editions Seghers, 1974), p. 203.

3. Tor Andrae, *Les Origines de L'Islam et le Christianisme* (Islam's Origins and Christianity) Trans. by J. Roche (Paris: Adrien Maisonneuve, 1955).

4. Dominique Sourdel, *L'Islam médiéval* (Medieval Islam) (Paris: Editions PUF, 1979), p. 216.

5. *Rivarol*, No. 29, (October 1981).

6. See bibliographies compiled by H. Peres, in *Studi Orientalistice in onore di Georgio Levi della Vida* (Orientalist Studies in Honor of Georgio Levi della Vida) (241 titles); W.J. Fischel, at the end of Vol. III of the English translation of the *Muqaddima* by F. Rosenthal (430 titles); A. Badawi, *Mu'allafat Ibn Khaldun* (The Works of Ibn Khaldun) (Cairo: 1962) (60 titles in Arabic and 214 in other languages); A. al-Dakhli, in *Al-hayat al-thaqafiyya* (The Cultural Life), No. 9 (Tunis, 1980) (329 titles, of which 176 are in Arabic).

7. Bernard Lewis, "The Question of Orientalism," *New York Review of Books*, June 24, 1982.

8. Edward W. Said, *Orientalism* (New York: Random House, 1978), p. 27.

9. P.E. Kemp, "Orientalistes éconduits, Orientalisme réconduit" (Orientalists Rejected, Orientalism Renewed), in *Arabica*, XXVII, fasc. 2 (Paris, 1980): 154.

10. M. Arkoun and L. Gardet, p. 195.

11. Louis Massignon, *Annuaire du Monde Musulman* (Directory of the Islamic World) 1954, revised and updated with the collaboration of Vincent Monteil (Paris: Presses Universitaires de France, 1954).

12. Michel Lelong, *L'Islam et l'Occident* (Islam and the West) (Paris: A. Michel, 1982), p. 39.

13. Quoted by Lelong, p. 23.

16 THE ISLAMIC CRITIQUE OF THE STATUS QUO OF MUSLIM SOCIETY

Isma'il Raji al Faruqi

The Sources

In the present generation, there is no single Islamic political thinker whose ideas have dominated the consciousness of Muslims around the world. Instead, that consciousness has been deeply affected by three leaders, each of whom has founded a movement. These three contenders are Abu al-'Ala' al-Mawdudi, Ruhallah al-Musawi al-Khomeini, and Hasan al-Banna.

Al-Mawdudi produced sixty-seven works, some of them monumental in length and depth, and edited two journals.[1] He founded the Jama'at-i Islami in 1941 and led it until 1972. His ideas unquestionably dominate Islamic political thinking in the Indo-Pakistani subcontinent. This has become all the more evident as Pakistani secular nationalism has scored one failure after another, and thereby removed itself from the growing surge of Islamic political thought and action. Al-Mawdudi's influence is limited outside of the subcontinent, however. Certainly, the man, his thought, and his movement are well known in all Islamic circles, but his dozen or more books[2] on Islamic politics have yet to become integral to Islamic political thinking worldwide. There are two reasons for this. First, al-Mawdudi's accomplishment has mostly remained bookish and scholarly; the Jama'at-i Islami has failed to achieve political victory or to transform a significant portion of the *umma* in Pakistan into agents of Islamic activism. Second, al-Mawdudi's thought does not go beyond the condemnation of the un-Islamic political status quo of the *umma*. It does not draw up an Islamic blueprint for the state, for the political and socioeconomic relations of the citizens. It does not translate the general principles into prescriptions for the programmatics of Islamic action, at least not in a way that goes beyond what is already known.

The second contender is Imam al-Khomeini. His case is the reverse of that of al-Mawdudi. As a professor of *kalam* (philosophy) and a thinker at Dar al-Tabligh University in Qum, he wrote little, but his leadership and organizational energies were inexhaustible.

His speeches, circulated secretly in taped cassettes, not only aroused and awakened his people, but inflamed and rallied them under the religious leaders to march against the "Shahanshah" and all that the monarchy stood for in one of this century's major upheavals. In the imagination of Muslims everywhere, Imam al-Khomeini has achieved towering status as the ideal *mujahid* against the overwhelming forces of evil. Moreover, Imam al-Khomeini's *wilayat al-faqih*, a series of lectures delivered at Najaf in 1979 in Arabic,[3] has been read by Islamic thinkers around the world, as have been (in English and/or Arabic translation) the scant works of 'Ali Shari'ati,[4] Abu al-Fadl 'Izzati,[5] and Murtada al-Mutabhari,[6] who also inspired and contributed to the Islamic revolution in Iran. However, there is little in these writings that Muslims do not already know. The idea of eliminating the political status quo and replacing it with an Islamic ideal through revolution is not only known to Muslims but has even been tried in many Muslim lands in the last hundred years. But since the days of Jamal al-Din al-Afghani there has been little discussion of the problem of preserving and developing the Islamicity of the revolution, of re-forming society and citizens so as to make the Islamic transfiguration workable and hence permanent. To be sure, the revolution in Iran is a source of tremendous pride and inspiration to Muslims everywhere. Because the status quo in most parts of the Muslim world is as unacceptable as that of pre-revolutionary Iran, the revolution is deemed by nearly everyone to be worthy of emulation. But the Iranian Revolution has so far shed little new light on what should be done *after* an Islamic revolution takes power.

The third contender is Hasan al-Banna and the movement he founded, al-Ikhwan al-Muslimun. This movement is proscribed everywhere in the Arab world except in Jordan and Sudan, where it is accorded some legitimacy on the basis of a precarious arrangement of mutual assistance between it and the government in order to avert the threat of radical Arab nationalists first, and Marxists second. Nonetheless, the movement still contains most of the intellectual and activist energies of the Islamic forces of the Arab world. Beside its classical thinkers and authors (Hasan al-Banna, Sayyid Qutb, 'Abd al-Qadir 'Awda, Sa'id Ramadan, Mustafa Mashhur, Mahmud Abu al-Su'ud, Mustafa al-Siba'i, Mustafa al-Zarqa, Muhammad al-Mubarak, Muhammad Nadim al-Jisr, etc.), a new generation has arisen to carry on the tradition of the movement. The amount, variety, and intensity of literature the movement has produced is tremendous by any standard.[7] In terms of action, the movement has not achieved any successes as spectacular as the Iranian Revolution, but it has had the experience of trying, failing, compromising, resisting, and cooperating in relation to government and society. In intellectual terms, the movement led Islamic activism in the Arab world, and it inspired other movements in many places. Nonetheless, a certain inadequacy has marked both its visions and its program of action, and this inadequacy may well have been the reason behind the Ikhwan's failure at home and failure to implant the movement throughout the Muslim world.

The three movements discussed thus far are not the only sources of contemporary Islamic thought. Indeed, the ideas stemming from these sources constitute little more than general or preliminary guidelines which Islamic thinkers learn and quickly transcend. Islamic thought is alive and intense among Islam's supporters, who have formed themselves into a kaleidoscope of local organizations and a number of national or international associations.[8] Their meetings, seminars, and conferences — whether at a local or world level — their newsletters, periodicals, books, and other publications constitute the sources of contemporary Islamic thought. It is a mighty river. Only a fraction of the thinking that takes place at Islamic meetings is printed, and only a fraction of what is printed is widely available, yet my university receives between 100 and 200 items of this literature every week of the year. Naturally, the material has little systematic order, and is extremely hard to classify. It is loaded with both repetitions of what has already been said and firsthand reports of brilliant intellectual breakthroughs. This chapter will focus on this material, however, because in my judgment it is the most representative of contemporary Islamic thinking. The job is difficult and hazardous; but the danger is more than offset by the excitement, dynamism, and challenge it presents to the observer.

To simplify the task, we shall classify the material under two categories: the criterion under which Islamic contemporary thought regards each issue considered here, and the judgment it pronounces on it. Our discussion of the former will inform the reader about the contemporary understanding of the norms of Islam, and our examination of the latter will reveal how the contemporary Islamic youthful adherent, professional, or thinker perceives the status quo. This approach will be applied to current Islamic thought about the fields relevant to politics and political legitimacy, namely government, the state, political structure, economic structure, sociocultural structure, and foreign relations.

The Critique: Government

Criterion

Contemporary Islamic thought understands Islam as prescribing, first, that government be by consultation: "Government [of the Muslims] is by consultation with one another" (Qur'an 42:38). The Prophet as chief of state was not absolved from this requirement, for the divine word commanded: "Consult them [the Muslims] in the affairs [of government]" (Qur'an 3:159). True, the form of consultation was not specified, and was left for Muslims to determine. But no Muslim may flout the command altogether, or assign to it a form that violates its substance by rendering it ineffective. Throughout the whole range of contemporary Islamic thinking, hardly an article or essay on politics does not invoke the two verses of the Qur'an mentioned above.

Second, Islam is seen as prescribing that government must be by the more competent, the more fit to rule. This norm is derived from the following *hadith*: "Whoever exercises power over Muslim affairs and appoints a person to a post while finding another who is more competent has committed treason to Allah and His Prophet." The Sunna has defined the traits of a competent ruler as consisting of firm *iman* (faith) and a clear vision of Islam, trustworthiness with respect to the people, and initiative and leadership to bring about the good and prevent the evil. Of government, the Prophet said: "It is a trust; and, on the Day of Judgment, a cause for shame and contrition, except to those who assume its duties with righteousness and fulfill well all the tasks it implies." For the contemporary Muslim, then, government is an awesome responsibility, certainly noble but fraught with dangers.

Application

As regards government, there is a worldwide consensus among Muslims that only two countries in the Muslim world have governments that may be called Islamically legitimate: Malaysia and Iran. The former possesses an electoral system that has not been violated since the country's foundation. It has put in power the United

Malaysian National Organization (UMNO), a union of Malays and a cooperative majority of the minorities (mostly Chinese and a few Indians) committed to work for the national welfare. Nobody has accused anybody else of tampering with the voting process, in which both the Muslim Youth and the Islamic Party participate. Thus the federal government is truly representative. Equally, there can be no doubt of the truly representative nature of the present Iranian government, for it was brought to power by the will of the people, a will expressed both by the recent revolution in which the overwhelming majority of Iranians participated and by honest elections. Not one of the Arab or other Muslim countries has done as well today. Every one of them is a police state where there are either no elections at all or elections in which the results are ridiculously unrepresentative.

Moreover, the consensus of the contemporary Islamic literature is that hardly any Muslim government leader today satisfies the requisites of competence, except in Malaysia and Iran. In Islamic meetings, it is common practice to ridicule the political leadership of most Muslim states by repeating, ad nauseam, their bunglings on every front of public life. Most of the political leaders of the Muslim world retain power by force of arms, thus proving their untrustworthiness as far as their own subjects are concerned. As for the qualities of *iman* and clear vision, of knowledge and leadership, the shortage is evident: today's leaders range from military people with little more than a high school education to royalty with little more than an elementary education, all betraying crass ignorance of the vision of Islam and the *shari'a*.[9]

The Critique: The State

Criterion

The Islamically committed are unanimous in believing that the relevance of their faith to the state consists of two prescriptions: universalism and sovereignty of the *shari'a*. The first is taken to mean that the state ought to be universal, if not in actuality, then in potentiality and tendency. No committed Muslim has ever agreed to any regional unity (the Nile Valley, the Maghrib, Greater Syria, the Fertile Crescent, the Arabian Peninsula) except as a first step and instrument to a greater unity of all Muslims. Until such unity is achieved, they maintain, every Muslim state should be organically related to the other states, so as to cooperate with them for the good of all Muslims. They never tire of quoting the following Qur'anic verses: "The believers are all brothers of one another" (49:10); "[The believers are so close to one another that] they issue from one another" (9:68); "This *umma* of yours is indeed a single *umma* and I alone am your Lord. Serve Me, therefore" (21:93); "cooperate [with one another] for the good, and in righteousness" (5:3); "And hold fast to the rope of Allah and never separate" (3:103); "Your *umma* is indeed the best *umma* given to humanity" (3:110); and "Enter and join the peace [of Islam] all together" (2:208).

Today's Muslim thinkers continuously exhort all Muslims to obey the commands and fulfill the ideal unity of the Muslim world. They point to the regional and intercontinental economic, cultural, political, and military unions taking place around the world and argue that the Muslim peoples ought to do at least as much. They are not impressed by inter-Muslim tensions and conflicts, which they maintain are all instigated or encouraged by external imperialist enemies. Islam, they hold, provides the ideal solution. Wherever conflict arises between any two states or groups, the *shari'a* directs all Muslims to rise and act jointly to end the conflict, to reconcile the parties in justice, and to fight and subdue the recalcitrant party (Qur'an 19:9–10). Even if, because of presently insurmountable difficulties, the Muslims do exist in multiple Islamic states for the time being, the *shari'a* requires their participation in a universal *Pax Islamica*, an Islamic order or organization institutionalizing and implementing the divine precepts.

The second prescription of Islam seen as relevant to politics and state legitimacy is the sovereignty of the *shari'a*. The Islamically committed are as unanimous on this point as on the first. The requirement that Islamic law be the law of the land is absolute and permits no compromise. For a country with a Muslim majority to have any other law is for the committed Muslim a tragic aberration, an evil that must be removed. Again, the imperative to order one's life according to the *shari'a* is divine, and hence indisputable. Islamic workers remind one another continuously of the relevant Qur'anic verses and raise them as mottos on their banners: "We have established a law for you pertinent to all matters. Observe it" (45:17); "Judge therefore between them by what Allah has revealed" (5:48); "Judgment belongs exclusively to Allah" (6:57, 12:67); "What? Shall I seek any judgment other than Allah's?" (6:114); "Allah has revealed for them the Book in truth that they may adjudicate between the people [by its verdicts]" (2:213). The Islamic state, they argue, is not Islamic by virtue of all its citizens being Muslims, for this has hardly ever existed anywhere. Nor would it be Islamic by the fact that its rulers are Muslims, or because it follows the monarchical or republican form of government, or even by including all the Muslims of the world within its borders. The ultimate criterion, the necessary condition of state Islamicity, is the sovereignty and implementation of the *shari'a* in its entirety. The Islamic state is therefore a genuine nomocracy upholding the *shari'a*, or it does not exist at all.

Application

There is little disagreement among the Islamically committed as to the validity of the assertion that no Muslim state possesses complete Islamic legitimacy. Even though most Muslim lands have been purged of colonial occupation, they stand today as nation-states, dedicated to national welfare and guided by laws of territorialism. Citizenship is restricted to the native, and the native is not free to move and reside where he pleases. Despite Islam's principles that the house of Islam is one, open to any Muslim to inhabit, traverse, or leave, that Muslims should receive one another with open arms, Muslim countries today shut one another out and make Islamic brotherhood a farce. The richer countries have enacted citizenship and entry-exit rules that would make the most racist states of the world blush in shame. Observant Islamic workers throughout the world point to the fact that "Egyptianization" was acceptable as long as it was directed against the colonialist foreigner. Later, however, Libyanization, Kuwaitization, Saudization, Pakistaniza-tion, Malayanization, and so forth militated against and were meant to shut out other Muslims. Diplomatic and military conflicts between Muslim states have been tearing up the Muslim world without anyone being able to settle them or bring the parties to their senses. Likewise, despite the tremendous popularity of the goals of unity and cooperation, no Muslim states have been able to carry out jointly any significant permanent project. The Organization of the Islamic Conference, the only Islamic interstate organization with any clout at all, is still largely an impotent agency. Even such nonpolitical associations as the Union of Islamic Universities or the Muslim States Science and Technology Authority remain devoid of funds or productivity, or both.

As regards the second prescription for state legitimacy, namely the sovereignty of the *shari'a*, the dominant judgment of contemporary thinkers is that the *shari'a* is not sovereign in its entirety in any country at this time. Some states like Turkey have avowedly repudiated the *shari'a* altogether, and have adopted non-Islamic legal systems in toto. Others, like Pakistan, continue to keep in force laws inherited from colonial regimes such as the ordinances relating to public order. Others, like Egypt and Jordan, have constitutions that declare that the *shari'a* is source and inspiration for all legislation, but enforce un-Islamic laws or decrees in areas such as contracts, torts, and criminal law (for example, laws pertaining to private property, alcohol, or interest). Still others, like Saudi Arabia and the peninsular Emirates, have constitutions that affirm the *shari'a* to be indeed the sovereign law of the land, but permit practices that violate the spirit of the *shari'a* (for example, royal privilege, un-Islamic banking, discrimination among Muslims, and appropriation of public funds [belonging to the *umma*]).

In the fields of immigration and naturalization, of *dhimmis* (non-Muslims who have covenanted with the Islamic state to live under its protection), of foreign relations — with regard to these matters, all states have enacted laws that violate both the letter and the spirit of the *shari'a*. These violations of the *shari'a* by the Muslim states have produced, in the minds and hearts of the Islamically committed as well as the Muslim masses at large, a tremendous resentment which will sooner or later explode into violence.

Political Structure

Criterion

All humans, Islam affirms, are born free. The Prophet proclaimed, "All humans are born free," and 'Umar ibn al-Khattab chastised his provincial governors, "How did you come to tyrannize over the people when God caused them to emerge from their mothers' wombs free persons?" No ruler may deny the people their freedom, whether religious, cultural, social, economic, or political. Their right to bodily safety and private property, to associate with one another, to practice their faith, to perpetuate their culture, and to express themselves is sacrosanct under the *shari'a*. In this the *shari'a* does not discriminate between Muslim and non-Muslim. All people are equal before it. Indeed, it lends its unrestricted support to the victim of breaches of the above freedoms; it entitles such a victim to resist and imposes upon all Muslims the obligation to assist the victim in the struggle and to vindicate the right that has been violated: "And to whosoever rises in opposition to injustice there is to be no blame" (Qur'an 22:41). The basis for this egalitarianism is the equal creatureliness of all humans before God, their One and Only Creator, Who said: "O People! We have created you all of a single pair — a male and a female — and We have constituted you into tribes and nations for the purpose of identification. Nobler among you is the more righteous" (Qur'an 49:3). And the Prophet declared in his farewell address: "All of you stem from Adam and Adam stemmed from dust. Know that no Arab has any priority over a non-Arab, a non-Arab over an Arab, a white person over a black person, a black person over a white person, except in the degree of righteousness." It is men's deeds and accomplishments in knowledge, piety, and virtue which distinguish them, not their birth, color, class, wealth, or citizenship. Moreover, the *shari'a* presumes any person innocent until proven guilty in a court of law, and it entitles every person accused of anything to a fair trial under the *shari'a* or his own traditional law. As to the political process, personal participation in it is in Islam not only a universal right, but a personal duty incumbent upon all resident adults. All residents of the Islamic state are obliged to obey the government, but only so long as its orders accord with the *shari'a*. As Abu Bakr, the first caliph, counseled the Muslims upon his election to the caliphate: "Obey me as long as I obey Allah and His Prophet . . . No obedience is due to the ruler which consists of disobedience to Allah." Finally, Islam denies any vicarious guilt or credit, reward or punishment. In His Holy Book, God said: "Allah does not hold a person responsible but for that of which that person is capable. To everyone belongs what he himself has earned, whether good or evil" (2:286); "No person may be responsible for the burden of another" (53:38); "Every person is subject to the merit or demerit which he has acquired [by his deeds]" (52:21). These and many quotations like them from the Qur'an and Sunna constitute the bases on which the critique of political structures in the Muslim world is made. From them, Islamic thinkers, workers, and committed professionals deduce the ideals of political organization. Personal and group liberty, private property, security, privacy, peaceful dissent, equality before the law, presumption of innocence in all, participation in the political process — all these are basic rights which, the

Muslim believes, belong to all humans as humans. Every Islamic association or movement has declared its subscription to them, its promotion of them as the necessary and inviolable rights of all, for they are sacrosanct in the *shari'a*. The rights of the non-Muslim are protected by the *shari'a* in no uncertain terms. The Prophet himself, the Hadith reports, will on the Day of Judgment be the prosecutor of those who violated any of these rights. The loftiness of the political ideals of Islam gives committed Muslims great cause for pride, which is evident on every page of their literature.

Application

Islamically committed writers and workers measure the performance of Muslim states by the above-mentioned norms and find nearly all Muslim states wanting. There is no disputing the fact that today the overwhelming majority of Muslims live in police states that deny them their basic human rights. Neither in the lands of the Nile Valley nor in those of the Maghrib, the Peninsula, Western Sudan (the Islamic collective name for the Muslim lands of West Africa), the Fertile Crescent, the Indo-Pakistani subcontinent, or Southeast Asia do Muslims enjoy the freedom to associate, to form parties, to participate freely in the political processes of their countries. The ban against political activity is ubiquitously enforced in the Muslim world. Where it was imposed years ago by the colonialist administration, it is still alive, with all its sinister provisions still in the same English or French terms in which it was couched by the colonialists. In this, the Muslim states are one with Israel, where the security ordinances of the British mandate continue to be operative against the Arab residents, whether Muslim or non-Muslim. In Iraq, Syria, Jordan, Egypt, Sudan, Libya, Algeria, Morocco, and the Peninsula, as well as in other Muslim lands, no one is free to engage in political activity critical of the government and its policies. By means subtle or otherwise against which the citizen has no recourse, dissenting individuals or groups, along with relatives and associates, are discouraged and silenced, threatened or punished. The mass murders in Syria, the arrests and shootouts in Egypt under Abdel Nasser and Sadat, the systematic destruction of whole villages and their inhabitants in Iraq, the hot pursuit of dissident Syrians and Libyans around the globe, and much more — these examples are symptoms of serious sickness in the political systems of most Muslim countries.

Economic Structure

Criterion

Being a comprehensive religion, Islam is as relevant to the economic structure of society as it is to its religious, ethical, and political structure. To emphasize this aspect of Islam, Muslims are fond of recalling the Qur'an's specific injunctions against *riba* (interest),[10] cheating in business,[11] breach of contract,[12] hoarding,[13] and theft,[14] as well as its promotion of *zakat* or *sadaqa*[15] of justice and equity,[16] of the writing down and fulfillment of agreements,[17] and of concern for the deprived.[18] The Qur'an's general statements regarding economic life, namely that God planted man on earth to colonize it,[19] that He made creation subservient to man,[20] that He filled it out with His bounty of useful provisions and objects of beauty[21] — indeed, that He created life and death to the end of giving man occasion to prove his moral worth in his usufruct and enjoyment of creation[22] — are equally in the background of every Islamic economic discussion. Basing themselves on these ideals, the Islamically committed regard man as a steward of creation and wealth and believe that his usufruct of same ought to comply with the divine injunctions. Certainly, the bounty of the world is his to acquire, but in honesty, not fraud. It is his to keep, but without injury to others; and his to enjoy, provided he shares it with the destitute. It may not be taken away from him except for due cause under the *shari'a*. In their view, Islam's economic ideal was realized in yesteryear under 'Umar ibn 'Abd al-'Aziz, the Umayyad caliph (717–720), when everybody was contented enough to reject any portion of the *zakat* funds offered to him. In today's world, the bounty is not less, but more. If it appears to be beyond the reach of the majority, the Islamically committed thinker concludes with certainty that this must be due to the mismanagement of economic resources and a bad distribution of wealth — in short, to the Muslim states' departure from and violation of Islam's imperatives. Wealth, resources, and manpower are obviously present in abundance. Knowledge and technology are also present; not with equal conspicuousness, perhaps, but they are attainable by those who seek them in earnest. If in the Muslim world knowledge and technology seem to be in short supply, that is again due to misman-agement — but in this case of human resources.

Application

Measured by the criteria of Islam, the present economic situation of the Muslim world is found by the Islamic movement everywhere to be pitiable. Within the Arab world, a few thousand families own and control the wealth of 150 million people. The percentage is even worse in the Muslim world as a whole. Millions of Filipinos, Indonesians, Indians, Afghans, Egyptians, Sudanese, and Somalis live at subsistence level or below. Vegetation is grown in the desert with desalinated water at 100 times or more the cost in other areas. Vast resources of land, water, and people remain idle. Except for the deltas of the Nile and Ganges and the island of Java, the Muslim world is very thinly populated. Customs walls built around each state permit little economic cooperation with other states, or remove it as a potential producer or consumer in any industrial project, thus denying industry the possibility of success. Where industries are founded, they are meant to support national pride rather than the Muslim world or even a regional economy. Moreover, these industries are for the most part cosmetic, projects where the parts are manufactured outside and only assembled in the given country. Hence, these industries are at the mercy of the foreign producer, both in actual production and in the price of the finished product.

Instead of being a blessing, oil wealth has proven to be a curse. Very little of it is diverted to genuine economic development either domestically or elsewhere in the Muslim world. While a portion of it is fraudulently siphoned by the few who seek personal security in investments outside the Muslim world, the greatest portion is lent at little interest to the alien powers, or spent on consumption-oriented development, such as the construction of new cities that are bound to deteriorate and decay once the stream of oil revenues begins to dry up. The tremendous construction industry, which is speculative in purpose, raises the price of land and the rents of apartments beyond what many possible users can pay. Yet it attracts the farmers whose poverty has uprooted them from their villages and brought them to work in construction projects and who live in shantytowns around the cities. They constitute a plebian mass ready to be manipulated by any demagogue and to explode in rebellion at the slightest shortage or price change of the imported staple foods on which they depend.

Muslims point with dismay to the fact that in no state is the collection of the *zakat* enforced. In many places, the importation or production of alcohol thrives and interest-financing prospers. The rich exploit the poor. The hands of a few unfortunate thieves are cut off in some countries to appease the public and fool it into believing that the *shari'a* is being observed. But the "weightier matters of the law" are never raised or observed.

Sociocultural Structure

Criterion

Islam believes that every man is entitled to education, training, and socialization into the *umma*.[23] It assigns the highest possible premium to knowledge and its pursuit, and countenances no excuses for illiteracy, ignorance, or social delinquency. The Prophet declared that "Pursuit of knowledge is a duty for every Muslim male and female." Islam places responsibility first on the parents and then on society to fulfill these requirements. It legislates the values pertaining to brotherhood and makes imperative the greeting of one's fellow, giving him counsel and advice, assisting him in need, correcting him when he errs, protecting him when he is weak, guarding his family and property in his absence, visiting him when he is sick, and burying him when he is dead.[24] Equally, Islam acknowledges every person's right to get married, found a home, and raise a family.[25] It has raised the status of women and conferred upon them rights unmatched by other civilizations.[26] The *shari'a* girded the family in its extended form with laws of dependence, support, and inheritance, in order to maintain the family's physical and moral well-being.[27] Islam teaches a humanistic philosophy of life, a world view of affirmation and activism, of quiescence and self-fulfillment, of culture- and civilization-building.[28] Finally, Islam appreciates and promotes beauty and refinement so much that it has upheld the divine status of revelation by pointing to the sublime literary qualities of the Qur'an.[29] Unlike any other sublime literary work, the Qur'an has permeated the minds and tastes of ethnically diverse peoples around the world. It has united them in appreciation of its form as well as of its precepts, constituting itself as the esthetic lens through which Muslims everywhere see and enjoy or create beauty.[30]

Application

Judged by these norms, the Muslim world of today offers little cause for satisfaction to the committed Muslim. Illiteracy is on the rise nearly everywhere in the Muslim world because of the inability of the governments to keep pace with the increase in population. Schools, colleges, and universities are springing up everywhere as if the pursuit of education was truly an obsession; but everywhere there are shortages in facilities and teachers. Moreover, the whole system is marred by a dualism of Islamic and Western views locked in competition with each other. Four international congresses on Muslim education were held in Makka al-Mukarrama, Islamabad, Dacca, and Jakarta (1976–1982), where the problem commanded the attention of participants from every corner of the Muslim world.[31] Furthermore, the academic standards of most Muslim institutions of learning have declined. The first cause of decline is the lack of Islamic vision in the leadership. The second is the disproportionate growth of enrollment as compared with facilities, faculty research, and resources. The third is the politicization of education — the subjection of academic decision-making to political interests, the infiltration of the university by the state police, and the lack of vision and experience in academic administration. Muslim women have not advanced in education to the same extent as men and thus they are being denied the rights Islam has conferred upon women.

By a cruel stroke of fate, modernization has come to mean Westernization. The Muslim world is aping the West, much to the detriment of the Islamic style of life. Muslim towns are fast becoming like Western towns and Muslim homes like Western homes. Muslims are getting married and founding families, but nowhere is housing adequate. The extended family is becoming a rarity in the city because of housing shortages as well as the unfitting architectural style imported from the West. To all this one must add the demoralization of the masses due to the failure of the political leaders to uphold the traditional values, either in their own personal lives or in official functions.

Foreign Relations

Criterion

Besides what was mentioned earlier in connection with state legitimacy, Islam calls upon Muslims to build a world order of peace and justice, to unite and cooperate among themselves so as to be able to contribute to the well-being of humanity in all fields.[32] Islam redefines man in terms of the valuational hierarchy to which he adheres, in terms of what he cherishes most. It blinds the true Muslim to race and color and makes him ever more sensitive to religious and cultural values. It instills in him the deepest revulsion for aggression and injustice; and it teaches him the noblest lesson of respect for other humans, even if they are non-Muslim, of tolerance of their differing views, and of the urgency of cooperation with all peoples in peace, freedom, and justice.[33]

Long before any Muslim state can meaningfully participate in world events and influence them for the better in accordance with the international law of Islam (a perfect corpus of international law and a system of international relations based upon it that Islam brought into being and applied a millennium before Grotius), the Muslim states must give up their nation-state character and adopt that of the world-*umma*. This is equally the road to international respectability and to the power to contend in interstate affairs. For unless the Muslim states are identical in policy, united in effort and strategy, and unless their union and common efforts are backed by a solid and efficient political, social, and economic infrastructure within their societies, they have no role to play except that of puppet and/or prey to the world powers. Muslims perceive a necessary connection between observance of the *shari'a* — God's law — in all its aspects and success in history. Their faith in God and in His revelation through Muhammad prescribes this connection as a law of history.[34]

Application

Despite a spiritual heritage which could give them great strength in the arena of foreign relations, at present the Muslims have lost ground on every front. In the Philippines, China, Thailand, Bangladesh, India, Afghanistan, Palestine, Lebanon, Somalia, Chad, and Western Sahara, Muslims are being killed by non-Muslims and their Muslim puppets. No Muslim state has succeeded in integrating its own population or making itself socially and politically viable. Moreover, many a Muslim state, often with the "help" of an outside power, has succeeded in alienating its neighbors, indeed in creating cause for hostility and aggression. Muslim blood, Muslim property, and Muslim honor are cheaper than they have ever been. East and West have colluded to see their puppets succeed, puppets who are enemies of Islam and the Muslims. Even the little, persecuted foundling called Israel has now built for itself the greatest firepower in the world next to those of the United States, the Soviet Union, and China, to pile defeats upon those Muslims who have not yet awakened, and to assume airs of imperialistic grandeur against the whole Muslim world. Divided between "radicals" who cooperate secretly with the enemy, or who fight him blindly and without much success, and "friendly" governments that cooperate with the enemy openly, the Muslim states today stand at the farthest possible remove from the interest of Islam and its cause.

Note on the Author

Isma'il Raji al Faruqi and his wife Lois (Lamya') al Faruqi died tragically on 27 May 1986. Isma'il al Faruqi was a Muslim and a Palestinian; both were integral parts of his personal and professional identity. He was a scholar-activist, committed to the development of Islamic studies in the United States and the welfare of the worldwide Islamic community. For several decades Professor Faruqi was a major figure in Islamic studies teaching at McGill, Syracuse, and finally Temple University. At the same time he traveled extensively throughout the Islamic world lecturing and advising Muslim organizations and governments. His books and articles reveal the breadth of his intellectual interests and the depth of his commitments. He will be sorely missed. — John Esposito

Notes

1. For a complete list of al-Mawdudi's works, see Khurshid Ahmad and Zafar Ishaq Ansari (eds.), *Islamic Perspectives: Essays in Honour of Sayyid Abu al-'Ala' al-Mawdudi.* (Leicester: The Islamic Foundation, 1979), pp. 1–14.

2. Ibid.

3. Published in Tehran and Cairo (n.d.), and in English translation by Hamid Algar under the title *Islam and Revolution* (Berkeley, CA: Mizan Press, 1981), pp. 27–168. See also *Mukhtarat min aqwal al-Imam al-Khomeini* (Selected Messages and Speeches by Imam al-Khomeini) in Arabic and English; Muhammad 'Ali Husayn, *Nida' al-thawra al-Islamiyya: 'Ard li-ta'ifa min nida'at al-Imam al-Khomeini ila abna' al-'alam al-Islami; Matla' al-fajr;* Sahib Husayn al-Sadiq, *Al-thawra wa-al-qa'id* (Tehran: Ministry of National Guidance, n.d.). See also *'Ala tariq al-thawra* (Tehran: Al-Haraka al-Islamiyya fi Iran, 1979).

4. *On the Sociology of Islam*, English tr. by Hamid Algar (Berkeley, CA: Mizan Press, 1979). Other works by 'Ali Shari'ati (various translators): *Selection and/or Election, From Where Shall We Begin, The Machine in the Captivity of Machinism, Reflections on Humanity, Reflections of a Concerned Muslim on the Plight of*

Oppressed Peoples (Houston, TX: Free Islamic Literature, n.d.); *Marxism and Other Western Fallacies: An Islamic Critique*, tr. by R. Campbell (Berkeley, CA: Mizan Press, 1980); and *One Followed by an Eternity of Zeroes, Yea Brother! That's the Way It Was*, and *Red Shi'ism* (Tehran: The *Shari'ati* Foundation, n.d.).

5. Abu al-Fazl 'Ezzati, *The Revolutionary Islam and the Islamic Revolution* (Tehran: Ministry of National Guidance, 1981).

6. *Al-mujtama' wa-al-tarikh* (Tehran: Wizarat al-Irshad al-Islami, 1979).

7. The list is too long to include here. For a summary, see Ishaq Musa al-Husayni, *Al-Ikhwan al-Muslimun: kubra al-harakat al-Islamiyya al-haditha* (Beirut: Dar Beirut li-al-Taba'a wa-al-Nashr, 1955), pp. 277–308. An excellent annotated bibliography of their works may be found in Muhammad Bayyumi, "The Islamic Ethic of Social Justice and Modernization," doctoral dissertation submitted to the Department of Religion at Temple University, 1976, pp. 611ff.

8. Local organizations focused around Muslim community centers, and professional or ethnic groupings, have mushroomed throughout the world. The most active of them in the West are in the United States, Canada, United Kingdom, Germany, France, and Italy; in the Muslim world, they are in Egypt, Sudan, Nigeria, Turkey, Pakistan, India, Bangladesh, Malaysia, and Indonesia; and outside the Muslim world, in South Africa, Ceylon, Australia, and Surinam. International organizations with worldwide constituencies and a significant potential for influencing the youth and intelligentsia of the Muslim world have emerged during the last twenty years. These include the Muslim Students' Association of the United States and Canada, with over 300 branches on the campuses of North American colleges and universities, the International Islamic Federation of Student Organizations, the World Assembly of Muslim Youth, the Islamic Council of Europe, the Islamic Medical Association, the Association of Muslim Scientists and Engineers, the Association of Muslim Social Scientists, and the International Institute of Islamic Thought.

9. This essay was written prior to the application of the *shari'a* in Sudan and its transformation into an Islamic republic through cooperation between al-Ikhwan al-Muslimun and the Numayri regime.

10. "Allah has made sale legitimate and interest illegitimate." (Qur'an 2:275.)

11. "Do not appropriate the wealth of others unrighteously." (Qur'an 2:188.)

12. "Fulfill your contracts; for every agreement is a responsible covenant." (Qur'an 17:34.)

13. "Those who hoard gold and silver [the wealth of society] and do not spend it in the way of Allah, to them announce punishment painful." (Qur'an 9:34.)

14. "As to the thieves, whether male or female, cut off their hands in retribution for what they earned [by their misdeed]." (Qur'an 5:38.)

15. The commandment to pay the *zakat* and give in charity may be found on practically every page of the Qur'an. Indeed, to pay the *zakat* is in the Qur'an constitutive of *iman*, or faith.

16. The same is true of justice as has been said of *zakat*. Indeed, justice is divine virtue and the first attribute after creatorship.

17. Qur'an 17:34; "O Believers! If you lend or borrow anything for a fixed term, write it down . . . Be it a little matter or great, do not neglect to commit it to writing." (Qur'an 2:183.)

18. "And give the relation his due, as well as the destitute and the wayfarer." (Qur'an 17:26); "Those [the believers] who recognize a specific right to the poor and the destitute in their own wealth." (Qur'an 59:9.)

19. "It is He Who brought you out of the earth and planted you therein to colonize it." (Qur'an 11:61.)

20. "He [Allah] has made subservient to you all that is in heaven and earth." (Qur'an 45:13.)

21. "Say, [O Muhammad], who prohibited the beautiful and goodly things which

Allah has provided? Say, they belong to the believers to enjoy in this world."
(Qur'an 7:32.)

22. "It is He [Allah] Who created life and death that you may prove yourselves
worthy in your deeds." (Qur'an 67:2.)

23. "Read in the name of your Lord, the Creator! Read! For your Lord is the most
generous. He taught [man] the use of the pen; He taught him that which he did not
know." (Qur'an 96:1–5.)

24. "The believers are truly brothers of one another." (Qur'an 49:10.)

25. The Prophet urged the Muslims to marry, saying: "I . . . fast as well as eat, I
pray as well as sleep, and I marry and have a family. This is my example. Whoever
does not follow it is not one of mine."

26. This is the claim made by most Muslim writers on "women" and "family" in
Islam. See, for example, Hammuda 'Abd al-'Ati, *The Family Structure in Islam*
(Indianapolis, IN: American Trust Publications, 1977); Kamal Ahmad 'Awn, *Al-mar'a fi al-Islam* (Tanta, Egypt: Matba'at al-Sha'rawi, 1374 A.H.), pp. 30ff; Mustafa
al-Siba'i, *Al-mar'a bayna al-fiqh wa al-qanun* (Aleppo: Al-Maktaba al-'Arabiyya,
1386 A.H.), pp. 25ff.

27. Amin Ihsan Islahi, "A Critique of the Modernist Approach to the Family Law
of Islam," *Studies in the Family Law of Islam*, ed. Khurshid Ahmad, (Karachi:
Chiragh-i-Rah Publications, 1961), pp. 87–199.

28. For a typical statement, see Muhammad Husayn Haykal, *The Life of
Muhammad*, tr. I.R. al Faruqi (Indianapolis, IN: American Trust Publications,
1976), pp. 517, 594.

29. Sayyid Qutb, *Al-taswïr al-fanni fi al-Qur'an* (Cairo: Dar al-Ma'arif, 1393
A.H.). Classical statements on the sublime nature of the Qur'an may be read in the
works carrying the common title "I'jaz al-Qur'an," by al-Jurjani, al-Baqillani, al-Suyuti, al-Khattabi, al-Rummani, and more recently by 'Abd al-Karim al-Khatib.

30. Lois Lamya' al-Faruqi, "The *shari'a* on Music and Musicians," *Islamic
Thought and Culture*, ed. Isma'il R. al-Faruqi (Herndon, VA: International Institute
of Islamic Thought, 1982), pp. 27–52; Lois Lamya' al-Faruqi, *Islam and Art*
(Islamabad: National Hijra Council, 1985). See also this author's "Islam and Art,"
Studia Islamica, Fasc. 37 (1983), pp. 91–109.

31. Proceedings of the said conferences are available at the World Center of
Muslim Education, King 'Abdul 'Aziz University, Jeddah, Saudi Arabia. Four
volumes containing some of these proceedings have already been published by
Hodder and Stoughton, London, under the general title of *Islamic Education Series*.

32. Khurshid Ahmad, "A Muslim Response," *World Faiths and the New World
Order*, ed. Joseph Cremillion and William Ryan (Washington, DC: The Inter-Religious Peace Colloquium, 1978), pp. 171–198. See also Khurshid Ahmad (ed.),
The Muslim World and the Future Economic Order (London: The Islamic Council of
Europe, 1979).

33. Altaf Gauhar (ed.), *The Challenge of Islam* (London: The Islamic Council of
Europe, 1978); Salem Azzam (ed.), *Islam and Contemporary Society* (London:
Longman Group, Ltd., 1982).

34. "If you ally yourself with Allah, then surely Allah will give you victory and
make you stand firm on earth . . . For certainly, Allah will give victory to those who
obey Him." (Qur'an 47:7; 22:40.)

17 A SEARCH FOR ISLAMIC CRIMINAL JUSTICE: AN EMERGING TREND IN MUSLIM STATES

M. Cherif Bassiouni

It is only in one Muslim state — Saudi Arabia — that Islamic criminal justice (i.e., Islamic criminal law and procedure) has been consistently applied for many years. In recent times, a number of other Muslim states, including Iran, Pakistan, and certain Arab Gulf states, have adopted systems of criminal justice based on Islam. In addition, some other states which either declare themselves to be Muslim states in their constitutions or simply consider themselves Muslim states have sought to incorporate or have at least considered the possibility of incorporating within their legal systems a system of Islamic criminal justice. In these countries some Muslim leaders followed by an increasing number of people have been urging the adoption of Islamic law as the basis of their countries' respective criminal justice systems.

A number of Muslim states have adopted a variety of normative proscriptions within their legal systems which derive from the *shari'a*, in particular with respect to private law (a leader among these states is Egypt). The application of Islamic criminal justice has been slow in developing, however. The reasons for this will be discussed in greater depth below, but it must be understood at the outset that the urge for the adoption of an Islamic criminal justice system can almost invariably be identified with what the Western world has called "Islamic fundamentalism." Therefore, it is necessary to begin by examining the meaning or meanings of this concept.

Islamic Fundamentalism and Criminal Justice Reform

To many non-Muslims, "Islamic fundamentalism" has come to be associated with various excesses committed under the ostensible banner of Islam. The very concept conjures up visions of violent revolutionary action and conduct that goes against hard-earned civilized standards of humane treatment and lawfulness of the legal process. This perception is distorted, however, because the revival of Islamic fundamental precepts, at least in theory, is nothing more than the age-long search by Muslim masses and their leaders for the true path of justice, once referred to as the path of *al-salaf al-salih*. This notion, which was eloquently propounded by Shaykh Muhammad 'Abduh in Egypt at the beginning of this century, was not new even then. In fact, the *muwahhidun* brought such reforms to Morocco in the twelfth century, while Ibn Taymiyya developed much the same philosophy of reform in Syria during the thirteenth century, and during the eighteenth century the Wahhabis of Saudi Arabia began a similar movement which still survives.

It is important, therefore, to distinguish between an Islamic reform movement in which the element of fundamentalism is merely part of an attempt to return to basics, and the context in which such a reform movement has erupted or appears to be burgeoning as part of political transformation in contemporary times. It is interesting to note that such movements have invariably been in societies that at one time or another were subject to a form of colonial or neocolonial domination by an alien culture seeking to implant a social system based on values different from those of Islam. The rulers of these countries relied on their dominant power, and on the support of usually corrupt or pliable indigenous elites emulating the West, to achieve the goals either of a dominant foreign power or of those who succeeded it. Even post-colonial indigenous regimes, whether truly nationalistic or only assuming that appearance, have more often than not either perpetuated some of the policies of their foreign predecessors by continuing or intensifying political oppression, or have sought to implant Western values and systems that are alien to the indigenous population. Irrespective of the manner in which these regimes emerged and subsequently developed, to the masses it remains strikingly apparent that often-dismal economic conditions, coupled with significant social disparities and lack of basic democracy and individual freedom, have continued unabated. Even some regimes not marred by poverty are characterized by inordinate social disparity, the absence of democracy, and a lack of individual freedom. In this regard, the emergence or resurgence of Islamic fundamentalism is simply a consequence of the unfulfilled need for social, economic, and political change, which in the Muslim context translates into the quest for justice in all its social and personal aspects. Thus the uneducated masses, frequently manipulated by an unenlightened or insufficiently educated leadership, have found their rallying point to be the more simplistic aspects of Islam as they understand it. In short, these masses believe that the resort to Islam is the only available means of social and political reaction against economic, social, and political conditions that do not allow any other viable expressions of discontent.

The most vivid example of this situation is Iran's Islamic revolution as articulated by the Ayatollah Khomeini and carried out by his followers. Irrespective of any political judgment one may make regarding the revolution, it is the opinion of this writer that the revolutionaries' application of Islamic criminal justice is in many respects contrary to the basic tenets of Islam. Thus, although certain laws that were promulgated may be in conformity with a certain interpretation of Islam, the manner in which these laws have been applied, as well as the ways in which other processes have been carried out (not the least of which are the absence of basic guarantees of a fair trial and the use of torture and other violent means), are without question contrary to the spirit and letter of Islamic criminal justice clearly embodied in the *shari'a*. Both Muslims seeking a revival of Islamic fundamentalism in Muslim countries and non-Muslims, especially in the Western world, share some of the same distorted perceptions of the Islamic criminal justice system, but their reactions are very different. In non-Muslim societies, conduct, such as has been witnessed in post-revolutionary Iran, is considered primitive and barbaric. In certain Muslim societies, on the other hand, the uneducated masses would not necessarily condone such actions but would nevertheless justify or rationalize such conduct for a variety of reasons unrelated to the subject in question. One set of reasons is the perception that the totality of circumstances in certain societies necessitates an inevitable radical political transformation, including revolutionary dismissal of a corrupt or oppressive regime. Thus, the ability of Iran's Islamic revolution to defy and almost hold hostage the United States (which is frequently if not always perceived by many people in Muslim countries as being associated with the corrupt regimes whose transformation is being sought), and its military achievements under difficult conditions against Iraq give it credence with other Muslim revolutionary movements. (But this confluence of beliefs is not necessarily translated into political affinity for or linkage between the various revolutionary or transformative movements or organizations.)

The emerging demand for the establishment of Islamic criminal justice in various Muslim societies is not always the product of thoughtful articulate development on the part of either theoreticians or legislative bodies. Rather, it is a response to political considerations that have nothing to do with the Islamic criminal justice system proper. In short, the call for Islamic criminal justice does not occur in those Muslim states which do not apply Islamic criminal justice because their current system is unfair or inadequate, though it may be. Instead, the demand stands as a symbol for a much larger issue — that of radical sociopolitical and economic transformation.

The Development of the Islamic Criminal Justice System

The Qur'an is the principal source of Islamic law (*shari'a*). It contains the rules by which the Islamic system of criminal justice is to be applied. The Qur'an does not set forth a complete system of criminal justice, but it does contain the elements necessary for the construction by believers of a system of justice capable of being responsive to the needs of the society of a given place and time. In this connection, Islamic jurisprudence recognizes a number of sources of law that permit the development of a comprehensive system of criminal justice. In addition to the Qur'an there is the Sunna, which is complementary to the Qur'an and consists of both the sayings (Hadith) of the Prophet and accounts of his deeds during his lifetime. The other sources of Islamic jurisprudence are given priority in the following order: *ijma'*, which is the consensus of opinion; *qiyas*, or a judgment based on juridical analogy; *ijtihad*, meaning independent reasoning; *istihsan*, the deviation from certain rules based on precedents deriving from other rules based on legally relevant reasoning; *istislah*, an unprecedented judgment derived by analogy to an explicit rule in the Qur'an or in the Sunna and necessitated by public interest and public policy; and *'urf*, custom and usage.

The Qur'an contains a variety of lawmaking provisions and legal prescriptions and proscriptions which are interspersed throughout its chapters and verses, some dealing with specific questions of substantive law, others with questions of criminal procedures, and still others establishing the bases for analogy and interpretation. Needless to say, the rules for interpreting the Qur'an itself are subject to a science — the science of interpretation (*'ilm usul al-*

fiqh). Among these rules is the notion of interpretation based on the policy of *shari'a* (*siyasat al-shari'a*). As a result, Islamic jurisprudence has had to take into account these different sources and rely on certain rules and theories of interpretation. This process has developed over a period of fourteen centuries from the time of the original revelation of the Qur'an in the early seventh century.

Since Muhammad's time, various schools of jurisprudence have emerged, in particular the four major Sunni schools (Hanafi, Hanbali, Maliki, Shafi'i), each one in turn spawning a number of sub-schools with different interpretative approaches and applications. Then there is the Shi'i school with its sub-schools. Furthermore, the historical development of Islamic jurisprudence has been influenced by the various cultures and social systems in which Islam has been applied. Indeed, the historical baggage of Islamic jurisprudence has assumed such overwhelming proportions that proponents of a return to "fundamentals," that is, a simplistic application of Islamic criminal justice as it is perceived to have been applied in the days of the Prophet and the four ensuing caliphs, have found it easier, rather than to sift through that great historical record, to urge a return to the so-called basics or fundamentals of Islam. The problem, however, does not lie in the return to the starting point. It lies in the fact that for many the return to the starting point is also the end of the inquiry. Adherence to such an approach is explained by the fact that revolutions seldom have the time for deliberative thought and study, and that the masses following such a movement are usually more inspired by simplistic clichés and applications than by sophisticated concepts of justice.

A significant disparity exists among Muslim scholars as to whether or not Islam in general and the *shari'a* in particular are dynamic or static. That significant schism obscures, or is maybe symptomatic of, another question that can be viewed essentially in terms of power relations. Clearly, if the proponents of a static Islam prevail, they will be the ones able to interpret that vision of Islam and in applying it they would become the controlling power. If, on the other hand, the notion of a dynamic Islam prevails, modern reformists and revisionists will wrest the power from the traditionalists. In short, those who dominate the Muslim world today could claim to be reformist or progressive and could use their interpretation of Islam to justify their regimes. Consequently, those who seek a return to a static fundamentalism of Islam are those who are seeking to wrest power away from those in control. The debate obscures and to a large extent distorts a basic reality in Islam. A key tenet of Islam — that Islam is not only a religion, but also a way and system of life that is applicable to all peoples and for all times — clearly implies that Islam cannot be static. This does not mean that certain basic rules of the *shari'a* can be altered by subsequent distorted reinterpretation (as many opponents of the dynamic interpretation claim). Rather, the above tenet means that the *shari'a* is essentially a policy-oriented legal system which requires dynamic evolution and evolving application to remain strong. For example, nothing in the *shari'a* would prohibit the development of a criminal code, a code of criminal procedure, and a code of corrections, provided that these different codes embody the basic rules of the *shari'a*. Furthermore, it is clear that the *shari'a* has not provided certain rules which can and should be embodied in a codified system in order to insure the integrity of the legal process itself and its proper application, and in order to guarantee the basic human rights of the accused as required in the Islamic criminal justice system no matter how fundamentally it is viewed.

Regrettably, the understanding of Islamic criminal justice and its policy bases is not sufficiently widespread in Muslim societies, and is particularly misconceived by proponents of Islamic fundamentalism. Those who call for a return to a static Islam frequently, but mistakenly. refer only to certain periods of Islamic history without understanding how the rules of those periods developed and how and why they were applied at those times. In addition, they clearly lack understanding of how these rules should be adapted and differently applied in a contemporary framework. For example, in the days of the Prophet there were no prisons, yet the notion of imprisonment existed and in fact there were instances of imprisonment during the time of the Prophet and of the subsequent four caliphs. Should that be interpreted in a contemporary context to mean that no institutional prisons should be established today? And if a prison is established, should there be no code of corrections or rules concerning the detention of persons? Indeed not — and the early practices of Islam are among the most humane and understanding expressions of an enlightened system of corrections, penology, and criminology.

Types of Crimes

There are basically three categories of crimes in the Islamic criminal system. The first are *hudud* crimes. These consist of seven crimes that are proscribed in the Qur'an. For some the penalty is not provided in the Qur'an but was meted out in the days of the Prophet and consequently is now carried on as part of the Sunna. The second category is that of *qisas* crimes — essentially voluntary killing and maiming and injuring. For these crimes the penalties provided are essentially those of either retaliation or compensation (*diya*). The third category is *ta'azir*. This category of offenses has no exact definition and in effect is intended to permit legislative development in the areas of the protection of the welfare, well-being, and safety of society. In a modern context, the *ta'azir* offenses could range from traffic violations to crimes related to treason such as sedition or espionage, and could include many other types of offenses such as pollution and the creation of hazardous conditions.

It is interesting to note that with respect to the seven basic *hudud* crimes (adultery, defamation, alcoholism, theft, brigandage, apostasy, and rebellion), virtually every legal system in the world penalizes much of such conduct. Thus the question is the definition of these crimes in contemporary terms and the application of an appropriate penalty in relationship to a possible interpretation of the *shari'a* in the light of contemporary social policy.

Qisas crimes (murder, voluntary manslaughter, involuntary manslaughter, and intentional crimes against the person, whether battery or maiming) are also covered in every criminal justice system in the world, and each of these crimes can be defined and codified in a manner consistent with contemporary Islamic values and social policy.

Although the final category, that of *ta'azir*, is not encompassed in either one of the first two categories, it certainly can be the basis of a contemporary codification because of its very nature and intended purpose, which even in early Islamic history reflected social policy.

With respect to all three categories of crime, there are some additional requirements in the *shari'a* concerning proof and applicable penalties. These too can be interpreted and codified in an appropriate contemporary manner. Thus, with respect to substantive crimes there is nothing in the *shari'a* that would prohibit their codification based on existing requirements; allowance would have to be made for reconsideration of some of the elements of these crimes and their application in the light of the *shari'a*, which would permit such a reconsideration of developing jurisprudence through *ijtihad*. Opponents of this particular view claim that *ijtihad* is no longer permissible. That is simply nonsense; there is no reason why *ijtihad* could not continue to go on *ad infinitum*. The decision by theologians of the Middle Ages that Islamic jurisprudence had reached its peak of development and that as a result *ijtihad* was no longer needed is unacceptable and has no basis in the *shari'a*.

Criminal Procedure

The same reasoning developed with respect to crimes and penalties would apply to criminal procedure. It must be noted, however, that Islam brought about a legal revolution which centered essentially on the protection of the rights of the individual without foregoing the rights of society. It carefully attempted to balance between the two. In fact, it provided the individual with such radical rights that many non-Muslim legal systems did not mature enough to apply them until centuries later. Consider the fact that under Islamic criminal justice since the seventh century there has been a right not to be compelled to be a witness against oneself, and testimony obtained through such compulsion would not be admissible. In contrast, in the Western world the resort to practices of torture, such as the oath *ex officio* and trial by ordeal, in order to obtain incriminating evidence continued for several centuries thereafter.

Conclusion

(1) The Islamic criminal justice system with respect to substantive crimes, criminal procedure, and corrections is perfectly susceptible to (a) modern codification and (b) modern interpretation and application, consonant with the basic principles of the *shari'a* and in the light of Islamic social policy, provided — and this must be emphasized — that any such development does not go contrary to a specific or clearly enunciated rule in the Qur'an (as opposed to one whose interpretation is merely stated by theologians of a certain school at a certain time in the development of Islam).

(2) Opponents of the progressive development of Islam are usually the proponents of a return to "Islamic fundamentalism," as

they interpret it. Theirs is a process of selective application of those portions of Islamic jurisprudence which they consider to be "fundamental." Under a fragmentary approach, certain aspects of the Islamic system as it existed at a certain historical time are frequently taken out of jurisprudential, historical, or social context. No regard is given to the essentially dynamic nature of Islam, and no consideration is taken of its policy-oriented approach.

(3) The legal developments described above can be carried out through *ijtihad*, a process that encompasses reliance on all sources of the *shari'a*, including the Qur'an, the Sunna, *qiyas*, *istihsan*, *istislah*, *ijma'*, and *'urf*. Here *ijtihad* would not limit itself to consideration of narrow specific interpretations given at various times by one or another of the four Sunni schools of interpretation or their sub-schools, but instead would rely on the letter and spirit of what is prescribed in the Qur'an as a whole and would take into account the total fabric and socioreligious goals of Islam.

(4) In order to achieve these goals, enlightened scholars must combine a knowledge of the past with an understanding of the present and a vision of the future. That is an educational challenge that has yet to be met in the Muslim world.

(5) There must also be a comprehensive process for gathering the vast legacy of Islam's historical-jurisprudential record. At present, Al-Azhar University in Cairo is in the process of collecting and publishing a compendium of the *shari'a* on the basis of the Qur'an, the Sunna, the four Sunni schools (Hanafi, Maliki, Shafi'i, Hanbali), and the Shi'i school of thought. When completed, this topical digest will be the most complete and authoritative source of Islamic *fiqh* (Islamic jurisprudence).

(6) The application of Islamic criminal justice requires a contextual framework and environment. Such a framework and environment necessarily requires socioeconomic justice, individual freedom, and democracy. Thus, the search for the true application of Islam has yet to find its realization, and in its absence, an Islamic criminal justice system is difficult to establish. To some extent, it would be unfair to apply Islamic criminal justice in the absence of such a predicate.

(7) Fundamentalist political activists, who oppose political regimes in Muslim states for a variety of reasons, seek a return to what they perceive to be "Islamic fundamentalism." They are, however, relatively unconcerned with the scholarly studies needed to bring about any true Islamic reform, or the dissemination of the

knowledge obtained from such studies so that the largest possible segment of the population (and not only the ruling elite) would become aware of it. Instead, these "fundamentalists" advance simplistic views as panaceas for complex problems.

The search for a return to Islamic criminal justice is therefore intricately tied to struggles in which not the reform of criminal justice but the gaining of power is the real objective. Islamic criminal justice reform thus becomes the victim of movements that have other goals, and which would eventually use and abuse the criminal justice system to strengthen their authority.

References

Books

Abu-Zahra, M. *Al-jarima wa-al-'uquba fi al-Islam* (n.d.).
Adams, D.H. *Islam and Modernism in Egypt* (1933).
Anderson, J.N.D. *The Maliki Law of Homicide* (n.d.).
Anderson, J.N.D. *Islamic Law in the Modern World* (1959).
Baroody, G. *Crime and Punishment under Islamic Law* (1961).
Bassiouni, M.C., ed. *The Islamic Criminal Justice System* (1982).
Farhun, I. *Tafsirat al-hukkam* (1937).
Gibb, H.A.R. *Modern Trends in Islam* (1947).
Hamidullah, M. *Muslim Conduct of State* (4th ed., 1961).
Ibn Hanbal, A. *Manar al-sabil* (n.d.).
Al-Kasani, A.A.M. *Badi' al-sani' fi tartib al-shari'a* (1st ed., A.H. 1327–1328, 7 vols.).
Ibn Malik, A. *Ahkam al-khilafa* (c. 1500).
Mawdudi, A. *Towards Understanding Islam* (5th ed., A. Ghandi, trans., 1954).
Mawdudi, A. *Human Rights in Islam* (1977).
Al-Mawardi, A.A. *Al-ahkam al-sultaniyya* (n.d., c. 1058 A.D.).
Mostafa, M. *Principes de Droit Pénal des Pays Arabes* (1973).
Moussa, M. *Muslim Jurisprudence* (1958).
Odeh, A. *Al-tashri' al-jina'i al-Islami* (3rd. ed., vols. I & II, 1977).
Qutb, A. *Islam: The Misunderstood Religion* (6th ed., 1964).
Rahbar, M. *God of Justice, Ethical Doctrine of the Qur'an* (1960).
Ramadan, S. *Islamic Law, Its Scope and Equity* (1961).
Al-Tusi, A. *Al-nahiya* (A.H. 1342).
Al-Tusi, A. *Al-mabsut* (2 vols., 1967).
Wenisinck, A.J. *La Pensée de Ghazali* (1946).

Articles

Abdel-Malek al-Saleh, "The Right of the Individual to Personal Security in Islam," in M.C. Bassiouni, ed., *The Islamic Criminal Justice System* (1982), p. 55.

Abdel-Wahab, "Meaning and Structure of Law in Islam." *Vanderbilt Law Review* XVI (1962).

Ahmad, "Islamic Civilization and Human Rights." *Révue Egyptienne de Droit International* XII (1956): 1.

Alfi, "Punishment in Islamic Criminal Law," in M.C. Bassiouni, ed., *The Islamic Criminal Justice System* (1982), p. 227.

Awad, "The Rights of the Accused under Islamic Criminal Procedure," in M.C. Bassiouni, ed., *The Islamic Criminal Justice System* (1982), p. 91.

Badr, "Islamic Law: Its Relation to Other Legal Systems," *American Journal of Comparative Law* XXVI (1978): 187.

Bassiouni, "Islam: Concept, Law and World Habeas Corpus," *Rutgers-Camden Law Journal* I (1969): 163.

Bassiouni, "The Protection of Diplomats under Islamic Law," *American Journal of International Law* LXXIV (1980): 609.

Bassiouni, "Qisas Crimes," in M.C. Bassiouni, ed., *The Islamic Criminal Justice System* (1982), p. 203.

Bassiouni, "Sources of Islamic Law, and the Protection of Human Rights in the Islamic Criminal Justice System." in M.C. Bassiouni, ed., *The Islamic Criminal Justice System* (1982), p. 3.

El-Berri, "La Prestation des Serments Comme Processus d'Instruction des Crimes d'Homicide dans la Législation Islamique." *Révue International de Droit Pénal* XLVI (1975): 373.

Hussein, "Due Process in Modern Constitution and the Process of Sharia." *Karachi Law Journal* VII (1971): 57.

Mansour, "Hudud Crimes," in M.C. Bassiouni, ed., *The Islamic Criminal Justice System* (1982), p. 195.

Nawaz, "The Concept of Human Rights in Islamic Law," *Howard Law Journal* XI (1965): 325.

Salama, "General Principles of Criminal Evidence in Islamic Jurisprudence," in M.C. Bassiouni, ed., *The Islamic Criminal Justice System* (1982), p. 109.

Schacht, "Islamic Law in Contemporary States." *American Journal of Comparative Law* VIII (1959): 133.

Weiss, "Interpretation in Islamic Law: The Theory of Ijtihad," *American Journal of Comparative Law* XXVI (1978): 199.

18 THE RECENT IMPACT OF ISLAMIC RELIGIOUS DOCTRINE ON CONSTITUTIONAL LAW IN THE MIDDLE EAST

Gamal M. Badr

The call for a return to an Islamic form of government is the culmination of both frustration at the failures of the present regimes and rejection of institutions borrowed from the West and therefore perceived as un-Islamic. Failures of the existing regimes have included their inability to redress economic injustice (a source of widespread discontent) and their external policy setbacks, of which the defeat of 1967 was the most painful. Governments that appeared capable neither of improving the quality of life for their citizens nor of defending the homeland against a hostile neighbor, let alone achieving proclaimed national goals at the regional level, lost much of their legitimacy in the eyes of their peoples. Under these circumstances, the search for an alternative was understandable.

The above failures were attributed, in part, to constitutional structures and political institutions introduced into the Middle East since the nineteenth century. Whether borrowing from the West was spontaneous, as in the case of Egypt, or the result of colonial domination, as in some other Islamic lands, did not matter much. In both cases adoption of Western norms and values was considered the result of cultural penetration of the Islamic world by the West and was therefore resented. It was believed that a return to the Islamic cultural heritage, in politics as well as in other fields, was the sound alternative to foreign influences that failed the practical test of living history so far as the elusive social and national objectives of the Islamic peoples of the Middle East were concerned. Perhaps more viscerally than deliberately, people compared Islam's present modest position in the world to the achievements of their ancestors during the Golden Age of Islam. The easy victories of the Muslim armies over two militarily and technologically superior empires were seen as nothing less than miraculous. They were the vindication of the divine promise in the Qur'an to make God's righteous servants inherit the earth (21:105) and of the Qur'an's description of the believers as the best nation brought forth for humanity (3:110).

Since, generally speaking, present-day Muslims were not remiss in matters of creed and ritual, the decline of the fortunes of Islam could only be ascribed to its political (rather than purely religious) manifestations. The adopted Western-type political institutions were seen as deviations from true Islam and therefore present-day Muslims were said to be no longer following divine guidance or deserving of divine protection. Both secular nationalism and secular "Arab socialism," with their respective forms of government, had let the Muslims down. A return to an Islamic form of government appeared to offer the best promise for the future and to provide a substitute for the diminishing legitimacy of the present regimes.

Proponents of a return to an Islamic form of government are long on criticism and short on constructive proposals. They are articulate in their repudiation of Western-type constitutional forms and political institutions. They are less forthcoming when it comes to offering a specific and detailed description of a form of government that they would consider Islamic. Their call sounds more like a millenarian longing for the return of a Golden Age than a well-articulated political program. This may be understandable in the light of the fact that neither doctrinally nor historically was there one exclusive form of government that may be called Islamic.

From the doctrinal point of view, the Qur'an and the Sunna contain only generalities when it comes to the political organization of society. Important principles are laid down, such as the sovereignty of the Almighty (which precludes any claim to sovereign status by a human being), the supremacy of the law, the equality of all believers (including the rulers) under the law, concern for the needs of the economically weaker members of society, and the requirement that the ruler consult the community in the affairs of state. These lofty principles represent the *ends* to be served by the political system. The *means* to achieve those ends have not been spelled out. On the mechanisms of governing the community the Qur'an is not explicit. Nor did the Prophet determine the form of government after him before his earthly life came to an end.[1] Since divine guidance of the believers is by definition comprehensive, this silence on the part of the two main sources of the law can only mean that constitutional matters were deliberately left to the Islamic community (*umma*) to determine. This is perceived as yet another instance of divine omniscience and a further sign of mercy. A preordained, immutable form of government could have caused future generations of the community great hardship. By choosing not to impose a particular form of government, Islam allows the believers to devise different forms of government to meet the changing needs of different times and different social conditions. In this exercise the community still enjoys indirect divine guidance through the use of such supplementary sources of the rules of law as the consensus of the community (*ijma'*) and the consideration of the public good (*maslaha*). In its recourse to *ijma'* the community has been declared infallible by the Prophet ("My community shall never agree on an error") and the determination of the public good at any time and in any place may not ignore any general principle or violate any peremptory rule of the Qur'an or the Sunna.

From the historical point of view, Islam did not know only one particular form of government or only one particular set of constitutional rules in the course of its fourteen centuries of existence. The basic distinction here is between the universal caliphate and the various limited dynastic realms. Under the universal caliphate, whether in its pure Medinan form or its subsequent monarchical form under the Umayyads and the Abbasids, the head of state was the successor to the Prophet in his political function and claimed universal authority over the whole domain of Islam. His power rested on a process of selection by prominent and representative members of the community, known as *bay'a*. Such a process of *bay'a* was required even when dynastic succession became established and the ruling caliph designated his own successor. Such designation did not convey title in itself; a *bay'a* was required in favor of the chosen successor either in his predecessor's lifetime or upon the latter's death. When political fragmentation caught up with the empire, autonomous realms came into being, first in the remote provinces. These local rulers made no claim to being the successors to the Prophet or to being universal rulers of Islam; they even recognized the caliph's authority and sought legitimacy through formal investiture in office by him. The power of these regional rulers rested on de facto control or on heredity. Such a form of government came into being even at the center, in Baghdad, where the Buyids and later the Seljuks took over from the caliph without overthrowing him or contesting his authority. This phase of Islamic history treats us to the spectacle of a caliph who rules in theory and a sultan who governs in practice and with whom all the real power lies. There even came to be pseudo-caliphates of limited territorial jurisdiction that contended with the universal caliphate rather than recognize its authority and seek its approval and investiture. Such were the Umayyad caliphate of Cordoba and the Fatimid caliphate of Cairo. The few ephemeral Shi'i and Khariji local states also fall in this category.

Each phase of Islamic history and its corresponding form of government had their own rationalization in the writings of Islamic scholars. Their works on the subject of government were mostly descriptive of the status quo, which they sought to justify. They did not, except at the philosophical speculative level (e.g., al-Farabi), lay down a prior normative model based on principle. We thus find in the words of al-Ghazzali (d. 1111 A.D.) statements to the effect that a bad ruler is better than no ruler because order is preferable to chaos, and that necessity makes legal a form of government that otherwise would not be legal. When we reach Ibn Jama'a (d. 1333 A.D.) we find him describing the ruler as "God's shadow on earth" and teaching that mere seizure of power justifies the ruler's authority. He also stated that although the ruler is required to uphold and observe the law, his removal should not be sought if he fails to fulfill this requirement, in order to avoid civil strife. There is a world of difference between the form of government condoned in these last statements and a typical Islamic model conducive to serving the societal ends formulated in the Qur'an and the Sunna. Under such scholarly doctrines absolutism became its own justification and the noble goals of equality, of supremacy of the law, and of consultation with the governed had to give way to the exigencies of sheer power.[2]

Is it any wonder, then, that today's champions of an Islamic government, laboring by choice under those doctrinal and historical constraints, are at a loss to specify the concrete form of the government they are advocating, to determine the basis of its power, to enumerate its branches, or to describe the inter-branch relationships within it? Should their model be the universal caliphate in an age when the universality of Islamic authority is but a memory? Or should their model be the local autonomous realms, based on the seizure of power, of which they should be the first to disapprove? Beyond such questions a larger one looms: if the lawgiver, in his infinite wisdom and his concern for mankind, abstained from prescribing a particular form of government for the *umma*, thus permitting continued evolution and renewal, why should early historical models, pertaining to an age of relative simplicity in the social structure, be imposed on a society that has become much more complex and that faces problems and has to find solutions that were not even thought of in the earlier phases of Islamic history? It appears that what is required is not a *return* to an Islamic form of government but a *quest* for a new form of government able to respond to today's challenges within the general framework of Islamic principles and values.

The dilemma of the activists in the field of the Islamization of government is compounded by the fact that they are not in agreement among themselves on several points of substance. For example, they differ on the extent to which consultation with the governed (*shura*) is required or its outcome is binding.[3] Some hold that the ruler is required to consult, while others say that the Qur'anic verses on *shura* (3:159 and 42:38) only recommend consultation to the ruler without requiring that he necessarily consult before reaching a decision. Once *shura* takes place, there is more disagreement as to whether its outcome is binding on the ruler. One opinion considers the ruler free to follow or to disregard the conclusion reached by the majority of those whom he consulted, while others hold that the ruler is obliged to act according to the outcome of the process of consultation. Another dispute revolves around the party system and whether it is Islamic or un-Islamic.[4] Some maintain that organized political parties competing for power are alien to Islamic tradition and culture. According to this view, the whole *umma* should be considered as one party ("God's party") while the dissidents are "Satan's party."[5] This is, in fact, nothing more than a verbal play on the Arabic word *hizb*, which in modern usage means "political party," but which in the Qur'an means simply "faction" and has no political connotations. Adherents of the opposite view argue more convincingly that political parties were known, albeit not under that name, from the early years of Islam, that the Qur'an and the Sunna contain no injunction against the establishment of political parties, and that, on the contrary, the implication of such verses as 3:104, 4:114, and 58:9 is that it is permissible. Furthermore, it is argued, in the *shari'a* what is not expressly prohibited is allowed (*mubah*). Finally, the proponents of this view declare the existence of parties to be a necessity of political life that is its own justification in the absence of any clear prohibition.

A point on which some advocates of Islamic government put much emphasis is God's exclusive sovereignty, for which they use the term *al-hakimiyya li-Allah*. If they intend this merely as a denial of claims by rulers to absolute power unfettered by any higher norms, there can be no dispute on the point. If, however, they take literally the transcendental concept of divine sovereignty, they would have to explain how this sovereignty can be translated into political reality and how it can operate at the level of human relations between rulers and subjects.

The above observations may explain why in the writings and oral pronouncements of the proponents of a return to an Islamic government one finds mostly what may be said to correspond to the first part of a modern constitution, namely the enumeration of the purposes of government and a listing of political and civil rights. The modalities of reaching those ends and safeguarding those rights are not dealt with in any detail. There is hardly a full description of a workable form of the institutions of the desired government, of the method for designating the head of state or for replacing him, of the relationship between the various branches of government for which the need cannot be denied. One point on which there is agreement is that an Islamic government exists in order to uphold and apply God's law, the *shari'a*, and the present governments are taken to task for having ignored this duty and for being therefore un-Islamic. Since governments of differing forms are equally capable of fulfilling that duty, agreement on this point does not amount to a political program. It may therefore be said that the impact of contemporary Islamic doctrine on constitutional law in the Middle East is still ill-defined and that Islamic doctrine has not yet resulted in any specific constitutional changes except in the one case of Khomeini's Iran. Detailed consideration of the Iranian case is beyond the scope of this presentation, and this author does not claim expertise in the Shi'i doctrine. It is clear, however, that under the new Iranian constitution[6] there is a central role for the *faqih* (i.e., the highest and most authoritative Shi'i jurist), who is in fact considered to be the deputy of the Hidden Imam. This is therefore a typically Shi'i model which has no applicability in the Sunni context. It is noteworthy, however, that the new Iranian constitution was put to a popular vote and that it preserves the parliamentary form of government with an executive responsible to a legislature elected by universal suffrage.

In the final analysis, any form of government is Islamic that fosters and promotes the basic principles and values of Islam in the area of public affairs. Of these, three are of immediate practical importance: (a) the supremacy of the law, and the subjection to it of the ruler and the ruled alike; (b) concern for the economically disadvantaged, short of leveling individual wealth; and (c) participation by the governed in the affairs of government. The first two call for no elaboration. With regard to the third, participation traditionally took the form of consultation, but it need not necessarily stop there. *Shura* was prescribed for the Prophet with all his immense authority and his personal infallibility. Fallible rulers of lesser stature may well need more extensive and more institutionalized forms of participation by the people in public affairs. *Shura* is merely a form; the underlying principle is participation. A multiparty parliamentary regime provides the most effective form of such institutionalized participation. This system's principal merit is that it does away with the need for the forcible overthrow of an oppressive or inefficient government, thus preserving the peace of the community which is a major value in the Islamic concept of government. The multiparty parliamentary system certainly cannot be said to be un-Islamic merely because it first came into being among non-Muslim nations.

Notes

1. Mustafa al-Rafi'i, *Al-Islam nizam insani* (Islam is a Humanitarian System), 2nd ed. (Beirut, n.d.), pp. 19–20.
2. References in English to al-Ghazzali and Ibn Jama'a are to be found in Albert Hourani, *Arabic Thought in the Liberal Age* (London: Oxford University Press, 1962), pp. 1–14; and in G.E. von Grunebaum, *Medieval Islam* (Chicago, IL: Chicago University Press, 1946), pp. 168–69.
3. Abdulhamid Metwalli, *Mabadi' nizam al-hukm fi al-Islam* (Principles of the System of Rule in Islam) (Alexandria: Munsha'at al-Ma'arif, 1974), pp. 243–50; A.K. Abulmagd, "Qadiyyat al-shura," *Al-'Arabi* (Kuwait, September 1980), pp. 18–24.
4. Al-Rafi'i, *Al-Islam*, pp. 48–49; S.S. Ahmad, "Political Parties and [the] Islamic Political System," *The Muslim World League Journal*, No. 4 (Mecca, February 1983), pp. 28–31.
5. Wa'il 'Uthman, *Hizb Allah fi muwajahat hizb al-shaytan* (The Party of God in Confrontation with the Party of Satan) (Cairo, 1975), pp. 79–80.
6. *Constitutions of the Countries of the World: Iran* (Dobbs Ferry, NY: Oceana Publications, April 1980) (mimeographed).

19 RELIGIOUS IDEOLOGY, WOMEN, AND THE FAMILY: THE ISLAMIC PARADIGM*

Barbara Freyer Stowasser

I

In Muslim conviction, the ideal social paradigm of Islam is that blueprint of the perfect social order which God revealed to His community in the Qur'an and which was realized, applied, expanded, and detailed in the Sunna of the early Islamic *umma*. As the Qur'an and Sunna legislate both man's duties to God, i.e., the religious observances (*'ibadat*), and his duties to his fellow man (*mu'amalat*), the blueprint is comprehensive; it provides the believer with clear guidance in all matters of the faith and of social relations.

This definition of the ideal paradigm's basis and nature, however, can be a problematic one as used by many Muslim authorities who understand it to mean that, once this perfect order was revealed and established, it then took care of all contingencies while remaining immutable itself. The same Qur'anic commentators who interpret the Holy Book in the light of their own contemporary reality, for instance, usually fail to consider the factors of growth and development, adaptation and change which have characterized the ideal blueprint through the ages and which are thus indicative of its flexibility.

Indeed, the development of classical Islamic *fiqh* proves not only the considerable inner dynamism of the legislative-interpretive processes leading to its formation, but the flexibility and adaptability of the blueprint enshrined therein. The fact that *fiqh* eventually developed from a dynamic process into a stagnant, then ossified discipline has certainly had very negative effects on the normative order it proclaims, by causing it to be presented as immutable. But the fault here lies with latter-day jurisprudence, not with an original, insurmountable rigidity or inherent stagnant quality of the blueprint itself.

The development and eventual stagnation of Islamic family law,

* Research for this article was funded by a National Endowment for the Humanities summer grant in 1982. It was presented as a paper at the Social Science Research Council conference on "Family, Law, and Change in the Middle East" in 1983.

as well as the problems of modern law reform, particularly as they relate to the need to regain the inner dynamism characteristic of early Islamic *fiqh* in its formative stages, have recently been described with great insight by John Esposito in his *Women in Muslim Family Law*. This paper would be duplicating and repeating many of his ideas if it were to address itself to the legal aspects of the status, rights, and obligations of women as daughters, sisters, wives, concubines, divorcees, widows, mothers, etc. It will be more useful here to attempt a description in more general terms of what it is that makes a woman's life "Islamic." To achieve this task, it is not sufficient merely to study the relevant detail in the Qur'an, precisely because of the general, broad, and flexible nature of most of its directives. Since the the Qur'anic text for the most part spells out "what the aims and aspirations of Muslims should be," since it gives "the *ought* of the Islamic religious ethic,"[1] an important part of such an undertaking is showing how these broad and general directives were translated into the terms of a specific social reality by various later interpreters. The result of such an undertaking will be a series of "ideal paradigms," some very different from others. Their differences will reflect the ongoing social changes and/or the stagnation of the social order in the Islamic world. It will not come as a surprise to find as the result of such a comparative study that the interpretations of the Qur'anic guidelines concerning women's status become more and more restrictive through the centuries, until the nineteenth century with its first reform movements is reached. In spite of the importance of the Qur'anic interpretations of the reformers — such as Muhammad 'Abduh and Rashid Rida's *Tafsir al-Qur'an al-hakim* or Sayyid Ahmad Khan's *Tafsir al-Qur'an* — the late medieval restrictiveness continues to prevail, at least in the areas of social relations, women's status, and the family in the works of nineteenth and twentieth century conservative Qur'anic interpreters, such as Sayyid Qutb's *Fi zilal al-Qur'an*.[2]

As far as the Sunna and its function as a mirror of the ideal paradigm of women's role and status are concerned, the problems here are of a different nature. By virtue of its provenance and its role in shaping the Islamic order, the Hadith is both a record of the way of life of the early community and a dynamic vehicle of the process of Islamization. While the normative function of the Hadith as a source of Islamic values is a prime importance, the question of the authenticity of individual *hadiths* recedes into the background if we understand the Hadith correctly, i.e., as a dynamic, "gigantic and monumental commentary of [sic] the Prophet by the early Community,"[3] which mirrors the growth and development of Islam as shaped by the consonant and dissonant voices of the individual traditionalists. Given the inevitable gap between the actual and the idealized, as well as between the genuine and later ascriptions, it is only to be expected that the Hadith contains much varied and often contradictory information on the society it describes.[4] This makes of the Hadith, even after its compilation, an instrument in the hands of later Muslim interpreters that is as flexible as the broad and general directives of the Qur'an. While they can interpret their own social reality into the broad terms of the latter, they have an abundance of contradictory detail available in the former to substantiate their various teachings. It is not surprising to find that the late medieval Islamic authorities and their modern, conservative successors lean heavily toward the restrictive *hadiths* when they map out the blueprint of the ideal social order and the woman's place in it.

II

To substantiate the thesis put forth above that any number of "ideal paradigms" can be formulated on the basis of the Qur'an and the Sunna, this paper will introduce, in much condensed but otherwise unchanged form, a contemporary conservative interpretation of the role, the rights, and the responsibilities of the Muslim woman, especially as regarding her family. A few of the criteria by which the interpreter measures whether a woman's life may truly be termed "Islamic" will then be put into the context of the larger Sunna to show the availability of contradictory *hadiths* that the author disregarded in order to arrive at his particular "ideal paradigm." Second, these criteria of what makes a woman's life "Islamic" will be compared with the Qur'anic legislation itself. Third, it will be pointed out that while conservative Muslim thinkers continue to interpret the Qur'anic material in the tradition of the ossified medieval *tafsir*, there are now also some progressive and reform-minded contemporary Muslim specialists in the areas of law and theology who are striving for a new methodology for Qur'anic exegesis that will enable them to interpret and apply the Qur'anic principles and values more freely to the exigencies of modern life.

The particular conservative interpretation we will examine is to be found in a very popular contemporary guide for the Muslim woman by Shaykh Muhammad Mutawalli al-Sha'rawi entitled *Qadaya al-mar'a al-muslima* (Issues Concerning the Muslim Woman, Cairo: Dar al-Muslim, 1982). Shaykh l-Sha'rawi is the editor of *Minbar al-Islam*, which is published by Al-Majlis al-A'la li-al-Shu'un al-Islamiyya. He also writes regularly on Islamic issues for *Al-Ahram* and several other Egyptian newspapers and journals. Shaykh al-Sha'rawi has his own, widely viewed weekly television show in Egypt which is broadcast from a different mosque each week, and the cassettes of his sermons are available at street-stands and a variety of shops, and sell in large numbers. Shaykh al-Sha'rawi, in other words, is an important voice in contemporary Egypt. He is now in his mid-seventies.

While it was partially because of his status and measurable impact as a voice of conservative Islam that his treatise was selected for the purpose of this paper, the choice was also influenced by the fact that his book encapsulates and summarizes in a most representative fashion much of what is presently being said by conservatives on the role of the Muslim woman within and outside the family in the Islamic world.

I have divided Shaykh al-Sha'rawi's guidelines for the Muslim woman, following more or less the outline of the book itself, into five parts: 1. Anatomy is destiny; 2. Women's rights; 3. Women and work; 4. Veiling and unveiling; and 5. Women and the family.

1. Anatomy is Destiny

Men and women have God-given different natures which predetermine the task which they are qualified to perform on earth. When one of the sexes becomes jealous of the rights and duties of the other, the result is the corruption of the whole order of being.

> God has determined for each sex its task beyond which it may not go. If this is ensured, each sex can perform its function without conflict. Corruption arises when one sex is jealous of the rights and duties of the other; from this results the corruption of the order of being. (p. 64)
>
> It is strange that equality should be demanded for the two sexes whose mold is different and whose make-up is contrary: contrary not in the spiritual, but in the organic sense, in an objective way, even as to the cells of their bodies and the external, physical symptoms of their appearance. Those who advocate equality of woman with man, why do they not demand

that man should do woman's work, so that they may be equal? Otherwise, they commit an outrage against the principle of equality which they desire. If the woman does the work of the man, while continuing to do her own special type of work that only she can do, then the meaning of all this is to burden her with an additional load. (pp. 11–12)

We are asking the man who wants the woman to go out and toil like a man: Why do you want her to perform your jobs although there are many jobs that she cannot perform? As long as you want her to do your work, you should do hers; go ahead and bear and nurse the children. Therefore, let's leave the woman out and leave the matter of her working to cases of established necessity. He who wants a good life has to pay the price, which is: endeavor and enterprise. To reap the fruits without toil is corruption. Those who demand woman's equality with man are clamoring for her damage and oppression. If the woman were impartial, she would see those who demand her equality with man — including all that the concept of equality entails — as enemies. And if those who demand her equality were fair, they would require that she perform all the jobs of the male and not restrict her quest of equality of those jobs that are easy and soft, neither tiresome not strenuous nor fatiguing. (pp. 25–26)

By virtue of her anatomy, then, the woman is predestined to perform only the task for which she was created: the bearing and raising of children. The woman is "the crooked rib" (see below); this metaphor expresses her main characteristics.

2. Women's Rights

The main rights of the woman in Islam, as listed by al-Sha'rawi, are: her full personhood; her equality with the man in the relationship with God; her full freedom in the matter of the faith; civil and property rights (which, however, are not described in any detail); the right to carry her own name after marriage rather than that of her husband or his family; and the right to pursue the proper type of education. Her right to maintenance by the husband is described later in the section dealing with her status in the family. It is within the family setting that a woman's real rights lie.

As to man's and woman's joint characteristics, God created them from one fundamental substance. As the Qur'an says: "He created you from one being, then from that [being] He made its mate." (Qur'an 39:6)[5]

It is not — as other sects and religions teach — that it was Satan who created the woman, or that the god of evil created her while the god of good created the man. Rather, according to Islam, they belong to one species. As humans, they are equals in responsibility for all that they do. As the Prophet says: "The man is a shepherd over and responsible for his flock, and the woman is a shepherdess over and responsible for her flock." And they are also both responsible before God. As the Qur'an says: "Whosoever doeth right, whether male or female, and is a believer, him verily We shall quicken with good life." (16:97) (pp. 9–10)

Islam has also established the woman's complete freedom in the matter of her faith. But after she has chosen, she becomes responsible for her choice. She may go against her husband's righteous choice, as did the wives of Noah and Lot, or against her husband's sinful choice, as did the Pharaoh's righteous and believing wife. (p. 10)

Islam has furthermore provided the woman with complete civil rights which do not exist in any other religion. The Jewish woman is subject to the guardianship of her father before marriage and to her husband after marriage. In French positive law, she does not have the right to stipulate individual property for herself against her husband. (p. 11)

If we were to take a good look, we would find that Western civilization deprives the woman of her particular attributes. What are the primary characteristics of the human being? They are: shape, characteristic features, and name. When a woman marries in Europe, she calls herself by her husband's name. She does not have the right to retain her name or her father's or mother's name. As a result of the infatuation of the "imitators" with the West at the beginning of the Renaissance, women found themselves compelled to eliminate their fathers' and their families' names and retain only their own. This was difficult to do, although in Europe and America a woman relinquishes her name altogether and is addressed by the name of her husband and his family as a matter of course. What equality exists there for a woman after she has been deprived of her name? In Islam, however, even the wives of the Prophet — who was the noblest of all creation and whose name to carry would have honored every single one of them — were not called Madame Muhammad ibn 'Abd Allah, or wife of Muhammad, but 'A'isha bint Abi Bakr, Hafsa bint 'Umar, Zaynab bint Jahsh. They retained their names and those of their fathers. But the West does not give the woman any rights, neither concerning her name, nor concerning her wealth. Rather, the freedom that women obtained there came about only because of the war, when the males were soldiers and needed the women to replace them in their civilian jobs; so they gave them some rights, to benefit from their labor. (pp. 13–14)

Socrates, for instance, has said that the woman is not prepared by her nature to understand rational knowledge . . . but that she is prepared to cook, and raise the children. Plato gave her a share in education, which made him unpopular. The satirist Aristophanes made fun of educated women in his play "The Pedantic Women," and Molière after him wrote a play entitled "The Women's Parliament." Islam, however, does not have this attitude toward women. Indeed, the Prophet has said that "the pursuit of knowledge is a religious duty for every Muslim man and woman." For example, Hafsa bint 'Umar studied some reading and writing with an Adawite woman and when the Prophet married her, he requested from 'Umar that this woman should continue to come to the house to teach Hafsa the remaining knowledge, to improve what she had already learned. In Islam, the women should study, but they should pursue the proper type of education. Just as men pursue the education that behoves them (industrial, business, agricultural, etc.), so also should the women pursue what behoves them. (pp. 14–15)

3. Women and Work

As is predetermined through her God-given physical and mental attributes, the woman's place is in the home. In the home, hers is the noblest of all professions, one far higher in rank than any profession pursued by men. Even those Western women who have achieved high positions on the job ladder are known to yearn for a return to being housewives. When a woman stays at home she contributes through her labor there far more to the family budget than when she earns a salary outside and has to pay for the expenses of the support staff that is taking her place in the home. While it is acceptable by Islamic standards for a woman to work with her husband, it is most problematic if she leaves the home to work elsewhere. Such a course is acceptable only if there exists a true and established need for her to do so, if she comports herself with all modesty when outside of the home, and if she gives up her work and returns to the home at the very earliest possibility.

The woman should be grateful, because while the man works with the lower species — as a farmer with the earth, the cattle, and other animals, or as an industrial worker with dead matter — the woman works with the most noble part of creation, the human being. The woman who is dissatisfied with this duty is worthless indeed. (p. 18)

If she wants to carry out her task as mistress of the house, wife, mother, and educator, she will not find the time to work elsewhere. Let her study and teach her children, thereby saving the cost of a private teacher, or weave and embroider and thereby save the tailor's expenses. If a woman applies herself in this way, she can save the household multiples of the salary she would ever earn, as well as the cost of clothing and other things which she would need if she were to go out to work. (p. 18)

Does a professional woman demand more work, the higher she climbs the professional ladder? Or does she rather want to be the mistress of a house, the more prominent and older she gets? This is so even with Western women. Marilyn Monroe was weary of the limelight and said that, if she were to do it all over again, she would prefer to be only a housewife. This is an attitude that is shared by many working women. (pp. 18–19)

Islam, however, is a realistic religion. If the circumstances necessitate that the woman should work, different interpretations are possible. There is woman's work in her husband's job, house, field, or for his and his children's care . . . The problem arises with that type of work which makes the woman leave her house and mingle with men. Here, Islam is realistic in establishing that if a woman is compelled to work, this represents an emergency situation. The necessity to work should be understood as such. The woman should be aware that she is a woman and should behave accordingly in public, and do her work without coming into bodily contact with anybody, to the extent possible. (p. 20)

When society at large becomes aware that a female is compelled by circumstances to leave her natural domain, society has to perform this woman's task for her to enable her to return to her home. As for the woman, she has to be swift about getting this necessity taken care of. . . . Islam's assessment of the need to work then involves the following points: the need itself, the assessment or rating of the need, the obligation of society to take care of the job for the woman, and the obligation of the woman herself to remove the need to work at the first available opportunity, and to always remember that she is female, when she works and when she walks. (pp. 22–23)

In assessing "need," people are of different opinions. There is the need to sustain life, and then there is the entirely different need to obtain luxuries. Necessary living expenses are those for food. But we are dealing with luxuries when someone says: I cannot get married because I cannot find a four-room apartment and equip it with a stove and a refrigerator. He wants to begin his life in a style that his father never achieved . . . But do not propose to a woman without being ready for her, under the pretext that life is a partnership and that she will work along with you . . . Society lost its equilibrium when man forgot his natural worth and aspired to live beyond his level, which compelled him to steal or accept bribes or cheat. (pp. 23–24)

These statements may seem to entail some harshness for the woman, while in reality this is a harshness that exists for her sake. (p. 25)

4. Veiling and Unveiling

It is interesting to note that in al-Sha'rawi's primer for the Islamic woman, the material on the veil is more voluminous than that on any other topic. His remarks on this subject are about four times longer than his treatment of women's rights or women and work, and in their totality surpass in length even what he has to say about women and the family. Al-Sha'rawi clearly equates the wearing of the veil with belief in God and religious devotion. He warns that the veil has to be worn for the love of God only and not for any other, inferior reason. The veil earns its wearer recompense and rewards in the hereafter. Hence, only carelessness regarding God's rewards and punishment can explain the conduct of those women who fail to wear it. This explains why old women turn with such vigor toward religiously correct behavior at the end of their lives, shortly before they meet their maker.

What is the meaning of "Islamic"? It means that I take something upon myself by choice. Where there is no choice, there is no obligation. The obligation establishes what to do and what not to do. Failure to be convinced by the obligation indicates a lack of faith in Him who has imposed it. People say easily: "He has charged me to do this, but conditions do not permit me to carry out this obligation, because of such and such . . ." But this is a refutation of God's authority. If a human being believes in God, but is unable to carry out God's command- ments, he is a disobedient believer. He is better than the unbeliever who totally refutes God's authority, just as Adam's disobedience is different from Satan's. Satan refuted God's authority, while Adam said: I have sinned. (p. 43)

A woman may not forgo the veil claiming that she is in a special situation. This order is imposed upon you by God as an act of religious devotion. (p. 44)

I have seen many veiled women and have asked them to explain their reasons for veiling themselves: some wear the veil because it is some kind of fashion article, others adopt it as a social matter, while others think that young men who are desirous of marriage turn toward those who abide by the rule of the veil. None of these reasons have to do with God and therefore some women actually give up the veil after they have worn it. The sound purpose of veiling is that it be for the love of God, in obedience to Him, and out of belief in Him and His order. All who wear the veil for this purpose will come to live it more each day, since no act endures except if its underlying reason endures . . . If you do something for an enduring reason, it will endure, but if you do it for a reason that is prone to change, so will the act. I act for the sake of God, whether people like what I do or not, since their approval is not to be taken into consider- ation by the believer . . . If a human being acts righteously and then stops, tell him: you acted for the sake of something other than God. (pp. 44–45)

Worldly embellishment, ornament, and adornment have to be weighed by the discriminating woman against the punishment which they will earn for her who indulges in them. The believer who is charged with the obligation to observe the precepts of religion only fails to carry out God's commandment because he fails to perceive the reward for obedience and the punishment for disobedience. If the woman perceived clearly what God's punishment for the violation of His rules will be, she would not go astray. The reason for abandoning God's commands and injunctions is the carelessness concerning the recompense. (pp. 45–46)

The young woman at the beginning of her life should look toward those women whose lives are coming to an end; without a doubt she will see that they attempt to revive their values, are devoted to modesty, and wear out the religious authorities with requests for legal opinions concerning what is lawful and what is not, and how they should relieve their consciences of things that occurred in the past. Instead of postponing this awakening of faith until old age, the young Muslim woman has to understand that she does not own her appointed time and thus cannot ensure that she will have time for repentance. And even if she does, why should she want to postpone this sweetness to the end of her life, instead of making it hers swiftly in purity and sincerity? (p. 47)

While immodest behavior necessarily means that the faith has been shattered, for which the woman will clearly be punished by God, the harm caused by such behavior is not restricted to the culprit herself, since she also becomes guilty of corrupting all the males who come in contact with her. Only men who are themselves corrupted will permit their wives to expose themselves in this fashion. On the other hand, such exposure will not win a young woman a husband, since all those she will be able to seduce will be married men or young, dependent males who are not yet marriageable.

The purpose of the veil is to make it impossible for a man to become sexually aware of a woman, by seeing her. This is necessary, because all sexual awareness necessarily leads to sexual desire.

Satan deceives many a young woman into believing that civilization and progress require strutting about and the wearing of ornament, and the displaying of one's charms, and that these do not indicate moral decline and the shattering of the faith, and that she herself can be committed to her faith in spite of indulging in these. This is quite untrue. (pp. 47–48)

Furthermore, her appearance excites the sexual instincts and attracts the attention of all those who see her. Even if her modesty had no other purpose but to curb their pretexts, this alone should suffice [to induce her to be modest]. Furthermore, a husband's masculinity desires that the woman be exclusively his. He who does not desire this in his wife intends to see other women himself. To permit her to do this is the license [for him] to enter into that polluted society [as well]. (p. 48)

The woman must not be deceived by those who encourage her to strut about and to abandon the veil. The feminist thinkers who inflate the woman to bring her out [into the open, unveiled] intend to defame Islam. When a woman goes out for work or education, what does that have to do with the exposure of her bust and legs? The corruptors want to corrupt the woman and want to prepare . . . the tools of her perversion. (pp. 48–49)

The young men we see in the streets today do not lack in inflamed sexual drive, but rather have more than an abundance of it already. Do you, Muslim sister, want to excite even further the adolescent who is already charged with sexual voracity? It is an obligation to veil from him all that may further excite his sexual drive, because he has plenty and more than plenty of that as is. (p. 49)

The only criterion by which Islam defines sexual maturity is the matter of looking at a woman: because of the desire that arises from it . . . Awareness is of three kinds: sexual awareness, emotional passion, and sexual desire. The Law forbids [unlawful] sexual desire; as for sexual awareness and emotional passion, the Law forbids them only in those cases when the man sees the woman, because . . . when a man sees a beautiful woman, his pleasure in her is like an internal motor that churns up in him his sexual desire. Islam thus prevents the process of becoming sexually aware of a woman [by seeing her], because if that were permitted, but sexual desire were not, anxiety and discomfort would result. (pp. 52–53)

When the woman has the intention of corrupting, through provocation, enticement, embellishment and cheap tinsel, whom does she corrupt? A married man [mostly], who has been married for thirty years, whose wife's face has become wrinkled from bearing his children. When he sees a girl in her twenties walking in his path with a swinging gait, and then goes home and sees his wife with the wrinkles of old age on her face, he compares, becomes nervous, and concocts reasons for a domestic quarrel. The food is salty today . . . the house is dirty today . . . etc. Or the young man who is still a student and wants to build his life but cannot [yet] get married, and whose father is having great trouble with [financing] his education — he finds the scourge that inflames him in the streets, and what can he do? (p. 50)

The veil is God's gift to the woman in that it ensures for her respect and veneration in her old age, neither of which she will enjoy if she fails to wear it when young. Her worldly punishment will be even worse than that, in actual fact, as in her old age a young woman will appear and entice her husband and her son away from her.

Only when she wears the veil can the woman truly fulfill her God-given and preestablished task, which is to symbolize peace and serenity for her husband, and to bring up the most noble of all species, the human.

> When God veiled the woman, He did it to protect her [whole] life. Woman's youthfulness comes to an end, and then society is less welcoming to her. When she goes shopping, she is neglected by the shopkeeper who used to draw out his chats with her when she was young. Society no longer honors her because she has lost her femininity. God says to her: In your youth, I want to bind you to a noble and pure way of life, and when you get old, your value will increase. When your son sees you, all wrinkled and white haired, he will sit down and kiss you and eulogize your white hair. Society, which used to forsake you when you got older, will hold you in ever higher esteem. We want you to sit down . . . don't do anything, just pray, and remember us in your prayers. (pp. 50–51)

> Hence, when God desires to prevent the woman from leaving the house and strutting about to excite the sexual drive in the man, it is to protect her old age: so God does not bestow upon her a young woman who will entice her husband and her son away from her when she has gotten old. (p. 51)

As for the features of the Islamic veil, al-Sha'rawi emphasizes that it was an important part of the early Islamic way of life. The early Muslim women wore it joyfully, without consideration of "modernity" or "lack of comfort," because of the intensity of their faith. Great detail is then given on the appropriate length and thickness of the veil and the style in which it should be worn.

> [As to the Islamic veil], we have to establish right at the start that the rules of the veil were part and parcel of early Islamic society because these rules protected a people who believed in God and His Prophet and his mission as God's authorized agent

to legislate for His community . . . This original faith which gladdened the hearts of the early Muslims induced the women of the Ansar, when they heard the Qur'anic verse ". . . and to draw their veils [*khumur*] over their bosoms [*juyub*], and not to reveal their adornment save to their husbands or fathers . . ." etc. (24:31), to tear their mantles and veil themselves with the material until at the morning prayer they looked as if black ravens were nesting on their heads. For this reason, they were praised by the Mother of the Believers, 'A'isha. Not one of them was afraid of a loss of elegance, or the hardship of the summer heat in that barren land, nor did any words about "modernity" come from their lips. Not one of them spoke in high-sounding terms about "having to be convinced of the necessity to do this." Not one of them turned toward emancipation and unrestraint or what else the devils were hoping for. It sufficed for these women that this commandment had come down from God . . . to turn this blessed community into a direction pleasing to God. (pp. 54– 55)

It requires a return to the strength of belief and moral character similar to that of the first, outstanding women of Islam before the women of today will behave in like manner.

There are some women who will give in willingly and completely to God's command; these are the women who will enter Paradise. Then there are those who believe in some of God's commandments and not in others; their compensation will be disgrace and shame. And then there are those who are infidels altogether, who will suffer the consequences; they will taste the punishment of disgrace and degradation for their unbelief, God willing. (p. 56)

In his examination of the proper shape of the Islamic veil, on the basis of God's Book and the Prophet's Sunna, al-Sha'rawi then quotes the following Qur'an verse: "And tell the believing women to lower their gaze and be modest [literally: cover their private parts] and display of their adornment only that which is apparent, and to draw their veils [*khumur*] over their bosoms [*juyub*] and not to reveal their adornment save to their husbands or fathers or husbands' fathers, or their sons or their husbands' sons, or their brothers or brothers' sons or sisters' sons, or their women, or their slaves, or male attendants who lack vigor, or children who know naught of women's nakedness. And let them not stamp their feet so as to reveal what they hide of their adornment. And turn unto Allah altogether, O believers, in order that ye may succeed." (24:31)

The *khimar* [plural: *khumur*] is the cover for the head, *jayb* [plural: *juyub*] is the throat and the forepart of the chest. And the request here is for the head covering to be pulled over throat and chest. How? You women know more about this than we men do! This Qur'an verse gives the limits [of veiling] from above. How about from below? We find the answer in the same verse: "And let them not stamp their feet so as to reveal what they hide of their adornment." The adornment of the feet are the anklets. And when the women hid these with long and loose-fitting gowns, as this verse indicates, they used to stamp their feet so that this ornament would become audible from behind the veiling garment. On the basis of this verse, then, it is established that the legs have to be covered down to the place where the anklets are worn, i.e., the heels. (p. 49)

The Prophet said to Asma' bint Abi Bakr when she entered his room in a thin garment: "O Asma', when a young woman has reached the age of menstruation, it is not fitting that anything should be visible of her [body] but such and such," and he pointed to his face and hands. And 'A'isha says: "The women of the believers were praying the dawn prayer with the Prophet, veiled in their cloaks. After the prayer they went home, indistinguishable from the darkness of the night." (pp. 57–58)

Al-Sha'rawi uses these stories as indications that these commandments from God and His Prophet were translated into "actual behavior and reality" among the believers. He then quotes *hadiths* which indicate that the garment may not be dragged arrogantly or proudly, but has to be lifted up enough to avoid the dragging of its train on the ground while at the same time continuing to cover the feet (pp. 58–60). Furthermore, he points out that the garment, in order to fulfill the conditions to be called "Islamic," may not in itself be decorative, a requirement which he bases on the Qur'an verse that the women may not "display of their adornment" (see above) as well as on the Qur'an verse: "And stay in your houses. Do not bedizen yourselves with the bedizenment of the Time of Ignorance" (33:33). He furthermore uses *hadiths* to prove that the garment should be heavy, not light; that it should not be molded to the body and revealing of it; that it may not be perfumed or smell of incense; that this garment should not resemble men's clothing; and that it should not be showy (pp. 60–62). He concludes this section by saying:

> I do not know anyone who can claim to believe in God and the Last Judgment and then arrogantly persist in what she does as if she had not heard a thing of what the Qur'an says: "Woe unto each sinful liar; Who heareth the revelations of Allah recited unto him, and then continueth in pride as though he heard them not. Give him tidings of a painful doom." (45:7 and 8) (p. 63)

5. *Women and the Family*

The sexual instinct in men and women and the pleasure the sexes bring to each other in lawful marriage are part of God's plan for the world. He has endowed the act of cohabitation with the most pleasurable of all delights.

> God has joined this act of impregnation [of the woman by the man] to the most pleasurable of all delights, i.e., sexual pleasure. Some unclean aspects may be found in it, but these occur always at the end. The prelude is the most delightful thing which a human being experiences in a state of ecstasy. The consideration of uncleanness does not come up until after the ejaculation is over. The prelude is as desirable as is the act itself. The impurity derives from what comes afterwards. Such is what spoils all pleasure in this world. (p. 28)

The sexual instinct serves to preserve all species of living beings. But, in distinction from animals, "the sexual instinct in humans is excessive. The rational mind has to restrain it . . . The method by which the instinct is regulated is the institution of marriage" (p. 29).

> One of the purposes of Islam in legislating marriage is to prepare a fitting place in which to raise the offspring that results from the spouses' encounter. The Islamic guidelines here precede the child's existence as Islam takes into consideration both of the prospective parents. Islam legislates equality [*takafu'*] of the spouses. This equality does not entail equality of

wealth, but is an equality in essential nature, such as the mind, health, character, and values. (p. 30)

Islam directs its full attention to the suitability of the marriage partners in order to ensure for the child a sound "vessel" whose qualities he will inherit by the laws of heredity and which will be crucial for his later Islamic upbringing.

Hence, the Prophet's words: "Choose well where you put your sperm, since heredity is plotting and scheming." (p. 30)

Both the Sunna and the Qur'an, according to al-Sha'rawi, admonish us not to marry our close relatives because this weakens the offspring whereas marriages with non-relatives strengthen the progeny.

Hence the Prophet's words: "Marry foreigners and do not weaken [your children]."
Experiments with plants have established that mixed breeding yields stronger and more abundant results.
The same idea is expressed in Arabic poetry . . . (p. 30)

The present-day dilemmas of unhappy marriages, high divorce rates, and faulty polygamous unions do not stem from an imperfection in these institutions themselves as legislated by God, but result from the imperfection of the partners who enter into these marriages with non-Islamic intentions and standards.

Some superficial people look at the failure of some marriages, at the high rate of divorce, and at the troubles caused by polygamy, and blame all of these on the laws of Islam. This is the wrong point of view. First, we have to ask if the order is implemented according to the will of the Legislator; or are there things that are blamed on the law without justification? Only then can we grasp whether the ill is in the law or in its application — in which case it is wrong to object to the law itself. On this basis we must not blame Islam for the failure of marriages, family-threatening divorce, or faulty polygamy. Because those who encounter difficulties entered into marriage without Islamic standards. It is right that this should happen to them, as it is a natural consequence. If we look in fairness at the reasons for both divorce and the failure of polygamy, we find that both result from the spouses' violation of Islamic standards. The same applies to the bride's guardian when he accepts a husband for the bride in his charge by non-Islamic criteria. It is only just that all [these eventual ills] should occur, or else we would [have to] doubt God's teachings. The difficulties of divorce and polygamy in this day and age are a testimony for Islam, not against it. (pp. 33–34)

The happy marital union is one in which, according to God's command, "Men are in charge of women, because Allah hath made the one of them to excel the other" (4:34). This "being-in-charge" of the men over the women is a burden on the man and a privilege for the woman.

> The meaning is that the men are charged to protect the women, to work for them, and to serve them, and includes all the obligations involved therein. Hence, this . . . is a burden on the man. (p. 35)
>
> On the other hand, it does not represent a discrimination against the woman, because her and the man's tasks complement each other. "Because Allah hath made the one of them to excel the other" does not mean, as some allege, that God prefers the men over the women, or He would have said "because He has made the men to excel the women." The meaning, rather, is that the "being-in-charge" necessitates preference with regard to exertion, action, and toil . . . on the part of the man, and is equalled by preference in another sphere, i.e., that the woman has a task which man cannot fulfill in which she is preferred over him, since the man cannot carry or give birth to or suckle the children, or menstruate. (p. 35)

It is sinful, however, to attempt to change this God-willed order of task distribution and task preference.

> God says: "And covet not the thing in which Allah hath made some of you excel others" (4:32). That means, we cannot compare two individuals who each have a different task.
>
> When we look at the tasks, we find that they complement each other. The man has the preference of "being in charge" with regard to exertion and toil, while tenderness, care, and feeling

are lost to him because he is absorbed in the demands of the "being in charge." Therefore, God preserves the woman for her special task and does not burden her with the obligation to pay, but frees her for the other, arduous task for which she was created. The Lawgiver has established that the man should help the woman. When the Prophet entered his house and found his wives at work, he helped them. This is an indication that the woman's task is a major one and that the male should come to her aid in it. (pp. 35–36)

As for the woman, she should be grateful for her lot, since it is she who deals with the highest species — the human — and brings up the lord of creation, while the man works with "minerals and earth, plants, stones, and animals" (p. 36).

It is worthwhile to point out that al-Sha'rawi wastes very little effort in his discussion of the issue of polygamy. He deals with polygamy only to defend the Islamic order, which provides polygamy for the man but monogamy for the woman, for the following reasons:

The Orientalists have snatched up some things to bring to the attention of the women and are saying to them: God has oppressed you, because He has established for the men a plurality of wives on earth and in heaven as well as *huris* while you may not have more than one husband. All of this is done in order to prove that God has singled out the male in special favor over the woman. These Orientalists used an angle by which they thought they could win the women over and provoke them [to stand up] against Islam. They forgot that God in reality is honoring the woman because the woman who holds herself in high esteem does not accept or like to have many men. Therefore, when God did not provide for her a plurality of men, he bestowed honor upon her and did not leave her as a spoil for every stud wishing to mount her. Some high-minded women even refuse to take on another man after the husband's death, even though God has permitted this. But these people want to put the idea into her heart that God has deprived her, while forgetting that God has honored her by testifying that she is pure, precious, and does not like to have more than one man. (p. 37)

Once, I asked some people in America who put this objection to me — that men can have several women but women cannot have several husbands simultaneously — whether prostitution was legal in America and they answered that it was in some states. I asked them how they took precautions so as to ensure public health, and they said that these women are medically examined twice a week to protect them and their customers against venereal diseases. I asked if they had to examine married women every week or month as well, and they answered: no, since the married woman is exposed only to the husband's semen . . . and that venereal disease only occurs when the semen of many men comes together in one place. I said that, therefore, God was right to permit plurality of wives, but not of husbands. (p. 38)

I also asked them that since they had these places for young men to find release for their sexual drives, why did they not have them for young women? Why was there no place staffed with young men that young women could visit to release their sexual tensions? They said that this had never happened and I answered that this was proof that it would bring disgrace upon the woman. This is how sound natural disposition works. Hence God, when he gave the man the right to polygamy without giving the same right to the woman, neither in this world nor the next, awarded the woman protection and high rank. (p. 39)

It is strange that we find in some societies women who unlawfully permit for themselves a plurality of men. These women we term whores. A whore's characteristics are that the more men she tempts, the more God arouses people to dislike her and the more He lowers her chances of an afterlife, until all hold her in contempt. He who wanted to obtain the favor of a single glance of hers would spit on her if he saw her in the Hereafter. All of this shows how the accounts are balanced in this world. (pp. 39–40)

The woman's only natural task in life is to be a wife and mother. It is through the fulfillment of these functions that she achieves not only rank and honor, but realizes her selfhood.

In her relation to her husband, the woman's role is to provide warmth, serenity, and support in the home. While he goes out to toil for her, as Adam did under God's commandment, he renews his energies with her after the work is done.

In the story of Adam in the Qur'an, God said to Adam and his wife, warning them against Satan: "Therefore We said: O Adam!

This is an enemy unto thee and unto thy wife, so let him not drive you both out of the Garden so that thou [singular] should come to toil." (20:117) God here addresses both Adam and his wife Eve; so the language we would expect is "so that both of you should come to toil." In actuality, however, the Qur'an is here explaining to each of them his task in life and says: You [Adam] will be in hardship. This means that the toil is Adam's alone, as if Adam is created to fight and to face life's difficulties, while the woman is created only as a means of rest for him. Adam expends all of his energies in life and then comes to her to find tranquility with her. She is the source of tenderness that caresses away all of his troubles so he can resume life's struggle more energetically thereafter. (p. 66)

The woman's basic task is to give the man tranquility and peace. And thereafter come the children and the grandchildren . . . If the woman were to fulfill this task, she would find that it would take up all of her time — to work for him, prepare for him what relaxes him, so he can come and find a peaceful and stable home in which all affairs are well arranged, and to be the vessel of procreation. (pp. 66–67)

The woman was entirely created for motherhood. The metaphor of the "crooked rib" signifies woman's inherent nature which is the preponderance of emotions over rationality. These are the very characteristics that motherhood requires.

The Prophet said about the women that "they were created from a crooked rib; the most crooked part is its highest portion, and if you were to straighten it, you would break it [the breaking signifying divorce] so enjoy her as crooked as she is." He was not blaming the woman when he said this, but was defining women's natural disposition and the preponderance of emotions over rationality, with which God has distinguished them in contradistinction to the male in whom rationality surpasses the emotions. Neither man nor woman are inferior to the other. The "crookedness" in the *hadith* does not imply any corruption or imperfection in woman's nature, because it is this crookedness of hers that enables her to perform her task, which is to deal with children who need strong compassion and sympathy, not rationality. The words "the most crooked portion of the rib is its uppermost part" signify the compassion the woman feels for her child, and the supremacy of her emotion over her rational mind. On this basis, her "crookedness" has become a praiseworthy attribute for the woman, because this "crookedness" is in reality woman's "straightest" qualification for her task. (pp. 32–33)

It is the mother who should bring up her children to ensure that they turn into healthy human beings.

> The Qur'an has established that the mother has the right to suckle and take care of her child. As the Qur'an says: "Mothers shall suckle their children for two whole years." (2:233) Psychological and medical studies indicate that this is the necessary time period to nourish the child with his mother's milk. Islam desires that the mother suckle the child even if she and the father have separated and that he pay her remuneration for her suckling and caring for the child. Likewise, Islam desires that after the suckling it be the mother who brings up the child, because when the child is small, he does not need judicious and decisive rationality, but tenderness and soft feeling, both of which are consistent with the mother's constitution. (p. 41)
>
> When the woman is busy with another job away from the children, she thereby leaves them to a caretaker, for instance, a servant girl. This servant may be trustworthy but can never have the mother's heart. When the child grows up, he lags behind if he is brought up by anyone but his mother. (p. 67)
>
> When the child is with mother and father and siblings of different ages, and grandfather and grandmother, he learns from the members of each generation. (p. 67)
>
> [When the child is small], he will not be ready for a teacher for a long time, but this does not mean that he is not fit to be educated. In this situation, there is no one appropriate to educate him but the mother, the father, and the closest relatives. From the very first, all the goings-on about him influence his psyche as formative elements. Therefore, Islam desires to foster in all people tender feelings toward their small children, to prevent the development of abnormality, deviation, and inferiority complexes. (p. 42)

As a mother, a woman will find rank, honor, lifelong support, care, and love in Islam.

When the West designed a "Mothers' Day," we aped them in this without thinking about the reasons for creating this festival. The European thinkers found that the children were forgetting their mothers and failed to protect them, hence they designated one day in the year on which the children should remember their mother. We, however, are celebrating "Mothers" Day' at every moment of the year. Most of us, when we leave the mother's house, still kiss her hand, ask for her prayers, and bring her presents when we visit her. Hence, we do not need this festival; still, we have adopted it, as if it were a glorious feat of the West, while in reality it is a disgrace. (pp. 15–16)

In Europe, the son abandons his mother to live in a home for the aged, while his father lives somewhere else. Islam, however, has given us the principle of mutual support and solidarity, according to the parents' need. The mother is thrice more entitled to a son's companionship and support than the father, as the Prophet has said. This is so because the father is a man who could survive even if he were reduced to begging; not so the mother. (p. 16)

The Qur'an says: "We have commended unto man kindness toward parents." But the remainder of this verse deals exclusively with the mother: "His mother beareth him with reluctance and bringeth him forth with reluctance, and the bearing of him and the weaning of him is thirty months." (46:15) Here, the father is not mentioned. It is the mother who deals with a human being before he reaches awareness and understanding. She carries and raises him. Since all things turn around the father in the child's later life, God wanted the mother to be given special consideration. Hence, the mother is given her rights in Islam. (pp. 16–17)

III

Al-Sha'rawi's assembly and interpretation of both Qur'anic and Sunnaic detail concerning women and the family are strictly traditional and are actually quite representative of medieval Islamic thought. What makes them "modern" — beyond the occasional allusion to natural science which more often than not misses the mark — are the defensiveness and xenophobia that pervade the text and labor to blame all social change on the corrupting influences of the West. Indeed, all social change is here represented as "un-Islamic," while "The Islamic Order" is seen as an unchanging, strictly patriarchal one characterized by features such as the extended family, total authority of the male over the female, segregation of the sexes, etc.

Restrictive interpretations of the traditional Islamic sources of this kind are highly characteristic of contemporary Islamic thought. In spite of the fact that al-Sha'rawi is neither a professional theologian by training nor an Islamic revolutionary, but a highly visible media personality and popularizer who enjoys the support of the Egyptian government, his ideas belong directly to the contemporary vision advocated by Muslim traditionalists *and* revolutionaries of women's role in Islamic society. As Yvonne Haddad points out in "Islam, Women, and Revolution in Twentieth Century Arab Thought," contemporary committed Islam or "Islamism" ". . . has become a kind of moral rearmament in which women are spearheading the construction of a new social order and playing active roles in the anticipated vindication of the Muslim people," as bearers and maintainers of cultural and religious values in the face of a dominant, imperialistic West with its hostile challenges to Islam.[6]

There are at least two ways to criticize al-Sha'rawi's restrictive and inflexible blueprint of the Islamic social order. One is to look into the early sources themselves and to refute certain details by bringing into view contradictory detail indicative of the fact that early Islamic society was much more flexible and hence quite different from what this type of later, restrictive adaptation makes it out to be. The Hadith material is of prime importance for this purpose. As for the Qur'anic verses, they are also in most cases much broader and vaguer in their thrust than interpretations of this genre avow. It is through the early sources themselves that we will here attempt to criticize and "adjust" al-Sha'rawi's restrictive paradigm in one of its aspects, i.e., the issue of women's seclusion in the private sphere of the home and their veiling when abroad, that is, their exclusion from public life. The second way to deal with al-Sha'rawi's restrictive and inflexible system is to deny it its relevance altogether by understanding the Qur'an — as some modern, reform-minded Muslims are now doing — as a source book of Islamic *values* in which the general, moral-religious norms are more important than the specific political, social, and economic detail that the Holy Book proclaims. This much more difficult and fundamental critique will here be attempted on the question of woman's equality with man.

On the issues of veiling and seclusion, as on most others, the Hadith material is quite contradictory. Three main characteristics are discernible without difficulty. First, "permissive" and "restrictive" material is found side by side, often anchored in the same early authority (such as Ibn 'Abbas). Second, the relevant material often exists in the form of clusters of related traditions. In this context, it is noteworthy that the longer and more detailed variants more often than not include restrictive detail that is absent in the shorter versions. What comes across as an addition, in other words, is often restrictive. Finally, the restrictive material is therefore generally more abundant in the later, as opposed to the earlier, Hadith collections.

On the basis of these general observations which will have to suffice here, one can clearly argue that the traditions depicting women's visibility and full participation in society should be studied with the greatest care, for there is good reason to assume that they more or less faithfully reflect aspects of early Islamic society that were left behind by later generations.

In pre-Islamic times, the veil was probably not unknown among the women in the Hijaz, since it may have been used as a mark of distinction by the urban high-born as against the slave women.[7] In any case, however, its wearing apparently did not constitute an essential part of the early Islamic way of life. In the initial pledge of allegiance (*bay'a*) that the women as a group made to the Prophet, the veil is not mentioned. Rather, the women pledged that "they would not take partners unto God, steal, commit adultery, kill their children, lyingly invent slander, or disobey the Prophet in a lawful matter,"[8] which "lawful matter" is then explained as "that they would not scratch their faces or tear their breasts or undo their hair, and wail"[9]; nor would they "use obscene language"[10] or "act dishonestly toward their husbands (by favoring others or giving them of the husbands' wealth),"[11] or "sit with men in isolated places"[12] "except with those closely related,"[13] "as the Qur'an says."[14] Thus, the veil is not one of the conditions imposed upon the women, and as a matter of fact only one single *hadith* among the very large number of *hadiths* reporting on the women's *bay'a* in Ibn Sa'd's *Tabaqat* mentions that the women were "wrapped in their cloaks" when they went to see the Prophet.[15] But even this "wrapped in their cloaks" certainly does not signify a complete veiling.

It was a matter of course for women in early Islamic society to accompany their men into battle[16] and even to participate actively in battle, either by trying to instill the courage to fight in their men who had been defeated or whose spirits were lagging,[17] or by nursing the wounded, fetching water, and recovering the dead.[18] Women could also grant protection in war and asylum to a fugitive.[19]

In the early years of Islam, many women accepted the new religion and joined the community of believers on their own without the consent of their husbands, even making the *hijra* on their own.[20] Muhammad's paternal aunt Arwa may serve here as a representative voice speaking for the soul-searching that must have preceded such a drastic step:[21]

> To the son of her first marriage who has become a Muslim, Arwa laments the fact that women can't do what men can do: "By God, if we could do what men can do, we would follow and defend him [Muhammad]." As her son inquires what prevents her from doing the same, she answers that she has to find out first what the other women are doing. He then implores her to convert and pledge allegiance to Muhammad, and she does.

These women who joined the believers in Medina on their own, without their husbands, were submitted to an examination to establish "that love of God and His Prophet only, not love of a man or flight from a husband" were responsible for this decision.[22]

Women were traveling widely in the early years of Islam. While Muhammad's wives — at least according to some authorities — were secluded on their travels with the Prophet to a point where the Prophet himself mistook the litter of one of his wives for the litter of another,[23] other women appear to have been much freer of movement. Notably, we find a discussion in the Hadith on how long (e.g., twenty-four hours, three days) a woman may travel by herself without a husband or male relative accompanying her.[24] By the time of Ahmad ibn Hanbal, however, we find a *hadith* indicating that she may not travel without her husband or *dhu mahram* (closely related male who falls within the incest rule).[25]

As to women's participation in the prayers at the mosque, there is overwhelming evidence in the Hadith that women prayed in the mosques together with the men.[26] They even visited the mosques at night.[27] The sheer number and variety of traditions indicating that women had the right to visit the mosque and should not be prevented from doing so,[28] or that they should be admonished to visit the *musalla* on the days of festival,[29] or that they must leave the mosque before the men,[30] or that one gate of the mosque is reserved for women,[31] or, finally, that the women are advised to perform the prayers in their houses,[32] in all probability reflect the various stages of the debates on this point that were taking place in the early Islamic community. These debates eventually ended with the women's disappearance from public prayer, "as the harsh disapproval of the learned succeeded in driving them out of the mosque."[33] Even the question as to whether or not menstruating women must avoid the mosque is part of this debate; here we find, e.g., the imposition that the prayers of menstruating women are only accepted *if they wear a veil.*[34]

The debate was later extended to include women's access to the bathhouse[35] and, not surprisingly, the later religious authorities wished to see the bathhouse prohibited to women.[36]

The men and women of the early Islamic community often met in the streets and greeted each other.[37] Even in the homes, however, there was ample social contact between the sexes, so that men and women knew each other personally, even if they were not closely related. Some traditions report that men visited their wives' houses and saw and talked with the female guests present,[38] just as they visited sick women to talk to them.[39] We also find reports on women acting as hostesses to the husband's guests.[40] One of the many available and well-documented categories of situations which may be used as evidence for the considerable amount of social contact between men and women in early Islam is that wherein a man proposes directly to a woman (in all cases the women described are widows or divorcees), without the benefit of a male intermediary. These proposals often occur in the house of the woman whom the man is visiting. We hear, e.g., of a woman who tells a suitor of a previous proposal by another man. The (second) suitor proposes right then and there and gets the bride.[41] Similar evidence may be found in the Prophet's proposal to Zaynab bint Jahsh, whose house he entered after her divorce from Zayd, but prior to his own marriage to her, without even having asked for her permission to enter.[42] We also hear about Umm Salama, to whose house the Prophet came to pay his condolences during a lengthy visit after her husband's death. After her waiting period he then proposed to her personally, and, after some negotiations, she accepted him.[43] It is not surprising that in this story, as in many others, additional *hadiths* exist which indicate either that a curtain existed between her and him on this occasion, or that the groom sent an emissary to express the proposal, or that he proposed "to the son of her brother or to her son, or to her guardian." Through emendations/additions such as these, the story was brought into agreement with later expectations.

Finally, there are even some isolated instances of "women who offered themselves in marriage" (*hiba*). Ibn Sa'd relates two such stories of the Islamic era, both of which involve the Prophet as the prospective husband. In neither case did the proposal lead to actual marriage, as the Prophet rejected one of the offers, while the other one was withdrawn.[44] Likewise, we find some indications that repudiation of the man (again the Prophet himself) by the woman was possible; Ibn Sa'd relates three incidents of this nature.[45] Highly interesting as these occurrences are,[46] they remain isolated instances and play too small a part in the bulk of the information on early Islamic society as a whole to be regarded as vitally constituent parts of that society's traditions. They remain relatively ephemeral, because their weight does not equal that of the material relating women's visibility, accessibility, and participation in communal life.

The fact that the Hadith very strongly indicates that women were visible and played a role in public life certainly reflects the Qur'anic commandments on this point. The Qur'an contains no exhortations to women in general to stay in their houses or to shun "man's work." As for the "law of the veil," the two verses directed at Muslim women in general which deal with this issue are:

O Prophet! Tell thy wives and thy daughters and the women of the believers to draw their cloaks round them [when they go abroad]. That will be better, that so they may be recognized and not annoyed. Allah is ever Forgiving, Merciful. (33:59)

And tell the believing women to lower their gaze and be modest [literally: cover their private parts], and display of their adornment only that which is apparent, and to draw their veils [*khumur*] over their bosoms [*juyub*, literally: breast-pockets], and not to reveal their adornment save to their husbands or fathers or husbands' fathers, or their sons or their husbands' sons, or their brothers or brothers' sons or sisters' sons, or their women, or their slaves, or male attendants who lack vigor, or children who know naught of women's nakedness. And let them not stamp their feet so as to reveal what they hide of their adornment. And turn unto Allah altogether, O believers, in order that ye may succeed. (24:31)

These two verses were, of course, later used as the basis for increasingly restrictive interpretations until they came to be understood as a divine order to the woman to hide every inch of her body behind an all-enveloping garment. Their literal meaning, however, which is both vague and problematic, does not at all necessitate such a course of interpretation.

A different story appears, both in the Qur'an and the Hadith, where the Prophet's wives are concerned. The pertinent Qur'anic commandments are to be found in 33:28–34 and 33:53 and 55. The Qur'an here clearly indicates that the wives of the Prophet "are not like any other women" (33:32); the context and the wording establish that the legislation applies to them specifically and not to the believers in general. As a group, the Prophet's wives have special rights and privileges as well as special duties, among which is the duty to "stay in your houses.[47] Bedizen not yourself with the bedizenment of the Time of Ignorance . . . " (33:33), and to remain behind a curtain in the presence of strangers — ". . . And when ye ask of them [the wives of the Prophet] anything, ask it of them from behind a curtain" (33:53). Likewise, they are not permitted to remarry after the Prophet's death (3:53).

The Hadith tends to reflect the application of these injunctions in the lives of this very special group of women, but clearly sets them apart from the more ordinary members of Islamic society.

After this critique "on technical grounds" of al-Sha'rawi's exhortations to the Muslim woman to veil and seclude herself because "that is the tradition of Islam," we now have to address the other and more complicated issue — male authority in Islamic society.

It has been widely recognized that, if one is to gain a correct understanding of its scope and importance, the Qur'anic material pertaining to the status of women should be studied against the background of the Jahiliyya. Islam is a religion of the city. Far from being a mere "projection of the Bedouin mind,"[48] the new faith with its mutually integrated religious, social, political, and economic institutions was born in and shaped by a city environment. Furthermore, Islam arose within the context of a situation of deep-going changes brought about by economic development that had already profoundly altered the political, social, and spiritual structures in Western Arabia.[49] It may indeed be the increasing urbanization and the social changes it had caused at the end of the Jahiliyya period which, combined with a deplorable lack of pertinent sources, are the reasons for our uncertainty concerning the status of women in pre-Islamic Arab urban society. On the one hand, we hear of publicly visible, independently wealthy women who are active in their own rights. The best-known example here is, of course, Khadija, Muhammad's first wife. As I have suggested elsewhere,[50] some details of Khadija's marriage to Muhammad are reminiscent of what Wellhausen[51] has suggested about matriarchal marriages in pre-Islamic Arabia. While the issue of the Arabian matriarchate is an old controversy,[52] it has recently been revived by Fatima Mernissi,[53] who makes a very strong case indeed that, since there apparently was no well-defined system of (patrilocal) polygamy in the pre-Islamic urban centers of Western Arabia and since marriages were frequently uxorilocal, these marriage patterns by themselves suggest a much greater degree of women's independence from their husbands and female sexual self-determination, both of which stand clearly in the face of the Islamic patriarchal order. As for marriage by capture or purchase, which implies a structure of virilocal polygamy, Mernissi maintains that this was "a novel idea in the Prophet's time as evidenced by his own inconsistent attitude towards it."[54] While Reuben Levy in his *The Social Structure of Islam* also indicates that "traces of an old system in which marriage did not necessarily mean the husband's definite mastery over the wife" are occasionally encountered in literature concerning a small number of privileged women,[55] he insists on the other hand that the majority of pre-Islamic urban women appear to have lived in a male-dominated society in which their status was low and their rights negligible. Most women were subjugated to male domination, either that of a male relative or that of the husband. The men's rights over their women were the same as the rights over any other property. This was certainly the case in marriages by capture, where the captured woman was completely under the authority of her captor. According to Levy, marriage by capture was common in pre-Islamic Arabia and still widespread during the Prophet's lifetime, but gradually disappeared thereafter.[56] Even marriages by purchase or contract, however, were characterized by the same lack of status for the woman. Here, the suitor paid a sum of money (*mahr*) to the guardian of the bride-to-be (and, possibly, another sum, *sadaq*, to the woman herself), thereby purchasing her and making her his exclusive property. The marriage contract, in other words, was a contract between husband and guardian, with the bride as the sales object.[57] Furthermore, neither conventions nor laws seem to have existed to put a limit to the number of wives that a man could have simultaneously, so that the only restrictive considerations were economic ones.[58] As to divorce in the Jahiliyya, it was entirely up to the will of the husband who, having purchased the wife, could dismiss her at will.[59] The divorce formula, pronounced three times, was effective instantly. Finally, there is some indication that women in pre-Islamic Arabia may not have been permitted the uncontrolled disposal of their possessions.[60]

While it would be most valuable in this context to continue this investigation in order to establish whether the Qur'anic laws regarding women's rights and status represent a deterioration or an improvement on what had gone before, the scope of this paper does not permit such an inquiry. It will suffice to take into consideration that both of these interpretations of the status of women in pre-Islamic urban society may very well be right, since, as W. Robertson Smith was the first to point out, marriage patterns in Arabia underwent momentous change in the sixth and seventh centuries.[61] What can be safely said is that in this period of fundamental change, the laws of the Qur'an supplanted what appear to have been many different social and legal patterns and traditions. As for the Qur'anic laws themselves, the most important among them are the following:

1. The marriage laws of the Qur'an that proclaim marriage as a meritorious institution and invest it with importance and dignity (e.g., 30:21; 2:223; 2:187; 33:51). Furthermore, the laws of the Qur'an restrict the number of wives a man can have simultaneously to four, with the recognition that this number may be so large as to make it difficult to treat them all impartially (4:3).

2. The property laws of the Qur'an that guarantee women the right to inherit and to bequeath property (e.g., 4:7; 4:11; 4:12).

3. The property laws of the Qur'an that guarantee women the right to have full possession and control of their wealth, including the dower, while married and after divorce (e.g., 4:4; 4:24; 4:20 and 21; 2:229).

4. The right of the wife to be properly fed and clothed at the husband's expense (e.g., 4:34).

5. The divorce laws insofar as they stipulate a waiting period during which the marriage is suspended, but not terminated (e.g., 2:228 ff).

In spite of these rights, however, the woman is not given full equality. Ultimately, the Qur'anic "blueprint" provides the male with status, control, and authority over the woman:

1. The testimony of a woman is worth half that of a man (2:282).
2. In most cases, women inherit half of what men inherit (4:11).
3. The marriage laws enjoin women not only to strict monogamy, but to marriage with a Muslim only, while men may marry from among the women of the "people of the book" (2:221; 5:5).
4. The divorce laws of the Qur'an stipulate that the woman may seek arbitration (4:35) or "ransom herself from her husband" for a sum agreed upon by both of them (2:229), while the decision and the power to divorce are left to the man (2:227).
5. The Qur'anic laws that regulate the structure of authority in the Muslim household stipulate that within the context of marriage and as a member of his household, the wife is in the charge of her husband and that he has authority over her, including the authority to admonish and beat her if she is rebellious. The Qur'an thus endows the man both with authority over the woman in the family setting, and with the obligation to provide for her by way of material support.

> "Men are in charge of women, because Allah hath made the one of them to excel the other, and because they spend of their property [for the support of women]. So good women are the obedient, guarding in secret that which Allah hath guarded. As for those from whom ye fear rebellion, admonish them and banish them to beds apart, and scourge them. Lo! Allah is ever High Exalted, Great." (4:34)

The superior status that is here given to the men over the women originates from the men's greater responsibility as protectors and providers within the socioeconomic context of seventh century Hijazi urban society. As this social order may have been more flexible than appears to us now through the distance of centuries in which it became more and more rigid, the verses themselves indicate that they were meant either to establish or, more probably, to strengthen an already functioning patriarchal society in which the men, as heads of extended families whose members relied on them both for support and defense, held more rights and, therefore, a higher status in society. With issues such as these, there is not enough contradictory detail even in the Hadith to refute or readjust totally the restrictive "ideal paradigm of Islamic society" as mapped out by the medieval and conservative modern Muslim thinkers who simply carry this particular detail of the teachings of the Qur'an to its logical conclusion when they equate "Islamic society" with the patriarchal order.

Modern, reform-minded Muslim thinkers in the fields of law and theology, however, have begun to deal with this very complex and centrally important issue (and others like it) in a different way. They are initiating a fresh study of the value system of the Qur'an and are beginning to work toward what John Esposito calls a "hierarchiza-tion" of the Qur'anic values in ways reminiscent of the process by which the Qur'anic values were first applied to newly encountered social situations in the formative period of Islam.[62] These Muslim thinkers differentiate between the socioeconomic and the ethic-religious categories in Qur'anic legislation. While women's status is inferior to men's in the former, they are full equals in the latter as to the spiritual and moral obligations imposed upon them, in their relationship to their Creator, and in the compensation prepared for them in the Hereafter (e.g., 33:35; 9:71; 40:40; 9:72; 48:5; 57:12; 3:195; and others). While the status difference of men and women in the socioeconomic sphere belongs to the category of *mu'amalat* (social relations), which are subject to change, their moral and religious equality belongs to the category of *'ibadat* (religious duties toward God), which are immutable.[63] By applying the principle of "hierarchization" of Qur'anic values, the Muslim reformists argue that the moral and religious equality of men and women "represents the highest expression of the value of equality,"[64] and therefore constitutes the most important aspect of the Qur'anic paradigm on this issue.

Notes

1. John Esposito, *Women in Muslim Family Law* (Syracuse, NY: Syracuse University Press, 1982), p. 3.

2. Muhammad 'Abduh and Rashid Rida, *Tafsir a-Qur'an al-hakim* (Cairo: Manar

Press, 1930/1349); Sayyid Ahmad Khan, *Tafsir al-Qur'an* (Lahore: n.p., 1880–1895); Sayyid Qutb's *Fi zilal al-Qur'an* (Beirut: Dar Ihya' al-Turath al-'Arabi, 1961).

3. Fazlur Rahman, "Sunna and Hadith," *Islamic Studies*, I (June 1962): 13, as quoted in John Esposito, *Women in Muslim Family Law*, p. 115.

4. Barbara Freyer, "Formen des geselligen Umgangs und Eigentümlichkeiten des Sprachgebrauchs in der frühislamischen städtischen Gesellschaft Arabiens (Nach Ibn Sa'd und Buhari)." *Der Islam*, XXXVIII (1962): 55ff.

5. All Qur'anic translations, unless otherwise indicated, are quotations from Mohammed Marmaduke Pickthall, *The Meaning of the Glorious Koran* (New York: The New American Library, n.d.).

6. Yvonne Haddad and Ellison Banks Findly, eds., *Women, Religion, and Social Change* (Albany, NY: State University of New York Press, 1985), pp. 275–306.

7. Reuben Levy, *The Social Structure of Islam* (Cambridge, UK: Cambridge University Press, 1969), p. 124.

8. Ibn Sa'd, *Kitab al-tabaqat al-kabir* (Biographien Muhammeds, seiner Gefährten und der späteren Träger des Islams), Vol. VIII, ed. C. Brockelmann. (Leiden: E.J. Brill, 1904), p. 1. Hereafter referred to as I.S., first figure is volume number, second figure is page number.

9. I.S., VIII, 3.

10. I.S., VIII, 4.

11. I.S., VIII, 4.

12. I.S., VIII, 4.

13. I.S., VIII, 5.

14. I.S., VIII, 5.

15. I.S., VIII, 6.

16. I.S., VIII, 90.

17. I.S., VIII, 28.

18. Al-Bukhari, *Sahih* (Le recueil des traditions mahométanes par el-Bokhari), vols. I–III, ed. L. Krehl (Leiden: E.J. Brill, 1862–1868), Vol. IV, ed. Th. W. Juynboll (Leiden: E.J. Brill, 1907–1908). The first figure represents the number of the *kitab* as indicated in Wensinck, *A Handbook of Early Muhammadan Tradition* (Leiden: E.J. Brill, 1927), pp. XIff.; the second figure represents the number of the *bab*: 13:20; 25:81; 56:65–68; 63:18; 64:18, 22; 76:2. Hereafter referred to as Bu, followed by *kitab* and *bab* numbers. I.S., VIII, 214, 301ff, 334, 335. Ahmad ibn Hanbal, *Musnad* (Cairo: n.p., 1313 A.H.), Vol. III, pp. 108ff, 112, 198, 279, 286, etc. Hereafter referred to as A.b.H., with first figure the volume number, the second the page number.

19. I.S., VIII, 21–22.

20. I.S., VIII, 20ff, 27.

21. I.S., VIII, 28.

22. I.S., VIII, 7, in accordance with Qur'an 60:10.

23. I.S., VIII, 67.

24. For example, Bu 18:4; 20:6.

25. A.b.H., I, 222; III, 66.

26. For example, I.S., VIII, 37, 49; Bu, 8:13, 14, 15; 10:93, 164; 77:19, and many others.

27. Bu, 10:162, 163, 165; 11:13.

28. Bu, 10:166; 67:116.

29. Bu, 13:15, 20.

30. Abu Da'ud, *Sunan* (Cairo: n.p., 1292 A.H.); the first figure represents the number of the *kitab* as indicated in A.J. Wensinck, p. XIII; the second figure represents the number of the *bab*: 2:196. Hereafter referred to as A.D., followed by *kitab* and *bab* numbers.

31. A.D., 2:17, 53.

32. A.b.H., VI, 301, 371.
33. R. Levy, *The Social Structure of Islam*, p. 131.
34. A.b.H., VI, 96, 150, 218, 238, 259, and many others.
35. A.b.H., I, 20.
36. A.b.H., VI, 173, 179, 267.
37. For example, I.S., VIII, 5.
38. For example, I.S., VIII, 59.
39. For example, I.S., VIII, 17, 51, 53.
40. For example, I.S., VIII, 89.
41. For example, I.S., VIII, 27.
42. I.S., VIII, 73.
43. I.S., VIII, 62ff.
44. I.S., VIII, 107, 110.
45. I.S., VIII, 100, 102, 106.
46. Fatima Mernissi, *Beyond the Veil* (New York: Halsted Press, 1975), pp. 18ff.
47. There is good reason to agree with those who reject the translation "stay in your houses" or "stay quietly in your houses" for grammatical reasons (in spite of the lengthy arguments on the part of those Qur'anic exegetes who favor it). Nazira Zayn al-Din, for example, points out that the verb in this verse cannot be *qarra yaqirru* ("stay") or *waqara yaqiru* ("stay," "remain"), but must be *qara yaqaru* ("to walk noiselessly on the sides of the feet, [so as to avoid the jingle of anklets which incites men's lust]"). Nazira Zayn al-Din, *Al-sufur wa-al-hijab* (Beirut: n.p., 1928), pp. 180ff.
48. Paul W. Harrison, *The Arabs at Home* (New York: Thomas Y. Cromwell Co., 1924), p. 42.
49. Eric R. Wolf, "The Social Organization of Mecca and the Origins of Islam," *Southwestern Journal of Anthropology*, VII (1951): 329–30.
50. B. Stowasser-Freyer, "Formen des geselligen Umgangs . . .," *Der Islam*, XLII, 49.
51. Julius Wellhausen, "Die Ehe bei den Araben." *Göttinger gelehrte Anzeigen* (Göttingen: n.p., 1983), p. 466.
52. Robert F. Spencer, "The Arabian Matriarchate: An Old Controversy." *Southwestern Journal of Anthropology*, VIII (1952): 478–502.
53. F. Mernissi, *Beyond the Veil*, pp. 29ff.
54. Ibid., p. 31.
55. R. Levy, *The Social Structure of Islam*, p. 94.
56. Ibid., pp. 92–93.
57. Ibid., p. 95.
58. Ibid., p. 100.
59. Ibid., p. 121.
60. Ibid., pp. 95–96.
61. W. Robertson Smith, *Kinship and Marriage in Early Arabia* (Cambridge, n.p., 1885).
62. J. Esposito, *Women in Muslim Family Law*, pp. 106ff.
63. Ibid., p. 108.
64. Ibid.

20 ISLAM BETWEEN IDEALS AND IDEOLOGIES: TOWARD A THEOLOGY OF ISLAMIC HISTORY

Mahmoud M. Ayoub

Among the world's spiritual and political leaders, Muhammad, the Prophet of Islam, occupies a unique position. Consciously and deliberately, he set out to establish a community of faith whose goal would be a state embodying both the political and religious genius of its founder, and the revelation that inspired it. From the start, the aim of the Prophet Muhammad was to win the Meccan Arabs to the new faith. To this end he directed his most determined efforts, so much so that the Qur'an in several places counseled that he be patient and not rush matters. The uniqueness of the message of Islam was not that it was political and this-worldly, but that it combined in a well-balanced system economics and the poor tax (*zakat*), prayers and commerce, worship and *jihad* (struggle) in the way of God, and individual freedom and the bonds of "God's limits" (*hudud*) in an impressive social code of moral law, the *shari'a*.

This is not, however, the only basis of the attachment of millions of human beings through fourteen centuries and across a variety of cultures, races, and languages to Islam and its polity. A more basic reason is that this system is, in the final analysis, established by God Himself. This claim, however its cogency may be argued, is well substantiated by the Qur'an, whose language and idiom remain different from anything else that has come down to us from the Prophet. In fact, tradition as Hadith and Sunna is simply the interpretation and elaboration of the concepts, injunctions, and precepts of the Qur'an. It is, therefore, with the Qur'an that we must begin for an understanding of Islam as a socioreligious system.

After sketching the main outline of the system from the Qur'an and Sunna, we shall examine three major movements that sought to interiorize and apply it in the life of Muslim society: the Khawarij, the Wahhabis, and the Society of the Muslim Brothers. All three movements, and others like them, in the end failed because they did not have the universal and pluralistic vision of the Qur'an and its recipient. We shall briefly look at the Sufi and the moderate Shi'i approaches to Islam as counterparts of the three movements just mentioned. To anticipate the conclusion of this study, let it be

297

observed that both Sufism and Shi'ism, and especially the former, have had greater success because they remained truer to the popular piety that characterized early Islam. By this I do not imply any judgment of right or wrong, but rather state a fact to be substantiated in the course of this discussion.

The Ideal Society: The Qur'an and Prophetic Tradition

The Meccan period of Muhammad's mission was largely one of preaching and warning, threatening (*wa'id*) the wicked with God's imminent judgment, and promising those who repent and make amends God's mercy and rich rewards in the hereafter. It was perhaps no accident that the need of the nascent community (*umma*) of Muslims coincided with the message of the Qur'an. Unity and brotherhood of the people of faith were two essential conditions for the formation and success of the first Islamic state in Medina, a city long torn by strife and conflict. Thus, the fact of brotherhood among Muslims established by the Prophet in Medina[1] was repeatedly reinforced in the Qur'an. "Hold fast, all of you, to the rope of God and do not be divided." The same verse goes on to remind the new Muslims of Medina of God's favor toward them: ". . . You were enemies, yet He created amity among your hearts, and thus by His grace you became brothers."[2] This bond of brotherhood is not to remain theoretical; rather, it must manifest itself in a fellowship of faith and good deeds. Faith, not blood or any other relationship, or love of fame and social status, is to be the sole basis of social obligations and responsibility. "O you who have faith, be vigilant before God, witnesses to justice,"[3] the Qur'an enjoins further, "even if it is against yourselves or those nearest of kin."[4]

The responsibility of a Muslim for his brother Muslim is expressed more directly and practically in the Hadith tradition. In one such tradition, the reality of faith is conditioned by the truth of this fraternity of faith. "No one of you shall have true faith," declared the Prophet, "until he wishes for his brother what he wishes for himself."[5] This relationship must not be determined by a show of righteousness or self-righteousness; it must extend to all Muslims, be they righteous or wrongdoers. Anas ibn Malik is said to have heard the Prophet say, "Support your brother, be he a wrongdoer or wronged." People asked, "O Apostle of God, we would support him who is wronged, but how can we support one who is a wrongdoer?" He answered, "You restrain his hands."[6]

The Islamic prohibition of usury and hoarding was not dictated by economic considerations, but by the concern that the poor must not go hungry. The Prophet is said to have warned, "Whoever hoards food for 40 nights would dissociate himself from God, and God would likewise dissociate Himself from him. Any people of a land among whom a man wakes up hungry, the covenant or protection [*dhimma*] of God would not embrace them."[7]

In times of peace as in times of war, no distinction must be made among Muslims as to their own rights, privileges, and responsibilities. According to a widely reported tradition, the Prophet stipulated that "'the lives' [literally "bloods"] of all Muslims are equal. The lowliest of them may offer their protection (*dhimma*) . . . the strong among them shall defend the weak, and the one mobilized [i.e. for the *jihad*] shall protect the one who is obliged to remain inactive."[8] This protection was not limited to Muslims alone; it included the "people of *dhimma*" (Jews, Christians, and Zoroastrians) as well. A detailed discussion of the treatment of the people of *dhimma*, or non-Muslim subjects in Muslim lands, is beyond the scope of this chapter.

The Qur'an and early tradition conceive relationships within the Muslim community in the context of the unity of humanity, which is in turn a reflection of the universal truth of God's oneness and absolute sovereignty. Man, in the view of the Qur'an, is the vicegerent (*khalifa*) of God on earth. As a rational being, capable of both good and evil actions, man, if he chooses the good, is higher than the angels. This idea is dramatically affirmed in the story of Adam, who was the challenge to the angels, who were obliged, on account of his divinely inspired knowledge, to fall down before him in reverent obeisance. Yet it was Adam also who disobeyed his Lord and lost his place in the Garden of Paradise. Adam typifies the human condition at all times. He was the first sinner and the first prophet. Thus every man and woman is prone to sin and evil as much as he or she is to righteousness and repentance. "Adam received certain words from his Lord and He turned toward him, for He is truly relenting, compassionate."[9]

Adam was, however, made for the earth and not for paradise. The earth is the natural stage on which man is to execute his mission as the vicegerent of God.[10] An important aspect of this mission, moreover, is the necessary diversity in the human family dictated by the earth's variety of climate, geography, and plant and animal life.

Yet in spite of this variety, man must always be aware of the underlying human unity. "Humankind! We have created you from one
male and one female and made you into nations and tribes in order
that you may know one another. Surely the most noble of you in the
sight of God is he who is most pious."[11]

Both unity and plurality of human society are willed by God.
Human unity is the Qur'anic argument for the equality of all men
and women as the creatures of the one God, the Lord of all being.
But cultural and racial diversity is necessary for the unfolding of
human history, for only when divided into nations can humanity
receive divine guidance through revelation. From the Qur'anic
point of view, history is revelation-history. Prophets, as recipients
of revelation, are the guides of humanity to its ultimate fulfillment.
Thus revelation-history is salvation-history. Guidance or salvation
is made necessary not because of human diversity but because of
human disagreement or dissension. The Qur'an declares,
"Humankind were all one community (*umma*], then God sent
prophets as bearers of good tidings and warners. He sent down the
Book with them in truth in order that it may judge among men
concerning that about which they disagree . . ."[12]

With diversity, however, comes nationalism, ethnic pride, and
inequality of wealth and power. Yet this evil can itself be the source
of a greater good. It distinguishes the good men from the bad and
thus spurs the righteous to a greater effort to perform their works of
righteousness. These may be acts of prayer and devotion, or striving
(*jihad*) in the way of God with wealth and life. "Had God not
repelled some men by means of others, many cloisters, churches,
synagogues, and mosques in which the name of God is often remembered would have been demolished . . ."[13] Those who defend the
houses of God, and thus ensure His worship therein, are lending
support to God, which He will repay in manifold measure. There
are also those who protect the world with their prayers. These are
the friends of God whose existence is necessary for the well-being of
the world. "Had God not protected some men by means of others,
the earth would have been corrupted. But God is of great bounty
toward humankind."[14] The first group are the people of faith
organized into a society with all its institutions, armies, and leaders.
The second are the shaykhs of the Sufi orders, the guides (*murshids*)
of men to God. Each group is necessary for the making of the
umma, yet ideally the two must be one. True *jihad*, however, must
begin in the heart of every individual against the evils of his or her

own soul. This is the greater *jihad* without which the *jihad* of the sword, the lesser *jihad*, becomes simply warfare whose aim is the enslavement and domination of one community by another. It is to the role of these two ideals that we must now turn.

The ideal rule in Islam is that of a prophet. After the cycle of prophethood has come to an end, the ideal ruler must be a prophet's representative or successor (*khalifa*). He must follow the former's moral law (*shari'a*) and model his character on the prophet's character. Justice, courage, piety, and wisdom are the qualities required in a good imam or leader of the community. He must regard all Muslims as brothers and his primary aim must be to preserve harmony among them.[15] "Surely the people of faith are brothers. Make peace, therefore, among your brothers . . ." This may at times require the use of force, yet the aim must always be peace and harmony in the community. "If two groups of the people of faith fight with one another, make peace between them. Yet if one of them transgresses against the other, then fight against the one which transgresses until it submits to the command of God. However, when it submits, then make peace between them with justice. Act justly, for God loves those who act justly."[16]

While he lived, the Prophet was the actual representative of God in the community. Thus, obedience to him was obedience to God. Through his Sunna, the Prophet continues to live in the community and thus continues to demand its love and obedience. His physical absence, however, requires that his authority (which is an extension of God's authority) be extended to those who are empowered by the community to be his successors. Thus the Qur'an enjoins the people of faith to ". . . obey God and obey the Apostle and those who are in authority over you." It further enjoins, "But if you fall into dissension concerning a matter, turn it over to God and the Apostle . . ."[17]

The ideal Islamic ruler is not, however, a dictator. Even though the Prophet is believed by all Muslims to have ruled through divine inspiration, and thus his word was final, nevertheless, he was enjoined by the Qur'an to consult the people before he resolved on a matter.[18] The Qur'an furthermore counts consultation (*shura*) among Muslims as one of the acts of faith: "and those who respond to God and observe regular worship, whose affair is decided through consultation among themselves and who give in alms of what we have bestowed upon them."[19] In these days when democracy is so idealized the world over, Muslims have found in this verse a proof text for the erroneous claim that Islam is synonymous with modern secular democracy.

Islam is, in essence, faith in the one and only God. Faith in divine oneness (*tawhid*) means that an ideal society is one that reflects God's singularity in its own unity of faith and purpose. The Qur'an presents this ideal as a challenge to the human tendency of divisiveness: "This community of yours is one community and I am your Lord, so worship Me."[20]

This one community of faith is further enjoined to be "a community of the middle position between the extremes of too much [*ifrat*] and too little [*tafrit*]." As a prophetic community, the Muslim *umma* could then share with the prophets their role as witnesses before God on the day of resurrection over the rest of humankind. "Thus have we made you an *umma* of the middle position [*wasatan*] so that you might be witnesses over humankind and that the Apostle be a witness over you."[21] Finally, the Muslim *umma* is challenged to be "the best community given to humankind." This great honor carries with it equally great responsibilities. A good community is one whose members "enjoin the good, dissuade others from evil, and have faith in God."[22]

The moral and theological implications of this verse have occupied Muslims throughout their long history. It has served both as a great impetus for revolution and change, and as a source of false pride and complacency. Most important, however, this verse has kept the ideal goal both within sight and yet far from realization. It was perhaps partly in recognition of the community's inability to realize this goal fully that a future Mahdi, an ideal ruler who is divinely guided, was anticipated by both Sunni and Shi'i Muslims.

The Mahdi ideal gained and lost in popularity with changes of political and social circumstances. Other and more dramatic attempts to realize the ideal of the prophetic *umma* of Islam were made in every era of Muslim history. The first, and in my view the most radical, movement was that of the Khawarij. It is also the earliest significant movement that raised questions so basic to the ideal of Islam that they are as relevant today as when they were raised over 13 centuries ago.

"God's Judgment" and the "Liberal Law" of His Apostle

The Khawarij were so called because they went out (*kharaju*) from the camp of 'Ali — i.e., they rose against him. Their story is too well known to need recounting here. Of greater relevance to this discussion is their attitude toward other Muslims and their faith. The Khawarij launched the first truly revolutionary movement in Islam, but it was a movement that had no program or direction. Theirs was a revolution without a goal of reform.

In their uncompromising integrity, they regarded both themselves and 'Ali as having committed an act of *kufr* (rejection of faith) by accepting arbitration, or "the judgment of men in the religion of God." Thus when they rose against 'Ali because he accepted arbitration, which they themselves had insisted upon during the battle of Siffin, 'Ali sent Ibn 'Abbas to reason with them. They asserted in the course of a long debate with Ibn 'Abbas that "'Ali was the commander of the faithful, but when he agreed to arbitration in the religion of God, he had by this departed from the faith. Let him repent, after confessing *kufr*; then we would return to him." Ibn 'Abbas argued that it is not right for a man of faith to confess *kufr*. As for human judgment or arbitration in religious matters, it was, Ibn 'Abbas argued further, what God stipulated in the Qur'an.[23]

On another occasion, Ibn 'Abbas returned to the Khawarij to convince them to return to the community of Muslims, but to no avail. He argued as before that the matter of arbitration, grave though it may be, did not mean *kufr*, or rejection of faith, nor did it require such drastic action as they were advocating. He argued further that the Prophet himself had accepted human arbitration when he concluded the truce of Hudaybiyya with the Associators of Mecca. In fact, the argument between Ibn 'Abbas and the Khawarij on this point is so instructive that it deserves special attention. We should first, however, recall briefly the event and the Prophet's attitude and diplomacy.

As the Prophet and the Muslims approached Hudaybiyya outside Mecca, his she-camel knelt down. The men, regarding this as a bad omen, exclaimed, "The she-camel has knelt down!" The Prophet answered, ". . . Rather, He who detained the elephant [of the Abyssinian general, Abraha] from Mecca has restrained her."[24] He continued, "By God, they [the people of Quraysh] shall not ask me for anything in which there is an act of kindness toward a near relative, but that I shall grant it to them."[25]

From this and what followed, it was clear that the Prophet intended to conclude a peace treaty with them. When he saw Suhayl ibn 'Amr, the representative of the Quraysh, approaching he remarked, "The people want peace." As 'Umar ibn al-Khattab saw the two men discussing the terms of the treaty, he protested to Abu Bakr, "Is he not the Apostle of God?" "Yes," Abu Bakr answered. 'Umar continued, "Are we not Muslims?" "Yes," answered Abu Bakr. "Why should we accept humility in our faith?" protested 'Umar. Abu Bakr, reflecting the prudence that was to characterize the wisdom of Muslim jurists, counseled 'Umar, saying, "Hold fast to his saddle [i.e., the Prophet's counsel]; for I bear witness that he is the Apostle of God." 'Umar then put the same objection to the Prophet, who answered, "I am the servant of God and His Apostle. I shall never oppose His command, nor will He ever let me be lost." Long after this, 'Umar continued to give alms in expiation for his well-intentioned fault.[26]

The Prophet then called 'Ali to write down the agreement between him and Suhayl on behalf of the Meccans. "Write," he said, "in the name of God the All Merciful, the Compassionate." Suhayl protested, "I do not know this! Write, rather, 'in your name, O God'." The Prophet assented and ordered 'Ali to change the phrase. He then dictated, "These are the terms of the truce between Muhammad, the Apostle of God, and Suhayl ibn 'Amr." The latter protested, "Had I borne witness that you were the Apostle of God, I would not have fought against you. Rather, write your name and the name of your father."[27]

Let us now return to the disagreement between 'Ali and the Khawarij. When 'Ali agreed to the arbitration between himself and Mu'awiya, he also consented to change the phrase "God's servant 'Ali, the commander of the faithful" in the document of agreement to simply "'Ali ibn Abi Talib." The Khawarij accused 'Ali of having "erased his name from the commandership of the Muslims." Ibn 'Abbas reminded them that the Prophet had accepted a similar change in the document drawn up at Hudaybiyya. 'Ali had then said, "O Apostle of God, my heart would not accept such a sacrifice as to remove your name from prophethood." The Prophet asked him to show him where the phrase, "Muhammad the Apostle of God" was and he erased it with his own hand. He then told 'Ali, "You shall be forced to do as I did and you will accept it."[28]

The Khawarij not only withdrew their allegiance (*bay'a*) from

'Ali but regarded anyone who was not of their opinion to be a rejecter of faith (*kafir*). It was lawful for them to shed such a person's blood, take his women and children as war captives, and seize his property as booty. They thus terrorized the Muslim community until they themselves were decisively crushed by people far less pious than they. The Khawarij devised a test of faith by which they slew or spared other Muslims. They asked them questions reflecting what they themselves believed. They accepted the caliphate of Abu Bakr and 'Umar, and supported 'Uthman during the first six years of his caliphate, after which they regarded him as having committed *kufr*. Likewise, they accepted 'Ali's caliphate until he agreed to the arbitration. Thereafter they declared him to be a *kafir* as well as anyone who continued to give allegiance to him.

The Qur'an clearly states, "Do not say to him who offers you peace [or Islam], 'You are not a man of faith'."[29] Moreover, basing their decision on a widely accepted prophetic tradition (Sunna), jurists have legislated that anyone who, even outwardly, accepts Islam by uttering the *shahada* (profession of faith) must be regarded as a Muslim with all the duties, rights, and privileges that accrue to any other Muslim. In a brief but succinct *hadith*, the Prophet put it thus: "I was commanded to fight with people until they say, 'There is no God but God'. When they say it they protect their lives and wealth from me, except in accordance with what is their due. Their judgment shall be with God."[30] The Prophet is also said to have upbraided a man for killing one of the Associators after the latter declared his Islam. The man protested that his opponent uttered the *shahada* under his spear. The Prophet retorted, "Why did you not split open his heart so that you may know what is in it?" The man admitted, "Had I been able to do so, I would have known what was in his heart." The Prophet then said, "So you neither accepted what he said, nor did you know what was in his heart."[31] It is important to observe that 'Imran ibn al-Husayn, one of the Companions of the Prophet, related this anecdote to Nafi' ibn al-Azraq, the head of the most extremist sect of the Khawarij, in answer to the challenge by Nafi' that 'Imran should join them in fighting against the other Muslims.

The Khawarij contradicted the clear injunctions of the Qur'an and Sunna against harming anyone but those with whom one does battle. The extremists among them allowed the killing of women and children of Muslims whom they wrongly considered to be rejecters of faith. They also considered as rejecters of faith those who agreed with them but did not join them in the fight against other Muslims.[32] Even the most moderate group, the 'Ibadiyya, allowed torture of children of their opponents as an act of revenge.[33]

The Khawarij were, however, people of piety and extraordinary devotion. They opposed wrongdoing and injustice, and many were ready to die in defense of what they considered to be the right and the good. One example of this courage and piety will suffice.

A man of the Khawarij, Mirdas ibn Udayya, was so well known for his piety and learning that every sect of the Muslims claimed him as one of them. One day he was in the court of 'Ubaydalla ibn Ziyad, the notorious governor of Iraq, who was threatening the people with these words, "By God, I shall punish the good among you for the wrong of the bad. I shall punish the one present for the fault of the one who is absent. I shall punish the one in the right for the one in the wrong, and the obedient for the fault of the disobedient." Mirdas then rose up and said, "We have heard what you have to say, O man, yet this is not what God says . . . rather, 'No soul shall bear the burden of another . . .'. Yet you claim to punish the obedient for the wrong of the disobedient." Mirdas then left the city.[34]

Ibn Ziyad then had Mirdas brought back and imprisoned, but the jailer was so touched by his piety that he allowed him to spend each night at home and return each morning. One day Ibn Ziyad decided to kill all the prisoners early in the morning. Mirdas knew what awaited him, but he still returned to prison because he did not wish to break his promise to the jailer. He was again spared, but when he saw a woman lying in the marketplace of the city whose arms and legs Ibn Ziyad had cut off, he declared war against oppression and was joined by a group of like-minded men. They were all slain in battle. Mirdas was remembered long afterward and eulogized by other Muslims.[35]

The Khawarij were the first genuine "republican party" in Islam.[36] They were first to argue that the main requirement of a ruler is piety and justice, and that neither the tribal lineage of Quraysh nor ethnic Arab identity were necessary requirements of a ruler. In this they opposed both prophetic tradition and Muslim consensus, which state that "imams are to be of Quraysh." Shahrastani considered this to be their chief innovation (*bid'a*).[37] The Khawarij went even further, asserting that the imam could be a slave, provided that he is pious and just. Otherwise, it was a binding duty upon the community to rise up against him and depose him. In this respect they were centuries ahead of their time and also true to the primitive tribal democracy of pre-Islamic Arabia.

All this notwithstanding, the Khawarij were proud and unruly Bedouins who despised non-Arabs. Thus their ideal, potentially so attractive to the masses of *mawali*, or non-Arab Muslims, brought them no converts beyond their small, strictly Arab circles. Likewise, their fervent devotion and piety yielded no lasting reforms. A fact supporting the major thesis of this chapter is that only the most moderate element of their group, the 'Ibadiyya, survived. It remains to this day a strictly Arab school of thought (*madhhab*) in a limited area and of limited influence. It is a reminder of the first awakening of social conscience in Muslim history.

With the death of 'Ali at the hand of one of their own zealots, the Khawarij lost the raison d'être of their existence as a revolutionary force in Islam. It was 'Ali who perhaps best characterized their great principles and the way in which they sought to realize them. Of their basic principle, that "judgment belongs to God alone," 'Ali said, "It is a word of truth used in support of an untruth." He is said to have commented further, clearly reflecting later anxiety about the unity of the *umma*, "It is a word of justice which shall lead to injustice. They say, 'There should be no leadership [*imara*],' yet leadership is necessary, be it righteous or evil."[38]

The Oneness of God and the Muslim Sin of Association: The Wahhabi Movement

History often repeats itself so closely that only names and dates need to be rewritten. Nearly a thousand years after the Khawarij, and out of the same Bedouin stock in the hills of Najd in the Hijaz, another radical movement appeared. The earlier movement had rebelled against the legitimate ruler of the Muslims. The second rebelled against the masses of the community, against their faith and piety. Again, their long story is too well known for it to be repeated in great detail here. We shall, as before, be concerned with their ideology and attitude.

Shaykh Muhammad ibn 'Abd al-Wahhab, the founder of the Wahhabi movement which bears his name, was born in 1703 in 'Uyayna, a small town in Najd. Both his grandfather and father were respected scholars of Islamic sciences. His father was his first teacher, but Ibn 'Abd al-Wahhab traveled far and wide in Syria and Iraq to study with the famous scholars of his time. From his youth he was drawn to the works of Ibn Taymiyya, an important conservative jurist and theologian (1263–1328), who remained his model throughout his career. Like the rest of his family and most of the inhabitants of Najd, Ibn 'Abd al-Wahhab was a follower of the Hanbali rite. The motto of his movement was, "The truth and the right is what the Sunna and the Book [Qur'an] brought. It also was what the Companions said and did, and what the four Imams [founders of the four schools] who are to be followed and their legal precepts accepted, have chosen."[39]

Early in life, Ibn 'Abd al-Wahhab began to preach against saint veneration, pilgrimages to shrines and other holy places, and the making of vows to living and dead religious personages. Soon he put his protest into action, and with a group of devoted followers he began to cut down sacred trees and demolish the domes over the tombs of the Companions of the Prophet and other holy men. Finally, he was driven out of his city and, after some negotiation, he established his permanent headquarters at the age of 42 in the city of Dar'iyya. There he made a pact with the local emir, Muhammad ibn Sa'ud, whereby the shaykh would have religious authority and the prince, political power. This was the beginning of the Sa'udi dynasty.[40]

From their headquarters in the isolated hills of Najd, the Wahhabis set out to extirpate by force what they considered to be Islamic idolatry. They destroyed the shrines of the Shi'i imams in Iraq and planned to destroy the tomb of the Prophet in Medina because it stood between man and his devotion to God. In his many epistles, the shaykh spelled out his ideology, which we shall now briefly summarize.

The faith of Islam, with which God sent all his messengers, is faith in the oneness of God (*tawhid*). There are two kinds of *tawhid*: "Oneness of Lordship, which means that God alone creates all things and providentially manages the affairs of His creation . . . this is a necessary truth; yet it does not bring a person into Islam, because most people do profess it. That [faith] which actually brings a person into Islam is Oneness of Divinity. This means that God alone should be worshipped, and neither an angel brought near to God nor a messenger sent by Him."[41] On this basis, Ibn 'Abd al-Wahhab applied to the Muslims of his time the Qur'anic verses that reproach the Meccans of the Jahiliyya for asserting that God created all things, yet failing to worship him.[42] Like the early Meccans, said the shaykh, Muslims interpreted the *shahada*, "There is no God but God" to mean that no one creates, sustains, gives life, and causes to die except God. This, however, is only "Oneness of Lordship." Thus, like the people of the Jahiliyya, Muslims did not affirm the oneness of worship (*'ibada*). It was therefore incumbent upon the true Muslim (that is, the one convinced by this argument) to oppose the "satans" of learning and eloquence who prevent others from being guided into the straight way.[43]

The shaykh then stated that ". . . the *shirk* [ascribing of partners to God] of the ancients was less grave than that of our time in two ways. The first is that the ancients did not commit the sin of association [of other things with God] in that they did not pray to angels, saints, and idols except in times of comfort." In times of hardship they called on God alone. Second, the ancients prayed to beings who were near to God such an angels or to inanimate things such as trees and stones which are subject to His will. Muslims, on the other hand, were praying to the most wicked of men along with God. (Here he was referring to the Sufi shaykhs, whom he accused of neglecting the *shari'a* and committing other acts of disobedience to God.)[44] The shaykh argued that since the Qur'an permits shedding the blood and seizing the wealth of those who reject a single aspect of worship, even though they may accept all others, so much more should the blood and wealth of those who worship other things with God be lawful for Muslims to shed and seize.[45]

We have seen above that professing Islam, even if only by the tongue, was sufficient to make a person a member of the Muslim community. The Qur'an enjoins further, "Call to the way of your Lord with wisdom and fair exhortation. Dispute with them in the best manner; for the Lord knows best who strays from His way and He knows best who are truly God-fearing."[46] Nonetheless, the shaykh argued that the *shahada* in itself does not protect the life and wealth of the one who utters it if it is seen that he does not affirm true divine oneness and does not abide by the *shari'a*. He considered his opponents not only as *mushrikun* (Associators) but also as "enemies of God."[47]

The shaykh also held that since true faith in *tawhid* is to be expressed in both word and deed, anyone who invokes the intercession or help of any being beside God must be considered a rejecter of faith. In this connection, Ibn 'Abd al-Wahhab asserted that the early Muslims had not allowed prayers in the names of

prophets after their death. This last claim by the shaykh is question-
able. If it were correct, then the Qur'anic declaration, "Surely God
and His angels bless the Prophet," and the injunction, "O you who
have faith, bless him and salute him with a great salutation of
peace,"[48] would be meaningless beyond the Prophet's own lifetime.
Also noteworthy here is the story of how 'Umar ibn al-Khattab,
after a long drought, gathered the people together for the prayer for
rain (*istisqa'*) and himself prayed, "O God, we used to beseech you
through your Prophet and you gave us rain. Now we beseech you
through your Prophet's uncle, so grant us rain."[49]

In the end, as with the Khawarij, the failure of the Wahhabis was
due to their own intolerance. In general, the ideas they opposed are
not unacceptable to all Muslims, and should at least be open to
discussion and *ijtihad* (personal reasoning). In particular, as was
indicated above, the notion that prophets and the friends of God
can intercede on behalf of the living, or indeed that the dead in
general can hear, has some support in the Sunna. In one of the most
celebrated verses of the Qur'an (3:169), the martyrs in the way of
God are declared to be "not dead, but alive with their Lord
sustained." Classical commentators, including people like Ibn
Kathir (a strict disciple of Ibn Taymiyya), have taken this to mean
"life" in the full sense of the word.[50] Ibn Hisham relates that after
the battle of Badr and the victory of the Muslims, the Prophet threw
the slain men of Quraysh into a filthy well. Some days later, he came
to the well and called out each man by his and his father's name and
said, "Have you found what your Lord had promised you to be
true. . .?" The people then said, "O Apostle of God, you call out to
men who have already decomposed!" The Prophet answered, "By
Him in whose hand is my soul, they are more capable of hearing
than you are; but they cannot answer back."[51]

Partly on the basis of some oblique references in the Qur'an but
more on the basis of a wealth of Hadith literature, Muslims have
spent much thought and ink proving the ability of the dead to hear
and relate to the living. One of the most important treatises on this
subject was written by yet another disciple of Ibn Taymiyya, the
famous Ibn Qayyim al-Jawziyya. His book, *Kitab al-Ruh*, is a
standard text on life after death. Sufi critics generally attempted to
refute Wahhabism on this basic point. Thus, Dawud ibn Sulayman
al-Baghdadi (1222–1299), a shaykh of the Naqshbandi order,
argued that the capacity of the dead to hear in the grave is a divine
gift, a favor (*karama*) which God grants to His righteous friends

(*awliya'*). This is not granted only to the righteous but, as we have seen in the account of the well, to the rejecters of faith also. The Sufi shaykh therefore found it strange that some had ignorantly denied the ability of prophets and pious friends of God to hear in the grave.[52] Not only can the dead hear, but according to the Hadith, they experience happiness and anger, joy and sorrow. Tirmidhi relates that the Prophet said, "Fear God with regard to your brethren of the people of the tombs! For your deeds are brought before them."[53] The implication is that good deeds will cause the dead joy, and evil ones will cause them sorrow.

Human piety, be it Muslim, Christian, Buddhist, or primitive, has from time immemorial sought blessing (*baraka*) in the tombs of saints and sages or in any object associated with them during their lives. Bukhari relates that the famous savant, Ibn Sirin, told one of the successors (*tabi'un*) that he had obtained a hair of the Prophet. The latter answered, "Were I to possess one hair, it would be more precious to me than the world and all it contains."[54] On the basis of all this, the Sufi shaykh argued at length for the reality of miracles and favors that God creates in His prophets and friends; they do not themselves create them.[55]

This controversy, of course, is part of the old conflict between the empiricism of the mind and the faith of the heart. It is the mark of this and the last century not to believe in the unknown or fantastic. Yet Muslims cannot ignore the many miracles of the Qur'an. To give but a few examples, one of which the Sufi critic of Wahhabism also uses: "Solomon," the Qur'an tells us, "was brought in the twinkling of an eye the throne of the Queen of Sheba by a man who was lower in prophetic rank than he."[56] Jesus raised the dead, and Muhammad was taken up to heaven. Moses split the sea, and the fire was turned into coolness and peace for Abraham. These and many other examples of the supernatural are meant, I believe, to lift the human soul above the world of material existence. Their rationality, or lack of it, is not the point at issue.

It was not Muhammad 'Ali who defeated the Wahhabis and restricted their activities to the land of their birth, but rather their own narrow and intolerant view of Islam. In their bid to purify Islam in their domain, they only succeeded in alienating the Shi'i community by reducing it to an oppressed and persecuted minority. In their toleration of political authority, even if it were in the wrong so long as it patronized them, they made of their reform movement not a universal faith but an impenetrable wall of outmoded tradition protecting a political regime. Wahhabism as a movement was neither reformist in the true sense nor was it a true revolution. Still, it was a landmark in the long history of protest in the Muslim community. After the Wahhabis came the Salafiyya movement, and that was followed by the Society of the Muslim Brothers, to which we shall now turn.

Reform and Revolution: The Muslim Brothers

Unlike the Wahhabi movement, the Society of the Muslim Brothers was, almost from its beginning, an urban movement in the full sense of the word. Its founder, Hasan al-Banna, was deeply influenced by Sufism in his youth, and this influence was to play a major role in his exemplary leadership and the formation of the urbane character of his movement.

With a small group of devout men, al-Banna, then a school teacher in Isma'iliyya, Egypt, founded the society in March 1928. The men called themselves the "soldiers" (*jund*) of Islam.[57] At first the Society operated from Isma'iliyya. Al-Banna worked with laborers, shaykhs of Sufi orders, and social and religious clubs. He was a good organizer and a tireless worker. He found a ready audience for his new ideas in the mosque, the home, and the club. This initial period in Isma'iliyya prepared the movement for a shift of the center of its activities to Cairo, which took place in 1932. There, in spite of many internal and external problems, al-Banna, aided by his brother 'Abd al-Rahman, saw the Society through its moments of glory and decline until al-Banna fell victim to an assassin's bullet in 1949.

Al-Banna had a clear vision of the nature of his Society and its mission. It was erected on three important principles: (1) Islam as a total system, complete unto itself, and the final arbiter of life in all its categories; (2) an Islam formulated from and based on its two primary sources, the revelation in the Qur'an and the wisdom of the Prophet in the Sunna; and (3) an Islam applicable to all times and to all places.[58] Thus al-Banna defined the Society of the Muslim Brothers, whose name he chose, as "a Salafiyya message, a Sunni way, a Sufi truth, a political organization, an athletic group, a cultural-educational union, an economic company, and a social idea."[59] It would be beyond the narrow scope of this chapter to detail the activities of the movement which realized these ideals.

Suffice it to say that the group indeed penetrated every walk of life in Egyptian society. This massive and efficient organization caused the movement to be both feared and admired, and made it impossible for any government to tolerate it.

Like every religious movement of its kind, the Society soon experienced various internal ideological and organizational problems that led in 1939 to the first serious split. This in turn led to compromise and deeper political involvement, both internally and externally. While al-Banna lived, he was generally able to overcome problems. Yet his own talents as a leader worked against him and the Society in the end. He organized a variety of professional, educational, agricultural, military, and athletic groups to carry out the work. One of these was the secret apparatus, a military force responsible only to him but enjoying a large measure of autonomy. In the end it became nearly impossible to control all of these groups. The Society's political and military involvement was sparked by British imperialism and the Palestinian struggle, as well as Egyptian party politics following World War II.

The Society gained much prestige and mass admiration as a result of its support of the Palestinian struggle against Zionism. The struggle against British imperialism and those who compromised Egypt's unity and aspirations was to lead to head-on collision with the government. Thus, during and immediately after the war the Society experienced its first period of persecution and arrests, and often had to take measures opposed to its own interests and to judge both its friends and enemies not in terms of its ideals but instead in ways dictated by the political exigencies of a complex and crucial period in Egyptian and Arab history. Al-Banna, fearing his own arrest, had to remind the Brothers that they were not a political party, a benevolent organization, or a local society. "Rather," he said, "you are a new soul in the heart of this nation to give it life by means of the Qur'an . . ."[60]

The Egyptian revolution of 1952, which was organized and carried out by a small group of army officers, was in large measure the work of the Muslim Brothers. Many of the officers were either members or active sympathizers. The Society therefore regarded the revolution as its own "blessed revolution." The honeymoon with the revolution, however, was of short duration. In 1954 the same group of officers, under the leadership of Gamal Abdel Nasser, dissolved the Society and executed many of its leaders. Nasser's slogan, "Religion belongs to God and the country to all," as well as his socialist tendencies and alliances, went contrary to the spirit and ideals of the Society and indeed of traditional Islam in general.

As an Islamic movement, the Society of the Muslim Brothers was committed to *jihad* in all its forms. *Jihad* was the basic principle on which its ideology rested. Its ideologues interpreted *jihad* concretely as fighting and dying in the way of God. Al-Banna popularized the phrase, "*fann al-mawt*" ("the art of death" or, perhaps, "death as art").[61] Thus, dying in the way of God was regarded as the shortest step from this life to the next life in paradise.

These are, of course, old Islamic ideals. The problem has always been how to determine the legitimate causes of *jihad* and how to distinguish between rash actions stemming from blind fanaticism or euphoria and the true *jihad*, whose basic aim must always be the reform of society as well as the individual fighter himself. When is *jihad* striving for God and in His way, and when is it simply a means of self-aggrandizement and self-righteousness even through martyrdom?

The spirit of *jihad* continues to dominate the movement of the Muslim Brothers and others that have subsequently followed its example and even borne its name. It was this spirit which made it impossible for leaders after al-Banna to exert any meaningful control over the rank and file of the movement. Moreover, it led to an unhealthy attitude of superiority and isolation and a narrow puritanism unsuitable for urban life. This exclusivism also raised many suspicions about the Society and its works in the minds of many Muslims in Egypt and elsewhere. Thus, in the Middle East today, "Muslim Brother" equals fanatic. No doubt Nasser's government with its powerful media played a major role in creating this unfortunate and often distorted image of the Society. This, coupled with the virtual liquidation of its leadership, dealt the organization such a hard blow that it has not been able to recover.

The Muslim Brothers perceived the problem of the Muslim world clearly. It is both internal and external. Internally, it is the decline of Muslim civilization after the period of the first four caliphs, the degeneration of true Sufism into orders and classes, superstition and saint worship, the inadequacy of the religious schools, the blind imitation by the Muslims of the West, and, above all, Muslim disunity. Externally, the problem is the imperialism of Europe, the United States, and the communist world. Western domination has struck such deep roots in the psyches of Muslims that they are no longer able to understand or appreciate their own faith and culture. Thus al-Banna counseled, "Eject imperialism from your souls, and it will leave your lands."[62] This Western disease which afflicts Muslims and non-Muslims, notably Eastern Christians, must be extirpated at all costs.

The solution that the Brothers offered is not new. It is the return to true Islam, the Islam of the first generation, in all areas of life. The way the intellectuals of the Society advocated was essentially that of the earlier reformists of the Salafiyya movement. Like them, they took the "pious forebears" (*al-salaf al-salih*) to be the norms for reform. This reform would begin first with Egypt, from where it would spread to the rest of the Arab world and from there to the Muslim world and the East in general. Thus, the Muslim Brothers were sharply critical of any form of limited nationalism in the Arab world.

Perhaps the tragedy of the Society of the Muslim Brothers is that their vision was not tried in an actual modern nation-state. In so many ways their ideals are understandably similar to those of the Islamic revolution of Iran. The Iranian venture, however, has not yet had time to prove itself. Yet if it fails, its failure will have much to say about the feasibility of an Islamic polity in a world of conflict and power struggle with cataclysmic possibilities. In any case, the last word from the movement begun by al-Banna and others like it (but under different names) is yet to be heard.

Conclusion: Revolution, Reform, or Evolution?

Islam in its early beginnings was a unique success story. Less than a century after the death of the Prophet, the Muslims dominated most of the known world. This universal commonwealth, unparalleled since the time of Alexander the Great, gave birth to a brilliant civilization that was both ancient and new, Western and Eastern. Out of the wealth and power that Muslims acquired arose the chronic mistaken view that Islam was synonymous with success and that the only cure for all ills is the recovery of past glory by present means of revolt and revolution.

Two important movements of protest against this view arose very early in Muslim history: Sufism and Shi'ism. The latter went through much travail before its ethos of suffering and martyrdom developed. This was in turn to produce the hope of an ideal polity that God can and will in His own good time establish under the "One raised up" (*qa'im*) by God, the Mahdi of the household (*ahl al-bayt*) of the Prophet Muhammad. Until recently, Shi'a were content to wait for God to act. In Iran, decades before Khomeini, the ideal of the authority of the jurist (*wilayat al-faqih*) as a political authority was advocated. Khomeini gave this idea both force and eloquence. In this sense, the Iranian experiment is one more example of the many movements of reform and revolution that are part of Muslim history. Its long-term success will depend on the extent to which it can retain, not only in theory but also in practice, its ethos and idealism.

The prayer of Shi'ism which the faithful repeat daily is "O God, we beseech You for a state [*dawla*] in which You exalt Islam and its people and humiliate hypocrisy and its people. [We pray] that in it You make us among those who call others to obedience to You and leaders to Your way. In it [we pray] that You grant us the honor of this world and the next." This prayer is the passionate hope that the Shi'a express in their devotion to the memory of the imams and especially the twelfth who, they believe, alone can and shall fill the earth with equity and justice as it is filled with inequity and injustice.[63] If any other leader succeeds in filling a role similar to that projected for the Mahdi, then Shi'ism will lose its raison d'être.

It is interesting that a man now living in Qum, the heart of Iran's Islamic revolution, perceives this danger and advocates a different approach to Islamic reform. Ayatollah Muhammad Mahdi al-Shirazi looks forward "to the government of the thousand million" Muslims.[64] He conceives this great commonwealth as being in structure a traditional Shi'i state that would include any necessary modern institutions. But the shaykh sees this state evolving through a long process of education and reform of the Muslim masses through small, active cells of dedicated workers. The shaykh regards all military coups and revolutions as un-Islamic and doomed to eventual failure. It is through evolution, not revolution, that the new and lasting Islamic commonwealth will be built. He predicts that with hard work and dedication, this hope could be realized in ten to fifteen years. In private, however, he admits that even if it takes fifty years, it shall be worth the wait. This old, venerable man is fully confident that his dream will be realized. This confidence is based on the prayer just cited, with which he ends his small, unusual book.[64]

We turn now to a brief consideration of Sufism, a movement that arose not long after the Khawarij, not far from the latter's birth-place, when a small, pious group isolated themselves from the wealth and corruption of Muslim society, a society which they felt had lost its ideals. They worshipped God in ascetic seclusion, weeping for paradise whenever they encountered a verse of the Qur'an describing it, and weeping in dread of hell, as in their recita-tions of the Qur'an they encountered its torments. Their devotion, piety, and detachment from the world earned them the name Sufis, that is, "people clad in coarse white wool" (a symbol of their asceticism and purity).

The Sufis touched the hearts of millions of Muslims with the fire of love. Their poetry and music, song and dance, but above all the states (*ahwal*) and stations (*maqamat*) of the Sufi journeyers to God have transformed Muslim history. Sufis did not neglect the *jihad* of the sword; indeed, without the Sufis it would be difficult to conceive of the independence and the preservation of the Islamic identity of the states of North Africa. Yet their *jihad* of the sword was always subordinate to the *jihad* of the soul, and it was this latter struggle which won for Islam large populations in India, Indonesia, Africa, and Malaysia. If Islam is to have any real influence in Europe and America, it will again have to be through the efforts of the Sufis.

The Khawarij came and went leaving only Muslim aversion to their extremism, an extremism that obscured many of their lofty ideals. The Wahhabis were also rejected by the Muslim community at large and now exist only in fossilized form in a state that speaks through its wealth rather than the enthusiastic voice of a reformer. The slow death, or perhaps recovery, of the Muslim Brothers and their approach calls for withholding judgment. Shi'i hopes and patient struggle may all be dashed on the rocks of the Islamic revolution in Iran, or perhaps with that revolution may bring forth fruits for all Muslims to enjoy. The future of the Muslims remains uncertain; it is in the hands of God. But "God does not change what is in a people until they change what is in themselves."[65] But as for Islam, the Prophet said, "[It] began a stranger and will return a stranger. Blessed are the strangers."[66]

Notes

1. See Ibn Hisham, *Sirat al-Nabi*, ed. Muhammad Muhyi al-Din 'Abd al-Hamid

(Beirut: Dar al-Fikr, n.d.), Vol. 2, pp. 119–20.

2. Qur'an 3:103; see also 49:10.

3. Qur'an 5:8.

4. Qur'an 4:135.

5. *Sahih Muslim* (Beirut: Dar al-Fikr, n.d.), Vol. 2, pp. 16–17.

6. *Sahih al-Bukhari* (An offset reproduction of the old Istanbul edition) (Beirut: Dar al-Fikr, n.d.), Vol. 3, p. 98.

7. *Musnad Ibn Hanbal* (Beirut: al-Maktab al-Islami, 1969), Vol. 2, p. 33.

8. *Sunan Abu Dawud*, ed. Muhammad Muhyi al-Din 'Abd al-Hamid (Cairo: Dar Ihya' al-Sunna al-Nabawiyya), Vol. 3, pp. 80–81.

9. Qur'an 2:37.

10. Qur'an 2:30.

11. Qur'an 49:13.

12. Qur'an 2:213; see also 10:19.

13. Qur'an 22:40.

14. Qur'an 2:251. See also my book, *The Qur'an and Its Interpreters* (Albany, NY: SUNY Press, 1983) Vol. I, for a comprehensive discussion of this verse.

15. See Abu al-Hasan 'Ali ibn Muhammad al-Mawardi, *Al-ahkam al-sultaniyya wa-al-wilayat al-diniyya*, 1st edition (Cairo: Mustafa al-Babi al-Halabi, 1960), Chapter 1, pp. 5ff.

16. Qur'an 49:9–10.

17. Qur'an 4:59.

18. Qur'an 3:159.

19. Qur'an 42:38.

20. Qur'an 22:92.

21. Qur'an 2:143.

22. Qur'an 3:110.

23. See Qur'an 5:95 and 4:35. See also Abu al-'Abbas Muhammad ibn Yazid al-Mubarrad, *Al-kamil (bab al-Khawarij)*, 2nd edition (Damascus: Dar al-Hikma, 1972), p. 9.

24. See Ibn Hisham, Vol. I, pp. 52–53.

25. Ibn Hisham, Vol. 3, p. 358.

26. Ibid., p. 365.

27. Ibid., p. 366.

28. Al-Mubarrad, p. 49.

29. Qur'an 4:94.

30. *Sunan Ibn Maja*, 2nd edition (Beirut: Dar al-Fikr, n.d.), Vol. 2, p. 457.

31. Ibid., p. 458.

32. 'Abd al-Karim al-Shahrastani, *Al-milal wa-al-nihal* (printed in the margin of Ibn Hazm's *Fasl al-milal wa-al-ahwa' wa-al-nihal*) (Baghdad: reprinted by Maktabat al-Muthanna, n.d.), Vol. 1, pp. 163–64.

33. Ibid., p. 181.

34. Al-Mubarrad, p. 52.

35. See al-Baladhuri, *Ansab al-ashraf*, ed. Ihsan 'Abbas (Beirut: al-Matba'a al-Katulikiyya, 1979), Part IV, Vol. I, pp. 180–86. See also 'Umar Abu al-Nasr, *Al-Khawarij fi al-Islam . . .*, 3rd edition (Beirut: Maktab 'Umar Abu al-Nasr, 1970), pp. 9–12.

36. Ibid.

37. Al-Shahrastani, Vol. 1, pp. 157–58.

38. Ibid., p. 160.

39. Amin al-Rihani, *Tarikh Najd wa-mulhaqatihi*, ed. Albert Rihani, 4th edition (Beirut: Rihani Publishers, 1972), p. 39.

40. See al-Rihani, pp. 38–40.

41. Amin Sa'id, *Sirat al-Shaykh Muhammad ibn 'Abd al-Wahhab* (Beirut:

Sharikat al-Tawzi' al-'Arabiyya, n.d.), pp. 79–80.

42. See Qur'an 39:38–39.

43. Sa'id, p. 302.

44. Ibid., p. 307.

45. Ibid., pp. 308–310.

46. Qur'an 16:125.

47. Sa'id, p. 312.

48. Qur'an 33:56.

49. Sahih al-Bukhari, Vol. 2, p. 16.

50. See 'Imad al-Din Abu al-Fida' Isma'il ibn Kathir, *Tafsir al-Qur'an al-'azim*, 2nd edition (Beirut: Dar al-Fikr, 1979), Vol. 2, pp. 153ff.

51. Ibn Hisham, Vol. 2, p. 280. For other examples see Dawud ibn Sulayman al-Baghdadi al-Naqshbandi al-Khalidi, *Al-munha al-Wahhabiyya fi radd al-Wahhabiyya* (Istanbul: Yizik Kitabavi, 1971), Pamphlet I, p. 7.

52. Al-Khalidi, p. 6.

53. Ibid., p. 16.

54. Ibid., p. 29. See also Sahih al-Bukhari, Vol. 1, pp. 50–51.

55. Al-Khalidi, pp. 29–32.

56. See Qur'an 27:38–40.

57. See Richard P. Mitchell, *The Society of the Muslim Brothers* (London: Oxford University Press, 1969), pp. 7–9.

58. Ibid., p. 14.

59. Ibid., p. 14.

60. Ibid., p. 60.

61. Ibid., p. 207.

62. Ibid., p. 230.

63. Mahmoud Ayoub, *Redemptive Suffering in Islam* (New York: Mouton Publishers, 1978), p. 217.

64. This is the title of his small book, *Ila hukumat al-alf miliyun* (Qum: Dar al-Qur'an al-Hakim, n.d.).

65. Qur'an 13:11.

66. *Sunan Ibn Maja*, Vol. 2, pp. 477–78.

Richard T. Antoun earned a Ph.D. in anthropology and Middle Eastern studies from Harvard University. He is currently a professor of anthropology at the State University of New York at Binghamton. Among his many publications are *Low-Key Politics: Local-Level Leadership and Change in the Middle East, Arab Village: A Social Structural Study of a Transjordanian Peasant Community*, "The Islamic Court, the Islamic Judge and the Accommodation of Traditions: A Jordanian Case Study," and "The Gentry of a Traditional Peasant Community Undergoing Rapid Technological Change: An Iranian Case Study." Dr. Antoun's current research interests include the social organization of tradition in Islam, comparative religion and symbolism, local-level politics, social change among peasants in Jordan, and the integration of Iranian peasants into the national legal system.

Mahmoud M. Ayoub received his doctorate in the history of religion from Harvard University, and is presently a research associate at the Centre for Religious Studies at the University of Toronto. His publications include *Redemptive Suffering in Islam: A Study of the Devotional Aspects of 'Ashura' in Twelver Shi'ism*, "Towards an Islamic Christology I and II," "The Speaking Qur'an and the Silent Qur'an: A Study of the Principles and Development of Imami Shi'i Tafsir," and "The Problem of Suffering in Islam." Dr. Ayoub is currently engaged in a translation of selected parts of Islamic exegetical works representing major schools of thought and different periods in Islamic history. The first volume in this projected ten-volume series, *The Qur'an and Its Interpreters*, was published in 1984. In addition, Dr. Ayoub is also completing an annotated translation of the Shi'i Hadith collection, *Kitab al-Hajjah*.

Gamal M. Badr obtained his LL.D. degree from Alexandria University in Egypt. A former justice of the Supreme Court of Algeria and a former deputy director in the United Nations Office of Legal Affairs, Dr. Badr is currently a consultant in the laws of the Middle East and is legal adviser to the Permanent Mission of Qatar

320

to the United Nations and Adjunct Professor of Law at New York University. He has written widely in English, French, and Arabic on the subjects of international law and Islamic law. His articles include "A propos du nouveau code civil algérien," "Whither State Immunity?," "The Exculpatory Effect of Self-Defense in State Responsibility," and "Islamic Law: Its Relation to Other Legal Systems." His recent book, *State Immunity: An Analytical and Prognostic View*, was published by Martinus Nijhoff in 1984.

M. Cherif Bassiouni studied law at Dijon University, University of Geneva, University of Cairo, Indiana University, The John Marshall Lawyers Institute, and George Washington University. He is a member of the faculty of the College of Law at DePaul University and the nonresident dean of the International Institute of Advanced Studies in Criminal Sciences in Siracusa, Italy. Dr. Bassiouni has written or edited over twenty books and seventy articles, including *The Islamic Criminal Justice System*, *International Criminal Law: A Draft International Code*, *The Palestinians' Right of Self Determination and National Independence*, and "An Analysis of Egyptian Peace Policy Toward Israel: From Resolution 242 to the 1979 Peace Treaty." Dr. Bassiouni's many other activities include the position of co-editor-in-chief of *Revue Internationale de Droit Penal* and membership in the board of editors of *The American Journal of Comparative Law*.

Hanna Batatu received his Ph.D. in political science from Harvard University. He is the Shaykh Sabah Al-Salem Al-Sabah Professor of Contemporary Arab Studies at the Center for Contemporary Arab Studies. The author of *The Old Social Classes and the Revolutionary Movements of Iraq*, Dr. Batatu has also made important contributions to many scholarly journals including *Arab Studies Quarterly*, *Peuples Mediterranéens*, *al-Thaqafa al-Jadida*, *MERIP Reports*, and *The Middle East Journal* as well as to books on such subjects as Islam and communism, hierarchy and stratification in the Arab world, and the future of higher education in the Middle East. Dr. Batatu's current research interests include social structure and political power in Syria and Saudi Arabia.

Joel Beinin obtained his Ph.D. in history from the University of Michigan. Since 1983 he has been Assistant Professor of History at Stanford University. He is a member of the editorial committee of

MERIP Reports and the author of several articles on Egypt and Israel. He has recently completed a book (co-authored with Zachary Lockman) entitled *Class and Nation: Workers and Politics in Egypt, 1899–1954*.

Habib Chatty studied at Tunisia's Sadiki College and the Institute of Higher Studies in Arabic. While at the latter institution, H.E. Mr. Chatty embarked on a career in journalism. He has served as editor-in-chief of a number of French-language papers as well as of such Arabic-language newspapers as *El Zohra*, *As-Sabah*, and *El-Amal*. In the 1930s he became actively involved in the Tunisian nationalist movement. Beginning in 1955, he held a succession of distinguished positions within the Tunisian government, including a period from 1974 to 1977 as the Minister of Foreign Affairs. In 1979 he was elected to his present position as Secretary General of the Islamic Conference Organization.

Eric Davis received his Ph.D. from the University of Chicago. He is an associate professor of political science and director of the Middle East Studies Program at Rutgers University. His publications include *Challenging Colonialism; Bank Misr and Egyptian Industrialization, 1920–1941*, as well as numerous articles, including "Ideology, Social Class and Islamic Radicalism in Modern Egypt" in S. Arjomand, ed., *From Nationalism to Revolutionary Islam*.

Ali E. Hillal Dessouki received his Ph.D. from McGill University. He is an associate professor of political science at Cairo University, a member of the editorial boards of *The International Journal of Middle East Studies* and the *Cairo Papers in Social Science*, and head of the Comparative Politics Unit at the Al-Ahram Center for Political and Strategic Studies. In English he has been editor of, and contributor to, *Islamic Resurgence in the Arab World*, *Democracy in Egypt*, *Islam and Power*, *The Iraq-Iran War*, and *International Relations in the Arab World 1973–1982*; co-author of *The Political Economy of Income Distribution in Egypt*, *Rich and Poor States in the Middle East*, *Managing International Crises*, *Islam in Foreign Policy*, and *International Security in South West Asia*; author of *Canadian Foreign Policy and the Palestine Problem*, and *Egypt and the Great Powers 1973–1981*; and senior author of *The Foreign Policies of the Arab States*. Dr. Dessouki has also published numerous articles in Arabic and English.

Mansour Farhang received his Ph.D. in political science from Claremont Graduate School. Currently a professor at Bennington College, Dr. Farhang was active in Iranian exile politics from 1960 to 1979. He held a variety of formal and informal posts within the Iranian Foreign Ministry from 1979 to June 1981, including a period as Iran's ambassador and permanent representative to the United Nations. In addition to many newspaper articles, Dr. Farhang has written such monographs as *The U.S. Press and the War in Lebanon*, *Khomeini and Saddam Hussein: One Must Go*, *U.S. Imperialism: From the Spanish-American War to the Iranian Revolution*, and *The Iranian Revolution and the American Press*. He is currently completing work on a manuscript entitled *The Iranian Revolution and U.S.-Iranian Relations*.

Isma'il R. al Faruqi obtained his Ph.D. from Indiana University. He studied Islamic religion and thought at Al-Azhar University and Christianity and Judaism at McGill University. Until his tragic death in 1986 Dr. al Faruqi was professor of religion and director of graduate Islamic studies at Temple University, director of the International Institute of Islamic Thought in Washington, DC, and since its foundation in 1982, president of the American Islamic College, Chicago. He is the author of over 125 publications in the fields of Islam, Christianity, Judaism, and world religions. Among his works are *Islam and the Problem of Israel*, *Christian Ethics: A Systematic and Historical Analysis of the Dominant Ideas*, *'Urubah and Religion: A Study of the Fundamental Ideas of Arabism*, *The Great Asian Religions*, *Historical Atlas of the Religions of the World*, *Tawhid: Its Implications for Life and Thought*, and *Trialogue of the Abrahamic Faiths*.

Peter Gran, an associate professor of history at Temple University, earned a Ph.D. in history from the University of Chicago. Among his publications are *Islamic Roots of Capitalism, Egypt 1760–1840*, "Political Economy as a Paradigm for the Study of Islamic History," and "Medical Pluralism in Arab and Egyptian History: An Overview of Class Structure and Philosophies of the Main Phases." Dr. Gran is currently working on a book on historians and historiography in India, Iraq, and Mexico and writing another on social history and religious culture in nineteenth century Egypt.

Iliya Harik is a professor of political science and the former director of the Center for Middle Eastern Studies at Indiana University. He received his doctorate from the University of Chicago. His many publications include *The Political Elites of Lebanon* (in Arabic), *Distribution of Land, Employment, and Income in Rural Egypt, The Arabs and the New International Economic Order* (in Arabic), and "The Economic and Social Factors in the Lebanese Crisis." Dr. Harik is presently studying the politics of economic development with an emphasis on the problems of socialism and denationalization.

Ibrahim Ibrahim received his Ph.D. in history from Oxford University. He taught at Warwick University (England) and at the American University of Beirut. Formerly an adviser to the Minister of Foreign Affairs in Abu Dhabi (United Arab Emirates), Dr. Ibrahim is currently a research professor at the Center for Contemporary Arab Studies, Georgetown University. He is the editor of *Arab Resources: The Transformation of a Society*, as well as the author of many articles on modern Arab thought, Islam and nationalism, and society and politics in the Gulf.

Bruce B. Lawrence is a professor of Islamic studies and the history of religions at Duke University. He has written four books and numerous articles on many aspects of Islam, and is presently preparing a monograph on *Fundamentalism: Jewish, Christian, and Islamic*.

Richard P. Mitchell earned a Ph.D. in Oriental languages and history from Princeton University. He was professor of Middle Eastern history at the University of Michigan. Prof. Mitchell is the author of *The Society of the Muslim Brothers* and (with Lois Aroian) *The Modern Middle East and North Africa*. Prof. Mitchell died of cancer in Cairo in September 1983 while continuing his research on contemporary Islamic movements.

Ergun Özbudun obtained a Ph.D. in public law from Ankara University Law School. He is a professor of law and chairman of the Department of Constitutional Law and Comparative Politics at Ankara University Law School as well as director of Ankara University's Institute for Middle Eastern Studies. He has recently been a visiting professor at Columbia and Princeton Universities.

Dr. Özbudun is the author of *The Role of the Military in Turkish Politics, Party Cohesion in Western Democracies: A Causal Analysis,* and *Social Change and Political Participation in Turkey.* He has contributed articles to several collected works and to many prestigious academic journals.

Barbara Freyer Stowasser received her M.A. in Middle Eastern studies at U.C.L.A. in 1959, and her Ph.D. in comparative semitics and Islamic studies at the University of Münster in 1961. A former Fulbright fellow, she has taught at the University of Maryland and is now on the faculty of Georgetown University where she is presently chairman of the Arabic Department. Dr. Stowasser's publications, both in German and in English, have dealt mainly with the early Islamic Hadith. She is presently preparing a comparative study of Qur'an commentaries, both medieval and modern, as relating to the question of women's status in Islam. For this project, she has recently completed field research at theological faculties and schools in Turkey, Jordan, and Egypt under the sponsorship of the Fulbright program, the Social Science Research Council, and the American Research Center in Egypt.

Bassam Tibi was born in Damascus and studied in Germany. He received his Ph.D. from the University of Frankfurt and his Dr. habil. from the University of Hamburg. He is currently a professor of international relations at the University of Göttingen. In 1982 he was a visiting scholar at Harvard. Dr. Tibi is the author of five monographs and over eighty articles, including his books *Nationalismus in der Dritten Welt am arabischen Beispiel* (English translation: *Arab Nationalism*), *Die Krise des modernen Islam,* and *Der Islam und die kulturelle Bewältigung sozialen Wandels.*

INDEX